The Notorious "Bull" Nelson

The Notorious "Bull" Nelson

Murdered Civil War General

Donald A. Clark

Southern Illinois University Press
Carbondale and Edwardsville

14 13 12 11   4 3 2 1

Library of Congress Cataloging-in-Publication Data
Clark, Donald A., 1941–
  The notorious "Bull" Nelson : murdered Civil War
general / Donald A. Clark.
       p. cm.
  Includes bibliographical references and index.
  ISBN-13: 978-0-8093-3011-9 (alk. paper)
  ISBN-10: 0-8093-3011-3 (alk. paper)
  ISBN-13: 978-0-8093-8603-1 (ebook)
  ISBN-10: 0-8093-8603-8 (ebook)
  1. Nelson, William, 1824–1862. 2. Generals—United
States—Biography. 3. United States—History—Civil
War, 1861–1865—Biography. 4. United States—
History—Civil War, 1861–1865—Campaigns. 5. Murder
victims—Kentucky—Biography. 6. United States.
Army—Biography. 7. Maysville (Ky.)— Biography. I.
Title.
  E467.1.N45C58 2011
  355.0092—dc22
  [B]   2010016746

Printed on recycled paper. ♻
The paper used in this publication meets the minimum
requirements of American National Standard for
Information Sciences—Permanence of Paper for
Printed Library Materials, ANSI Z39.48-1992. ∞

To Barber,
for her loving patience and support

Contents

Illustrations

Preface

any years ago, a first look into the life of Dr. Joshua Taylor Bradford revealed that my distant relative once served as a personal physician to Maj. Gen. William "Bull" Nelson. It was puzzling to find that a kind and gentle man like Bradford enjoyed the company of a notorious brute who, when "irritated or opposed," was disgustingly "dictatorial and dogmatic." The mystery of that relationship started to unravel when I discovered he considered Nelson "a perfect library of social wealth" who could "repeat verbatim, page after page of his favorite authors." Bradford also found that when Nelson "was in good humor and free of care (which . . . was not often the case), he was [the] most genial and entertaining of conversationalists," who had a "gift of gab" that made him remarkably "companionable."[1]

This "noble, warm-hearted" man possessed "extraordinary character." He was "absolutely fearless," and close admirers regarded him as one of "the very foremost of Kentucky's loyal sons." Those friends also found it hard to honor Nelson with that tribute during the deeply troubled times that followed his ignoble death. Some two decades later, William H. Perrin said it was still too difficult and dangerous to write about every event connected to the Civil War; particularly those disagreeable episodes that were "too recent" for a historian to treat without prejudice.[2]

At that time, many veterans wanted to believe that the publication of the *Official Records of the War of the Rebellion* would overcome a broad spectrum of self-serving distortions and lies that arose during the Civil War. Many found the outcome deeply disappointing, and that inspired a phenomenal increase in the number of published memoirs and newspaper accounts. The last category inspired James B. Fry, the former adjutant general in the Army of the Ohio, to write to Dr. Bernard J. D. Irwin, ex-medical director in the Fourth Division. Fry said a recent newspaper story about "the killing of General Nelson by General Davis . . . [was] grossly incorrect, and . . . unjust to Nelson," and he wanted to correct that false impression. Irwin agreed to help "do justice to the reputation and memory of as true a patriot and as brave a soldier as ever confronted an enemy. Indeed I [Irwin] have often wondered that some one of the many friends of General Nelson had not at least endeavored to set the matter right in regard to an occurrence [his murder] that seemed destined to be misunderstood or misinterpreted by those who proposed to know anything about the unfortunate affair." When Fry published *Killed by a Brother Soldier* in 1885, he employed the same melodramatic dialogue that appeared in the numerous news accounts at the time of the murder. There was no mention of why it took twenty-three years to reveal that Brig. Gen. Jefferson C. Davis provoked Nelson into hitting him, nor did Fry offer any significant insight into why the Federal government failed to bring that Union general to justice.[3]

A long and arduous examination of primary and secondary records exposed lies and misinterpretations about Nelson, and it likewise confirmed certain truths. That investigation led to Benjamín Vicuña Mackenna, a previously unnamed "Chilean correspondent" and prominent revolutionary, who greatly admired Nelson. It also uncovered a long-overlooked biographical sketch by Anderson Nelson Ellis. That former aide and close family friend of the Nelsons authored an 1894 piece in the *Biographical Cyclopaedia and Portrait Gallery with a Historical Sketch of the State of Ohio.* In 1906, the *Register of the Kentucky Historical Society* carried a similar version by Dr. A.[Anderson] M.[Nelson] Ellis. Many have relied on that piece without knowing the true connection to Nelson.

A year after the Ellis article appeared Capt. Thomas Speed's *The Union Cause in Kentucky* praised a throng of Kentuckians who fought to keep the nation together, but it gave scant attention to Nelson's contributions. Six years later, Charles Cunningham, a former private in Company K, Sixth Regiment Ohio Volunteer Infantry, noted that although "William Nelson was one of the greatest Generals . . . He appears to be forgotten, as his name is never seen in print."[4]

The situation remained the same until Kentucky historian Hambleton Tapp wrote about the murder for the *Filson Club Historical Quarterly* in 1945. Lt. Cdr. Arthur A. Griese did a similar piece in 1952 that included an excellent appendix, which was quite helpful in putting together Nelson's naval service. Over the next three decades, there were many other articles of varying substance and quality. In 1997, Kirk C. Jenkins produced an excellent piece about the death of Nelson for *Civil War History.* That essay and others like it have contributed to our understanding of Nelson, but because of their brevity and incessant focus on a tragic ending, they do not provide a full appreciation of his strengths and weaknesses, triumphs and failures.

This Maysville, Kentucky, native served at sea for "twelve years and six months . . . performed shore and other duty for over four years, and was nearly five years unemployed [on extended leaves], making a total of twenty-one years of service to his nation before the Civil War." Sixty-seven Kentuckians served as general officers in the Federal army, and Nelson was one of four (less than 6 percent) who rose to the rank of major general. For that reason, Nelson frequently comes to the forefront of any serious discussion about the Civil War in Kentucky, or the early stages of the war in the West. Unfortunately, that interest is too often focused on his ignominious death at the hands of a small, frail, sickly Union general with the unlikely name of Jefferson Davis.[5]

That sudden demise added to the challenge of writing an authoritative interpretation of Nelson's life. He left no pile of letters or insightful memoir that might lay open the inner personal thoughts that we would all like to see. To deal with that limitation, this work relies on a host of long-neglected sources that give us the words of those who knew him well. The contrasting information should enable the judicious reader to arrive at better balanced conclusions about the character of William Nelson and at the same time enrich the historical record.

Acknowledgments

A fantastic group of people helped bring this work to fruition. I am particularly appreciative of my wife, Barber, for the understanding, love, and patience she gave to this effort. I am also very indebted to Sylvia Frank Rodrigue, executive editor at Southern Illinois University Press. Her thoughtful guidance and support are special gifts. Likewise, I sincerely appreciate the dedicated skills of Karl Kageff, editor-in-chief, Kathleen Kageff, project director, and copy editor John Wilson. Many others helped ensure the quality of this work, and that includes a host of anonymous readers that will always be remembered for the valuable input they gave.

National treasure Edwin C. Bearss graciously read the first rough draft and offered characteristic rousing advice to push forward. From start to finish, Stephen D. Engle of Florida Atlantic University provided extraordinary encouragement that will always be remembered. Kentucky's state historian, James C. Klotter, took time from a demanding schedule to go through an early draft, and his invaluable knowledge and advice helped the project become better focused. Melba Porter Hay assisted with elements of style and made thoughtful suggestions. William J. Marshall, curator of manuscripts at the University of Kentucky, helped push the original draft forward with his careful reading and constructive advice. Likewise, Stacy D. Allen, chief ranger at Shiloh National Park, provided very thoughtful and invaluable input.

Cartographers Dick and Donna Gilbreath did a terrific job with all the maps. Nancy Brannen, a collateral descendant of Nelson, graciously shared pictures and information on the Nelson/Doniphan lines. Likewise, I am indebted to James M. Prichard of the Kentucky Department of Libraries and Archives, Michael McCormick, the Vigo County (Indiana) historian, Trevor Plante and Rebecca Livingston, with the National Archives and Records

Administration, Ron D. Bryant, Kentucky historian, and Deborah Petite, for research at the National Archives.

I will always value the supportive smiles, encouraging suggestions and serene patience of the many nameless persons who staff the libraries, historical societies, and other institutions that helped make this possible. They include, but are not limited to: Kreitzberg Library Special Collections, Norwich University, Norwich, Vermont; Nimitz Library, U.S. Naval Academy, Annapolis, Maryland; Naval Historical Center, Washington, D.C.; Library Archives/Special Collections, U.S. Military Academy, West Point, New York; United States Military Institute, Carlisle, Pennsylvania; Vigo County Public Library, Terre Haute, Indiana; Lexington (Kentucky) Public Library; University of Kentucky Libraries, Lexington; Kentucky Historical Society, Frankfort; Indiana Historical Society, Indianapolis; Filson Historical Society, Louisville, Kentucky; Cincinnati and Hamilton County (Ohio) Public Library; and the Kenton County (Kentucky) Public Library, Covington.

All of us who strive to understand and explain the past rely on the noble efforts of the professional and nonprofessional historians who preceded us. It would be particularly ungracious if I failed to note their painstaking efforts that took place before the electronic age, a true phenomenon that gave me extraordinary benefits and advantages.

The Notorious "Bull" Nelson

The Roots of Imperfection

William "Bull" Nelson was an ox of a man who carried his three-hundred-pound weight on a sturdy six-foot four-inch frame. A meticulous dresser who always stood ramrod straight, this dashing tar had a booming voice, long curly black hair, and piercing black eyes that gave the appearance of someone who was ready to fight at the drop of a hat. One newspaper reporter captured the essence of his manner when he described him as "a go ahead, driving person, full of impatience and energy, a good soldier, and a profane man, with as little of the gentleman about him as well can be."[1]

Harvard-educated Nicholas Longworth Anderson took no comfort in the brutal way in which Nelson reprimanded subordinates, but this volunteer commander accepted it as the only way "to exact that iron discipline which makes an army" capable of overpowering the foe. No one impressed Lieutenant Colonel Anderson with the idea of genius as much as Nelson did, and he noted that Nelson's "faults were those of a commander anxious to secure the highest efficiency of his troops by the most rigid discipline of his officers." That latter practice caused him to be "beloved by his men," but despised by the volunteer officers that he publicly humiliated in a way they would never forget or forgive.[2]

Those victims had no appreciation for how a demanding heritage and brutal training helped make Nelson a martyr to that "severe duty." They did not care about the influence Dr. Anderson Doniphan had on his maternal grandson. As a young man, that Virginia aristocrat was known as a "rather fast young blood" who loved to engage in "fun and frolic of almost any kind." Doniphan's rash behavior is seen in a story about a chance encounter he had with a deer grazing by the side of the road. Without hesitation, Doniphan leaped off his horse, took a hurried shot, and missed the target. At this same time, his valuable horse dashed off into the woods. Doniphan tried to entice the high-spirited steed to return, but his impatience got the best of him. Throwing all common sense aside, he shot the defiant animal and returned home—with no apparent regrets.[3]

Throughout any given day, Anderson Doniphan enjoyed sipping toddies and taking snuff to extreme excess. He relished visits from the grandchildren and treated them to sumptuous meals prepared by the household slaves. Afterward, Doniphan would tell grand tales about forebears with dubious connections to Ireland, Spain, and Scotland. The actual records leave no doubt that he was a descendant of Alexander Doniphan, who migrated to Virginia in 1674.[4]

In 1793, Anderson and his brothers, George and Joseph, took a flatboat down the Ohio River to Limestone Landing (Maysville, Kentucky). At Germantown, a small village on the Mason/Bracken county line, Anderson established a thriving medical practice. By 1803–4, he had gained the acquaintance of Thomas Nelson, a merchant trader from Baltimore who had set up a retail dry-goods store in Augusta, Bracken County, Kentucky. In 1805, Nelson's wife Matilda died, leaving behind four young children. That same year he acquired $3,200 by flat-boating goods to New Orleans, and on his return trip through Scott County, highwaymen took that money from him. Four weeks later, Nelson recovered nearly half of the stolen funds when authorities apprehended one of the thieves. As a booming trade with New Orleans continued to increase the wealth of many Kentuckians, that eased the way for Nelson to become a town trustee, buy slaves, purchase in-lots, and acquire thirty-six acres near town.[5]

During the second year of the War of 1812, Thomas Nelson enrolled as a surgeon's mate under Dr. Anderson Doniphan in Col. John Poague's Fourth Regiment of Volunteers. That regiment assembled in Mason County on August 31, 1813. At Newport, Kentucky, they became part of the 3,500 mounted volunteers who marched to Detroit for the advance into Ontario, Canada. Under the cry, "Remember the Raisin," two thousand Kentuckians defeated the British, overwhelmed their Indian allies, and killed Tecumseh, leader of the Shawnee. Several years later, Andrew Jackson expressed the true significance of the war when he noted how eighteen discordant states had cast aside their distrust for each other and formed the first true union.[6]

That cooperation brought increased trade and unprecedented wealth to the Ohio Valley. It also created an ever-growing number of emancipated slaves who worked at various trades in the towns along the Ohio River. Some of them had been freed because of illnesses that prevented them from earning "a sufficient livelihood and maintenance" for their owners. On March 1, 1816,

Thomas Nelson used those words when he emancipated a six-year-old mulatto girl named Ann and a three-year-old mulatto boy called Oliver Nelson. Thomas continued to own two blacks over the age of sixteen, and in the fall of that year, he resigned as town trustee and moved to Lexington, a dominant trade center intent on molding itself into the "Athens of the West." The following spring, his second son, Thomas Washington Nelson, announced that he wanted to marry Frances (Fannie) Doniphan. Thomas Nelson dashed off a letter to Dr. Anderson Doniphan to tell his "Esteemed Friend" that he apologized for not being able to visit him on a recent trip to Bracken County because his leg had been broken in a fall from a horse.[7]

Doniphan replied that he readily approved of "Tommy" marrying his "very attractive, handsome and intellectual, daughter." The two exchanged vows in Mason County on May 20, 1817, and a year and a half later, "Tommy" enrolled in the Medical Department at Transylvania University. On March 17, 1820, the *Kentucky Gazette* reported that twenty-three-year-old T. W. Nelson of Georgetown, Kentucky, had obtained a degree to practice medicine. His father had given up on plantation life and returned to full-time work as a commission merchant. Matilda, his eighteen-year-old sister, remained at home with their father, stepmother, a half-brother, and three slaves.[8]

Fig. 1. "Captain" Thomas Nelson, William Nelson's grandfather. Unsigned oil painting, possibly by John Grimes (1804–37). Courtesy Mrs. Nancy Barkley Brannen, Maysville, Ky.

Fig. 2. Dr. Thomas W. Nelson, William Nelson's father. Unsigned oil painting, possibly by John Grimes (1804–37). Courtesy Mrs. Nancy Barkley Brannen, Maysville, Ky.

Dr. and Mrs. Thomas Washington Nelson moved to Maysville, where he established his medical practice on West Second Street. On September 27, 1824, his third son, William, was born and named for his recently departed uncle. The following year "Tommy" became a state representative from Mason County. That brief stint ended in 1826, and the thirty-year-old then announced he had "returned to Maysville . . . disposed henceforward to be perfectly satisfied with the dull pursuits of private life, and . . . determined to devote his whole time and attention to the Practice of Medicine. His shop is . . . where he may always be found, except when absent on professional business." Dr. Nelson employed a black girl named "Sophy," but he never owned slaves. As a member of the Old Blue (Presbyterian) Church, he very likely supported the congregation's active involvement with the Auxiliary Colonization Society.[9]

In Lexington, his father served on the Board of Trustees of Transylvania University. Those men had to address the growing concern over how students of the institution were spending their free time, and the *Kentucky Reporter* suggested it would be much better if hours spent in "frivolous amusement . . . [were] devoted to military exercise, and a proficiency in that useful art attained." That news caught the attention of Capt. Alden Partridge. The former commandant of West Point was quite interested in using military-style training to educate young men to be of service to their nation, and he asked Thomas Nelson and the other trustees if Transylvania would be interested in having a military department.[10]

Captain Partridge had established the American Literary, Scientific, and Military Academy at Norwich, Vermont, in 1819. It was the nation's first private military school, and many upwardly mobile professionals saw the rigid discipline of that institution as a good way to instill a sense of duty, honor, and country in their unruly sons. They also believed "the courses of study . . . appear better calculated to prepare young men for becoming useful and practical members of society, than those generally pursued in the literary colleges of the country."[11]

Dr. Nelson saw military schooling as one way for his three sons to "keep up the ancient renown of the family and have a public career." By 1836–37, it was apparent that eldest son Anderson Doniphan Nelson did not have the requisite temperament needed to study medicine under his patrician namesake. Anderson appeared better suited for a career in the army, and in order to obtain an appointment for him to attend the "West Point Academy," Dr. Nelson moved to Chillicothe, Ohio. Sons Thomas Henry Nelson and William Nelson remained in Mason County and attended Maysville Academy (Seminary), a school that embraced the rigid Scots-Presbyterian faith of their forebears. Both brothers could have boarded at the academy or with their Uncle Robert, who later operated the Washington Hotel (Lee House).[12]

Kentucky historian Richard Henry Collins lived nearby, and he remembered William Nelson as being "by nature rough and high tempered." Family friend Anderson Doniphan Ellis noted that a classmate of William's considered him "a bright, warm-hearted impulsive child, devoted to his mother and sister, firm in his convictions, true to the right as the needle to the pole, intolerant of all petty dealings and developing as he grew older qualities which stamped him as a born leader among his playfellows." Another said William was "a beloved companion of my childhood—brave, honorable and original, attentive to his studies, never neglecting his duties, winning golden opinions from all, and carrying his flute as regularly as his books, and spending his noons learning to play it."[13]

In the summer of 1837, Dr. Nelson enrolled thirteen-year-old William in the Collegiate Department of Captain Partridge's military school. It had received a charter as Norwich University three years earlier, and like West Point, the upperclassmen (cadre) had the authority to indoctrinate and orient the incoming students (rooks). For a "rough and high-tempered" boy from Maysville, this was a critical turning point. He could no longer rely on the emotional comfort that comes from family and friends. Now William had to deal with a hard-nosed cadre who thrived on imposing their will on others. The bullies among them had been through the ritualistic hazing, and this was their time to test the new students' mettle and establish themselves with the new class. Without close supervision, these immature, self-absorbed young men could turn a well-intentioned practice into cruel and abusive forms of entertainment that amused them and brutalized the recipients. Tradition absolved them from personal responsibility and sustained the gross indignities they heaped on others. Those special few of their victims who readily adapted to that maltreatment rose above the degradation to become exceptional military leaders. Most became part of the bureaucratic class that preserved and protected the overall system. The severely scarred found it difficult to serve in any capacity, but their less-crippled companions would seek to validate their self-worth by engaging in the same abusive treatment that damaged them. After William Nelson finished this indoctrination, he would experience additional heartless behavior that ensured he ended up in the latter category.[14]

For now, he slept on a slatted, three-foot-wide wooden bed with a gun rack directly above that held a 12-pound Springfield musket. With the exception of Sunday, each day began with Reveille at daybreak, the call to formation, roll call, and hoisting of the flag. They then rushed to put their rooms in order and dashed off to breakfast at 6:00 A.M. From there, the cadets went to scripture and prayer services at the chapel before starting classes at 8:00. After the noon meal, instruction resumed at 1:00. From 4:00 until Retreat sounded at sunset, Nelson and his fellow cadets engaged in drill and dress parade. After the flag lowering, they ate supper and returned to their rooms to study infantry tactics, field artillery procedures, and various academic assignments. Recitations received a grade of 1 through 4. Captain Partridge personally reviewed each report, and at the Saturday evening Dress Parade, each cadet publicly accounted for his efforts by announcing the results before the entire student body and faculty.[15]

This was a place where boys from the North and South mixed for the first time. Military science drove the curriculum, and "those hours of the day which are generally passed by students in idleness or devoted to useless amusements" were to be used to drill on the 6-pound guns. Partridge made sure there was no time to engage in contentious debates over slavery, and the cadets were surprised when he gave a dissertation on the antislavery movement that included "portions of Daniel Webster's Liberty and Union Speech given before Congress in 1830." This inspired some cadets to discuss the morality of slavery. When a heated debate erupted, they stopped in order to prevent politics from taking precedence over training that taught them to serve in defense of their country.[16]

In August 1838, news of the long-awaited United States Exploring Expedition came to the forefront as Nelson started his final year at Norwich. Accounts of those South Sea adventures enthralled the corps of cadets, and they seem to have inspired Nelson to seek a career in the navy. When he returned home in the early fall of 1839, Congressman Garrett Davis of Bourbon County was already in the process of seeking a warrant for him to become a midshipman. Secretary of the Navy James K. Paulding approved that request, and the appointment arrived with an effective date of January 28, 1840. On February 7, Nelson wrote Secretary Paulding from Washington, Kentucky, to acknowledge his acceptance.[17]

In April, orders arrived for Nelson to report to Commander Lewis Warrington for duty onboard a U.S. receiving ship at Norfolk, Virginia, until his services were required at sea. That vessel turned out to be the *Delaware*, a 44-gun ship based at Gosport. Appointed Midshipman Nelson learned:

1. No particular duties are assigned this class of officers.
2. They are promptly and faithfully to execute all the orders for the public service which they shall receive from their commanding officers.

3. The commanding officer will consider the midshipmen as a class of officers meriting in a special degree their fostering care; they will see therefore that the schoolmaster performs his duties toward them by diligently and faithfully instructing them in those sciences appertaining to their profession, and to use his utmost care to render them proficient therein.
4. Midshipmen are to keep regular journals and deliver them to the commanding officer at the stated periods in due form.
5. They are to consider that they owe to their country to employ a due portion of their time in the study of naval tactics and in acquiring a thorough and extensive knowledge of all the various duties to be performed on board a ship of war.[18]

Bullying and rough fighting were commonplace. In order to appear older, some young men grew whiskers, chewed tobacco, drank brandy, and swore like common sailors. These errand boys were always going and never arriving. Should they accidentally bump into an officer, any attempt to apologize would only receive something like, "Sir, do you take me for a post to scrub your pig's hide against? It is your duty to keep a respectable distance from an officer and not soil his clothes." For those who saw themselves as would-be commodores, the need to regain a sense of self-worth might cause them to cock their caps at an angle, put on a contorted face, and threaten a crewman with a good "licking" if he disobeyed an order. A special few saw the value of being considerate. They never cursed or abused the men who sailed the vessel; and that humanity could bring an old tar to say, "Ah, good luck to you, sir. You have a soul to be saved." Later events make it seem doubtful that William Nelson ever received that blessing.[19]

After six months of basic training, he received orders to join the *Yorktown*. On December 13, 1840, Acting Captain John Henry Aulick, the father of Nelson's classmate Richmond Aulick, ordered that 16-gun sloop-of-war out of Hampton Roads, Virginia. Some thirty days later, she was standing in for land (anchored at sea while waiting for permission to land) at the famed harbor of Rio de Janeiro, a key leg in the triangular slave trade between Africa and the West Indies. After a brief stay to take on provisions, the sailors hoisted anchors on February 5, 1841, and the *Yorktown* was soon back out to sea.[20]

The midshipmen usually gathered on the half-deck for schooling in the afternoon. Near the long 24-pound guns, the ship "professor" would explain the theory and practice of gunnery or show the "middies" how curvilinear lines described the trajectory of shells flying through the air. As they continued toward the treacherous waters of Cape Horn, a sudden gust of cold wind from the Antarctic could send the massive Nelson aloft with "All hands [to] reef top-sail." Darkness lasted up to seventeen hours during the journey through the hazardous straits; hail and snow pelted the reefers without mercy, and good captains made sure that "grog was given to the morning watch." No recordable incidents occurred on this passage, and by March 20, 1841, the *Yorktown* was safely on her way to Valparaiso, Chile.[21]

At the Bay of Callao (Lima, Peru), Captain Aulick had the crew prepare the vessel for the primary mission of protecting whaling ships and other commercial vessels sailing the South Seas. At the end of May, the *Yorktown* steered a course for the Marquesas, the Society Islands, and New Zealand. In the Fijis, one man died from an outbreak of smallpox. To avoid communicating "that horrible disease to the helpless natives," Captain Aulick then ordered the *Yorktown* to head straight for the Sandwich (Hawaiian) Islands. On October 9, 1841, the vessel dropped anchor at Honolulu. This was the hub for American whaling interests in the Pacific Ocean, and for Nelson, it would be the first of many visits to the obliging port.[22]

Thirty whaling ships arrived during the stay, and their reports to Captain Aulick indicated there was no reason for him to remain any longer.

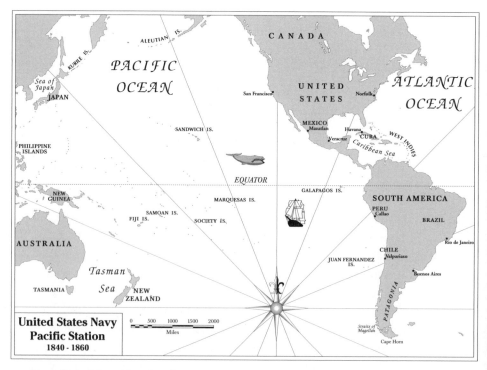

Map 1. United States Navy, Pacific Station, 1840–60

The *Yorktown* departed for Mexico on November 6, 1841, and she reached Mazatlán on December 8. Having been at sea for ten months, the vessel went on to Callao for a thorough overhauling of the sails and rigging. There, Capt. Thomas ap Catesby Jones relieved Aulick of command, and he took command of the Pacific Squadron. Nelson joined the *Shark*, a small sloop, after Jones made the *United States* his flagship because the *Yorktown* was regarded as a third-class ship.[23]

Many now viewed the Old United States Navy (1798–1861) as one of "the most backward and poorly organized of all the world's navies." Noted writer Richard Henry Dana advised any who dared to sail the sea should expect "a mixture of a little good with much evil, and a little pleasure with much pain." Herman Melville saw the ocean as a place where brutes, whoremongers, and drunks kept company "with the snake, the shark, and the worm." Captains of merchant ships offered better pay and shorter enlistments, and that meant the U.S. Navy commanders had to accept the services of seamen rejected by them. To enforce discipline among those castoffs, officers relied on flogging and other practices that had been in use since the days of slave galleys in the Roman Empire. The secluded world of the sea made it easy to ignore any public outrage over their inhumane practices, and that disregard brought increased pressure to disband the U.S. Navy if it could not or would not correct the problem.[24]

Many of the old commodores had weathered similar storms, and they were not about to concede without a fight. By late November 1842, concern with shipboard discipline reached a new level when Capt. Alexander Slidell Mackenzie arrested Appointed Midshipman Philip Spencer for "suspected" mutiny aboard the *Somers*. Mackenzie ignored the requirement to hold a court-martial and declared that Spencer, a boatswain, and a seaman were guilty of discussing the idea of mutiny. Mackenzie brought about his own court-martial when he ordered the men hung from the yardarm of the *Somers* on December 1, 1842. A group of his peers found him not guilty, and that seemed to vindicate the extreme discipline of the "Old Navy." In reality, "the *Somers* affair" had aroused very strong support for reform from officers who believed it would not have happened if the navy had a land-based school.[25]

Throughout the Mackenzie trial, the Mexican minister at Washington had insisted on the recall of Commodore Jones for the absurd seizure of Mazatlán in October 1842. That brought orders for Capt. Alexander J. Dallas to succeed Jones on January 24, 1843. While Dallas traveled across the Isthmus of Panama in June, Jones sailed out into the Pacific. Dallas did not assume command of the Pacific Squadron until July 12, 1843. He found the

Shark was the only vessel available to him, and when the broad blue pennant went up the main mast, Appointed Midshipman Nelson became part of the celebrated effort to find Jones.[26]

Dallas reached Honolulu in April 1844. He transferred his flag and Nelson from the *Shark* to the armed store ship *Erie*, but soon found the effects of brain disease made it necessary to return to Callao where he died on the evening of June 3, 1844. A little over a month later, Nelson recorded: "8 [P.M.] to Meridian [midnight watch] light breezes and cloudy standing in for the Harbor of Rio de Janeiro Raza Islands ahead." As required, he informed the secretary of the navy of his impending return and availability for other duty. When the *Erie* docked at the Brooklyn Navy Yard on November 10, 1844, the twenty-year-old Nelson had been at sea for nearly four years.[27]

He returned home to visit with family and friends who were full of news about how James K. Polk's call for the annexation of Texas enabled the Tennessee Democrat to win a narrow victory over Kentucky's stalwart Whig, Henry Clay. On January 14, 1845, Nelson headed off to Pensacola, Florida, for duty aboard the *Falmouth*. That vessel belonged to the recently formed Home Squadron, and this would give Nelson his first experience in protecting coastal commerce, aiding ships in distress, suppressing piracy, and interdicting the slave trade.[28]

During that assignment, his mother, Fannie Doniphan Nelson, died. He was detached from the *Falmouth* on July 24, 1845, with a two-month leave of absence. On September 10, Nelson received orders to attend the new land-based naval school. The *Somers* affair had convinced the navy of the need for this school, and Capt. Isaac N. Mayo suggested it be located at Annapolis, Maryland. Two days prior to the opening, Nelson advised Secretary of the Navy George Bancroft that he had reported to the superintendent, Commander Franklin Buchanan. When classes commenced at 11:00 A.M., October 10, 1845, the senior class (the first class) was comprised of fifty midshipmen. Superintendent Buchanan warned these young men, "The regulations of the navy require you to pass through a severe ordeal before you can be promoted."[29]

Nelson and the other seniors considered themselves officers, and for them this final stage of training was little more than temporary leave from sea duty. For five years, these jack tars had lived in a world where the double-reefed dressing gown often served as the regular uniform, and they intended to keep that custom. There were no military formations or drilling, but the curriculum did include "infantry-drill and fencing." "Bully" Nelson resided in a former blacksmith's shop known as the "Gas House" because of his "rather inflated tendency." The rowdy ways of all the midshipmen defied the purpose of the nearby classrooms. All-night drinking parties, rolling 32-pound shots down the halls— every class had a need to be among those who "dared violations." The demerit system borrowed from West Point did not fit the "seniors" who had trained under the roughhouse traditions of the gunroom. They believed that anyone who dared give "evidence on others" should end up covered with tar and feathers.[30]

By the spring of 1846, these hard-edged young men found that the prospects of war with Mexico had increased substantially. U.S. Army units were under orders to patrol the disputed land between the Rio Nueces and Rio Grande, and on April 25, 1846, Gen. Anastasio Torrejón's force of two thousand cavalry attacked the seventy men in Capt. Seth B. Thornton's Second Dragoons at Carricitos Ranch. In the Thornton Affair, sixteen Americans were killed, five wounded, and forty-nine taken prisoner. At Corpus Christi, Texas, Brig. Gen. Zachary Taylor ordered additional troops forward. The Kentucky native then informed President James K. Polk, "Hostilities may now be considered commenced." On May 4, the always prim and proper Commodore David E. Conner headed north from Veracruz to meet with the "Rough and Ready" Taylor at Pointe Isabel. President Polk had already consulted with his cabinet and decided, "The cup of forbearance had been exhausted." Northern Whigs rightly feared that this expansionist Democrat was pursuing a course of action that would lead to a call for slavery in territory acquired by sale or force. Congress saw no need to debate the implications, and it gave this first ever commander-in-chief the unprecedented authority to start a war against a foreign nation.[31]

England and the United States were still at odds over the boundary with Oregon, and the *Times* of London rarely had anything good to say about America. The paper noted that Mexico could field 32,000 troops whereas the United States had a mere 7,300 men. It mockingly predicted that the "conquest of a vast region by a state which is without an army" would be a unique historical accomplishment. Another edition said it would take years for the United States to assemble a competent army, and even then, it would have to rely on a base of supply that was too far away from the field of operations. The situation in the Oregon territory was an entirely different matter for the British. They recognized it was in their best interest to reach a pragmatic agreement with the United States, and they accomplished that end in mid-June.[32]

On June 19, 1846, seven of the fifty-six midshipmen who had recently applied for service in the Mexican War were under orders when Capt. Lawrence Kearney and the Board of Examiners arrived at Annapolis. Nelson went before the Board of Review on July 1, 1846. He had reached the age of twenty-one years and nine months, had no outstanding debts, and had served five years at sea aboard the *Delaware, Yorktown, Shark, Erie,* and *Falmouth.* Nelson handed over five badly damaged journals with the explanation that a steam explosion had smashed them along with all the letters from his commanding officers. The board reviewed the dilapidated mess, found nothing amiss, and approved Nelson for the rank of passed midshipman.[33]

The graduates received a three-month leave of absence from July 10 to October 10, 1846. News accounts indicated "about thirty of the young men have been passed to the grade of 'passed midshipmen;' but, by some strange arrangement, under act of Congress, only ten of the whole number of the graduating class will be admitted of the pay of that post, (there being ten vacancies;) the other portion are liable to do duty with midshipman's pay simply, having the title, and necessarily incident to all the expenses of passed midshipmen."[34]

Instilled with the Spartan values of duty, loyalty, and courage, Nelson appeared well suited for sailing the seas he loved. In that world of dominance and domination, he had learned the ways of profane braggarts who were prone to fits of intense anger—behaviors often associated with warriors looking for approval and recognition by superiors. Nelson now had orders to head off to war and prove his worth. This duty would also return him to the eccentric environment of the ship at sea, an isolated place ruled over by "harsh, exacting, and overbearing" despots who believed the men under them should "fear their own officers more than the enemy."[35]

A Taste of War   [2]

As Nelson wrapped up his affairs at Annapolis, Don Antonio López de Santa Anna, the exiled dictator of Mexico, was meeting in secret with special diplomatic agent Alexander Slidell Mackenzie and other United States officials at Havana, Cuba. During their talks on July 6–7, 1846, Santa Anna convinced those men that if they arranged for his return to Mexico he would facilitate the sale of contested territory to the United States. After Santa Anna passed through the blockade at Veracruz, he went on to Mexico City and quickly resumed the role of president. He then advised President Polk that all negotiations for peace would cease.[1]

At that time, U.S. Congressman David Wilmot managed to stymie a congressional bill that would have funded the purchase of the disputed Mexican lands. Wilmot strongly opposed the expansion of slavery, and he borrowed a phrase from the Northwest Ordinance to introduce a proviso that stated, "Neither slavery or involuntary servitude shall ever exist in any part of" the territories that might be acquired from Mexico. This action only added to the inevitability of war with Mexico. With no funding to purchase disputed lands, expansionist supporters of Polk were determined to use force against a dictator who had no interest in negotiating a settlement.[2]

Over eight hundred miles of forbidding terrain lay between the Rio Grande and Mexico City, and military planners decided to seize the port city of Veracruz and move against the capital city from there. Maj. Gen. Winfield Scott received overall responsibility for this first-ever joint operation by the army and navy. The Home Squadron under David E. Conner maintained a blockade of the Gulf of Mexico with thirteen ships carrying 217 guns. They were based at the island of Antón Lizardo, twelve miles below Veracruz, and Scott planned to acquire fifty transports of 500- to 750-tons capacity and transport fifteen to twenty thousand soldiers to that isle.[3]

Santa Anna had no ships, and he built his strategy around the traditional military belief that a large professional army would prevail against a mostly volunteer ground force with no proven success. That calculation, however, ignored the significant role of expansionist war hawks supporting well-trained West Point officers working side by side with a seasoned U.S. Navy. In early September 1846, those hawks were demanding to know why the 54-gun flagship of the Home Squadron spent so much time in the Pensacola Navy Yard with "her sails furled to the yards." A closer check revealed the *Raritan* was making regular runs between Pensacola and the island of Antón Lizardo when Nelson reported for duty in mid-October.[4]

General Scott arrived at the mouth of the Rio Grande at the end of December 1846, and the following week he had his land force boarding over two-hundred leased transports. Four thousand soldiers reached the Lobos Isles on February 18, and Scott arrived the following day with another nine thousand troops. On March 2, 1847, this huge armada headed for Antón Lizardo, and two days later the billowing sails of the fleet appeared on the horizon. Nelson and the men of the *Raritan* could see a blue pennant with a red center flying from the main of the steamer *Massachusetts,* and that signaled the imposing six-foot five-inch Scott was about to join them.[5]

Scott and Conner spent much of Friday, March 5, 1847, working on the final plans. Jacob Oswandel, Company C, First Regiment Pennsylvania Volunteers recalled, "the whole scene was full of wild excitement. . . . The soldiers mingling with the sailors in singing their favorite songs . . . [just before] the longest day of their lives." At dawn, March 9, the *Raritan* hoisted her anchors at Antón Lizardo and started toward the Sacrificios Isles. At 2:30 P.M., she was in position for Nelson and the other junior officers to help supervise the loading of fifteen surfboats that carried forty soldiers, a naval officer, and a crew of eight to ten sailors. Similar procedures occurred on the other vessels, and by 3:30, all sixty-five surfboats were bobbing about in the choppy waters. At 5:30, the fourth flag went up the main of the *Massachusetts.*[6]

The surfboats moved forward and landed with precision. The soldiers jumped out and took up positions in the sand hills where they proudly planted the standards for their regiments beside the United States flag. Nelson's brother Anderson, who served with the U.S. Sixth Regiment of Infantry, was among the 8,600 soldiers and marines who "were eating their biscuit and pork on the sand or preparing to bivouac" about midnight. Over the next few days, the hard-pressed sailors managed to land only fifteen carts and one hundred horses at the point of debarkation. This led the *Times* of London to report that the Americans had done everything wrong and the Mexicans appeared ready to push them back out to sea. In truth, the defenders were about to become completely isolated.[7]

On Sunday, March 21, Commodore Matthew C. Perry assumed command of all naval operations and ordered the Home Squadron to unleash a horrendous barrage on Veracruz. The enemy focused its fire on the ships, and this allowed work details to pull seven 10-inch army mortars across creeks, stagnant ponds, and thickets to a position about one half mile south of the city. On Monday, United States forces had the objective completely encircled, and Scott asked Gen. Juan Morales to capitulate. The Mexican commander refused, and that brought the order for the seven mortars to commence fire. Scott was particularly impressed with the damage caused by the "heavy metal" of the navy, and he accepted an earlier offer to bring ashore three long 32-pounders and three French 8-inch Paixhans that fired 64-pound exploding shells.[8]

Scott wanted the navy to turn their guns over to the army, but Perry insisted that his "officers and men must go with them." Naval regulations of the time required that vessels like the *Raritan* have seventy-five men who could operate on land with artillery, and when Perry appeared under the stern of that ship, Nelson and his fellow midshipmen were thrilled to learn they would go ashore with one 32-pounder. Lots were drawn, and Nelson came up with a long straw. It took a force of fifteen hundred soldiers and

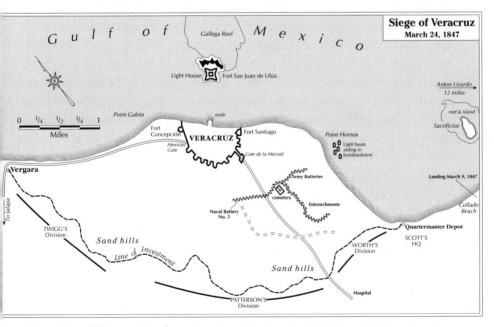

Map 2. Siege of Veracruz, March 24, 1847. Adapted from Justin Smith, *The War with Mexico*, vol. 2, and Marcus J. Wright, *General Scott* (New York: D. Appleton, 1897)

sailors to move the heavy cannons off the vessels and onto surfboats that brought them to the beach. The first two guns were loaded on the only two-wheeled carts available. The battery site was two and a half miles away, but an extra ration of rum helped the men pull the carts through axle-deep sand and across a seventy-yard-wide lagoon. One sailor had a "falling out" with an intoxicated Tennessee volunteer who then killed him. Another man was mortally wounded by an enemy shell.[9]

A shortage of carts and horses made it necessary to leave two guns at the landing, but on Wednesday, March 24, all six guns of Naval Battery No. 5 were in place. Capt. John H. Aulick ordered that last gun on the right be cleared of sand and sponged. The last bit of chaparral was cut away, and moments later the Mexican defenders opened fire on the *Raritan's* 32-pounder. For the next five hours, the two sides engaged in a continuous exchange of fire. At 2:30 P.M., the overheated naval guns had spent all fifty rounds (approximately ten per hour). Damage to the fifty-five feet of the wall included a thirty-six-foot-wide breach. Loud, mournful cries from the city made it seem the enemy had many casualties, but that offered little comfort. Four seamen were dead. One officer and five men lay wounded, mostly from chaparral splinters, cactus thorns, and spurs.[10]

At 4:00 P.M., Capt. Isaac N. Mayo arrived with the second relief party, comprised of one hundred fifty sailors and marines. William Nelson was one of three passed midshipmen who served with six naval lieutenants, one marine lieutenant, one assistant surgeon, one acting master, and six midshipmen. The new arrivals went to work performing maintenance on the guns, and the army engineers started shoring up the breastworks. At the same time, a group of foreign consuls came forward under a flag of truce to request a ceasefire that would allow for the evacuation of the women and children. That same group had turned down an earlier opportunity, and Scott ordered them back with the warning that unless the entire city surrendered, the firing would continue in the morning.[11]

At sunrise, Thursday, the boatswain's mate was about to pipe all hands to the guns when twelve Mexican batteries opened fire. A 13-inch enemy round struck the sand about five yards behind the naval battery, and as the quarter-gunner tried to push the hot projectile away it exploded into a cloud of dust and smoke. Everyone in the naval battery expected to find at least one blackened corpse, and instead they were delighted that Seaman John Williamson and three others escaped with only light wounds. Midshipman Thomas B. Shubrick was determined to get revenge, and he shouted for his men to be "quick about loading . . . the one [round] that is going to knock out the big cannon . . . Ram it down, my lads." As the eager Shubrick stepped forward to sight the barrel, he was suddenly decapitated by an incoming round.[12]

That shocking loss made the fighting intensely personal. Lt. Raphael Semmes, a future nemesis of the Union navy, found that whenever the naval battery hit a target the sailors stood on top of the parapet and taunted the Mexican defenders by "waving their hats and crowing like roosters." At the same time, the "crash of the eight-inch [Paixhan] shells" shook the earth so hard that church bells [in Veracruz] rang of their own accord. Shrieking civilians ran for safety at the mole between the city and the castle of San Juan de Ulúa. A Mexican round struck a 10-inch army mortar and hurled it thirty feet away. Other enemy rounds struck a nearby cemetery, sending coffins, bones, and skulls flying everywhere. The army battery responded with

Fig. 3. *Bombardment of Veracruz* by André J. Castaigne. On the second day of firing, Passed Midshipman William Nelson joined Naval Battery No. 5. From left to right were the *Potomac's* 32-pounder, the *Albany's* 64-pound shell gun, a parapet of sandbags six feet deep, the *St. Mary's* 64-pound shell gun, the *Mississippi's* 64-pound shell gun, another parapet of sandbags six feet deep, the *Potomac's* 32-pound gun, and the *Raritan's* 32-pound gun. All the guns were mounted on platforms with their carriages. The recoil was checked with sandbags and run out with sidetackles and handspikes. Picture Collection, The New York Public Library, Astor, Lenox and Tilden Foundations

screeching Congreve rockets, and by 3:30 P.M., the naval battery had fired all of its ammunition. In the quiet stillness that followed, the enemy could be seen fleeing through the gaping holes of the walled city. Nelson and his cohorts were still standing on the parapets and shouting taunts at the hapless foe when the third relief detachment under Capt. Samuel L. Breeze arrived a half-hour later. Passed Midshipman Edward Barrett relieved his old classmate of command of the Ambulance Corps, and the boisterous Nelson returned to Collado Beach in an army wagon pulled by wild mules.[13]

In two days of fighting, Naval Battery No. 5 lost one midshipman and four seamen. They had fired 25 percent of the 463,000 pounds of metal thrown against Veracruz. Most of the fire struck the redoubt of Santa Barbara. One-third of the city lay in ruins, and "fires were raging several places." Nineteen civilians had died when a shell struck an infirmary. Seventeen more perished in the adjacent female hospital, and that sent crying children into the streets to seek solace at Divina Pastora. One observer stated, "From the gate of La Merced to the Parish, not a single house was uninjured." If the enemy continued to resist, Scott intended to assault the city with three columns of infantry: two from the army and the third comprised of sailors and marines. The need to implement that plan ended when a flag of truce appeared at 8:00 A.M., Friday, March 26, 1847. Hours later, a huge gale and sandstorm halted negotiations on shore and carried away the foresail and spritsail of the *Raritan*.[14]

On March 29, approximately five thousand Mexican defenders surrendered with five hundred artillery pieces. An estimated four hundred had died in battle and some two hundred lay wounded. United States forces had thirteen dead and fifty-five wounded. Scott would now go forward with the primary mission of conquering Mexico City, and Perry would pursue plans to secure Tabasco (also known as San Juan Bautista and Villahermosa). At that place, it appeared that Gen. Domingo Echagaray had about nine hundred men posted along the Rio Tabasco, a narrow river with steep banks covered with dense foliage. At any point, a small force of hidden enemy soldiers could wreak havoc if they fired down on sailors and marines in tightly packed boats. There were no fortifications behind those enemy positions, and Perry believed that a rapid advance would enable him to sweep into the rear of the foe with an improvised task force.[15]

Captain Mayo served as "the acting Adjutant-General" of that "infantry brigade," which was comprised of 1,173 sailors and marines with "field artillery." On Monday afternoon, June 14, 1847, Nelson and nine fellow classmates were with a flotilla of nine warships that towed forty ship's boats across the bar at Frontera. At dusk, the column stretched six miles up the Tabasco River. About midnight, it was learned that Col. Miguel Bruno had set ambushes at two points, fifteen and twenty miles further up the river. That halted the advance until daylight on Tuesday. Late that afternoon, the flotilla was forty miles inland and near Santa Teresa when about 150 Mexicans fired on the starboard sides of the boats. The *Bonita*, the flagship *Scorpion*, and the brig *Washington* joined with the *Vesuvius* to drive the foe back into the jungle. Perry now halted, because just ahead was Devil's Bend, "a long reach of a mile and a quarter in length; [where] the river narrows, and an obstruction [was] thrown across the bar with a strong breastwork [on the right shore] commanding it."[16]

At 6:00 P.M., the officers stood beneath the shredded awning of the *Scorpion* and talked about the holes in the side of *Vesuvius*. Lt. John A. Winslow commented on how the marines had "fired away, without going once to the right side of the quarter deck. . . . [He then joked about how they] shaved one of the Commodore's [Perry's] whiskers and knocked a cigar out of the mouth of another officer." Future assistant secretary of the navy Gustavus Vasa Fox served as the acting master of the *Washington*, and he had nothing memorable to say. That was not true of "Bully" Nelson. He could not resist announcing the boats had not been "fired into at all—that it was all gammon, etc." The foolish bravado offended Commodore Perry, and it delighted Midshipman William Parker when he saw that "Mr. Nelson was promptly suspended and sent below."[17]

At first light Wednesday, June 16, Lt. William May went forward to investigate the obstruction at Devil's Bend. At 6:40 A.M. enemy fire stuck May and several of his men. Perry promptly ordered Cmd. Franklin Buchanan to take the special infantry brigade ashore at Seven Palms, and while the *Bonito*, *Spitfire*, and *Scourge* sprayed the landing zone with fire, seven hundred sailors and marines boarded surfboats that lined up three deep in the middle of the river. Perry called a cease-fire, the men gave "three hearty cheers," and the boats landed at the edge of a thirty- to forty-foot hill. Nelson was now part of Capt. Alexander S. Mackenzie's Second Division of Artillery, and his enormous strength was probably a great help to the men who struggled to tug and pull seven 6-pounders up this nearly perpendicular wall of mud. On reaching the top, they fired those guns at entrenched defenders, who quickly withdrew into the jungle.[18]

The other three guns came forward while scouts investigated the situation to the front. Navy Lt. Lafayette Maynard's pioneers started hacking out a pathway behind the scouts, and Capt. Alvin Edson followed with a column of marines. Captain Buchanan supported the artillery with infantry, and the ambulance party followed in the rear. About one hour later, the forward scouts advised that Colonel Hildago was waiting with three hundred infantry, three hundred cavalry, and two 24-pounders. Edson's marines were well ahead of the main column, and Perry halted them so the overburdened artillery could catch up with the ten brass guns. As the artillerymen struggled through the high grass and thick chaparral, Nelson and other officers brought up canteens filled with liquor, "and the moment they saw a poor fellow fall they would give him 'a drop of comfort' which had an astonishing effect on him."[19]

Meanwhile, the men on the boats at the Tabasco River blew up the channel obstructions and rushed downriver. Those vessels moved in behind Tabasco and opened fire on Fort Iturbide, a well-defended position that had a battery of six guns with four hundred entrenched infantry. The protective fire enabled Lt. David Dixon Porter to land a party of sixty-eight men that drove the outflanked defenders back into the jungle. The *alcalde* (mayor) tried to surrender the town, but defenders in the woods ignored his efforts and continued to fire. At 11:40 A.M., Acting Master Isaac N. Briceland raced through that gunfire and planted the American flag on the governor's house. Four hours later, Nelson and the dog-tired artillerymen reached the edge of a town filled with jeering catcalls from Porter's men. That made their guns seem "a thousand pounds heavier, " and Perry quickly formed the crestfallen men into columns and marched them into town with a "fine band of music . . . and flags flying."[20]

This task force believed there was ample reason to toot their horns. The rapid advance deep into hostile territory had driven off nine hundred enemy soldiers at a cost of six wounded and three missing. By June 22, 1847, it was time to move on and Capt. Gershom J. Van Brunt took command of a detachment of 175 marines and 20 artillerymen supported by three small craft made up of the bomb brig *Etna*, gunboat *Bonita*, and steamer *Scourge*. Regular rotation called for the *Raritan* to return to Norfolk on July 1, and it appears that Nelson joined the *Scourge* before Perry ordered the final evacuation of Tabasco in mid-July. Throughout the rest of that month and into August, the *Scourge* remained at the mouth of Frontera. On September 14, 1847, she was patrolling one of the rivers below Veracruz when Anderson D. Nelson entered Mexico City with Don Carlos Buell and various other army officers who would interact with William Nelson during the Civil War.[21]

In January 1848, the twenty-three-year-old William became the acting master of the *Scourge*: a nebulous position between the rank of a passed midshipman and a lieutenant (executive officer). The core duties centered on navigating the vessel and entering mundane matters into the log. Nelson noted the "armorer repairing village church bells . . . [and the] engineer finished the propeller and transferred it to water's edge." Two days later, he recorded the "armorer and engineer [remained] at work on shaft and propeller." On January 18, the *Scourge* took the gunboat *Bonita* in tow. Several weeks later, Lt. William Smith and Nelson delivered the war prize *Laura Virginia* to New Orleans. On February 11, Nelson sailed by the castle at Veracruz. A week later, he engaged in the first recorded instance of meting out punishment when he saw that "John Allers, Quarter Master [received] one dozen lashes of the cats for disrespect and disobedience to the master [Nelson]." Days later, Nelson headed for new duties at Pensacola.[22]

Throughout the conflict, the Home Squadron blockaded the entire Gulf of Mexico. During the siege operation at Veracruz, Nelson was under the influence of distinguished leaders like Conner, Perry, Mayo, Buchanan, and Mackenzie. Perry's special infantry brigade exposed him to the deployment of infantry and artillery, and for his personal gallantry and skill as an artillerist, Nelson received a sword. Any exchange of information with Anderson D. Nelson has long since disappeared. That older brother and other professionally trained officers of the United States Military Academy had proved the *Times* wrong and placed their country on a par with the world powers. Through the vigorous recruitment, training, and deployment of a mostly volunteer force, the United States had defeated a large professional army that had the support of a huge population dispersed across a vast expanse of land.

Boundary disputes had been the foundation for sixteen months of fighting for what would become the states of California, Nevada, Utah, Arizona, and parts of New Mexico, Colorado, and Wyoming. This land grab also raised an extraordinary question. Did Congress have the power to prohibit slavery in the new territories? Those opposed to slavery believed the Constitution gave lawmakers that authority. Slave interests, on the other hand, believed that the power to regulate the peculiar institution was a matter for each state to determine. Nelson and many others were going to find that constant clashes over that question would divide the North and South in such a way that it would take an extraordinarily bloody war to resolve the issue.[23]

A t Pensacola, Nelson became acting lieutenant of the supply ship *Relief* while he waited for reassignment. There was a great deal of excitement over the discovery of gold in California, and that brought up talk of building a railroad across the Isthmus of Panama. Because Cuba served as a gateway to the isthmus, some feared that Spain would obstruct commerce in the region. That concern led President Polk and his cabinet to broach the subject of a "fair purchase" of that island in May 1848, and Spain summarily rejected the offer. At the end of July, Nelson's duty in the Gulf ended and he joined the *Michigan*, an iron-hulled vessel that carried two 18-pound guns while she plied Lake Erie, assisted ships in distress, and protected against any possible British encroachment of American soil.[1]

During the spring of 1849, Nelson learned that a devastating cholera epidemic had taken the life of his fifteen-year-old sister, Elizabeth, his forty-three-year-old father, Dr. Thomas W. Nelson, and step-grandmother, Elizabeth Cleneay Nelson. At this same time, the intervention of the Hapsburg and Russian governments in the Hungarian Revolution led the embryonic administration of Whig president Zachary Taylor to engage the U.S. Navy in the largest show of force in the Mediterranean basin since the conclusion of the Barbary Wars in 1815. On July 26, 1849, Nelson was on the *Independence* when she headed out of Norfolk for the base at Spezia, Italy.[2]

This action was regarded as the embodiment of a "Young America" at war with absolute monarchists, and it had support from many in the United States. This ambiguous cause in turn attracted a secondary group who encouraged Cuban ex-patriot Narciso López to assemble a 1,300-man filibustering (free-booting) expedition off the coast of Mississippi. General López had come to the United States in 1848, and he led a faction intent on ending Spanish rule of the island. A long-standing statute prohibited carrying out "any military expedition" against any foreign state at peace with the United States, and in September 1849 President Taylor ordered a naval blockade of Round Island and had the freebooters arrested.[3]

The situation in Europe posed an entirely different problem for the Taylor administration. Turkey had arrested Hungarian revolutionary Louis (Lajos) Kossuth, and the Russian and Austrian governments were demanding his extradition. In December 1849, George P. Marsh, the U.S. minister at Constantinople, approached Turkish officials and asked for the release of the "Magyar" (Hungarian). The following month, Congress approved having a U.S. Navy ship take the deposed leader to America. Commodore Charles W. Morgan received orders to cruise the Bosporus in anticipation of carrying out the mission. Morgan transferred Nelson to the *Cumberland* as acting master, disregarded that assignment, and headed for Lisbon to settle an indemnity claim against Portugal.[4]

At Cincinnati and Covington, John T. Pickett, an old Maysville acquaintance of Nelson's, was busy recruiting a second filibustering expedition for General López. Pickett had served under Gen. John Pragay during the Hungarian Revolution, and in April 1850, his two-hundred-forty-man Kentucky regiment departed for New Orleans to link up with three hundred men from Louisiana and Mississippi. The freebooters achieved victory at Cardenas, Cuba, on May 19–20, but López could not convince the people to overthrow the Spanish government, and he had to withdraw.[5]

In Washington, a complex series of five bills (later known as the Compromise of 1850) was under debate when President Zachary Taylor suddenly died on July 9. The need to overcome the stalemate between the fifteen free and fifteen slave states was acute when Vice President Millard Fillmore took the oath of office the next day. He appointed Daniel Webster secretary of state and asked outgoing Kentucky governor John J. Crittenden to join his administration as attorney general. Fillmore trusted that Crittenden and other slave state appointees would alleviate Southern fears while Webster did his best to engineer the difficult passage of the bills and deal with representatives from Santo Domingo who wanted the United States, Great Britain, and France to protect them from Haitian efforts to seize control of their country.[6]

Democrat Stephen A. Douglas, a newly elected senator from Illinois, worked with Webster and Henry Clay to push through the bill that made California a free state. Another law established territorial governments in New Mexico and Utah. Those territories also had the right to determine through the doctrine of popular (squatter) sovereignty whether they would be slave or free states upon entering the Union. The Fugitive Slave law, the most controversial measure, aroused the everlasting ire of antislavery advocates by mandating the recapture and extradition of blacks who escaped into free states.[7]

In the spring of 1851, the irrepressible López finalized plans to conduct a third invasion of Cuba. The activities of Maj. Louis Schlesinger, a former officer under Louis Kossuth, brought a great deal of attention to the expedition before the odd collection of 453 "ruffians" sailed from New Orleans to Bahia Honda, in Pinar del Río province, Cuba. In nearby Texas, Lt. Jefferson Columbus Davis bragged to James B. Fry that the expedition would succeed if it were under his direction, but it was sure to fail with the amateurs now in charge. Two weeks later, Spanish troops at Las Pozas overwhelmed the invaders. On August 16, 1851, Col. William Crittenden, the nephew of U.S. Attorney General John J. Crittenden, was among the fifty-one men executed by a firing squad.[8]

López went under the guillotine on September 1, and that same day, "Acting Lieutenant" William Nelson helped Kossuth, his family, and fifty exiled followers board the *Mississippi* at Smyrna (Izmir), Turkey. U.S. Minister Marsh no longer trusted Kossuth, and Capt. John C. Long was instructed to sail directly to the United States and "avoid any expression of opinion." Marsh warned Long that the "Magyar" might seize any opportunity to restart his revolution and recommended the *Mississippi* "touch as few ports as possible, and remain as short a period at them, as is possible."[9]

On September 21, 1851, the *Mississippi* dropped anchor in the Bay of Spezia at Sardinia. Kossuth wanted to confer with Italian revolutionary Giuseppe Mazzini in London and asked to use the telegraph on shore. Captain Long denied the request and quickly headed for Marseilles. Commodore Morgan informed U.S. consul John L. Hodge that Kossuth "is utterly ungovernable. . . . He is like a firebrand." Late Friday afternoon, September 26, the *Mississippi* anchored in the harbor at Marseilles. That evening Nelson went ashore to obtain *pratique*, the papers that an incoming ship received after it met quarantine regulations through the presentation of a clean bill of health. Nelson invited M. de Suleau, the *prefet des bouches du Rhone*, to visit Captain Long, and he presented two letters from Kossuth that sought permission for the Magyar to travel through France to England.[10]

French officials denied the request because they feared it would lead to a coup by Napoleon III. Kossuth was livid, and he unleashed a storm by publishing a diatribe that brought out a crowd of thirty-five hundred protesters in Marseilles. De Suleau informed Kossuth he was no longer welcome in Marseilles, and a throng of admirers followed their hero back to the *Mississippi* in hundreds of boats. Captain Long told Kossuth to withdraw from the adoring crowd, and instead he climbed up on the poop deck to deliver a speech. Long embarrassed Kossuth with a public rebuke, and the Magyar asked to leave the *Mississippi* at Gibraltar.[11]

Consul Hodge and Commodore Morgan provided the Magyar with added justification when they officially declared the events at Marseilles a blatant disregard for the neutral position of the United States. That pronouncement put the officers of the *Mississippi* at odds with each other. Acting Lieutenant Nelson led a group who supported the Magyar. In private, he expressed embarrassment for "the coarse conduct" that insulted a guest of the United States in such a way that it made him want to resign his commission. The *Mississippi* arrived at Gibraltar on October 1, 1851, and the Magyar disembarked in front of a crowd of adoring sailors who showed their appreciation by giving him "three hearty cheers."[12]

The *Mississippi* reached the Brooklyn Navy Yard on November 12, 1851. Nelson promptly sought and obtained an extended leave of absence to act as an escort for the Magyar's grand tour of the United States. Five days later, the *New York Times* published a private letter that appears to have been a joint effort of Nelson and other officers from the *Mississippi*. It refuted the attacks made against Kossuth and noted, "We had frequent opportunities . . . of listening to [Kossuth say that he will not] ask assistance from us [the United States]. He does not require it; but be assured *he will ask us*, as he has done in England, *to proclaim the principle of universal non-intervention* [in European affairs]."[13]

On December 6, 1851, a crowd of a quarter million New Yorkers gave Kossuth the sort of public ovation that only George Washington and Lafayette had received previously. Troops in the procession found it hard to restore order in the madness that seriously injured a woman and caused the death of one man. As the unruly crowd pressed against the escort detail, "even Lieutenant Nelson, endowed . . . with a commanding Kentuckian frame . . . could not prevent Madame Kossuth from being repeatedly torn from his arm."[14]

Moments later, her diminutive husband was at the podium, dressed in a black velvet frock coat. With a sword belted to his side, he launched into a lengthy discourse on the Hungarian Revolution. Nelson wanted no more of the adoring crowd, and he saw that Madame Kossuth and Francis and Theresa Pulszky were safely waiting in carriage before the talk ended. A city official took notice, and he complimented the ladies on their command of English. He then looked at Nelson and asked, "Do you speak our language?" The deeply bronzed seaman answered, "I calculate that I do." The official then

Fig. 4. Lieutenant Nelson in strange dress uniform, c. 1851–52 or 1858. An imposing figure who always stood ramrod straight, the six-foot four-inch Nelson had piercing black eyes and long curly hair and weighed between 260 and 300 pounds. CDV done in Montreal for E. & H. T. Anthony, New York, N.Y. The Filson Historical Society, Louisville, Ky.

inquired how he had learned to speak English. Nelson replied, "In my father's house, about twenty-six years ago." The puzzled alderman replied, "How so! Is English taught to infants in Hungary?" Nelson said he did not know about that country, "but I learnt it in Kentucky." He pointed to his jacket and sourly asked, "Don't you know your own navy?" Kossuth arrived moments later to find the ladies laughing loudly at how their "Kentuckian friend had, *by his language*, been mistaken for a Hungarian." That evening everyone enjoyed extraordinary dining that rivaled the best European fare.[15]

Lexington, Kentucky, native George N. Sanders was acquainted with Nelson, and he had recently purchased the *Democratic Review,* the preeminent voice for the proexpansionist Young America movement. In 1848, Sanders had gone to Europe with the intent of selling forty thousand surplus American muskets to Kossuth. Now the Magyar wanted to acquire thirteen to fifteen thousand muskets, and Sanders tried to ingratiate himself with a letter to the *New York Herald* that said the laws against the export of arms were unconstitutional.[16]

On December 27, 1851, Nelson received an especially cordial greeting from Governor Enoch Lowe when the Hungarian entourage arrived in Baltimore. In nearby Washington, officials decided that when Kossuth went before the first session of the Thirty-second Congress there would be no departure from the non-intervention policy of the country. On January 5, 1852, those lawmakers were riled when the Magyar showed up with a personal armed guard. Reports said those men acted like subalterns who had "been reared in camps, as they caroused all day, and then tumbled into their beds booted and spurred, furnishing items of liquors, wines, cigars, and damaged furniture for the long and large hotel bill which Congress had to pay." On January 9, Kossuth called on the gravely ill Henry Clay. This former acquaintance of Nelson's grandfather quietly dismissed the Magyar as someone who was making a veiled attempt to elicit military support for a failed revolution.[17]

Kossuth believed the American heartland would rally to his cause, and at Columbus, Ohio, he went off to address the Ohio State Senate while Nelson joined Capt. Charles F. Henningsen at a meeting of Hungarians in the Representatives' Hall. Henningsen was a massive, blonde soldier of fortune who served with Kossuth in Europe and had come to the United States as a spokesperson for the Magyar. Now he vigorously promoted the idea that Hungary could subdue Russia and Austria if Britain or the United States kept the other European nations out of the fight. At the conclusion of that talk, the master of ceremonies introduced Nelson as a gallant naval officer and a "thorough gentleman in every sense of the word." At the podium, Nelson informed the crowd that "European Absolutism" could no longer deceive their subjects and asked that no one hesitate backing a cause in which the Austrian Empire would be subdued in three months "without wounding one man, or shedding one drop of American blood."[18]

On February 12, 1852, the *Cincinnati Enquirer* described the arrival of Kossuth as one of "the most remarkable events of this remarkable age." The Magyar went across the Ohio River to speak at the Newport Barracks, and at Covington, officials donated $175 to the cause and assured him Kentuckians would furnish ten thousand men if needed. That night, Kossuth was the guest of honor at a festive grand banquet given at the Burnet House. In addition to Nelson, the diverse group included Kentucky governor Charles S. Morehead, a future Know-Nothing who would find himself imprisoned for disloyalty in September 1861; Cassius Marcellus Clay, a fiery proponent of gradual emancipation with compensation; and astronomy professor Ormsby M. Mitchel, who would come to despise Nelson. The praise heaped on the Hungarian guest could not overcome the growing mistrust about his unwillingness to denounce slavery or stand up for the Catholic Church. When the Magyar reached Louisville, he seriously injured his cause by foolishly noting that George Washington had never intended for the policy of noninterference to serve as constitutional dogma.[19]

Nelson family acquaintance John J. Crittenden loathed the toadyism surrounding Kossuth, and he warned at an event celebrating Washington's birthday, "Beware of the introduction or exercise of a foreign influence among you! We are American! The Father of our Country has taught us, and we have learned to govern ourselves." That philosophy also expressed the thoughts behind "The Order of United Americans." They would evolve into the ephemeral American/Know-Nothings whose Ohio Valley constituents held that German and Irish immigrants helped defeat Henry Clay's bid to become president.[20]

Kossuth left St. Louis in late March and headed down the Mississippi River to New Orleans. Col. John T. Pickett was in the Crescent City looking for a way to overthrow Haiti. This acquaintance of Nelson met with the Magyar to propose raising fifteen hundred mercenaries who would overthrow Faustin I and become part of an army that Kossuth could deploy against Austria. Tentative plans called for six battalions to be under the command of officers from the United States Army and Navy that included Nelson.[21]

At the same time a badly divided Democratic Party met in Baltimore to nominate a candidate for president, Kossuth continued to campaign for the freedom of Hungary in the New England states. The Young America faction liked James Buchanan or Stephen A. Douglas. Others wanted Lewis Cass, a proponent of popular sovereignty, or the former secretary of war, William L. Marcy. The wide variety of candidates produced a deadlock, and that led the delegates to place Franklin R. Pierce on the thirty-fifth ballot. An unknown from New Hampshire, Pierce championed a conciliatory policy toward the South, and that resulted in his nomination on the forty-ninth ballot. The next day, Edmund Burke, an adviser to Pierce, recommended that he invite Kossuth to New Hampshire and obtain his support to win the German vote. Kossuth instructed Nelson to go in his place, and rather than wait for a report, he openly recommended Pierce as the best choice for German Americans. That blatant interference in domestic politics signaled to many that the European revolutionary could not be trusted.[22]

Nelson's meeting at Concord, New Hampshire, went well. In his July 3, 1852, report to Kossuth, he said Pierce's "views upon the mission of the

American people and the great Democratic Party are precisely what you wish." Nelson also recommended that Kossuth meet with Pierce. The Magyar declined because the $85,000 collected on the tour had been misspent. He desperately needed money to pay for 7,500 muskets in Brooklyn and 130 barrels of bullets at Morningville. There was an option on another 6,000 muskets, and Kossuth asked George N. Sanders to secure a loan for $10,000 by using the entire lot of 13,500 arms as collateral. On July 13, Kossuth authorized Charles F. Henningsen and William Nelson "to negotiate on my behalf, my cooperation with a company for the defense and colonization of So. Domingo . . . I further commission the said . . . Henningsen . . . to plan the campaign and represent me in it as political and military agent during its continuance." The following day, Kossuth sailed for London under the alias of Alexander Smith.[23]

Six months later, Senator John P. Hale of New Hampshire introduced a detailed motion that had the form and manner of a direct impeachment of Commodore Charles W. Morgan. The next morning everyone was shocked to learn that the sixty-three-year-old Morgan had died from gout of the spine at the Washington Navy Yard. On January 13, 1853, Senator James Shields of Illinois announced that Lieutenant Nelson had furnished him with a letter of reply to Hale's resolution. Shields noted that while the coarse style of expression was inappropriate for the Senate, Nelson insisted that the language remain in the letter. Objections and counters led to a postponement of the hearing, and a week later Hale withdrew his resolution out of respect for Morgan and his family.[24]

One month later, Francis Pulszky left Southampton, England, with plans to meet with the incoming Franklin Pierce and obtain support for intervention in European affairs. Pulszky's instructions also called for him to hold a secret meeting with Nelson and tell him to direct Colonel Pickett to prepare for an expedition to Italy, Hungary, Turkey, or anywhere that Kossuth might direct. Pulszky was to organize those volunteers while Kossuth urged Giuseppe Mazzini to delay plans to seize Milan. Mazzini went forward with the Milanese revolution and failed before Pulszky arrived in the United States, and that effectively ended the need for Pickett. It also ensured that Pulszky no longer enjoyed warm welcomes in official circles.[25]

On February 15, 1853, the *Baltimore Sun* reported that Judge Henry Stump prevented a duel between U.S. Navy Lieut. William W. Pollock and an "officer named Nelson" by putting Pollock under a bail of $1,000 to keep the peace. At that time, William Nelson was under orders to join the *Marion* as acting master. A subsequent order changed that assignment to the *Princeton*, a 1,370-ton screw-steamer that was to join Commodore Perry's expedition to restore relations with China and Japan. Nelson's opportunity to become a part of that notable voyage ended when the ill-fated *Princeton* developed engine trouble.[26]

Once repaired, the *Princeton* became the flagship of the Eastern Squadron under Commodore William B. Shubrick. At the end of June 1853, Shubrick left Norfolk and headed for Nova Scotia to negotiate on behalf of thousands of American fishermen who were being harassed by British vessels because of differences over what constituted "three miles from the coast to the bays." The *Princeton* arrived in Halifax on August 5, 1853, and Shubrick met with Britain's representatives the next day. They agreed on terms that would produce a treaty with Canada in 1854. During the return voyage, Shubrick had the *Princeton* moving under steam and making excellent time when a horrendous fire broke out in the boiler room. The disabled vessel struggled to reach the East River where tugs towed her to the Brooklyn Navy Yard.[27]

On October 17, 1853, Nelson received a thirty-day leave. After he visited with Kossuth in England, the Magyar was convinced the Haiti expedition could go forward if someone supplied Pickett with a ship. George N. Sanders was now the unconfirmed consul to London, but when he embarrassed the United States by holding a dinner for seven leading European revolutionaries, that indiscretion ensured the Senate would deny his confirmation. By the end of May 1854, President Pierce had signed the Kansas-Nebraska Act into law. Two months later the nation was clearly on the road to civil war when Kossuth asked Pierce if he intended to recognize Hungary's independence. There was no reply, and the Magyar never requested aid again. Later newspaper accounts said that Nelson joined Commodore Perry's *second voyage* to Japan in March–June 1854, but there is nothing in the records to support that claim.[28]

On September 1, 1854, Nelson returned to duty as acting master of the *Independence*. Just before the 54-gun flagship set sail, he celebrated his thirtieth birthday and received the full rank of sailing master. While the *Independence* sailed toward Cape Horn, the *Albany* disappeared at sea, and that unfortunate event opened two lieutenants' slots for Nelson and his classmate Samuel P. Carter. Both became lieutenants on April 18, 1855. The *Independence* sailed the South Pacific in support of whaling interests, and when she anchored at Mare Island, San Francisco, in December, Nelson received orders to take temporary command of the store ship *Fredonia* at Valparaiso, Chile.[29]

On May 23, 1856, Nelson requested that Consul George B. Mervine hold a court of inquiry and fix responsibility for the loss of black silk handkerchiefs, black hat ribbons, and cotton pocket-handkerchiefs. Nelson was ashore when the theft occurred, and in his absence, Lt. Dawson Phenix established that boatswain George Calow was the culprit. Calow received a sentence of five years in the penitentiary, and the court held Nelson personally responsible for a loss of $1,005.76.[30]

It was during this same time that Nelson became acquainted with Benjamín Vicuña Mackenna. This Liberal Party revolutionary had sought to overthrow the ruling Conservative Party several years before. He had escaped a death sentence by running away to Europe and the United States and returned to Chile just before Nelson's arrival. A noted historian, he later wrote "some striking anecdotes" for *Harper's Magazine* and a biographical article for the *Frankfort Commonwealth*.[31]

Mackenna greatly admired the enthusiastic way in which Nelson threw himself into the sports and amusements of his country. This Americano looked like a reincarnation of "Henry the Eighth" when he chased after cattle at the annual hunt or broke three or four horses at the rodeo. After sojourns to Lake Aculeo or the fig groves of Catrace, he would return to town and dance the *Zamacucca* with the "grace and agility of an *eligante*." Nelson also enjoyed a reputation as an "elegant and tasteful gentleman of the salons." He frequently revealed his spontaneous temperament by kneeling before the beautiful ladies and swearing "love as inconstant as the billows of his loved ocean."[32]

Nelson impressed everyone with his "spirit of fun and good humor." Once in a mixed crowd of English and Chileans, someone asked what regiments resembled the British soldiers. He replied, "Wait a moment, until I can see their backs, as that is the part of the English soldier we Americans are most familiar with." Nelson loved to foxhunt with his English counterparts, and on one occasion, he encountered a Chilean rider who had fallen under his horse while jumping across a ditch. It appeared certain the weight of the animal would squeeze the life out the young man. Someone suggested shooting the horse, but Nelson insisted that would surely kill the rider. He then took off his cravat, tied it around all four legs, and lifted the animal high enough for others to pull the rider safely away from the horse.[33]

Another example of that stupendous strength occurred during a port call at Rio de Janeiro. During a theater performance, the nonstop jabber of a loud-mouthed British officer angered Nelson to the point that reached into the box, picked the man up by his collar, and with one jerk threw him to the floor eight feet below. Some speculated on the prospects of a duel, but that ended when the English vessel departed early the next morning. Mackenna noted that years later the Brazilians still spoke about the actions of the "*gran Americano*." Chileans who knew the story believed Nelson would have prevailed in the duel because he often took target practice at a local shooting gallery. During one such occasion, Nelson noticed a servant make the customary pause at the threshold of the doorway. In the next instance, he turned and fired a ball straight through the top of the man's sombrero. With equal assurance, Nelson walked across the room to hand the terrified servant a fistful of coins to show he meant no harm.[34]

The assignment at Valparaiso ended in the fall of 1857, and Nelson took an extended leave of absence after his return to the Brooklyn Navy Yard. In late March 1858, he was in Washington making a call on an influential supporter of the navy, Congressman Stephen R. Mallory of Florida. Nelson was looking for relief from the charge against "his account for certain moneys lost [while in command of the *Fredonia*], for which he cannot account; which was referred to [Mallory and] the Committee on Naval Affairs." This put him in direct contact with Senator William McKendree Gwin, a prominent proslavery Californian who chaired that committee. On April 9, 1858, Gwin hosted "the most magnificent fancy ball ever given in the United States." That affair gave Nelson the opportunity to mix with the likes of President James Buchanan; members of the cabinet, Senate, and House; diplomats, army and navy officers. The seating placed him beside "Morning Star" (Miss Martha Ready), "the most attractive young lady at the ball." Nelson had come dressed as a "Commander" but some thought he looked more like "huge Falstaff." The description clearly fitted the hilarity and gaiety of the other costumes, and it helped Senators Jefferson Davis, Stephen A. Douglas, William H. Seward, and John J. Crittenden "to forget that they had recently been shivering lances on each other's reputations in the Senatorial arena."[35]

In late August 1858, Nelson received orders for duty aboard the *Niagara*, the largest screw-steam frigate in the navy and the only ship suited for the task of accommodating the 318 Africans rescued from the slave ship *Echo* (brig *Putnam*) near Kay Verde, Cuba. This duty was not new to the U.S. Navy. In 1808, Congress abolished the importation of slaves from Africa, and twelve years later, declared the transport of slaves an act of piracy punishable by death. Ineffective interdiction led to the formation of the African Squadron in 1843, and fifteen years later, the *Dolphin* became the first U.S. Navy ship to capture a cargo of slaves *and land them in the United States*. The motives were far from noble. Each slave liberated brought a bounty of $25.00, which the crew shared by rank once the captured vessel was sold at auction.[36]

The *Echo* had originally boarded 450 to 470 African slaves at Kabenda, Guinea, but when they arrived at Castle Pickney, Charleston, South Carolina, that number had dwindled to 306 due to poor medical attention and severe malnutrition. Dr. Thomas Rainey was appointed to represent the Africans, and he had them transferred to Fort Sumter where Lt. Jefferson C. Davis was given responsibility for their care. Congressional law required that on their return to Africa they receive subsistence for a year. A contract with the Colonization Society called for the payment of $150 for the transport and support of each refugee to Monrovia, Liberia, for an estimated total cost for the 300 survivors of $45,000. Dr. D. H. Hamilton and other dignitaries chartered a steamer to bring out 360 blankets, "a bale of cotton cloth, a hogshead of bacon, and four casks of rice." Pipes and tobacco were to come later. It pleased those officials to find the "savages . . . appeared in fine spirits, and entertained their visitors with a display of . . . dancing and singing."[37]

On Sunday, September 12, 1858, two tugs guided the *Niagara* out of the Brooklyn Navy Yard. That night the officers and crew marveled at the sight of Donati's Comet, the second largest to appear in the nineteenth century. Early Monday morning, Capt. John S. Chauncey had the *Niagara* under steam, and on Saturday, September 18, he put her into anchorage fifteen miles below Charleston. At 1:00 P.M., on Sunday, U.S. Attorney General Jeremiah S. Black and the captain in charge, Lieutenant Davis, came aboard to speak with Captain Chauncey and discuss arrangements for transferring the Africans—now down to 271—who were suffering terribly from scurvy and dysentery. Nelson and Davis are reputed to have "formed a warm friendship" during this time, but the actual circumstances suggest they probably met only briefly and nothing more.[38]

Lieutenant Davis and Attorney General Black returned to Charleston, and late Sunday evening they relinquished control of the African refugees who were then hauled up through the stern port of the *Niagara* and put on the lower deck under the control of Frank, a Portuguese prisoner who served as an interpreter. On Tuesday, September 21, the *Niagara* headed back out to sea. Captain Chauncey expected "to make the run in 20 days, remain two or three weeks, and sail thence for New York." His cargo below deck showed no interest in using slop buckets for their waste, and conditions turned ghastly overnight. Captain Chauncey moved them to the quarterdeck, and the next morning, Acting Master's Mate Richard Parker found the accumulation of human excrement equally filthy and horrid.[39]

To Parker, the refugees were little better than beastly monkeys. He also felt great pity, particularly when he found a boy and girl dead on Tuesday morning. At 9:30 A.M., the call went out for "all hands, bury the dead." Captain Chauncey conducted an Episcopalian burial service for the two corpses sewed together in a blanket. Several of the crew placed the bodies on a plank and carried them to a gun port. The placed a 32-pound shot on the board, and after the remains slipped through the port, they disappeared with a barely noticeable splash. Each day, while the celestial rocket continued its course, Nelson dutifully recorded the sad fate of others. By Thursday, September 23, eleven bodies had been "committed to the deep."[40]

At 2:00 A.M. Friday a violent gust of wind took off the main topmast at the cap. The few veteran members of the crew scurried up the main mast to start repairs while their untrained cohorts struggled with the ropes and sails of the other masts. On the following Tuesday, Captain Chauncey had the *Niagara* moving "like the wind," and Friday, October 1, his human cargo shook with hopeful glee as they watched the steady glow of the brilliant comet.[41]

Over the next few days, a heavy northwest wind rolled the huge vessel to the point that her masts and rigging appeared to be in danger of going over the side. The crew dispensed with regular uniforms, and Parker started wearing "a short flannel Monkey jacket & pants sometimes [with] a collar . . . always with a shirt." By Thursday, October 14, forty-three Africans had died, eleven in the last two days. The fierce wind had taken the *Niagara* way off course, and to make up the distance, Captain Chauncey ordered the coal-powered screw propeller lowered into the water. At 4:00 P.M., Thursday, October 21, the fast moving vessel arrived at Porto Grande, a Portuguese town of fifteen hundred on St. Vincent's Island. Parker stumbled across another dead African that evening, and after disposing of the remains in eighteen feet of water, he simply noted the grim total had reached fifty-seven.[42]

On Tuesday, October 26, Captain Chauncey had the *Niagara* continue under steam and sail. The next evening, he ordered the anchors lowered two miles from Porto Praya. African boatmen arrived and ferried some of the crew to shore so they could pick up a supply of bananas and oranges. At the Naval Store House, Master Morse resupplied medicines and saw that the casks had ten thousand gallons of fresh water. Aboard the *Niagara*, Nelson placed one unruly seaman in double irons for striking a man, and he confined another for stabbing a man. On Friday, the *Niagara* started for the coast under steam and sail, and by 4:00 P.M. Sunday, November 7, Cape Mount came into view.[43]

On the approach to Liberia, Captain Chauncey slowed the engines, and by daylight Monday, the shoreline was visible. At 2:00 P.M., the *Niagara* anchored a mile and a half south of Monrovia in the Cape Mesurado Roads. Nelson helped hire sixty "Krumen" who loaded the empty water casks into launches and headed up the St. Paul River to refill them. The heavily tattooed "Krooboys" were "Magnificent, athletic fellows—all 6 ft & over in height & splendidly formed & speaking more or less English." They proudly called themselves "Jack No Fear, Jack Two Glass, Jack Half a Dollar, Jack Ugly," and so on.[44]

Seventy-one Africans had died during the fifty-two-day voyage, and Captain Chauncey spoke with Dr. Roberts, "two colored gentlemen . . . [and] the harbor master, a N. York Darkey" about arrangements for the two hundred survivors. On Tuesday, November 15, the officers and men on the *Niagara* watched the "Krooboys" deftly move the refugees ashore with rhythmic chants that kept perfect time with the rowing motion of their paddles.[45]

Two days later, the *Niagara* headed off at a speed of 10 miles per hour and covering 240 miles in a day. On Saturday, November 27, Donati's Comet had been with them for sixty-five days, and Parker carefully noted that it seemed to disappear soon after "the Capt's Monkey fell overboard and . . . drowned." Saturday, December 11, the *Niagara* anchored in New York Harbor, and the next day the *New York Herald* rudely announced the accomplishment of the mission with the headline "The Niggers Are Landed."[46]

Nelson received orders to report for duty with the burgeoning Home Squadron, which now had 5,075 men with 331 guns: an increase of 2,935 men and 148 guns since the conclusion of the Mexican War. The squadron was responsible for conducting operations against the slave trade in the Gulf of Mexico and Caribbean Sea, and Nelson reported for duty on the sloop-of-war *St. Louis*. By mid-August 1859, Nelson may have known that Chile had banished Benjamín Vicuña Mackenna and George Hunneus for their role in the Second Succession Revolution against President Emanuel Montt and the Conservative Party.[47]

Whether Nelson was with the *St. Louis* at Colon (Aspinwall) or at sea, a constant flow of letters and newspapers kept him informed about affairs at home. George D. Prentice, editor of the *Louisville Journal* and a prominent Old Whig from Connecticut, expressed concern over how the "Negroes are daily and nightly escaping from their owners in startling numbers." Those escapes aroused the fear of insurrection, and on October 16, 1859, that anxiety reached a fever pitch when John Brown and a small band of followers seized the Federal arsenal at Harper's Ferry.[48]

A quick conclusion to that bizarre episode did little to lessen the shock to the national psyche. The *Cincinnati Enquirer* saw the raid as the "legitimate fruit of the repeal of the Missouri Compromise." It also predicted that the same Douglas Democrats who pushed through the Kansas-Nebraska Act would also "increase the chances of insurrection, bloodshed and all the horrors of servile war." The *Chicago Tribune*, a strong supporter of Abraham

Lincoln, expressed a similar scenario, singling out William H. Seward and Salmon P. Chase as Republican presidential candidates who "stand ready to deluge the land in blood to carry out their fanatical views" on slavery.[49]

The prospects of a civil war were at the forefront of the news when Nelson returned to Maysville in the spring of 1860. He was suffering from the effects of "Panama Fever" (yellow fever), and while he convalesced at the Washington Hotel (Lee House), Secretary of Navy Isaac Toucey asked the Committee of Naval Affairs (headed by Gwin and Mallory) to decide if Nelson should pay for the loss of supplies from the store ship *Fredonia*. The committee saw no reason to hold Nelson liable, and on June 14, 1860, Congress approved his long-sought request for financial relief. Immediately after, orders arrived for choice duty with the ordnance department at the Washington Navy Yard.[50]

Secretary Toucey answered to old commodores whose fate rested in the hands of the navy board (Gwin and Mallory's committee). Whether by design or by circumstance, Nelson had obtained a pivotal assignment at a time when officers in Washington were divided into "carpet sailors" who dominated the bureaus that influenced decisions and the "sea-going fellows" who displayed an uncommon courage, cautious manner, and principled determination that they carried "from ship to ship." The latter category would have likely surmounted objections over Nelson's about the close association with a European revolutionary who had engaged in bizarre plotting with Colonel Pickett. More importantly, this egalitarian Democrat was a devoted patriot who was deeply concerned about the fate of his state and the nation.[51]

Older brother Thomas Henry Nelson was a lawyer and politician who strongly opposed the doctrine of popular sovereignty. Tom had helped found the Republican Party in Indiana, and he was determined to see Abraham Lincoln become president. That possibility worried John Marshall Harlan and other Kentucky Unionists who feared the commonwealth would become a battleground for opposing forces. Those moderate conservatives supported the Constitutional Union Party and candidate John Bell's platform of "the Union as it is and the Constitution as it is"; a very forthright motto that also matched the unyielding military personality of William Nelson.[52]

Measuring the Political Currents   [4]

I n early August 1860, Nelson crossed the neatly shaded grounds of the Washington Navy Yard and reported to Capt. Franklin Buchanan. This old friend was the commandant, but this was his first introduction to Capt. John A. Dahlgren, the chief of the Bureau of Ordnance. New buildings supported the production of light brass ordnance, boat howitzers, shot, shells, percussion caps, musket balls, and projectiles. Along the shoreline of the Anacostia River, there were two cavernous ship houses and an experimental gun battery that tested guns, propellants, and projectiles.[1]

A short ride up frenzied Pennsylvania Avenue put Nelson in contact with military officers and officials who gathered at Willard's Hotel to guzzle ten-cent drinks, gossip about the upcoming presidential election, or simply enjoy stewed terrapin and fried oysters. Abraham Lincoln's expected victory on November 6 confirmed the worst fears of those who supported slavery. In his native Kentucky, the extreme distrust over that issue brought a mere 1,364 votes. The majority of the commonwealth voted in favor of John Bell and the Constitutional Unionist Party. In Nelson's Mason County the antisecessionist Bell received 1,305 votes, states' rights Democrat John C. Breckinridge 799, popular sovereignty Democrat Stephen A. Douglas 247, and antiexpansionist Abraham Lincoln 26.[2]

In Maysville, the *Eagle* declared that Kentucky's Union Party (slaveholding Democrats who opposed secession) would "not look to Revolution, for the correction of any of the evils of this [incoming Lincoln] Government, or to secession; or to nullification; but to the ballot box, as the only legitimate means under the Constitution." At the state capital, the *Frankfort Commonwealth* asked its readers "to endure with patience what we cannot evade. . . . Give Mr. Lincoln a chance . . . he will not even have the power to appoint an officer without the consent of the Democratic Senate."[3]

It made Samuel F. Dupont "sick at heart" to learn that sixty southern naval officers had resigned by the end of November. The Delaware native spoke for Nelson and others with roots in slaveholding states when he said, "My oath declared allegiance to the United States as one to support the Constitution. . . . I stick by the flag and the national government as long as we have one, whether my state leaves the Union or not."[4]

Kentucky governor Beriah Magoffin had supported Lexington native John C. Breckinridge, and on December 9, he sent a circular to all the slave state governors that recommended they hold a convention to promote constitutional amendments to protect slavery. Magoffin said that if Northern abolitionist interests blocked those proposals, he would then recommend that Kentucky join the secession movement on the condition that all the slaveholding states act in concert rather than individually. U.S. Senator John J. Crittenden represented the Union Democrats, moderate/conservative slaveholders in Kentucky. Those John Bell supporters believed the constitutional right to own slaves would stand. They therefore backed this Old Henry Clay Whig when he sought to extend the Missouri Compromise line and enact laws that would protect slavery south of that line.[5]

The Deep South had no faith in a government that would be under the control of a Republican administration. On December 20, South Carolina shocked the nation into reality by seceding. In Washington, that action produced a rash of rumors. One said a mob of armed dissenters intended to take possession of the Navy Yard, which led Captain Buchanan to announce in early January 1861 that he expected the men in his "command to defend it to the last extremity; and if overpowered by numbers the armory and magazine must be blown up." Lieutenants Richard Wainwright, William Nelson, and John H. Russell served under Captain Dahlgren. He ordered "two trusty men" and a few clerks to secure "eight hundred muskets and rifles, three rifled 12-pounders and five smoothbore 12-pounders" in the attic of the main building. Dahlgren then advised Buchanan that he needed "only about one hundred good men (seamen preferred) to hold this building."[6]

At Frankfort, Governor Magoffin learned that the U.S. Senate had rejected the Crittenden compromise, and he called on the Kentucky General Assembly to convene a secession convention. Garrett Davis then informed Robert J. Breckinridge, the uncle of John C. Breckinridge, that if that special session "should pass a secession ordinance without submitting it to the people, it should be met by armed resistance." On January 17, the House convened and "the sergeant-at-arms [was directed] to hoist the American flag over the capitol."

During the session, Brig. Gen. Simon Bolivar Buckner, the secessionist-leaning Guard commander, asked for additional arms, equipment, and other munitions of war. A review of the Adjutant General's Report indicated that the four thousand men in the State Guard were "admirably drilled." They were organized into sixty-one companies armed with "58 pieces of ordnance, 11,263 muskets, 3,159 rifles and 2,873 cavalry arms." Those chilling numbers convinced a majority to vote against the military appropriations bill.[7]

In Mason County, Nelson's friends and neighbors held "an immense meeting" that denounced the "faithless and perfidious confederates" and promoted the idea of a "perpetual Union." This crowd believed it was the duty of all true patriots to prevent a "long protracted, civil war." They also affirmed that "the supreme right of self-protection" meant they could maintain an armed militia and recommend new laws to "avoid the evils of the past" (constitutionally protected slavery).[8]

Early Saturday, January 26, 1861, Nelson encountered a well-dressed Englishman who asked for directions to a particular room at the Supreme Court. The eccentric manners and pronounced Cockney accent of this man gave Nelson a unique idea. It seemed to him "that a funny banqueting scene might be gotten up, if he should draw up a card of invitation" and used this character to legitimize "a social repast . . . in honor of Queen Victoria and the British people." Senator Henry S. Foote of Mississippi did not know about the joke that he would later write about. That evening, Foote arrived at a renowned restaurant and found "the English guest . . . occupying the seat of honor." States' rights Democrat John C. Breckinridge, his loyal supporter Humphrey Marshall, Senator William H. Seward (R.-N.Y.), and Lieutenant Nelson sat near the counterfeit host.

After the Englishman gave a brilliant toast to Queen Victoria, the wine flowed freely, and the room filled with "songs both merry and pathetic." Seward offered a toast in which he noted how the "agreeable hilarity of the [Washington] dinner scene . . . [was too often] marred by the unhappy introduction of irritating sectional topics." That had not happened on this occasion, and Seward hoped that "many such pleasant banquets . . . hereafter occur among us." Most likely, there was a time when the future secretary of state did learn that this affair had no other purpose than to amuse William Nelson and his zany friend.[9]

On January 29, Kansas became the thirty-fourth state in the Union. Texas seceded two days later, and that meant six of the fifteen slave states had joined South Carolina in leaving the Union. A rumor spread that Southern dissidents intended to seize Washington and that caused Nelson and his cohorts to position 24-pound guns behind barricaded doors and line the walls and windows with sandbags. Captain Buchanan advised:

> In the event of an attack upon this navy yard by a mob, the following will be observed by the officers and employees connected with it:
>
> The main entrance to the yard will be defended by Lieutenant H. H. Lewis, in charge of a 12-pounder howitzer and the marine guard. The east entrance will be defended by Lieutenant [Charles H.] Simms, in charge of a 12-pounder howitzer.
>
> Three howitzers, under the command of Lieutenants [Richard] Wainwright and [William] Nelson and Gunner [John] Clapham will defend the ordnance buildings and the west side of the yard, all under the command of Commander Dahlgren.
>
> Lieutenant Commanding [Thomas Scott] Fillebrown, with the howitzer of the *Anacostia*, assisted by Carpenter [John] Rainbow and [retired] Boatswain [George] Willmuth, each in charge of a howitzer, will defend the lower part of the yard.
>
> The marines and howitzers will be concentrated as necessary at any point where their services may be required.
>
> Commander [William] McBlair will see this order executed and superintend generally, under my directions, the defense of the yard.[10]

At Springfield, Illinois, a letter from Charles F. Mitchell informed president-elect Lincoln about affairs in Kentucky. The Flemingsburg resident had just returned from Frankfort with state senator Landaff Watson Andrews of Bath County. Mitchell believed the border states would remain in the Union if Kentucky remained firm. He said the state senate remained opposed to the secession convention by a slim majority of four, but that figure would double if they presented the question in a different way. The House appeared to be in favor by two votes. Citizens with substantial means were "on the side of Union—But every poor white scamp, every adventurer, every demagogue & every office seeker & slavery fanatic are for convention & consequently for Secession. . . . Oh! if our friends in the North would but step forward with a magnanimous spirit & accept some plan of settlement acceptable to the border states—what joy it would give."[11]

In Louisville, travelers from the seceded states in the South now took great pride in signing hotel registers with addresses such as "The Republic of Mississippi" and so on. At Frankfort, lawmakers in the Kentucky House of Representatives put the secession convention call to a trial vote and the measure lost by 54 to 36. By February 11, 1861, it was apparent the Senate had no interest in voting approval, and the General Assembly agreed to adjourn until March 20, 1861.[12]

That same morning, Lincoln departed from Springfield with a huge entourage that included newspaper correspondent Henry Villard and three of Mary Todd Lincoln's cousins: Lizzie Grimsley, John Blair Smith Todd, and Capt. Lockwood M. Todd. Capt. John Pope had found a place as a military escort, and at the Indiana border William Nelson's brother Tom climbed aboard with fellow Indiana Republicans, U.S. Representative Schuyler Colfax, U.S. Senator Henry S. Lane, and Caleb B. Smith, a behind-the-scenes politician who had seconded Lincoln's nomination for president. About 3:00 P. M. the following afternoon, Cincinnati mayor Richard M. Bishop welcomed the president-elect to a city filled with a mix of opportunists and suspicious personalities that included Southern sympathizer George N. Sanders. Early the next morning, Tom Nelson, Indiana governor Oliver P. Morton, and other dignitaries from Indiana bid Lincoln farewell as Larz Anderson (Maj. Robert Anderson's brother) boarded the train with other prominent Ohioans who headed for Columbus with the president-elect.[13]

On February 24, 1861, Lincoln and his entourage took up residence at Willard's Hotel while seventy-three-year old John J. Crittenden said good-bye to his colleagues in the U.S. Senate. A week later the House of Representatives voted 95 to 62 to censure Secretary of the Navy Isaac Toucey for "accepting without delay or inquiry, the resignation of officers of the Navy, who were [now] in arms against the Government." That behavior was seen as a "grave error, highly prejudicial to the discipline of the service, and injurious to the honor and efficiency of the Navy." When Nelson learned that large numbers of naval officers were also being ordered to foreign duty stations, he rushed to the Navy Department and found orders for him to report to the *Bainbridge* in the Pacific Squadron. The underlying intent was to deter the resignations of Southern officers, but Nelson and other naval officers who had a strong sense of loyalty looked on Toucey's actions as treason. He angrily ripped the papers apart and stormed off to seek advice from some of the "leading men in the country."[14]

Tom Nelson helped his brother by introducing him to Henry Villard. That well-regarded correspondent was impressed with William's "unbounded loyal enthusiasm . . . tireless, infectious energy . . . [and the] altogether . . . remarkable personality." Others saw an "extraordinary individual—one of the type that often precipitate as well as participate in atypical events." On Monday, March 4, 1861, Villard chatted with the president-elect just before the inauguration. They spoke about the terrible pressure from place-hunters, and Lincoln replied, "I hardly have a chance to eat or sleep, I am fair game for everybody of that hungry lot."[15]

The second day after the inauguration, William Nelson walked into the Executive Mansion with the peculiar manner of Kentuckians that said, "Here I am; if you don't like me, the worse for you." Nelson had a natural affinity for the Southern way of life, and Lincoln sensed that subversive elements might seek out this "warm hearted, handsome," and "aristocratic" individual because he appeared likely to "cast his lot" with slaveholders. In view of that, it was suggested that Nelson mingle with Washington society while the president considered how to make the best use of his aggressive personality. During that interim, Nelson found that should Kentucky secede, his "warm personal friend" John C. Breckinridge was not averse to offering him a place in the Confederate military.[16]

In Lexington, the *Statesman* made it known that on March 19, "a Convention of States' Rights anti-coercion men of Kentucky will be held in Frankfort." This was the day before the state legislature went back into session, and President Lincoln asked Joseph Holt to meet with him and discuss the situation in Kentucky. The highly successful Louisville lawyer was a former member of the Buchanan-Breckinridge administration who wanted to keep his state loyal to the Union. Lincoln also looked to Green Adams, and that old political ally from Knox County, Kentucky, accepted the position of auditor in the Treasury Department.[17]

On Thursday, March 28, the *Times* of London correspondent William H. Russell attended the first state dinner held by the Lincolns. At the affair, Russell sat next to the largest naval officer he had ever seen. It stunned him when this 260-pound mariner suddenly launched a fierce and coarse attack "against members of his profession who had thrown up their commissions." Nelson went on to say that "Sumter and Pickens are to be reinforced, Charleston is to be reduced to order, and all traitors hanged, or he will know the reason why; and says he, I have some weight in this country." At the same dinner (or a similar affair), Nelson gave an extraordinary display of his "knowledge about medicine, church history, art, music, literature, and the military." The virtuoso performance held everyone spellbound until a fellow officer cleverly noted the speaker carefully avoided naval affairs because he had no mastery of that discipline. That wit might have been Gustavus Vasa Fox, the affable and rotund seaman who had served with Nelson at Tabasco. Fox had recently returned to naval service with the intent of providing relief for the forces at Ft. Sumter.[18]

The following day (Good Friday), Lincoln conferred with Fox and the new cabinet about provisioning Fort Sumter, and Nelson kept William Russell from nosing around by taking him on a grand tour of the Navy Yard. In Kentucky, the legislature had elected outgoing Vice President John C. Breckinridge to replace John C. Crittenden in the U.S. Senate, and the following week, Breckinridge made a transparent attempt to promote secession. He told the lawmakers that he viewed the United States as "a limited confederation of equal states" in which the individual states could leave with adequate cause. These legislators represented landed aristocrats, merchants, farmers, and immigrants who wanted to safeguard the financial vitality of the Upper Ohio Valley. They preferred neutrality, opposed secession, and their representatives voted accordingly. Before the General Assembly adjourned on April 5, 1861, they approved a Border State convention in Frankfort on May 27 and authorized $19,400 for the construction of an arsenal at Frankfort.[19]

Tom Nelson remained in Washington looking for the right opportunity to speak with the president about becoming the new minister to Brazil. He tried to meet with Lincoln just as he decided to go ahead with the resupply of Fort Sumter. The Confederates placed the fort under siege, and Maj. Robert Anderson surrendered the facility on April 13, 1861. Washington had fifteen volunteer companies, six regular companies, and thirty-seven marines at the Navy Yard. Lincoln immediately conferred with the War Department, the Navy Department, and the cabinet about how to mobilize additional forces. Lt. Gen. Winfield Scott recommended that the states supply seventy-five thousand militiamen to serve the three-month maximum allowed by law, and on Monday, April 15, Lincoln requested those troops from the states not in rebellion.[20]

In Louisville, the proclamation produced reports of companies "in the act of enlisting for the Southern Confederacy. . . . several start to-morrow." It also appeared that "every respectable [Kentucky] Union paper" was condemning the announcement "in unmeasured terms." The *Louisville Journal* and the *Louisville Democrat* denounced the call as "unworthy" and a "gigantic folly." George D. Prentice, the editor of the *Journal* was astounded by the request. In Maysville, the *Eagle* asked its readers, "Will we sustain such an Administration? Never, while the sun shines." On Tuesday, April 16, a crowd of three thousand citizens in Louisville voted to adopt resolutions that would prevent Federal troops from using Kentucky to march against any seceded state. They endorsed Governor Magoffin's proclamation that Kentucky would not supply the requested four regiments "for the wicked purpose of subduing her sister Southern States." The gathering also noted that no troops should be supplied the Confederacy. At Paducah, a mass meeting of citizens voted to "take prompt measures to place the State in a condition to defend her rights, her honor, and her soil." They further resolved, "We are unhesitatingly with the south in sympathy, in interest and in action."[21]

John Harney, the editor of the *Louisville Democrat*, noted that Kentuckians were about to be "ground between the upper and nether mill stone." He explained that "we whose interest is allied to both sections, who are dependent for an inlet to our commerce on the waters of the upper Mississippi [Ohio River], and for an outlet to the mouth of the same [New Orleans], are . . . plunged into a war in which, no matter which part wins, we lose." Paul R. Shipman, the associate editor for the *Louisville Journal*, understood the reluctance to declare allegiance to either side. He advised the Central Committee of the Union Party that they should promote a policy of neutrality because that unfathomable position would make it appear that Kentucky was taking a firm stand when in reality it would give loyal Union men much needed time to become better organized.[22]

The unpredictable nature of the stance worried Lincoln. He saw an immediate need to "arouse the young men of the State to action for the Union. We must know what [young] men in Kentucky have confidence of the people and who can be relied on for good judgment, that may be brought to the support of the [Federal government]." Lincoln had observed the thirty-six-year-old William Nelson for six weeks, and he appeared particularly well suited for determining how the political currents in Kentucky might be running. He had "intelligence, courage, and an accurate knowledge of men" that was further complemented by "the social gifts, the free manners, [and] the impulsive temperament peculiar to the South."[23]

On Thursday, April 18, the *National Union* at Winchester, Kentucky, announced that "any attempt . . . to put Kentucky out of the Union by force, or to compel Union men . . . to submit to an ordinance of secession is an act of treason . . . and . . . [it is] therefore lawful to resist any such ordinances." In Louisville, Nelson addressed the following letter to Mary Lincoln's cousin John B. S. Todd at the Executive Mansion:

> The people have gone absolutely mad. Some of the best Union men are talking of secession and acting as officers at secession meetings: I have met several people and a Union meeting arranged for to night—Mr. [James] Guthrie will speak—Gov. Magoffin is here doing all he can to encourage secession, damn him! Mr. Crittenden will take the stump on Tuesday. . . . An immense pressure is brought on all officers to resign

and some are weak enough to be bullied into it. . . . There are a thousand [men] enrolled, under the command of Col Blanton Duncan—I have taken opinion of friends on the idea of swearing out a warrant against Duncan for treason &c but they say that it will only do harm in the state of excitement. . . . I think Ky can be held still![24]

It appeared that Duncan and other Confederate agents had a clandestine agreement with Governor Magoffin that allowed recruits to be transported free-of-charge from Louisville to Nashville on Guthrie's L&N railroad. Guthrie declared that he wanted "Kentucky to take her stand for peace. . . . and let those who want to make the experiment of secession go as individuals." The secessionist *Kentucky Statesman* declared: "KENTUCKY CAN NOT BE NEUTRAL . . . The idea of a stolid indifference or an armed neutrality . . . when the remaining States are engaged in deadly strife is to our mind worse than absurd." In Hardin County, five officers of the State Guard announced, "Kentucky must arm for her defense against [Federal] INVASION. . . . we call on all able bodied young men . . . to come forward and enroll themselves in the State Guard."[25]

On Monday, April 22, 1861, Nelson informed President Lincoln through Captain Todd that the "poison of disunion . . . ideas have been industriously disseminated" in Kentucky. He incorrectly assumed that "Magoffin at the instance of [John C.] Breckinridge has refused to call an extra session of the Legislature because the Legislators are strongly *union*." The Louisville banks had denied the governor's request to borrow $500,000 for arms and Nelson believed it would be another three or four months before Kentucky secessionists could acquire a sufficient amount of money for guns. In that interim, it appeared that "armed neutrality" would be the best way to keep Kentucky "true to her colors."[26]

An unsigned memorandum had already gone forward to President Lincoln that said the senders represented a majority of forty thousand people who held 80 percent of the wealth in the commonwealth. That anonymous group also recommended that Kentucky adopt a position of "armed neutrality" from which it could act as a mediator who fanned "the flame of loyalty" in the present crisis. These men stated that the impending threat of a secessionist takeover made it imperative to form "companies and battalions in every neighborhood under the name of Home Guards."[27]

At the Washington Navy Yard, Captain Buchanan was incensed over news that Secretary of the Navy Gideon Wells had ordered a Federal guard placed on four U.S. Navy ships. On Tuesday, it appeared to Buchanan that his native Maryland was about to secede, and he assembled the command to tell them it was no longer possible for him serve his nation. Capt. George A. Magruder, the chief of ordnance, had been with Nelson at Tabasco, and he elected to go to Canada rather than choose sides. By the end of the day, Captain Dahlgren was left with 37 marines, 34 men in the ordnance department, and 267 men in three infantry companies. Col. Charles P. Stone learned that "should an attack be made to-night in the direction of the President's Mansion, the Massachusetts troops will promptly move to its defense, leaving the District of Columbia volunteers and Pennsylvania troops for the defense of the Capitol." At midnight, Stone saw a bright light in the East Room. On further investigation, he discovered that Captain Todd had authorized Kansas radical James Henry Lane and Kentucky firebrand Cassius Marcellus Clay to house 50 armed men in the Executive Mansion. Wednesday morning, April 24, Lane and Clay received orders to move those volunteers to the Washington Navy Yard by 9:00 P.M.[28]

At Louisville, 70 young men at Garrett Townsend's saloon showed their support for the Union by enrolling in the First Ward (Union) Home Guard. Hours earlier, Nelson had been disgusted by the sight of "regularly organized [secessionist] troops . . . [leaving] the State [of Kentucky], with drums beating and flags flying, for the avowed purpose of joining the Confederates." State Guard Capt. Joseph Desha had added to that distress when he departed from Cynthiana with 107 recruits that were to join Blanton Duncan's Confederate regiment at Louisville. When Desha reached Frankfort, Union "rowdies" expressed their disapproval by throwing rocks and boulders at the train. In Covington, the tension between secessionists and unionists worried the city council to the point they saw a need to authorize a special corps of volunteer police to "dispense with 'grass throwing' and resort to weapons more in keeping with the times."[29]

Governor Magoffin called for the Kentucky legislature to reconvene on the first Monday in May, and Garrett Davis felt certain this would bring about an appropriation of arms for the secessionist State Guard. Nelson had instructions to return to Washington, and Davis apparently joined him. President Lincoln agreed to meet with Davis, and they spoke about neutrality, the property rights of slaveholders, and the need for Federal support. Lincoln also assured Davis there were no plans to abolish slavery in Kentucky, and he contemplated no military operations. As Davis was about to leave, he told Secretary of War Cameron of his desire to place arms in the hands of "ten or even twenty thousand young and effective men" who would "put down any secession movement."[30]

Davis did not know "the President and Secretary of War [had just] committed to . . . [Salmon P. Chase] the principal charge of what related to Kentucky and Tennessee." The former Democratic governor of Ohio was highly regarded in Cincinnati. He would now be responsible for recruiting, developing strategy, planning initiatives, and issuing orders that "agreed with Lincoln's policy of respecting Kentucky's neutrality." Chase was interested in "the covert arming of loyalist elements," and he believed that "two Kentuckians" could move "Kentucky away from neutrality and into the Union." On the military side, Chase admired Nelson's "apparent leadership qualities." In Garrett Davis, he saw a politician who could handle the task of "cultivating Union opinion and working with the loyalists in the Kentucky legislature." This was done under the pressure of the moment and no one seemed to look at the issue of compatibility between the "temperamental" Davis and the "voluble" Nelson.[31]

Lincoln's personal secretary, John Hay, characterized the sixty-year-old Davis as "a gentleman, slight in stature, elderly, quiet, grave. A fine head—thin white hair, the baldness of the brow giving prominence to the benevolence and energy indicated by the phrenological development—clear bright eyes, a Wellingtonian nose—a firm, straight mouth—a complexion untarnished by dissipation, and an expression of feature honest and steadfast, without concealments and without fear." Cincinnati newspaperman Murat Halstead viewed Davis as "the last lingering relic of a class of little great men, who cannot, in their minds, disentangle the interests of good government from those of slavery, and in whose troubled dreams mingles always unwholesomely the flavor of the unresting contraband." The always-difficult Cassius Marcellus Clay noted how that exasperating acquaintance relished making "his points, a book at a time, in a thin, piercing voice."[32]

On Friday, May 3, 1861, Maj. Gen. George B. McClellan received command of the Department of the Ohio, which was comprised of the states of Ohio, Indiana, and Illinois. The next morning the "Stars and Stripes" were flying over every house in Nelson's hometown of Maysville as 820 people went to cast their votes for delegates to represent the Union ticket in the Border State convention. The States Rights' ticket had withdrawn, and statewide the Union candidates received 107,334 votes in 105 counties (5 did not report).[33]

The following day, Lincoln continued to deliberate over how to appeal to a nation dominated by emotional young men who looked on war as a romantic responsibility that would provide them with the opportunity for everlasting fame and glory. Nelson had shown the sort of spirit that inspires such men, and when he arrived at the Executive Mansion on Saturday, he intended to present "his plan for furnishing arms to the Kentucky Unionists." The president listened intently before he coyly asked his genial friend what kind of person would expose himself to such danger. Nelson declared with complete abandon, "Cast your eyes on a little man of my size." Lincoln instructed Nelson to meet with his old friend Joshua Speed in Louisville and work out the details for a distribution of arms in Kentucky. Before Nelson could board the train, Secretary of War Cameron released five thousand Prussian flintlocks converted to percussion-cap rifles.[34]

N elson reached Louisville Monday evening, May 6, 1861. The next morning, the Kentucky General Assembly was meeting in special session at Frankfort when he arrived at Joshua Speed's office. This was the first encounter between the two men, and they went into an adjoining room and engaged in small talk until each felt comfortable enough to openly discuss arming Unionists and meeting with the key leaders in Frankfort. The two men agreed to leave for the state capital that afternoon, and as Nelson started for the door, he warned that neither of them should acknowledge each other "on the cars this afternoon." If needed, Nelson said he would "insult" Speed to dispel any notion of friendship between them. Joshua and his brother James avoided Nelson by traveling in a separate car. At Frankfort Nelson dashed off to the residence of an old acquaintance while Joshua Speed went about notifying key Union leaders there would be a special meeting at the office of James Harlan later that Tuesday evening.[1]

At 9:00 P.M., Nelson met with the Speeds, James Harlan, John J. Crittenden, Charles A. Wickliffe, Thornton F. Marshall, and Garrett Davis. Davis told the others he had known Nelson for twenty years, that he was "a friend . . . and a gallant officer of the navy" who had recently traveled over a large portion of Kentucky meeting with Union men who wanted to arm companies formed in opposition to State Guard troops who favored secession. Nelson told the gathering the president had authorized him to bring in five thousand muskets and bayonets along with a supply of forty cartridges and fifty caps per gun. He placed blank authorization forms on the table, trusting that would intimidate these men into signing. Harlan and his colleagues were not the type who would give anyone that much discretion, and they made it clear the distribution would be solely under their authority. They decided that each of them should oversee their own district; Nelson would allocate weapons according to their requests; and Joshua Speed would endorse the consignments. When the meeting adjourned in the early morning hours of Wednesday, May 8, Garrett Davis boldly declared this might have been the most vital assembly ever held in Kentucky and possibly the United States.[2]

On Tuesday, May 14, 1861, Nelson and Davis were at the public landing in Cincinnati to superintend the unloading of the guns from the steamboat *Reliance*. A hard bunch of roustabouts was to separate the cargo into two shipments. One would be ferried across the Ohio River to railcars at the Covington & Lexington depot. The second was to go by steamboat to Maysville. The activity caught the attention of the Home Guard Central Committee and they alerted the Committee on Suspicious Characters. Wednesday afternoon several of the latter group went to Covington and ordered the telegraph operator to cease all transmissions. Another bunch went to the landing and demanded that Nelson produce papers that authorized him to ship guns into hostile territory. A stream of curses and the threat to arrest anyone who interfered with the loading sent those men scurrying back to the safety of the six-story Carlisle Building at Fourth and Walnut Streets.[3]

About midnight, the conductor on the last railcar signaled the loading at Covington was completed. Ten percent (500) of the muskets and bayonets were to remain under the control of local Union leaders Bushrod W. Foley and John W. Finnell. The other 4,500 went into the heart of Kentucky to inspire unionism and sour secession. At daylight, Thursday, May 16, some 2,250 arms arrived in Paris. Garrett Davis and John D. Hearne sent two wagons to Georgetown. Fourteen boxes stayed at Paris. The rest went to Fayette, Clark, and Montgomery counties.[4]

The second shipment arrived in Maysville on Saturday. Richard H. Stevenson wrote to Col. Thomas B. Stevenson that "about two o'clock [A.M.] Hamilton Grey [Gray] and others brought here in the Steamboat *Boston*, 2,500 percussion muskets, obtained from the Lincoln authorities, pretendedly to be used in arming the Home Guard . . . but really in support of the ursurpations [sic] of Lincoln." Stevenson believed that Garrett Davis was responsible for instigating the "high handed treachery," and it appeared that Nelson had directed this act of "neutrality with a vengeance."[5]

Garrett Davis indicated that "the officer" (Nelson) had fronted some of the costs, and it required "that every man to whom a gun was delivered should pay $1 . . . to reimburse the price of transportation, and some other charges and expenses." Davis said no arms or ammunition had come "into the State without authority of the laws thereof." He noted the United States Constitution guaranteed the right "to keep and bear arms," and the Constitution of Kentucky declared that the right of loyal citizens to "bear arms in defense of themselves and the State shall not be questioned." Davis went on to say the Home Guard companies were independent bodies with their own rules. He did not know where the arms came from, but "the officer" (Nelson) confided they had been "appropriated according to his discretion, without restrictions or instructions, except they were intended for true, faithful, and reliable Union men."[6]

At the General Assembly in Frankfort, lawmakers who sympathized with the seceded states readily accepted stories that Unionists had brought fifteen thousand arms into Kentucky. That exaggeration meant that Nelson's introduction of five thousand converted flintlocks had shifted the balance of power to the Union Home Guard. Harrison County state representative William W. Cleary immediately demanded an investigation of "the arms brought into this state [by Nelson] without authority of the laws thereof." Lovell Harrison Rousseau represented Louisville in the Senate, and along with other Unionists, this Mexican War veteran quickly countered Cleary's inquiry by asking for an investigation "into the mystic doings of the Knights of the Golden Circle and the supply of weapons to [Blanton Duncan's] troops who left our State to aid secessionists in Virginia."[7]

Friday, May 24, the last day of this second special session of the General Assembly, the Senate approved armed neutrality by a vote of 13 to 9. Lawmakers also granted the appropriation of $3 million to buy arms and that suggested the secessionists had obtained a great victory. However, a closer look revealed that a five-member board with a unionist majority would control all military affairs in the state. The neutrality bill also required a loyalty oath from each member of the State Guard. Failure to take the oath within thirty days meant they had to resign and return their arms to the state. A willful failure to return state property within forty-eight hours of notice would be punishable by a fine of not less than $5,000 and imprisonment until they paid the penalty in full.[8]

The ability to intimidate Union voters in the June and August elections was unlikely now that the legislature had effectively muzzled "Magoffin's State Guard" and Nelson had armed loyal Kentuckians with five thousand muskets. Judge Allan A. Burton of Lancaster had even higher goals and he sought additional arms from Washington to help ensure that Kentuckians would "elect an unconditional union legislature who will go flatly for Coercion."[9]

Joe Holt agreed with that aim and he declared the armed forces of the national government had as much "constitutional right to pass over the soil of

Kentucky, as they have to march along the streets of Washington. . . . Kentucky may be assured that this conflict, which is one of self-defence, will be pursued on the part of Government in the paternal spirit in which a father seeks to reclaim his erring offspring. No conquest or effusion of blood is sought."[10]

On May 28, 1861, newly appointed Brig. Gen. Robert Anderson assumed command of the Department of Kentucky, which was headquartered in Cincinnati. Anderson had no authority to take action in the commonwealth, and that meant the Home Guard companies were responsible for keeping Kentucky loyal. Joshua Speed noted, "so far, we have beaten them [the secessionists] at their own game." Indiana governor Oliver P. Morton doubted the effectiveness of those companies and he informed Secretary Cameron, "It is the opinion of all military men here [Indiana] that it would be little better than murder to send troops into battle with . . . muskets altered from flint to percussion locks." Unionists in Kentucky were pleased to have those arms, and on May 29, Speed seconded the request of the Union Committee for more muskets. His note concluded with the advice that "no one can serve us better than Capt. Nelson."[11]

In a matter of months, Kentucky had moved from "strict neutrality" to "intermediary neutrality" and finally "armed neutrality." During each stage, secessionist feeling had grown increasingly stronger in the westernmost part of Kentucky. Major General McClellan informed President Lincoln, "Nelson will explain to you that a convention in now being held at Mayfield which may declare the 'Jackson Purchase' separate from Ky, its annexation to Tenns, & that this will be followed by an advance of Tenna troops upon Columbus and Paducah. . . . Should it not be in the power of the Govt. to send Lt. Nelson back to distribute arms, I would be glad to have him attached to my staff, on account of intimate relations with the Union men of Ky."[12]

A second installment of five thousand guns arrived on June 5, 1861, and it included one thousand arms for Emerson Ethredge, a former congressman from East Tennessee. About that same time, six cannons and nine hundred muskets vanished from Paducah and turned up in Tennessee. Garrett Davis informed McClellan that by "the later part of the month [June] . . . You will have to move on Paducah and Columbus." Joe Holt responded with a lengthy argument against armed neutrality entitled "The Duty of Kentucky in the Crisis." The carefully worded tract avoided any criticism of the ordinary citizen and instead it attacked those who promoted secession as nothing more than a "band of agitators" with an "unholy lust for power." Prominent Cincinnatian Larz Anderson, the brother of Brig. Gen. Robert Anderson, joined Nelson in reprinting five thousand copies at their own expense. Holt was advised by Nelson that the "effect in the state was absolutely wonderful. I am told that 'your letter' and 'my guns' did the business. . . . The Union Party will soon stand solidly on it . . . neutrality is being abandoned."[13]

On June 9, Nelson was in Washington when he wrote to Secretary of State Seward about Larz Anderson's concern that the "Kentucky brigade" should go to Louisville. Nelson noted that the First and Second Kentucky Regiments were established at Camp Clay, so various officers could be mustered into service. He felt it would do the Union cause great harm if any Federal troops entered Kentucky before the June elections and recommended that the ailing Robert Anderson remain in command at Cincinnati. Nelson concluded by asking Seward, "Let us have our own way a little longer, and I promise to hold the State true to her allegiance."[14]

On June 20, 1861, Kentuckians elected nine of ten Congressional candidates on the single issue of keeping the state in the Union. At that same time, incorrect news reports said, "Seventy and eighty boxes of the 'Lincoln muskets' [stamped "1824"] were sent up the Covington and Lexington R. R. . . . for the Union men of the [East Tennessee] mountains." In Tennessee, the president of the Memphis & Charleston Railroad, Samuel Tate, wrongly advised Confederate secretary of state Robert Toombs that Andrew Johnson had shipped ten thousand guns from Cincinnati to Nicholasville and from there they would go by wagon to East Tennessee.[15]

Andrew Johnson, Green Adams, and others wanted an officer sent "to [East] Tennessee to muster into the service of the United States 10,000 men." Judge Burton was among the Kentucky Unionists who recommended Nelson for that assignment. Adams departed from Washington to enlist troops in Kentucky, and Nelson stayed so he could complete arrangements for more arms to come forward. On July 1, 1861, Nelson was officially detached from the navy and given temporary authority to act as a brigadier general and muster into service five regiments of infantry, one regiment of cavalry in East Tennessee, and one regiment of infantry in West Tennessee. That directive also called for him to receive "10,000 stands of arms and accouterments, six pieces of field artillery, two smooth and two rifle bore cannon, and two mountain howitzers, and ample supplies of ammunition."[16]

In Lexington, the *Statesman* reported fifty men from the town "are now at *Camp Boone* . . . and we understand twenty Kentucky companies are now concentrating [there]."At Louisville, the secessionist *Courier* reported, "there had been a perfect exodus of gallant stalwart Kentuckians through this city to [Camp Boone] Tennessee to join the Southern army." In total, it appeared that two complete regiments had gone "to fight for the defense of State Rights and Constitutional Liberty."[17]

James Guthrie's Louisville & Nashville (L&N) railway carried those men, and this brought a ruling from the Jefferson County Circuit Court that prohibited any practice that aided the cause of tearing the nation apart. Nelson was about to openly recruit and camp soldiers on Kentucky soil, and Joe Holt set the stage with a passionate address at Louisville on Saturday evening, July 13, 1861. Garrett Davis chimed in with advice to Secretary of War Cameron that Unionists expected to elect eighteen out of nineteen men running for the Kentucky state senate in two weeks. He stated "our purpose" is to gain the necessary two-thirds majority (26 out of 38 members) to impeach Governor Magoffin, and "when . . . [the August election] is over we will be ready for a more active policy."[18]

In Washington, Andrew Johnson obtained the release of Lt. Samuel Powhatan Carter from naval duty so he could assume a role similar to that of his old classmate Nelson. Samuel's brother, James P. T. Carter, was there seeking arms, and Secretary of War Cameron told him the only person with "the requisite authority to act" on that request was Nelson. James Carter came to Cincinnati, and after Nelson met with him, he informed Andrew Johnson the secessionists would be "on the lookout for Carter. . . . I fear he will find some serious difficulty in getting through." Nelson characterized Carter as a "chatterbox" who had seriously compromised plans by discussing them with people who could not be trusted. He complained such "blabbing" could cause more trouble than five thousand Secessionists could and sarcastically concluded, "I half wish they would catch and hang him." When James Carter arrived in Barbourville on Monday, July 15, he delivered a tirade against Nelson before continuing on to East Tennessee. That rant seemingly encouraged Green Adams to tell Secretary of the Treasury Chase that he believed "Nelson is more wind than substance, but hope in this I may be mistaken."[19]

Nelson had come forward to meet with the "principal gentlemen of Southeast Kentucky" at Lancaster. They decided the headquarters for the East Tennessee expedition would be at "the old Bryant tavern stand one and a half miles south of Crab Orchard" and sixty-five miles from the Cumberland Gap. Nelson planned to raise thirty companies of infantry and five of cavalry at a camp named in his honor. Speed S. Fry of Danville would become colonel of the First Regiment Kentucky Volunteer Infantry; Clay County politician Theophilus T. Garrard the colonel of the Second Regiment Kentucky Volunteer Infantry; and Adair County politician Thomas E. Bramlette colonel of the Third Regiment Kentucky Volunteer Infantry. The First Regiment Kentucky Volunteer Cavalry would have William J. Landram for colonel and Casey County politician Frank L. Wolford for lieutenant colonel. Nelson estimated it would take 350 wagons and 100 broken mules to transport "13,000 muskets, weighing 185,000 pounds; ammunition weighing 54,000 pounds; accouterments weighing 75,000 pounds; rations weighing 250,000 pounds."[20]

Nelson wrote to Capt. Leonidas K. Metcalfe, the son of former governor Thomas Metcalfe, and asked him to help raise men for the brigade. Nelson said he needed "to hurry matters a little for political reason[s]. I have seen the Old Fogies in Lexington. They are weak, but they will be compelled to come up to the scratch in the long Run." That remark apparently referred to Garrett Davis, John J. Crittenden, and other old Henry Clay Whigs who were reluctant to see Union recruits encamped on neutral soil. This thoroughly disgusted Nelson and he asked Crittenden, why should "native Kentuckians . . . assemble[d] in camp under the flag of the Union . . . upon their native soil. . . be [the] cause of apprehension." Richard Robinson agreed with Nelson, and he offered the use of his farm at Hoskins Cross Roads, a key intersection sixteen miles below the terminus of the Kentucky Central Railroad in Nicholasville. The gently rolling pasturage could easily sustain a thousand mules for four months out of the year. The main house served as a tavern, there was a storehouse, blacksmith shop, barn, mule-shed, and numerous outbuildings.[21]

Nelson returned to Lexington on July 21, 1861, and as he walked through the lobby of the Phoenix Hotel at 6:00 P.M., an aide handed him a telegraph from Brigadier General Anderson. It said, "Our army has been disastrously beaten at Bull Run [First Manassas], and we are in full retreat for Washington. That city may be in possession of the enemy before morning." Speed S. Fry recommended keeping this a secret, but Nelson disagreed, telling him that would be a serious mistake because all the telegraph operators all along the line were aware of that news.[22]

Nelson wanted to discuss the implications of this disastrous setback with the Central Union Committee, and after doing so, he headed for Cincinnati to meet with Lt. Samuel P. Carter. There were no arms and equipment for the East Tennessee expedition and the two classmates decided Carter should still go ahead and organize loyalists with the few shotguns and muskets that were available. In Lexington, the Old Whigs took advantage of Nelson's absence to convince Colonel Landram there would not be a Confederate advance into Kentucky if he stopped recruitment. When Nelson learned about this effort to undermine his mission, he sternly advised, "The [Tennessee] expedition is neither postponed nor abandoned. . . . I shall assemble the brigade and muster it into service as soon as possible."[23]

Green Adams had pronounced misgivings about the progress of the East Tennessee expedition, and he informed an unnamed governor that Nelson should "come on with his arms . . . immediately after the election . . . I will go to see Nelson in a day or two, & if things do not go to suit me, I may call and see you." Adams's counterpart, treasury agent William Mellon, asked Nelson if he could be of help, and Nelson brushed him aside saying all of his requirements would be met by other means. Mellon notified Chase, "[Nelson] may be entitled to all the confidence you have given him . . . but many are suspicious of him and make such serious charges against him which they say they can *prove*, I could not and still cannot help fearing he may be trusted too much." Another Carter brother, William B. Carter, added to the complaints with a letter to President Lincoln that ignored how his brother Col. James P. T. Carter held a command position under Lt. Samuel P. Carter, U.S.N. He advised, "We must have a *competent commander*. It is madness to entrust the control of the military movements in East Tennessee to a *Naval officer*." A scornful Garrett Davis told the president, "my mind cannot begin to grasp . . . in a few months [fighting will] begin to manifest itself, & it will rapidly expand and grow. . . . You must bring a larger force, at every point of operations, commanded by the most competent men."[24]

On Monday, August 5, Kentuckians elected 76 Union men to the House of Representatives versus 24 states' rights advocates. The Senate went to the Union, 27 to 11. Of the 138 seats in the General Assembly, 103 (75 percent) of them now belonged to the Union. Green Adams told the Union men in Knox County the time had come to discard neutrality, "take up arms," and "fight for the Government." Col. Speed S. Fry departed from Danville with a detachment of the Second Regiment Kentucky Volunteer Infantry (later the Fourth), and by Tuesday evening, he had joined Colonel Landram and the First Regiment Kentucky Volunteer Cavalry at Camp Dick Robinson. George D. Prentice complained to John J. Crittenden that this action was as "equipped for mischief as if it had been contrived . . . by the Devil himself. It is reckless to the last degree. It is insane." In Covington, the *Journal* gleefully reported that Crittenden and Garrett Davis "are making efforts to arrest the movement, and break up the camps." When Davis heard that the volunteers at Camp Dick Robinson considered him "as no better than Secessionists," he immediately rushed off for Washington to have them removed from Kentucky soil.[25]

An extra of the *Winchester (Ky.) National Union* reported that two to three hundred disunion troops had come through the Cumberland Gap with intentions of moving against Barbourville. Other rumors said the Rebels intended to steal fifty thousand pounds of bacon, rob the Barbourville bank, and advance against Lexington. True or false, any report of enemy activity gave the volunteers at Camp Dick Robinson a sense of purpose that put them in tune with the stern regimen of their hyperactive commander. Nelson required very little rest, and before any of the men awoke, he ate a light breakfast and made himself ready for the day. Few of the men "had ever seen a live general before." They liked his exuberant style and eagerly looked forward to seeing him at the drills behind the Robinson house until they realized he had a "marked temper" and "very overbearing ways."[26]

Guard duty gave the men the opportunity to cut off the feathers of any pompous officer, and when a new sentry came across Nelson in slippers and nightgown, he ordered him to halt and give the countersign. Nelson continued to puff away on his cigar and assured the soldier that it would be all right to let him pass. The private sternly replied, "No it isn't all right by a jug full." Nelson started to walk away, and the guard leveled his musket. With a very serious look in his eye, he announced, "I am the commander of this beat and you will mark time and march!" The hard tone of his voice convinced Nelson to keep "tramping air" until the officer of the day appeared and ordered his release. Nelson then turned to the young guard and with "a cheery tone said, 'Right my hearty! Always do your duty as you understand it.'" There are many embellished versions of the supposed incident, and all of them reveal a leader with a special connection that encouraged anecdotal stories.[27]

Camp sanitation was a top priority with Nelson, and he made daily inspections to ensure that the men properly disposed of all refuse. His piercing black eyes glared at every detail, and when he found a problem, his feral tongue gave the responsible party a severe lashing. Those volunteers also took great consolation in knowing Nelson had the "very redeemable trait" of treating wayward officers in the same manner. One such encounter occurred just after Colonel Landram relinquished command of the First Cavalry to Lieutenant Colonel Wolford. That Mexican War veteran "rode the framework of an ugly road horse," and the face of this country lawyer usually looked like it "had been undefiled by water or razor for some time." The officers and men were bitter about the rude way Nelson had scolded them, and after Wolford personally guaranteed they would always be in compliance, Nelson said he would never go into the First Cavalry area without their commander being present.[28]

Nelson had a "violent antipathy" for volunteer officers who engaged in endless campfire debates about how to end the Civil War and he truly appreciated the way in which the rough-hewn Wolford tried to drill his men to perfection. The best time for him to judge the overall success of the entire command was at daily dress parade, and on one particular evening, it looked like the whole center would collapse from the strain of overcrowding. Nelson supposedly rushed over and bellowed out, "Bear away there! Bear Away! About a fathom to the starboard, luff you damned lubbers!" Fact or fancy, this anecdote is another example of the comfortable familiarity and enjoyment of Nelson's commitment to his men.[29]

This seaman also had a "facility of profane expression" that made a lasting impression on the men. It went far beyond common crudeness, and one fictional narrative (based on known events) described an instance in which Nelson overheard some muttering about his being nothing more than a navy lieutenant. He let loose with a stream of vulgarity that led a waggish bystander to remark that if this jack tar could fight as well as he cursed, then Kentucky would soon be free of the secessionists. Nelson tired to hold back his temper, his face became beet red, and his jowls started to twitch. The staff could not hide the smirks on their faces, and that brought a self-deprecating laugh from Nelson. Many of his aides were from prominent families, and it distressed them to see their commander demean his position with foul language. Nelson did his best to honor that concern when Col. Samuel Owens inadvertently sat on his hat. He stammered and stuttered for a minute and commanded to the heaven above, "Christ give me patience!"[30]

During the second week, Brig. Gen. Robert Anderson received command of the Department of the Cumberland, and this made him responsible for all Federal operations in Kentucky and Tennessee. Dr. Jonathan Hale had recently escaped from Tennessee by way of Albany, Kentucky, and he agreed to work as a spy for Nelson who now had additional authority "to accept and muster in . . . regiments for service in Tennessee and Kentucky in such numbers and of such arms as you may consider necessary for the best interests of the country." Anderson had "but two men, Acting-General Nelson" and Lovell H. Rousseau. The later had resigned from the Kentucky state senate in June to raise troops at Camp Joe Holt in Jeffersonville, Indiana. Anderson preferred to have four brigadier generals from the regular army, and on Thursday, August 15, he met with Col. William Tecumseh Sherman in Washington to ask that he become second in command. At the same time, Anderson also requested the services of Don Carlos Buell, George H. Thomas, and Ambrose Burnside.[31]

That same day, thirteen carloads of food, military clothing, and arms destined for Camp Dick Robinson left Covington. At Cynthiana, a secessionist mob surrounded the train and threatened violence if the armed guards did not turn over three thousand muskets, a hundred and ten thousand ball cartridges, and thirteen boxes of canister shot for six 12-pounders. Rather than comply, Kentucky Central Railroad officials telegraphed the engineer to back the train out of town and return to Covington. From there the arms went down the Ohio River to Carrollton and up the Kentucky River to Owen County where secessionists halted the steamboat. After the vessel returned to Cincinnati, John Harlan and James Speed wired Garrett Davis to secure a mail packet that would take the arms to Louisville, where they would be forwarded to Lexington by train.[32]

At Paris, Kentucky, the *Western Citizen* declared the establishment of Camp Dick Robinson took place without the proper input from Union officials. In a similar vein, the paper noted that talk of a Confederate invasion from Tennessee had no basis in fact. At the Garrard County camp, Nelson called a meeting in which James Harlan presided and John M. Harlan and Joshua F. Bell delivered opening speeches. Jeremiah T. Boyle, Thomas E. Bramlette, and Frank Wolford recommended moving against the enemy. Speed S. Fry and William J. Landram disagreed because they considered the present intelligence inadequate and wanted the troops to receive additional training.[33]

The editor of the *Western Citizen* protested that "some of the principal officers" at Camp Dick Robinson stated neither they nor the Government had any intention of invading Tennessee or sending arms or munitions of war into that state. It appeared that Tennessee was "concentrating her troops in [the] thousands along our border" and the sole reason for troops in Garrard County was to defend against a possible invasion. Several miles north of Paris, the secessionist *Cynthiana News* falsely reported, "Many of the Lincoln soldiers encamped in Garrard County mostly are citizens of Ohio and Pennsylvania, they having come into Kentucky in small numbers, in citizen's garb, to keep down suspicion." A far more factual view appeared in the *Covington Journal*. The paper noted that a recent speech by Joe Holt in Buffalo, New York, declared that neutrality in Kentucky had been a ruse and "all disguise is thrown off" now that Union troops are camped on her soil.[34]

On August 18, future Confederate general Abraham Buford informed Arnold Harris that fighting in Kentucky could be expected because of the violation of neutrality by "Nelson, whom you know to be as God Dammed a Black Republican as is to be found anywhere in the country." Buford was "bitterly opposed to this Nelson movement," and he said, "if we succeed all will be well with Kentucky: if not our neutrality is gone and my sword shall be drawn in the defense of the South. My ambition would be gratified if I could just command a brigade and drive Nelson across the Ohio River." Buford had no way on knowing the Confederate Congress had just passed an act that authorized the enlistment of troops in Kentucky. He was also unaware that Lincoln had just informed a group of Confederate commissioners that if Kentuckians wanted Federal troops they would have them.[35]

At Camp Dick Robinson, the green volunteers readily believed a tale about how Governor Magoffin had ordered Brig. Gen. Simon B. Buckner to enforce Kentucky's avowed neutrality with State Guard troops. They also accepted the rumor that Confederate brigadier general Felix Zollicoffer was moving through Cumberland Gap and could attack within the next day or so. When drums sounded the long roll of alarm, these young men felt certain the Rebels were about to rush out of the dark firing their muskets. Amid the ensuing madness, Nelson mounted his big charger and rode with his amateurish officers to show them how to bring order out of the rowdy chaos.[36]

At noon, August 20, 1861, two new companies of Tennessee volunteers reached Danville. The demanding eighty-mile march had taken three days to complete and the sight of 214 ragged exiles with bloodied feet shocked the citizens. When they reached camp Dick Robinson, Nelson welled up with emotion and "tears rolled down his cheeks." He had promised Lieutenant Carter that if the men arrived with wagons he would see that those wagons went back to Camp Andy Johnston loaded with arms. That pledge could not be upheld because it was now believed the Confederates were about to invade Kentucky and Nelson told Carter to abandon Barbourville and come forward with all of his men.[37]

About 2:00 A.M. Wednesday, August 21, the twice-circumvented arms shipment arrived at the Louisville wharf. John M. Harlan and Judge Joshua F. Bullitt personally supervised loading the guns onto a waiting train, and they sent word to Nelson the arms would reach Lexington in the morning. He ordered a detachment to Lexington, and on entering town about noon they were quickly surrounded by a hostile crowd of Southern sympathizers. Colonel Bramlette conferred with John C. Breckinridge, and that defused the situation. The first load of weapons reached Nicholasville at midnight, and late Thursday morning, the soldiers at Camp Dick Robinson had the long-awaited arms. This was particularly pleasing to "young soldier boys" who carried out the mission, because Nelson publicly praised them for the capable way in which they carried out the mission.[38]

Green Adams did not see Nelson in the same light as those soldiers, and he wanted Secretary Chase to know that Nelson was making "himself unpopular with every person nearby." He "talks bold, defiant & threatening & some of our friends think him imprudent . . . perhaps Nelson drinks a little too much, & does not make himself as popular with the troops as he might[,] but his bold position suits the union men here." The latter point did not match the soft position taken by Garrett Davis. Nelson told him, "the time for talking had passed in Kentucky, and *the time for action* had come." Davis rushed back to Washington and found that Chase's patience had worn thin. Chase told Davis he needed to stop hindering the Union cause with contrary remarks. He added President Lincoln would not "disavow, directly or by implication, the action of Lieutenant Nelson under the sanction of his [Lincoln's] own authority, given at the urgent instance of some of the wisest & best Union men in Ky. & Tenn. Nelson may have been imprudent in language, & possibly in some modes of action. You [Davis] must caution him on these points. But action, even tho' somewhat imprudent, is better than total inaction."[39]

At the end of August, the *Cincinnati Gazette* published a letter from a Lexington "Union Man" who wanted it known that secessionist and unionist "picnics and barbecues . . . are still carried on . . . more actively after the [August] election than before it." That individual believed the so-called peace demonstration of an armed State Guard in Owen County had no other purpose than to disrupt the newly elected legislature when it convened at Frankfort on September 3. He said that former First District congressman Henry Cornelius Burnett had relied on George N. Sanders to acquire five thousand arms for Camp Vallandigham. Once another thirty-five hundred arms arrived at Glasgow, there would be an attack against "Kentucky Union men in Garrard County." Key military officers, legislators, and professionals met with Nelson and authorized him to organize a total force of ten thousand men composed of the four thousand troops at Camp Dick Robinson, the four thousand Home Guards, and the two thousand men that Lovell H. Rousseau had across the Ohio River at Jeffersonville, Indiana. Nelson was to be in Frankfort within six days, and Governor Magoffin received notice that Nelson had permission to use force if needed.[40]

In Washington, Secretary Chase wrote to Nelson that he valued the way in which this seaman exercised "true prudence . . . & proper economy." He counseled this high-spirited friend to exercise restraint with Garrett Davis and told him that military necessity dictated that Anderson and Sherman command the Department of the Cumberland. There was no mention of their distrust for a navy lieutenant who seemed incapable of exercising any "control over his wayward, passionate temper." Chase simply advised that they "fully acknowledge the value of yr. Services. You can be made a Brigadier if you wish; but I have all along understood yr. wish to be for a promotion on the sea."[41]

Over the course of the past few months, Nelson had upheld the trust given him by Secretary Chase and President Lincoln. His role in arming loyal Kentuckians helped the legislature approve "armed neutrality" and authorize a pro-Union board to take control of the state military forces. That success assured that nine out of ten congressional seats went to Union men on June 20. Ten days later Nelson received orders to organize an expeditionary force of ten thousand troops that would move in support of East Tennessee unionists. The successful election in the first week of August served as a mandate for bringing troops into Camp Dick Robinson, and now those newly elected legislators were about to convene in Frankfort.

"A Showman's Caravan" [6]

On Tuesday, September 3, 1861, Nelson was in Frankfort protecting the Kentucky General Assembly. Optimists among the newly elected lawmakers wanted to believe the threat of war would be over in three to four months. Pessimists, on the other hand, worried that "Southern leaders [would] force the fight up to the Ohio River, obstruct its navigation, seize Frankfort, occupy Louisville, threaten Cincinnati, . . . [and] carry the state out of the Union." Confederate major general Leonidas Polk viewed the mounting presence of Federal forces at Cairo, Illinois, with alarm. The next day he put an end to the speculation in Frankfort by sending his former Maury County, Tennessee, neighbor, Brig Gen. Gideon J. Pillow, to Hickman, Kentucky. Polk established a position on bluffs overlooking the Mississippi River at Columbus. This fortification became the anchor for the left flank of the Confederate line that extended down to Fort Henry on the Tennessee River and Fort Donelson on the Cumberland River. It would soon go up to Bowling Green and across to Brig. Gen. Felix K. Zollicoffer at Barbourville, Kentucky.[1]

Polk did see that this advance into an officially neutral state was about to open the way for an invasion of the heartland of the South, a region that extended some "430 miles from the Mississippi River in the west to the Cumberland Gap in the east." At Cairo, Illinois, Brig. Gen. Ulysses S. Grant ordered troops to Paducah and Smithland, where he expected to take advantage of the Tennessee and Cumberland Rivers to outflank the Confederates at Columbus and Bowling Green. From St. Louis, Maj. Gen. John C. Frémont could move forces down the Mississippi River corridor. At Louisville, Robert Anderson could advance troops south on a hard turnpike road that ran parallel to the Louisville & Nashville Railroad.[2]

In Washington, Secretary Chase answered Green Adams's complaint about Nelson's brusque manner. He greatly admired Nelson's daring accomplishments and truly appreciated how this navy lieutenant had "been careful & judicious in his disbursements, spending only Hundreds where other men would have spent Thousands." As to Nelson's supposed alcohol abuse, Chase exclaimed, "[God] forbid that so noble a man shd. fall into [a] habit likely to impair his usefulness." He advised that "true friends should be faithful, speak plainly and avoid all *talk about* him wh. might hurt his position or his usefulness." As clerk of the Kentucky Court of Appeals, Leslie Combs saw no need to employ such discretion when he told President Lincoln:

> My friend *Nelson* is excessively unpopular—with his command. Of-ficers and men—have been urging me to ask his withdrawal, but I was reluctant to do or say anything, that might wound his feelings—His whole education and all his habits, fit him for the sea; and I hope you will soon give him a *lift* in his profession and transfer him to a ship.
>
> He told me that he had not sought his present position and would much prefer promotion in the naval services—I have visited his camp, in order to satisfy myself.[3]

The expected arrival of Brig. Gen. George H. Thomas provided Brig. Gen. Robert Anderson with the leeway to relieve "Lieutenant Nelson, U.S. Navy, who has done such good service to the cause of the Union by the zeal and untiring energy he has displayed by distributing arms . . . and organizing . . . Camp Dick Robinson." In the interim, Nelson was to keep Frankfort secure during a second "Peace Convention" and work to overcome the severe reac-tion to Frémont's blatant disregard of the Confiscation Act. That action ap-plied to Missouri slaveholders, but its far-reaching implications had caused one company of volunteers in Kentucky to throw down their arms and walk away. Lincoln feared the very guns "furnished Kentucky would be turned against us," and he directed Frémont to withdraw the troublesome procla-mation. That welcome directive opened the way for the Kentucky General Assembly to request assistance from the United States government and insist that Governor Magoffin "call out the military force of the State to expel and drive out the [Confederate] invaders [at Columbus, Kentucky]."[4]

Nelson knew that he was about to be promoted to brigadier general in the volunteer army when he returned to Camp Dick Robinson. It also appeared to him that by accepting the appointment he would lose his beloved commis-sion in the navy. On September 15, 1861, Colonel Bramlette's Third Regiment Kentucky Volunteer Infantry prepared to say farewell to a general they had "come to love . . . with all his brusque manners." The future governor handed Nelson a personal note that said, "Goodbye my Genl—my friend; if I can ever

Fig. 5. Brigadier General Nelson, c. 1861. Library of Congress

serve you call upon me and my response . . . will show the earnest sincerity of my confidence." Nelson kept his feelings to himself, and he "expressed no word of dissent to an order that separated him from an army whose organization owed its existence to his courage and energy." He congratulated his men on the good fortune of having an experienced regular army officer take up the unfinished work that he, as an inexperienced navy lieutenant, had undertaken just two months earlier.[5]

Nelson's promotion became official on September 16, 1861. He also had orders to organize three new regiments at Maysville, advance them into eastern Kentucky, and end the threat of a Confederate buildup in the Big Sandy Valley. To aid in the recruitment of this Federal expeditionary force, broadsides announced that Tennesseans Andrew Johnson and Horace Maynard would join Kentuckians Joe Holt and John J. Crittenden at a grand Union barbecue near Maysville. Nelson wrote to Acting Secretary of the Navy Gustavus Fox, "I turned my Brigade over to Genl Thomas a regular (who can command troops if he cannot raise them)." He explained, "I raised a splendid Brigade in the heart of Kentucky, broke down the Governor and the neutrality party, and moved the State into an active participation of the war, all within the space of 42 days from the day I entered the State. I did it, when everybody refused to undertake so dangerous a mission. The *ability* with which I managed the affair is attested by its success. The *energy* by the short space of time it took me to do it." Brig. Gen. James A. Ripley, chief of the Ordnance Office, supported that position when he noted that since the first release on May 4, there had been seventeen thousand guns sent to Kentucky: thirteen thousand distributed from Cincinnati, three thousand from Louisville, and one thousand in Covington. East Tennessee received an additional six thousand, and that brought the total to twenty-three thousand.[6]

In Washington, Secretary Chase had dinner with Daniel Ammen, a naval officer who had grown up near Ulysses Grant in Georgetown, Ohio. Ammen noted that "a large number of brigadiers . . . would be found inferior" to Nelson; and he believed his "personal influence among his friends and relatives in Kentucky had been greater than that of any other person known to him in restraining that State from passing an act of secession." Chase's fourteen-year-old daughter "Nettie" interjected that from her perspective Nelson "was not a gentleman; he pinched her arms."[7]

Nelson arrived in Cincinnati on Friday, September 20, 1861, and Anderson relayed that news to President Lincoln by ciphered telegraph at 6:30 P.M. Nelson took a steamboat to Maysville on Saturday, and the next day he joined the speakers at the Grand Union Barbecue. The huge event also included Col.

Charles A. Marshall, a nephew of former chief justice John Marshall and first cousin of secessionist agitator Humphrey Marshall. Charles Marshall helped Nelson select an assembly point three miles south of Maysville and about one half-mile north of Washington, Kentucky. That land belonged to Dr. Alexander K. Marshall, another nephew of Justice Marshall and a first cousin of Humphrey Marshall. Initially called Camp Nelson, it would soon be renamed Camp Kenton.[8]

On September 24, Nelson pushed forward with the daunting task of assembling a new brigade. Sherman recognized the importance of the Big Sandy expedition, and he warily advised the commander of the Department of the Ohio, Brig. Gen. Ormsby M. Mitchel, that there was no officer to send. He believed that Nelson would "be energetic and pushing, and I hope successful." Those vigorous traits led Nelson to arrest seven "old friends and companions" for aiding the Confederate cause. Southern sympathizers complained to Sherman, and he quickly declared the action failed to provide those enemies of the national government the "opportunity for trial by the legal tribunals of the country."[9]

Nelson stayed focused on the mission by ordering Maj. John Smith Hurt to establish a staging area at Olympian Springs (Mud Lick Springs), eight miles below Owingsville and twenty miles east of Mount Sterling. From that position Hurt was to secure the mountain pass on the Mount Sterling–Pound Gap Road (Rt. 460), known as McCormick's Gap (later Frenchburg). On September 29, Hurt placed three armed companies at that gateway to prevent movement to or from the Rebel camp at Prestonsburg. On October 8, Col. Lewis Braxton Grigsby added his three hundred men to Hurt's two hundred. They then mustered into twelve-months' service six companies that would eventually become the nucleus of the Twenty-fourth Regiment Kentucky Volunteer Infantry. Col. James Perry Fyffe was at Camp Kenton with the Fifty-ninth Regiment Ohio Volunteer Infantry, and on Thursday, October 10, Col. Leonard A. Harris arrived in Olympian Springs with the Second Regiment Ohio Volunteer Infantry. At this same time, Col. Jesse S. Norton started forward from Nicholasville with the Twenty-first Ohio Volunteer Infantry.[10]

From his headquarters in Louisville, Sherman suggested to Nelson that Harris advance the Second Regiment from Olympian Springs toward Prestonsburg. In conjunction with that movement, Col. Joshua W. Sill's Thirty-third Regiment Ohio Volunteer Infantry could leave Portsmouth, Ohio, and go up the Big Sandy River to Prestonsburg. Because of a lack of arms and ammunition, "the general [Sherman] does not order this expedition, but hopes it can be undertaken. It is left entirely to your discretion." The true nature of the enemy situation was vague. Newspaper accounts indicated that Col. John "Cerro Gordo" S. Williams had between two and seven thousand recruits in the Confederate Fifth Regiment Kentucky Volunteer Infantry at Prestonsburg. In truth, Williams held command of an inexperienced group of one thousand or so men armed with squirrel rifles, shotguns, and several pieces of artillery.[11]

Harris's Second Regiment conducted a reconnaissance near Prestonsburg on Thursday, October 10, and they incorrectly reported there were at least four thousand well-armed Rebels with two pieces of artillery. Nelson telegraphed George H. Thomas at Camp Dick Robinson and asked that he send two regiments in support. Another copy went to Sherman with a notice that the advance into eastern Kentucky would commence once he hired wagons. Nelson then issued a call:

> TO THE HOME GUARDS OF THE NINTH AND ASHLAND DISTRICTS—You are hereby called on for active service for ninety days. You will be mustered in companies of 101, all told.—You will be furnished with everything necessary and required for the campaign. You will rendezvous at Olympian Springs. Let every man bring warm clothing and his blanket. Two cents will be allowed per mile traveled to that point. Let every man that has a government musket be on hand. If for any reason he cannot come for himself, let him transfer his gun to someone who can. Those having trusty rifles and preferring them.—Move at once to Mudlick Springs; you will then be organized and led against the enemy immediately.

The Home Guards gave no response, and the frustrated Nelson then characterized them as nothing more than "fireside rangers."[12]

On Thursday, October 17, Nelson informed Sherman that he would leave Olympian Springs at daylight to take possession of McCormick's Gap. He gave notice to the region that:

> many of you have been misled by wicked and desperate men, bankrupt in fame and fortune, who hope to profit by the ruin of the Commonwealth. . . . I say return home, lay down your arms, live in peace and friendship with your neighbors. . . . I offer you a complete amnesty for what is past; you will be held accountable for the future. But to secure this result you must return home within — days. After that time you will be treated as enemies and must never more hope to see in safety families or enjoy your property until you have carried out the purpose of your wicked misleaders. . . . I urge this offer upon you. Should you

reject it, the enlightened world as well as the laws of your country will hold you alone responsible for the shedding of fraternal blood.[13]

At 8:00 A.M., Friday, a cold, drizzling rain was falling on Nelson as he mounted a handsome black horse and rode out to speak with the troops. The Second Regiment Ohio Volunteer Infantry and Grigsby's militia were ordered "to Camp Garrett Davis, about 15 miles up the State Road on the Dry Ridge, and there he would fully equip" them. Grigsby's militiamen refused to march because they were "worn out with promises" from a government that would not accept their twelve-month enlistment agreement in place of the new mandatory three-year requirement. Nelson made a patriotic appeal that failed to sway the men. Then he suddenly shouted, "I will publish you in every paper in the state for the God Damned infamous act." Orderly Sgt. Thomas W. Parsons hollered back, "For a trifle I would publish you with a cartridge." Another man offered a feeble protest and Nelson yelled shut-up, "You talk like a God Damned Dunghill" chicken. Grigsby's officers then managed to convince one hundred twenty men to go forward, but the other men turned in their arms and headed for home. That brought a call for new recruits, the fife and drum began to play, and Harrison Gill, the proprietor of Olympian Springs, brought out a bucket of whiskey to enliven the affair.[14]

Nelson ordered Harris's Second Regiment Ohio Volunteer Infantry to Camp Garrett Davis with two pieces of artillery and a company of cavalry. He then headed for Paris to telegraph Sherman about the situation. It appeared the fifteen hundred Rebels were encamped eighteen miles southeast of McCormick's Gap at Hazel Green, and Nelson believed that if Harris had additional support those troops could prevent an incursion through McCormick's, Betty's, or Yokum's gaps. Joshua Sill's Thirty-third Regiment Ohio Volunteer Infantry was already on the march from Paris to Mount Sterling. At Covington, troops were boarding a train for Paris. Capt. James McLaughlin's Company B, First Regiment Ohio Volunteer Cavalry, was with Capt. Andrew J. Konkle's Battery D, First Regiment Ohio Volunteer Light Artillery, which had six bronze 6-pound rifled field pieces.[15]

Saturday morning, October 19, Konkle and McLaughlin arrived at Paris and started unloading horses, wagons, and associated equipment. Sunday evening they reached Olympian Springs and found Harris's Second, Sill's Thirty-third, and Fyffe's Fifty-ninth regiments of Ohio Volunteer Infantry with some mounted Kentucky troops. Col. Charles A. Marshall's Sixteenth Kentucky Volunteer Infantry Battalion had replaced Harris at Camp Garrett Davis. First Sgt. Ara C. Spafford was at Winchester, with Norton's Twenty-first Regiment Ohio Volunteer Infantry, and he said it seemed like a "Sambo's holiday [because the slaves] . . . swarmed around us like bees offering to carry our muskets, etc."[16]

On Monday, October 21, 1861, the men that Nelson had organized at Camp Dick Robinson were engaged in a protracted battle at Wildcat Mountain when the remaining three hundred volunteers in Colonel Grigsby's militia joined the nine hundred men in Harris's Second Regiment. Two guns from Konkle's Battery D and the cavalry from Capt. James McLaughlin's Company B augmented the detachment. At 2:30 P.M., Harris started them toward West

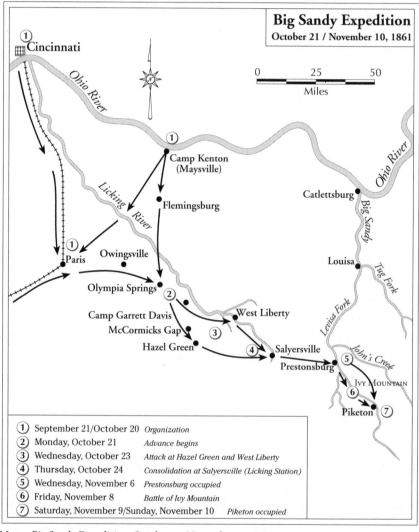

Big Sandy Expedition
October 21 / November 10, 1861

① September 21/October 20 *Organization*
② Monday, October 21 *Advance begins*
③ Wednesday, October 23 *Attack at Hazel Green and West Liberty*
④ Thursday, October 24 *Consolidation at Salyersville (Licking Station)*
⑤ Wednesday, November 6 *Prestonsburg occupied*
⑥ Friday, November 8 *Battle of Ivy Mountain*
⑦ Saturday, November 9/Sunday, November 10 *Piketon occupied*

Map 3. Big Sandy Expedition, October 21–November 10, 1861

Liberty in a drenching rain. Early Tuesday morning, Nelson marched against Hazel Green with about twenty-eight hundred men from the Twenty-first, Thirty-third, and Fifty-ninth regiments of Ohio Volunteer Infantry. He also had Kentucky militia under Col. Leonidas K. Metcalfe and the Sixteenth Kentucky Volunteer Infantry under Colonel Marshall. The two guns from Battery D had the protection of Capt. William McLaughlin's Company A.[17]

Pvt. Loyal B. Wort served as a drummer in the band of the Twenty-first Regiment Ohio Volunteer Infantry, and he wrote his wife that Nelson's advance was "a very hard march . . . up one mountain and down another . . . we hav got 25 teams and 4 horses to each and that makes 100 horses. . . . there is an artillery company . . . and they hav 6 peaces [pieces]." One local resident hollered at Nelson that his soldiers could not possibly move wagons across one particular hill. The old salt bellowed back: "By God Damned, sir, *nothing is impossible with these men!* . . . We shall go forward, sir!" Nelson ordered teams of twenty-five men to lift each wagon out of the mud and carry it across the hill with the assistance of spliced mule teams.[18]

By Tuesday afternoon, his southern prong was at the western edge of Hazel Green. At 5:00 A.M., Wednesday, Maj. Joshua V. Robinson Jr. advanced two companies of the Thirty-third Regiment Ohio Volunteer Infantry against the two hundred Rebels who guarded the town. Colonel Marshall's Sixteenth Kentucky Infantry and Colonel Metcalfe's mounted militia joined the brief fight, and thirty-eight Rebels promptly surrendered. Twelve miles north, the northern prong under Colonel Harris forded the Licking River three times before they found a creek bed that served as a road into West Liberty.[19]

A Rebel flag was flying above the courthouse, and the dilapidated condition of the homes suggested those structures could have "been built for Noah's occupation after leaving the ark." Col. John Ficklin commanded five to seven hundred Rebels, and this inexperienced Bath County politician assumed the Union advance of eighty to one hundred men was the entire force. In reality, Harris had twelve hundred Federal troops. The main force was on the rocky slope of a hill just west of town. Some were about one hundred feet from the river, and the rest were in a cornfield. About 8:30 A.M., Harris ordered Battery D to open fire. One 6-pound gun remained on a muddy road, and the other fired six shots in and around the courthouse. Capt. James McLaughlin's Company B, First Regiment Ohio Volunteer Cavalry, charged the steep, rocky hill, and Colonel Harris joined the flank companies that scoured the cornfield with Enfield rifles. Sgt. Thomas Parsons and about one hundred fifty men in Capt. James Carey's militia came in by way of Yocum Creek. Parsons watched as the first artillery shell went over the town and exploded on the opposite side of the river. A second shell landed about forty feet from the brick jail, and the explosion from it ripped a hole in the wall.[20]

A white flag brought a cease-fire, and the Rebels withdrew north of town with a loss of twenty-one dead, forty wounded, and thirty-four captured. The Second Regiment Ohio Volunteer Infantry seized fifty-two horses, ten to twelve mules, two jacks, a large bear, and a variety of guns and knives. A few minor incidents of bad behavior occurred, but overall the men under Harris acted in a way that cast a favorable light on Nelson's command.[21]

Sherman had no direct contact with this operation, and he sent word for Thomas to avoid pushing troops too far into southeastern Kentucky because Nelson "has got into difficulty with the militia and I have no person to send there." At Paris, the *Western Citizen* wrongly reported it had obtained through "undoubted authority that the rebels at Prestonsburg had been re-enforced with two regiments of Virginia troops . . . and now number between five and six thousand." In Macon, Georgia, the *Daily Telegraph* claimed to have the "authentic particulars" on "Sow Nelson's first victory" at West Liberty. It said "the enemy's General—a notorious debauchee, braggart, coward, and liar by the name of Nelson, an ex lieutenant (the 'fat lieutenant') of the U.S. Navy—is a man whose fort [e] lies in magnificent inventions of . . . pretended details of his performances." The Georgia paper further deluded its readers by saying the "indomitable" Jack May and a company of seventy-four sharpshooters had trapped the enemy and slaughtered them like sheep. It then concluded by saying the "enterprising" Captain May had no one killed or wounded and there were at least fifty enemy graves.[22]

Nelson waited for his wagon trains to catch up, and he resumed the pursuit on October 31. On November 6, a hard rain was falling when Nelson ordered Norton's Twenty-first Regiment to advance from Salyersville to the West Levisa Fork of the Big Sandy River. During the arduous, twenty-four-mile march, the dutiful youngsters did their best to keep the files well dressed and remain in step. At the conclusion, Nelson rewarded their earnest effort by gruffly telling them they should keep the ranks "closed up." Nelson then stepped aboard a ferryboat on the West Levisa Fork. The added weight nearly tipped the boat over and he yelled at the exhausted volunteer pulling the rope, "God Damn you. You are trying to drown me." The young volunteer snapped back, "God Damn you. Get over and help trim the boat." The old seaman did not hesitate a moment in responding to a familiar demand given in a moment of crisis.[23]

About midnight, the troops arrived at the abandoned "Gibraltar" of Prestonsburg. The camp followers among them were convinced a great victory was just ahead, and some unknown party from that group telegraphed Washington that the "result had been accomplished, and that a thousand prisoners had surrendered." Sadly, that deceit caused some to believe "the way was about to be opened for the relief and arming of suffering loyalists in East Tennessee. . . . Truth soon told a different story."[24]

At 11:00 A.M. Thursday, November 7, Colonel Sill started the northern prong of the Big Sandy expedition toward John's Creek. From there, he was to veer south for about forty miles and gain the rear of the enemy at Piketon. The Thirty-third Regiment Ohio Volunteer Infantry was comprised of about 839 men with one section of artillery that had two rifled 6-pound guns under Col. Roher Vacher. Maj. Thomas S. Hurt commanded a light flank battalion comprised of six companies of 100 men who came from the Second, Twenty-first, Thirty-third, and Fifty-ninth regiments of Ohio Volunteer Infantry. This included two Bath County militia companies under Capt. Roy D. Davidson. Colonel Metcalfe had 142 mounted men (made up from the wagon teams) and Col. Richard Apperson, a Montgomery County Circuit Court judge, was in charge of a strange assortment of 36 "gentlemen volunteers."

At dawn Friday, Nelson started the southern prong toward Piketon with two days' rations and no tents. Colonel Marshall and the 400 men of companies A, B, C, and D, Sixteenth Kentucky Infantry Battalion, led the way by wading across a waist-deep creek about twenty-five yards wide. Directly behind them, Lt. Col. Joseph Doniphan and Lt. Col. Joseph B. Harris had approximately 100 men from Company A, Second Regiment Ohio Volunteer Infantry under the command of Capt. Alexander S. Berryhill. The miners and sappers followed as Marshall's flank men dashed around gullies and moved across the rugged terrain like "deer." That important duty left them "wet with perspiration, faint, exhausted, yet determined." The main column had the luxury of using the Old State Road (Rt. 460), a "straight road on plain surface." This force was comprised of Col. Leonard Harris's Second Regiment Ohio Volunteer Infantry with 900 men and Norton's Twenty-first Regiment Ohio Volunteer Infantry with 1,000. Fyffe had 750 men in the Fifty-ninth Regiment Ohio Volunteer Infantry. Captain Konkle had two sections of Battery D, First Ohio Light Artillery. Col. Laban T. Moore commanded the newly formed 600-man Fourteenth Mountain Regiment of Kentucky Volunteer Infantry.[25]

At 9:00 A.M., the Federal advance was about eight miles east of Prestons-burg when they encountered Capt. James M. Thomas moving along the other side of the Levisa Fork with the fifty mounted rifles of the Confederate Fifth Kentucky Infantry. Each side fired at the other. Thomas had one man killed, another wounded, and he raced off knowing Nelson could not pursue because that would leave the heavily encumbered column vulnerable to further attack.

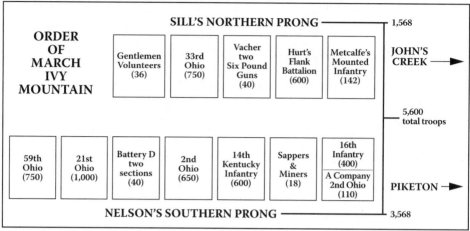

Fig. 6. Order of March Battle Ivy Mountain

A short while later, a civilian told Capt. Silas S. Canfield, Company K, Twenty-first Regiment Ohio Volunteer Infantry, that he saw the Rebels fortifying the side of Ivy Mountain.[26]

After another four miles, the road narrowed to a seven-foot-wide path, and torrents of rain were filling it with knee-deep water when Canfield saw the same man speaking with Nelson. The troops could not move to the left (north) because of the hogback, thousand-foot-high Ivy Mountain. On the right (south), they faced a twenty-five- to fifty-foot drop into the West Levisa Fork of the Big Sandy River. Captain Konkle ordered Battery D to unlimber their guns and rig them so they could follow the infantry in a single file. Three miles further, and some fifteen miles from Piketon, Marshall's Sixteenth Kentucky Volunteer Infantry disappeared from sight at a sharp elbow in the road that started down a steep decline toward the bridge at Ivy Creek. On the eastern side of the creek, Rebel captains John Shawhan, Hiram Hawkins, and James M. Thomas were waiting in the side of Ivy Mountain with two hundred fifty men armed with double-barreled shotguns and old muskets. About 1:00 P.M., Captain Gualt, "the guide, and Mister Reed" came upon the smoldering remains of the bridge. The guide spotted "the foe [80 to 100 feet up the hill] . . . concealed behind rocks, trees, and bushes," but he did not see the camouflaged position in a cornfield on the other side of Levisa Fork.[27]

Gualt and his companions were less than fifty yards from Capt. Jack May when he gave the signal for his men to open fire. The hillside exploded with blue smoke, and several bullets struck the guide before he could find cover behind a rock. Gualt leveled a five-shot Colt revolving rifle at the enemy, his horse went down, and he dived into the river. Colonel Marshall arrived as

Gualt was swimming toward the other side of Levisa Fork. Four scouts were dead, another thirteen men wounded, and within moments, Marshall's jeans were "badly riddled," his cap "ventilated," and his horse killed.[28]

It was impossible to form a line across a rutted path filled with panicked horses. Nelson came forward on a "splendid charger . . . saber drawn, excited, and fairly shouting his orders to aides and regimental commanders." Three musket balls went through Nelson's hat, and Sherman's assistant adjutant general, Capt. Oliver D. Greene, later recalled that his men so "hated him, they tried to kill him." Nelson supposedly replied, "Oh, never mind, they'll like me better by and by."[29]

Twenty-first Ohio Adjutant George Sheets said that Nelson dismounted, took out his field glass, and found "the God Damned cusses [across the creek] are firing at me." A sapper and miner from Company K, Twenty-first Regiment Ohio Volunteer Infantry, was standing beside him, and he said, "Bub, give me your gun." Nelson then climbed up on a prominent rock "and shouted to the men urging them on, and telling them that if the Rebels could not hit him they could not hit any of them." Nelson told Captain Konkle to place two light artillery pieces near the creek and fire directly into the enemy breastworks. He then ordered Harris and Norton around to the left and up the north side of the mountain to flank the enemy position.[30]

Colonel Fyffe tried to come forward with the Fifty-ninth Regiment Ohio Volunteer Infantry and found an overturned ammunition wagon blocking the narrow road. After his men overcame that obstacle, they encountered another wagon that halted them again. To his front, Fyffe saw:

> the blue overcoats & blankets of the 21st O.V.I. . . . . I ordered our men to drop theirs. . . . We started on and the sight that presented itself as we rounded the point was trying on the nerves of untried soldiers. . . . some few of my men were breaking, in alarm and terror, to the rear. . . . We soon ran up to where Genl. Nelson stood [nearly alone] in the road. . . . [He] pointed over the river into a corn field . . . [and told me] to rest my men a moment then to dismount and charge up the road along the hillside. I got off my horse & gave him to Ben Cliborn. He [Nelson] then ordered me to send forward my Rifle Co. . . . My Liut. Col. [Farran] Amstead leading them. . . . [Their] telling fire . . . completely silenced [the cornfield] and drew off the forces over there.[31]

William Elliot Johnson, Company A, Twenty-first Regiment Ohio Volunteer Infantry, recalled the "the balls fell all around us. . . . Capton [Berryhill] got shot [in the wrist]. . . . [Another] boy [David Hilt] was shot in the face on the left side . . . Nock out his eye. Tore the hole side of his face off." As the volunteers struggled to get around huge perpendicular rocks, Konkle's mountain howitzers sent two shells toward the ridge. About 2:00 P.M., the Twenty-first Ohio Infantry reached the top and began rolling boulders back down the hill into the Rebels below them. That sudden reversal stunned Captain May's men, and it became a severe struggle to regain control as he withdrew toward Piketon, ordering the men to fell trees and burn bridges to obstruct pursuit.[32]

The Twenty-first Ohio chased after the foe and "helped themselves to chickens, flour, meal, fruit, sorghum syrup, turnips, cabbage, or anything convenient." Nelson halted that pursuit after three or four miles and ordered the troops into bivouac just beyond the burned bridge at Coldwater Creek and near the home of Unionist Lindsay Layne. At Piketon, Colonel Williams posted a rear guard of four hundred men, and he began preparations to move all of his troops southwest to Pound Gap, Virginia. The Battle of Ivy Mountain (Ivy Narrows) had cost ten Confederate dead, fifteen wounded, and forty missing or captured men. Nelson had gained full control of the field at a loss of six killed and twenty-four wounded.[33]

Throughout the night, a soaking rain turned the old State Road into a quagmire. At 3:00 A.M., Saturday, the temperature was about 40°. Soon afterward, the Federal advance marched against a steady northeast wind that made the men miserably cold. The enemy rear guard fired on the Twenty-first Ohio as they removed felled trees and repaired burned bridges. Two enemy combatants were killed and one of them was Dr. James N. Draper of Prestonsburg. By nightfall, the column had advanced ten miles and come to within five miles of Piketon. On Sunday, November 10, the lead troops were within two and a half miles of Piketon when a detachment from Sill's Thirty-third Ohio Infantry arrived with news that Metcalfe's men had secured Piketon at 4:00 P.M. Saturday. Nelson arrived about 9:00 A.M. Later in the day, he wrote an official report from "Camp Hopeless Chase" that boldly declared the expedition would have "slain the whole of them with sufficient cavalry."[34]

At Pound Gap, Colonel Williams reported that Nelson had dispersed an "unorganized and half-armed, barefooted squad" that lacked everything but the will to fight. Williams had expected reinforcements, and he believed that with a thousand more men and six pieces of artillery his men could have destroyed the columns of Nelson and Sill. Williams admitted the speed of the Federal advance surprised him, and quite unlike Nelson, he believed that "infantry armed with rifles are the men for this country. Cavalry is almost useless except for picket duty." Williams noted that Maj. Richard Hawes, the brigade commissary officer from Paris, Kentucky, had secured hogs, horses, and wagons, but still needed more money. It seemed that Nelson had six thousand men at Piketon and fifteen hundred at Prestonsburg, and reports suggested he intended to destroy the Virginia & Tennessee Railroad, a line that connected the Confederate capital at Richmond, Virginia, to Chattanooga, Tennessee, and the Mississippi Valley. From there Nelson might move to Richland and destroy the railroad between Wytheville and Abington, Virginia.[35]

Judge James W. Moore had been in Virginia, and as he traveled through his hometown of Mount Sterling to Nashville, he spread the rumor that Humphrey Marshall, the commander of Confederate forces in eastern Kentucky, intended to advance troops into central Kentucky. The grossly overweight Marshall was far better suited to be a dinner companion for Nelson. He was neither a soldier nor a military genius and resorted to bogus reports to create the illusion of success. Marshall informed the *Charleston Mercury* that Union losses at Ivy Mountain had been "frightful—two hundred and seven killed (counted) and about a hundred and forty wounded. Our (Confederate) loss is reported as follows; One killed, four wounded and seven missing." The *Macon (Ga.) Daily Telegraph* said that "five or six hundred would . . . be a low estimate of the . . . enemy" dead piled up in the road.[36]

The North was anxious for a quick conclusion to the war, and that led the *New York Times* to look at Piketon as one "the few really brilliant events of the war." The *Cincinnati Commercial* remarked that "our military chieftains . . . [should note] the quiet, business like style" of the eastern Kentucky campaign. The paper noted that Nelson did not wait until everything appeared ready. He instead moved a newly recruited army across unforgiving terrain without adequate transportation and prevailed. The *Commercial* concluded, "Gen. Nelson is not the 'coming man.' He has arrived." The success won high praise from McClellan, and Nelson graciously thanked his men for their "constancy and courage."[37]

A week later, Brig. Gen. Don Carlos Buell arrived in Louisville to replace the deeply embattled Sherman. When the *Cincinnati Gazette* noted that change, it also announced that while the battle at Ivy Mountain had been "Reduced to a Skirmish," it remained "a glorious victory" because it had seriously weakened the Confederates in eastern Kentucky. The *New York Times* felt betrayed and it denounced the "brilliant" victory as "A Hoax." In Covington, the *Journal* warned against the "universal proneness to magnify our [Union] victories and lessen the extent of our defeats." That sage advice seems to have escaped the attention of John W. Finnell before he informed the Kentucky Military Board that Nelson "whipped Williams. 400 killed.—1,000 prisoners. [John S.] Williams and [Richard] Hawes prisoners. This is reliable."

"The grossly exaggerated" news accounts stunned J. Taylor Bradford, and that same sort of reality led the *Cincinnati Gazette* to conclude, "The costly campaign in Eastern Kentucky has had no more permanent effect than the passage of a showman's caravan. Five hundred rebel guerilla cavalry will undo in a week the ornamental work which Gen. Nelson's army has done at so great an expenditure of money and of most precious time."[38]

On Sunday afternoon, November 24, "Nelson's Brigade, numbering 5,000 men, left by [the Ohio] river." On Tuesday, Nelson arrived at Camp Jenkins (Camp Buell), a receiving point five miles below Louisville named in honor of "a snip of a Captain in the U.S. Quartermaster Dept. on Gen. Buell's Staff." Capt. Charles Gilbert was a regular army officer who served as adjutant, and he found Nelson's "ideas of army administration were the crudest." The next day Buell wrote McClellan, "Nelson . . . has already got into difficulty with [Ormsby M.] Mitchel; and, if I am rightly informed, has behaved very absurdly. As he is a veteran, [however,] some allowance must be made for him."[39]

This seasoned professional had proven his worth by boldly arming loyalists, assembling one brigade of Union volunteers on neutral soil, and conducting a successful campaign in the Big Sandy Valley with a second newly organized brigade. The fact that Nelson was the brother of a fellow West Point classmate helped Buell overlook the objectionable points of his volatile personality. This was an individual who placed duty to country above all else; an extraordinarily important attribute in a volunteer army fighting a civil war. While both men had a mutual appreciation for using harsh discipline to drive less-motivated men to perform under the stress of combat, the most important attribute Nelson brought to this relationship was an unquestioned loyalty to superiors.

Soon after Don Carlos Buell assumed command of the Army of the Ohio at Louisville, a letter published in the *Covington Journal* advised, "All eyes are turned to the impending battle in Kentucky. Gen. Buell will be provided with all the men he can use, and will have everything at his command to make his army irresistible. His success or failure is regarded as the turning point of the crisis of the Union. If he fails, all is lost; if he succeeds, the Union is saved. So [it now appears that] Gen. McClellan has already become a secondary character in the war."[1]

A correspondent for the *Cincinnati Gazette* at Camp Nolin declared the only real obstacle Buell faced in Kentucky was a force of eighteen to thirty-five thousand Confederates at Bowling Green. This armchair general surmised that Buell could easily move against Nashville and/or seize the Cumberland Gap and take control of the East Tennessee & Lynchburg Railroad. He concluded by asking for "our new general" to simply concentrate his forces or move aggressively against the enemy as he should.[2]

On December 2, 1861, Buell answered the first part of that challenge by organizing the seventy thousand men of the Army of the Ohio into five divisions and placing Nelson in command of the Fourth Division. On December 10, Nelson was about to march those men to a training site north of the Green River, when he spotted a disruptive drunken soldier. Nelson went after the man with a reckless abandon that made the tipsy volunteer think his commander was also "pretty drunk." The mischievous soldier coyly asked Nelson, "'perhaps you would like to take one yourself' . . . and pulling out his flask of whiskey,[he] says, 'help yourself, I aint proud.'" Nelson did not want to unleash his wrath in front of the huge crowd gathered along Bardstown road and he discreetly withheld it for another time. As the troops started forward several Negroes joined behind Col. William B. Hazen's Forty-first Regiment

Ohio Volunteer Infantry. Nelson promptly ordered all the followers returned when one owner complained that his slave had been wrongly encouraged to follow the boys in blue.[3]

That evening the column went into bivouac along the outskirts of Bard-stown Junction (Shepherdsville), and several members of the Twenty-fourth Regiment Ohio Volunteer Infantry used the opportunity to slip away to buy some "apple-jack." Hours later, the young volunteers tried to reenter the line, and the corporal of the guard, Alonzo C. Pocock, yelled out, "Halt! Who goes there?" Pocock received no answer, so he fired a cautionary shot in the air to encourage a response. Pvt. Michael Connell took that as a direct assault, and he fired four or five shots at Pocock. The entire regiment went on line, Connell was soon under arrest, and Nelson ordered a general court-martial to convene at the earliest possible date.[4]

Nelson reached the north side of New Haven on Friday, December 13, 1861, and he was promptly handed a wire from Buell that told him to have his troops ready to support Brig. Gen. Alexander McCook's Second Division "at the earliest possible moment." Nelson pushed on to White City, and from there he marched south along a cobblestone roadway (Rt. 470) for about three miles.

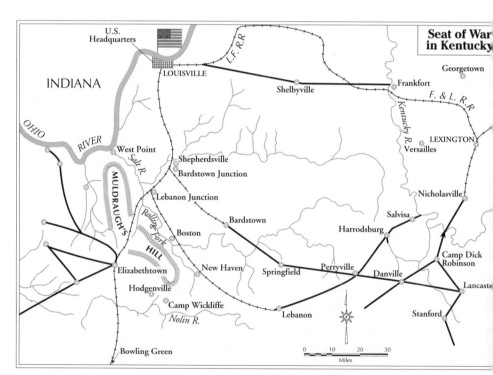

Map 4. The Seat of War in Kentucky, 1861. Adapted from *New York Herald,* November 14, 1861

About 1:00 P.M., Col. Milo S. Hascall's Fifteenth Brigade, Army of the Ohio, set up camp five miles northeast of the log cabin where Abraham Lincoln had been born fifty-two years before. The site was about twenty miles north of the Green River, and it covered "three small hills, the spurs of which run to the turnpike road [Rt. 470]." John McDougal, a prominent secessionist, owned the land that supplied "clear pure water" from McDougal Creek. His two-story brick home served as the headquarters that was just below "two beautiful meadows, containing fifty or sixty acres each . . . used for drilling and parade ground." On December 16, 1861, Nelson officially named the camp for former governor Charles A. Wickliffe of Bardstown.[5]

Col. Stanley Matthews had been with the Fourth Division two weeks, and the highly regarded Cincinnati barrister wrote to his wife that Nelson "has shown himself in his treatment of others, both officers and soldiers, not much better than a brute. He is coarse, savage, tyrannical, and continually insulting everyone with his bits of blasphemy." One particular incident concerned Dr. Bradford's Negro servant. Nelson had berated the man for an unintended offense, and he complained to Matthews that "Bradford had treated him" badly. Nelson asked for an honest assessment, and Matthews replied, "General I am compelled to say that I think you have done your friend a grievous wrong." Matthews disliked taking on the role of "a prophet," but he deemed it necessary to tell Nelson, "You are two different men. . . . The outside man is rough, overbearing, inconsiderate, tyrannical, easily giving offense, and not overlooking offense given by others; but the inside man is generous, open, frank, fearless, magnanimous. You forget that the inside man is known only to a few intimate friends, and that the world at large sees only the outside man. Some of these days you will come into contact with some person, in some offensive way, who not appreciating more than he can see from the outside will, in resenting your offensive manner, shoot the outside man, and in doing so kill the inside man." Matthews suggested that Nelson repair the relationship, and he agreed to see Bradford "and make the best amend I can offer."[6]

The weather was extraordinarily beautiful because of a late Indian summer, and Nelson took advantage of the last few days to drill the division as two brigades of eight regiments. In addition to marching and manual of arms, he emphasized skirmish maneuvers, weapons exercises, and bayonet practice. Matthews noted, "Gen Nelson has subsided a good deal & has been endeavoring to make himself more agreeable. Aside from his rough measures and profane language, I think he is a good officer, is vigilant, industrious, cautious, and brave." One private commented, "General Nelson has the confidence of the whole division, and more than this, is really liked by most of the men, not withstanding the coarseness, the regular quarter-deck style of his manners." What impressed that soldier was how "Old Buster" performed "an act of genuine kindness" when he encountered a volunteer with measles. Nelson demanded to know why the soldier had strayed so far away from his unit, and the young boy explained that in his weakened condition he could not eat hard tack and needed bread for nourishment. Nelson asked why he did not have the bread, and he replied that it cost ten cents and he only had five cents. Nelson handed him twenty-five cents and told him to buy five loaves of bread. His "blowing up" at the camp bakery then ensured the price of bread remained fixed at five cents.[7]

Alf Burnett remarked that "discipline, obedience and execution" represented the "Alpha and Omega" for "Big Buster." Burnett considered Nelson "one of the most 'coming men,' one whose mark will not be mistaken when the rebellion is over." He added, "What we want now is men of the same stamp—men of energy and action—men who will fight." Buell could see how the "officers [under Nelson] chafed under a control to which they were not accustomed, and which admitted no compromise between authority and obedience, yet in the end they learned to appreciate its importance, and the division became distinguished for its discipline and high tone." It was also his opinion that "No commander during the war enjoyed the confidence of his troops in greater degree than did General Nelson." They found "there is no measure of General Nelson's industry," and they appreciated that he "holds officers responsible for dereliction of duty . . . looks after the best interests of the common soldier . . . [and] gaining popularity."[8]

In order to weed out incompetent officers, improve the punctuality of the sentries, and prevent dereliction of duty, Nelson convened court-martials as often as circumstances permitted. In the matter of Michael Connell, the young private pleaded guilty to firing shots at a "superior officer." Court president Stanley Matthews accepted that plea and ruled the sentence would be death by firing squad. Connell's friends encouraged him to escape, but he brushed the suggestion aside, believing that with time the grim decision would be set aside.[9]

The story received scant attention from the press, in part because the public was far more interested in knowing when the Federal army would advance. For that very reason Nelson was in Louisville with Buell on Friday, January 3, 1862, to discuss moving against Bowling Green. On his return to Camp Wickliffe, a freezing rain had "enveloped [stoic camp guards] in a case of ice, presenting a glittering appearance" that pleased Nelson. However, on further examination, he found these soldiers negligent in their duties. That brought a call for "two more midnight long-rolls to be sounded, getting the boys out of bed to shiver in the cold." In the pitch-black dark, Nelson rode out alone in knee-deep mud and drenching rain to test the vigilance of the men by wearing no insignia. This death-defying feat led to the arrest of three captains, and it resulted in Nelson's coming down with chills, fever, and congestion.[10]

The *Cincinnati Commercial* noted how "sighing and grief continue to do their melancholy work on him [Nelson], as they did *poor* Jack Falstaff." His "even and amiable temper is not always proof against provocations furnished by the stupidity and carelessness he is required to control and punish." The paper admired that a "chaotic mass of undisciplined men . . . are fast being transformed into soldiers. This is attributable alone to the master spirit of the ground, Gen. Nelson." U. S. Senator Garrett Davis disagreed completely. He informed President Lincoln that Nelson was out "of his appropriate element, & not at all qualified to perform the duties of this place." Davis stated that while he remained a *steady friend* of the "web footed General," he wanted him removed from the brigadier's list. In his not-so-humble opinion, Nelson was "the most odious man I have ever known," and if nominated, "I shall feel it my duty to oppose his confirmation."[11]

On Thursday, January 9, Bradford recorded the "Genl. is better today. Free from fever." At midnight, the diary changed to, "Genl. Not so well. He has too much company—sat up too long—will pay for it." Nelson deteriorated through the night, and in the morning, Bradford noted the "Genl. is quite sick today . . . paying for his feast last night." Lt. Col. Nicholas Longworth Anderson, the son of Cincinnati aristocrat Larz Anderson and nephew of Brig. Gen. Robert Anderson, visited later. Nelson was still "very sick" but well enough to insist on an exchange of the Greenwood muskets for Enfields so that "no regiment should have rifles of different calibers."[12]

Sunday evening, Nelson and the commanders met in Bradford's tent and discussed their concern over "the mistake of inactivity." Dr. George C. Blackman, a noted Cincinnati surgeon who coauthored the *Handbook for the Military Surgeon* with Charles S. Trippler, had returned to the city to advise the *Cincinnati Times* "that no advance will be made for weeks, as the army is without adequate means of transportation." Lt. Col. Henry Von Treba, Thirty-second Regiment Indiana Volunteer Infantry, added to that unwelcome news by telling the *Indianapolis Journal* that it would take another three weeks for the Green River Bridge to be up to the standards needed for an advance on Bowling Green.[13]

On Monday morning, January 13, the continued illness of Nelson and Colonel Haskell was "keenly felt by the entire division." Nelson was equally concerned about the health of his men, and he wanted the old English Bell tents replaced by the newly arrived Sibley tents. Each one-hundred-and-one-man company received five tents that "held sixteen in a mess." They were thirteen feet high and eighteen feet in circumference, and Nelson believed the extra space would keep the men from infecting each other through an "exudation from the skin." The real problem was the bad weather that kept the men in those tents. With the exception of guard duty, they had little more to do than gossip among themselves while they listened to muffled drumbeats, death volleys, and the haunting notes of the bugles that sounded for companions who succumbed to disease.[14]

Nelson had uplifting news for the troops on January 20. The day before, Brig. Gen. George H. Thomas had defeated a Confederate army under Brig. Gen. Felix Zollicoffer at Logan's Cross Roads (Mill Springs), and this broke the center of the Confederate line in Kentucky. It also opened the way for an advance on Bowling Green and Nashville. Capt. Oliver D. Greene, the assistant adjutant general, recalled that everyone respected the ability of George H. Thomas, but at this particular time, the "regulars and volunteers" had an especially high regard for the spirited way in which Nelson threw "himself into every enterprise." The lead was therefore given to the Fourth Division because those exceptionally well-drilled soldiers were "considered superior" to all others in the Army of the Ohio. To better prepare his prized division, Nelson ordered the companies to conduct armed skirmish drills in the brush and woods each morning. Each battalion then went through the same drill in the afternoon.[15]

Buell characteristically guarded his plans and this kept him from coordinating with Maj. Gen. Henry W. Halleck's Department of the Missouri at St. Louis. He now sent Dr. Bradford forward with a cavalry escort to find a *healthier* location for the Fourth Division near the Green River. When they reached the pontoon bridge at Munfordville on Friday, January 31, 1862, it appeared that the adjacent wooden railroad bridge was about ready to handle a locomotive.[16]

Halleck in the meantime had sent Brig. Gen. Ulysses S. Grant down the Tennessee River against Fort Henry. That objective was seized on Thursday, February 6, 1862, and the Confederates withdrew twelve miles east to Fort Donelson on the Cumberland River. At Camp Wickliffe, the men of the Forty-first Regiment Ohio Volunteer Infantry believed that with Colonel Hazen absent on leave, Lt. Col. Graham N. Fitch, Forty-sixth Regiment Indiana Volunteer Infantry, or Lt. Col. James R. Slack, Forty-seventh Regiment Indiana Volunteer Infantry, would take command of the Nineteenth Brigade when they headed for Bowling Green on Friday, February 7. Those officers were very political, and Nelson preferred to meet with the brigade adjutant, Lt. Robert L. Kimberly, who found him sitting "coatless and stretched in a chair before the fire." Kimberly asked who would command, and Nelson curtly advised he would personally assume that duty in the morning.[17]

The advance toward Bowling Green ended on Monday, February 10, when Nelson was called back to support Grant's action against Fort Donelson. Brig. Gen. Ormsby M. Mitchel's Third Division replaced the Fourth Division and started forward Thursday morning. That evening, Nelson told Colonels Hazen and Ammen that early Friday morning, February 14, their brigades would make a forty-three-mile march to the confluence of the Salt and Ohio rivers at West Point, Kentucky. There, steamboats were to transport them to the mouth of the Cumberland River at Smithland, Kentucky. At 4:00 A.M., six inches of heavy snow had fallen on tents that had to be taken down and loaded on the wagons. At 6:30 A.M., the Tenth Brigade had Pvt. Michael Conner under guard when they marched south toward Buffalo. Colonel Ammen moved north (Rt. 61) through Hodgenville, and the Tenth and Nineteenth brigades went into bivouac two miles south of Elizabethtown. On Saturday, Nelson waited until 10:00 A.M. for the baggage trains to catch up. He then pushed forward in knee-deep mud, but had to halt the column five miles north of Elizabethtown.[18]

Sunday, Nelson drove his men forward on a grueling, twenty-mile march, not knowing that Grant had taken control of Fort Donelson. Just below West Point, he learned that over a thousand men had dropped out along the way. The thought of those men being left to die on the dismal, cold ground sent Nelson into a terrible rage. The officers responsible for this were publicly humiliated with vile cursing and personal insults that few would ever forgive or forget.[19]

Early Monday morning, twenty-five boats were waiting to board troops at the mouth of Salt River. As shivering soldiers trudged through knee-deep mud toward the belching black smoke, the always impatient Nelson rushed over to Maj. Enos Hopkins and directed him to divide companies C and H, First Michigan Engineers, between the *Autocrat*, with the Twenty-fourth Regiment Ohio Volunteer Infantry, and the Forty-sixth Regiment Indiana Volunteer Infantry on the *Golden State*. Hopkins did not board the men because it appeared the boats had reached their capacity. That disobedience turned Nelson "purple with rage," and he rashly threatened to march the men onto the boats at the point of bayonet. After giving those words a second thought, he directed Capt. W. L. Coffenberry to take command. As the two companies started aboard the *Lancaster* #4, Nelson placed Capt. Marcus

Grant and Major Hopkins under arrest and ordered them to Louisville for trial, saying it was a disgrace to have "such persons to accompany him in the presence of the enemy."[20]

Nelson intended to keep "boats of the same regiment and brigade together," but when the flotilla moved out into the high, fast water, that plan disappeared in dense fog and vanishing light. The entire double column of boats fell into disorder, and Nelson trusted he could regain control of the flotilla before reaching Smithland. At 9:00 P.M., the flagship *Diana* stopped at Canneton to take on coal, and this gave Nelson the opportunity to use the telegraph office. There was news about the seizure of Fort Donelson, and if there were further instructions at Smithland, he was to continue up the Cumberland River and report directly to Grant.[21]

Tuesday, February 18, the advance of Mitchel's Third Division was within thirty-seven miles of Nashville when Nelson arrived at Smithland. Lieutenant Colonels Fitch and Slack immediately appealed to Sherman to have the Forty-sixth and the Forty-seventh regiments Indiana Volunteer Infantry reassigned. Nelson then telegraphed Buell to say that any further detachment of regiments would dismantle the Fourth Division. Buell ordered Nelson to return, and by the time Secretary of War Edwin M. Stanton countermanded that order, Nelson had reached Cannelton. Nelson returned to Paducah at noon, February 21, and Grant saw that as an opportunity to overcome some of the "hard fighting" that lay ahead. He directed Nelson to come up the Cumberland River to meet with him at Fort Donelson.[22]

Lt. Henry H. Walke, an old Tabasco acquaintance of Nelson, commanded the *Carondelet*, a 13-gun ironclad that led the left column of ten steamboats on Sunday, February 23. The gunboat *Cairo* led the other ten transports of the right column, and about 10:00 P.M., the flotilla had reached Fort Donelson. Nelson went ashore and learned that Grant wanted him to seize Nashville without additional ammunition, and Nelson boastfully exclaimed that if needed he would go after the "enemy with the bayonets." Neither knew that Mitchel's cavalry had reached Edgefield, a town directly across from Nashville. They were also unaware of Mayor Richard Boone Cheatham's intention to surrender the city to Buell when he arrived on Monday.[23]

When Nelson returned to the *Diana* about midnight, he immediately ordered the flotilla forward in a horrendous rainstorm. Several captains pleaded for permission to stop at Dover because treetops were damaging the wheelhouses of their transports. Nelson insisted that they push through the night and at 8:00 A.M., Monday, February 24, the truce flags at Clarksville came into sight. While Nelson made a brief visit to that place, Grant reported to Henry

Halleck through the Department of Missouri at Cairo that "the gunboats have gone up to Nashville" and Nelson is under "verbal instructions, to have the men under wholesome restraint" when they enter the city.[24]

There were no direct communications with the Army of the Ohio, and that meant McClellan had to inform Halleck in St. Louis that Buell would be in front of Nashville on Monday evening. At this same time, McClellan recommended that "a combined movement of troops and gunboats [move down the Tennessee River] and seize Decatur [Alabama]." He said Buell would be instructed to "occupy and to re-establish the railroads from Nashville to Decatur and Stevenson [Alabama]. This will nearly isolate A. S. Johnston from Richmond [Virginia]."[25]

At dawn, Tuesday, February 25, Nelson reached the abandoned Fort Zollicoffer, and by 7:00 A.M., he could see a host of yellow hospital flags flying over Nashville. One hour later, a mass of excited citizens greeted the incoming boats by waving white sheets and petticoats. High water covered the lower part of town, and the *Diana* docked at the foot of a street between two huge warehouses. Amid closed stores and shuttered houses, a group of hesitant whites stood beside loaded wagons and carriages as the color sergeant of Company C, Sixth Regiment Ohio Volunteers, jumped ashore with the blue Guthrie Grey flag. Another soldier disembarked with the national colors, and next came five companies of the Sixth Regiment Ohio Volunteer Infantry marching to the "inspiriting strains of Dixie from the drums and fifes." At Cedar Street, a crowd of slaves clapped their hands and danced with joy when they heard the band playing "Yankee Doodle."[26]

Nelson was not deterred by the sight of angry white citizens who grumbled over how the commander of Confederate forces, Albert Sidney Johnston, had "behaved cowardly" by withdrawing to Murfreesboro. As he came forward to raise the national flag above the state capitol building, the Thirty-sixth Regiment Indiana Volunteer Infantry continued past the courthouse square. Further up Main Street, the Hoosiers kept a watchful eye on the Confederate cavalry who continued to linger along the edge of town. By 11:00 A.M., Nelson was in Edgewood to join the meeting with Mayor Cheatham and ten members of the city council. Mitchel could not confront Nelson under those circumstances, but he did obtain some satisfaction when a friendly correspondent for the *Pittsfield (Mass.) Sun* noted that this occupation of an abandoned city was akin to the "brilliant *newspaper victory*" at Ivy Mountain.[27]

Tuesday afternoon, Nelson ordered his troops two miles south on the Murfreesboro pike where they were to set up Camp Andrew Jackson. That night Capt. Robert Klein, Company I, Third Regiment Indiana Volunteer

Cavalry, arrived in camp with the escort troop. A short time later, the threatening clatter of horses along his front caused Lieutenant Colonel Anderson to advance a line of skirmishers from the Sixth Regiment Ohio Volunteer Infantry. In the next instant, Klein's hard-riding Germans chased after John Hunt Morgan's men, shouting curses in German and English. By the end of the chase, Klein had "lost two horses and one man killed."[28]

In Nashville, the Claiborne family invited Nelson to tea, thinking this would help develop cordial relations with the occupying army. The burly Kentuckian assumed that these Southerners would like to hear him expound on the causes of the war. Mrs. Claiborne was offended by the rudeness, and Nelson added to it by placing his thumb on his nose, wiggling his fingers, and stomping out of his guest's home.[29]

Sadly, that foolishness hid the mature side of Nelson that wanted to stop Andrew Johnson from becoming military governor of Tennessee. The East Tennessee native was "self-willed, uncompromising [,] and dictatorial." He could not abide with an "opinion in conflict with his own," and like Nelson, his rough speech and belligerent manner easily antagonized those who valued "the dignity of their positions." The two men held entirely different views when it came to reconciling with those Tennesseans who had rebelled against the Union, and for that reason, Nelson implored Secretary Chase, "Do not send Andy Johnson here in any official capacity. . . . [The people] seem to be awakening from some unpleasant dream . . . [and the] tide has already turned."[30]

Many in the North supposed the Confederate army in the West would collapse once the Federal army took control of the vital railroad junction at Corinth, Mississippi. Halleck was working on plans for that advance when he heard rumors that Grant had resumed his old habit of excessive drinking. He had clearly overstepped his authority by coming to Nashville to encourage Buell to continue after Albert Sidney Johnston at Murfreesboro. On March 4, Halleck informed Grant by telegraph, "You will place Major-General [Brig. Gen.] C. [Charles] F. Smith in command of the expedition [to Savannah, Tennessee] and remain at Fort Henry." This called for the headquarters to be 30 miles north of the principal objective of Corinth and 125 miles from Buell at Nashville. Smith ordered Brig. Gen. William T. Sherman to install advance elements of the Fifth Division, Army of the Tennessee, one hundred miles up the Tennessee River, nine miles below Pittsburg Landing, and some twenty miles from Savannah, which was on the opposite side of the Tennessee River.[31]

That same day, Nelson announced that the Fourth Division would assemble under arms to witness the execution of Pvt. Michael Connell at 3:00 P.M.,

Wednesday, March 5, 1862. Lieutenants Kimberly and Holloway still resented how Nelson slighted them at Camp Wickliffe, and they wrongly surmised that he saw this as "a fit time to give a lesson in army discipline." They also supposed that Nelson had not forwarded the matter to higher headquarters "as he should have done." Neither knew that Nelson still hoped "a reprieve might yet be granted by the department commander," and they certainly had no idea that this was someone who "never went to bed without saying his prayers."[32]

At the appointed time, the somber beat of the drums signaled for the band to strike up the funeral dirge. A young lieutenant marched a squad of ten men forward with arms reversed. Four men bore an empty pine coffin followed by the condemned Connell. He was dressed in civilian clothes in order to prevent any disgrace of the army uniform. Connell walked in cadenced step with a Catholic priest from Nashville and a chaplain from the Twenty-fourth Regiment Ohio Volunteer Infantry. Maj. Albert S. Hall announced the sentence, and Nelson told his aide to look for one more sign of a messenger from Buell.[33]

Moments later, Major Hall nodded to executioners. A mounted officer rode up just as the sword with a white handkerchief was about to go up. The detail brought their guns back down to their side, and five minutes later, Nelson's aide returned with no news of a reprieve. In rapid succession the blindfold went back on, the sword went up, and out came the commands: *Ready . . . Aim . . . Fire!* Connell fell back on the coffin, rolled over on his right side, and sank to the ground. Being forced to witness an "official murder" that was conducted by Nelson made the ordinary solider feel corrupted. Very few, if any, considered the fact that Stanley Matthews made the decision to put Connell to death or that Buell could have stopped it.[34]

For now, the prosecution of the war took precedence over personal feelings. The following week, Halleck succeeded in his efforts to have the three military departments in the West consolidated into the Department of the Mississippi. Buell received orders to move the Army of the Ohio to Savannah, Tennessee, and join forces with the Army of the Tennessee. Halleck saw no reason why the lead division for the Army of the Ohio would not arrive before the end of March, and Buell did not refute that inference.[35]

In order to evaluate the readiness of his division, Nelson chose the occasion of Andrew Jackson's ninety-fifth birthday to march his troops to Hermitage Plantation on March 12. The always-disapproving Kimberly and Holloway characterized this as another "one of Gen. Nelson's freaks": a political pilgrimage with no military purpose. They were further angered that Nelson "put a favorite regiment in the lead [the Sixth Regiment Ohio Volunteer Infantry], and exercised no control over the pace." Nelson was pleased with how the troops performed, and the disdain of those two disgruntled officers very likely went unnoticed. The next day, few knew that due to the incapacity of Charles F. Smith, Halleck had no choice but to order Grant to resume command of the Army of the Tennessee.[36]

On March 14, 1862, Buell advised Halleck the aggregate force in the Department of the Ohio was 101,737. With an effective strength of 71,233, Buell proposed concentrating eighteen brigades and six divisions of 55,000 men to strike the enemy along the Memphis & Charleston Railroad. Buell had his eye on Florence, Alabama, and he believed the enemy line should "be cut west of Decatur, not farther east than Corinth." He recommended using "two columns, one through Murfreesboro . . . the other through Columbia [Tennessee]." While Buell and the main force proceeded to Columbia, Brig. Gen. Ormsby McKnight Mitchel was to cover his left flank with the Third Division "mainly at Fayetteville; [and Col. William W.] Duffield's [Twenty-third] brigade, with a battery and battalion of cavalry at Murfreesboro, with a detachment at Lebanon."[37]

Halleck believed the enemy line extended from Decatur, Alabama, to Island No. 10, and therefore the Federal army "must attack it in the center, say at Corinth [Mississippi] or Jackson [Tennessee]." On Saturday, March 15, 1862, Buell said he would "commence moving tomorrow." The five divisions of thirty-seven thousand troops were to march forty-two miles to Columbia, Tennessee, by way of the turnpike road that ran parallel to the Nashville & Decatur Railroad. As the senior officer, Brig. Gen. Alexander McCook would lead with the Second Division. Saturday night a strong cavalry detachment rode south along the Franklin Turnpike (US 31) to secure the crossings at Rutherford Creek and Duck River, and they found that men from Col. John S. Scott's First Louisiana Cavalry had set the bridges on fire.[38]

Monday, March 17, 1862, Grant assumed command at Savannah while Nelson was marching the Fourth Division out of Camp Andrew Jackson. By Thursday, he had his troops encamped just south of Spring Hill. Brig. Gen. Alexander McCook had ordered Capt. Amos Glover, Company F, Fifteenth Regiment Ohio Volunteer Infantry, to start rebuilding the Duck River Bridge with a forty-man detail, and on Saturday, March 22, Nelson edged the Fourth Division forward while Glover's men finished flooring the four-hundred-foot-long trestle. On Monday, March 24, Glover's men began work on a 150-man flatboat. They finished the following day, and Nelson immediately "ordered the fording cleaned."[39]

Buell arrived on Wednesday, March 26, and after personally examining the progress of the rickety structure, he ordered the construction of a pontoon

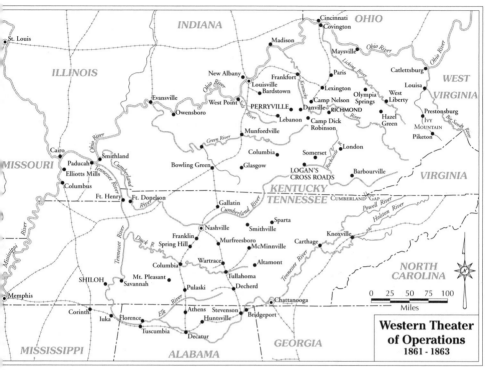

Map 5. Western Theater of Operations, 1861–63

bridge. Nelson then ordered Col. Jacob Ammen to move the Tenth Brigade two miles closer to the Duck River. The next day two couriers from Grant arrived as Nelson watched the interminable bridge construction. It stunned Nelson when he heard those men say the Army of the Tennessee was nine miles below Savannah on the west bank of the Tennessee River and not the east, as supposed. Nelson's "strong individuality . . . his prescience, energy, and readiness" erupted in full force. He yelled at a staff officer, "By God Damned! We must cross that river at once, or Grant will be whipped!" This old salt intended to meet "the needs of the hour" with a "rude, imperious emphasis," and for the moment, that style of leadership would win "him respect and a strange sort of feeling that was almost affection."[40]

Buell's new headquarters were on the opposite side of the road from Ammen's Tenth Brigade, and Nelson rushed there to seek permission for his troops to cross immediately. Buell listened patiently and then "pointed out the difficulty of resuming the march before . . . completion [of the bridge] . . . which would be finished . . . in a few days." Nelson felt certain that his division could be over "in six hours" because the river "had fallen rapidly and reached its ordinary stage." The sly smiles of disdain on the faces of the staff irritated the assistant adjutant general, Capt. Oliver D. Greene. He viewed Nelson as an individual who "always came up to his talk." Buell agreed, and as an added incentive, he told Nelson that if he "could get his men safely over, with all of his artillery and baggage," they could keep the lead for the Army of the Ohio. Nelson informed Colonel Ammen they would cross the Duck River at daylight, Saturday morning, and when Ammen asked if the bridge would be finished, Nelson responded, "No; but the river is falling; and God Damn you, get over, for we must have the advance and get the glory."[41]

Nelson intended to use Capt. Robert Klein's Company I, Third Regiment Indiana Volunteer Cavalry, as scouts, and he directed Capt. Emerson Opdycke, Company A, Forty-first Regiment Ohio Volunteer Infantry, to act as his bodyguard. Opdycke considered Nelson to be "very positive, and decided, and very much down on those he dont like, swears *some*; and has some officer under arrest most of the time. I manage with him very well, answer his questions promptly—yes or no—and never give advice except when asked, in short I know my duty and do it, without intruding upon his time, this pleases him, . . . he has never given me a sharp word, if he ever *does* abuse me, . . . I will bring him to justice, as I know *my* rights as well as *his*.[42]

On Friday, March 28, a bright sun made for a pleasant day as Bradford and the other surgeons culled out those soldiers who appeared unfit for hard marching. Nelson and Ammen were examining the fords on the Duck River and they found the crossing points were all quite crooked. There was a strong current and the water ran deep above and below where the two stood. They also saw that because there had been no rain for three days, the rapidly falling water was barely touching the beds of fully loaded wagons returning from Columbia. That evening the cheerful Nelson told his officers to get the men ready "for the march of their life."[43]

On Saturday, March 29, a cheerless cold rain was falling when first call was sounded at 4:00 A.M. In the pitch dark, the Twenty-fourth and Sixth regiments Ohio Volunteer Infantry and the Thirty-sixth Regiment Indiana Volunteer Infantry marched three miles forward to the ford at Duck River. The men of the Thirty-fourth Regiment Illinois Volunteer Infantry were "astonished" at the sight of Nelson "passing our camp." At 6:00 A.M., that amazement turned to resentment when they realized he intended to ford the river and take the lead away from the Second Division. Along the opposite bank, a crowd of curious men, women, and children from Columbia watched in amazement as Nelson's men carried out "one of the queerist military orders on record."[44]

The men stacked arms, took off their pants and blouses, rolled them up, and attached the clothes to their bayonets. With cartridge-boxes tied around their necks, they moved down the slippey river bank to a tortuous S-shaped ford that was 175 feet wide. The rock-hard bottom made for easy going, and Maurice Williams, Thirty-sixth Regiment Indiana Volunteer Infantry, recalled, "The water was about waist deep and very swift and most awful cold and still it was sport for us." Col. August Willich, Thirty-second Regiment Indiana Volunteer Infantry, had instructed the cavalry on how to ford the river by fours, and a regiment of those horsemen was at the lower edge of the ford to break the current and provide help if needed. When they moved up the other side, their water-soaked horses turned the slope into a slippery mess for those who followed. At the top, the muddy soldiers wrung their underwear dry and redressed amid the shouts and jeers of the civilian audience.[45]

It took four hours to cross the infantry. Next came the artillery and baggage. Each regiment supplied one company of stong men to assist with the loading and movement.The Polish military experience of Lt. Joseph Pietzuch was evident in "scows" made by turning one wagon body over and placing it on top of another wagon. Tents were packed in the bottom of the top part. The artillery ammunition was removed from the limbers and placed on the tents. By sunset, all but a few pieces of artillery were over, and the Tenth Brigade went into bivouac two and a half miles south of Columbia on the plantation of Gideon J. Pillow's father-in-law, William P. Martin.[46]

The Twenty-second and Nineteenth brigades remained ten miles back from the north bank of the Duck River, and to make room for them on Sunday, March 30, Nelson moved the Tenth Brigade five miles forward at noon. Sgt. Lyman S. Widney noted that "Nelson's movement . . . stirred our commanders into unwonted activity. . . . Several divisions in our rear closing up to the bridge, ready to cross at the earliest moment." That evening, Ammen encamped at "Captain [George N.] Polk's plantation" (Rattle and Snap), and Nelson occupied Gideon J. Pillow's Clifton Place, a baronial estate of seven hundred acres.[47]

At dawn, Monday, March 31, Sergeant Widey was "mortified" to see Thomas L. Crittenden's Fifth Division crossing ahead of the Second Division. After they had finished, McCook started his troops across the swaying pontoon bridge. C. C. Briant, Sixth Regiment Indiana Volunteer Infantry, Fourth Brigade, recalled it was still "dark as hades, except the flickering lights on the shore, which enabled you to see more clearly" the terrifying danger of crossing "a temporary bridge built on top of water." Ropes fastened to trees held the "frail structure against the swift current." The "screeching and cracking" beneath each step made the ropes strain so hard "you could fairly hear them sing in air." Some of the soldiers spoke of how pleased Nelson's men were to have the lead. Most seemed to believe the "fording exploit" was nothing more than "an uncalled-for piece of bravado" conducted by "a tyrant."[48]

Grant had expressed no interest in seeing Buell's forces before April 7, 1862, and Nelson told Ammen to set a pace that would not bring them into Savannah before then. Grant would later claim he tried to spend each day at Pittsburg Landing, but because Buell "was expected daily," that kept him in Savannah "longer than I otherwise should have done." That Monday evening, Nelson bivouacked at the foot of a large hill just beyond Mount Pleasant and some eleven miles from Columbia. Several citizens informed Colonel Ammen that the Rebels had six wagonloads of salt pork three miles outside of town, and while the men from the Sixth Ohio Infantry went after that bounty, Nelson learned from his scouts that the Buffalo River Bridge was intact. Klein's escort cavalry was ordered eleven miles forward to ensure the Rebels did not destroy the structure during the night. As it neared midnight, a camp sentinel mortally wounded a farmer who made sure his last words to the "Yankee invaders" were "a horrible imprecation upon" them.[49]

The invective of that Southern partisan fit with the certainty that the railroad, the telegraph, and the good, hard-surfaced road all ended at Mount Pleasant. The final seventy-nine miles would be over a dilapidated pathway that had been built as a farm-to-market road by Gideon Pillow in 1839–40. Now that old pathway was about to be of extraordinary importance to the Federal troops just below Pittsburg Landing.[50]

Beyond the once-thriving resort at Summertown, the landscape turned ugly, the travel became hard, and the "peculiar institution" of slavery was no longer evident. Here "poor whites" tilled "worthless yellow clay. . . . Ever and anon some lane or gateway was thronged with young and old . . . eager to witness the march of our troops. . . . with streaming eyes" saluting the flag and exciting the soldiers as they marched by.[51]

The movement of thousands of men and animals during a heavy spring rain turned the road into six inches of mud, and the subsequent mess called for constant repair. When Nelson saw that the fences along the narrow, rutted pathway hindered movement, he had the men tear them down and ordered their commanders to give the telegraph workers any assistance they required. On Tuesday, April 1, the sound of gunshots caused Col. Walter C. Whitaker to send a small detachment of the Sixth Regiment Kentucky Volunteer Infantry forward to investigate. Nelson rushed forward and hollered, "Why in The Heal are you not with your Regt?" Whitaker would have none of it and continued eating breakfast while Nelson looked into the false alarm. When he returned, Nelson avoided a confrontation with the fiery Whitaker and went directly to his headquarters.[52]

During the fourteen-mile march to Henryville, the unseasonably hot weather turned the road into choking dust. Nelson stopped at a plantation house to get a drink of buttermilk, and from the porch he could see a young soldier riding on a wagon. Nelson had forbidden the practice, and he jumped on his horse and raced forward with his hand on a revolver and yelling, "You God Dammed bastard get off the wagon or I'll put a bullet through you." The soldier stared back with a homicidal glare and coldly replied, "Try it, God Damn you!" Nelson knew better than to force the issue. That evening the division camped three miles on the other side of the Buffalo River, and at supper, Nelson laughed heartily about how "any mere lad with nerve enough to defy and threaten a general . . . would have shot me for sure."[53]

Wednesday evening the advance for the Fourth Division arrived at Proctor's Furnace, and Nelson sent pickets to Waynesboro, five miles away. Near the hill that supplied iron ore for the town, the commanders had a drink at the headquarters tent, and Dr. Bradford noted, "Genl Nelson is in good humor." Everyone recognized the momentous importance of what lay ahead, but none of them suspected that Albert Sidney Johnson and P. G. T. Beauregard were finalizing plans to attack Brig. Gen. William T. Sherman at Shiloh Church on Friday, April 4.[54]

On Thursday, April 3, Nelson marched the Fourth Division fifteen miles to Hardin Creek. When they reached Waynesboro, it truly delighted the men when they saw small United States flags in the windows of some homes. Several women asked one of the regimental bands to play "Yankee Doodle, &C," and while they did, an artillery battery signed up new recruits. Buell was about to leave Columbia, and he advised Grant and Halleck that the Army of the Ohio should probably be held in place at Waynesboro where there would be the option of moving south to Hamburg Landing or on to Savannah. Late that afternoon, Nelson was unaware that Halleck had agreed with that recommendation, when he heard the troubling sound of cannonading coming from the area around Pittsburg Landing. The firing most likely came from the U.S. Navy gunboats *Lexington* and *Tyler*, but Nelson interpreted this as a sign of trouble for Grant.[55]

Albert Sidney Johnson intended for his forces to advance at 6:00 A.M., Thursday, April 3. However, as fate would have it, the deputy commander of Confederate forces, P. G. T. Beauregard, confused the corps commanders with a complicated marching order that delayed the start. By noon, Grant had established telegraph communication with Nelson, and it seemed clear to him those troops would arrive on Saturday, April 5. Grant confidently advised Nelson that the transports needed to ferry the men across the Tennessee would not arrive until Tuesday, April 8, and "all difficulties in our neighborhood will be remedied before your arrival."[56]

At 3:00 P.M., the long-delayed Confederate movement started forward. Albert Sidney Johnston advised President Jefferson Davis, "Buell is in motion, 30,000 strong, rapidly from Columbia by Clifton to Savannah; Mitchel behind him with 10,000. Confederate forces, 40,000, ordered forward to offer battle near Pittsburg. . . . Hope engagement before Buell [Nelson] can form junction [with Grant]." Below Shiloh Church, the skirmishing was "so continuous" that Grant remained in the field until he was satisfied his army was not in danger.[57]

On Friday, April 4, Grant rode to the front in a driving rain that caused his horse to fall and left him "very much injured." Nelson would not allow the weather to thwart his movement, and by 3:00 P.M., he had reached Vansant's Plantation, ten miles east of Savannah. A half hour later, Maj. Elbridge G. Ricker, Fifth Ohio Volunteer Cavalry, Sherman's Fifth Division, encountered two regiments of Confederate infantry and troops from the First Alabama Cavalry. The Confederates fired three artillery rounds, and the distinct sound carried far enough to get Nelson's attention. Sherman rushed forward with two infantry regiments and found "the enemy is in some considerable force at Pea Ridge." He did not see that those troops from William J. Hardee's Third Corps were actually the vanguard for the entire Army of the Mississippi.[58]

Sherman continued to believe that if Albert Sidney Johnston should advance against the Federal forces, it would be from the west and not the south. When Grant arrived, the situation appeared "all quiet." Believing there was no immediate threat, he returned to board the *Tigress* at Pittsburg Landing. The wet conditions caused his horse to slip on the ramp, and that injured his ankle so severely that Grant now had to use crutches. Nelson remained uneasy over the unexplained sound of artillery, and as it neared midnight, he decided to move forward in the pounding rain. Reveille sounded at 1:00 A.M., Saturday, April 5, 1862, and he had the lead start forward in the dismal, wet darkness an hour later. Between 11:00 A.M. and noon, the first files of the Thirty-sixth Regiment Indiana Volunteer Infantry started across the eastern edge of Savannah.[59]

Nelson rode ahead to find Grant and discovered he was with the ailing Charles F. Smith at the headquarters in the William H. Cherry home. At least five hours of daylight remained, and Nelson suggested his division should continue on to Pittsburg Landing. Grant declared that Savannah would do for the present, and Nelson took no "comfort" in that answer. He asked about the disposition of the enemy, and Smith replied that the Confederates remained "in Corinth, and, when our [steamboat] transportation arrives, we have got to go there and draw them out, as you would draw a badger out of his hole."[60]

The smugness irritated Nelson, and that plainly showed when he asked Grant, "Do you not think that [Confederate general P. G. T.] Beauregard will attack you? The wonder is that he has not done so before. If he fails to attack your present position, sir, he is not the man whose military discretion should govern the movements of any army." Grant explained that Sherman did "not apprehend anything like an attack on our position" and "should [the Confederates] attack me, I . . . can hold my own." Nelson snapped back that if Beauregard could not beat Grant alone, why go against Grant *and* Buell? The rudeness offended Grant, and he abruptly ordered Nelson to put his troops into camp one half-mile east of Savannah. Grant would later claim he also told Nelson to bring his division forward to the east bank of the Tennessee River early Sunday morning; that transports would be available to move those men across to Crump's Landing or onto Pittsburg Landing.[61]

Grant advised Halleck that a large enemy force attacked Sherman's outposts on Friday. He added the "idea of an attack (general one) being made upon us" was quite remote, but "should such a thing take place" his troops would be ready. Grant said that Nelson had arrived, and it appeared the remainder of Buell's army would reach Savannah on Sunday and Monday. Because he anticipated sending those troops to Hamburg Landing, Lt. Col. James B. McPherson was "to examine the defensibility of the ground . . . and to lay out the position of the camps" some four miles south of Pittsburg Landing.[62]

About 3:00 P.M., Saturday, Grant joined Nelson for an inspection of the Fourth Division. At Colonel Ammen's tent, Grant counseled his old friend not to worry about the enemy situation. He reiterated that transports would not be available until "Monday or Tuesday, or sometime early in the week," and until then, Ammen should relax and make his men comfortable.[63]

The other four divisions stretched thirty miles back to the east when Buell rode into Savannah about sunset. There was no sign of Grant, and it appeared that he "probably" had gone to Pittsburg Landing. At Nelson's headquarters, Buell presumed he could do nothing more than call for a review of the Fourth Division at 9:00 A.M., Sunday. A full moon shined brightly, and Nelson, the "gifted conversationalist and charming companion," entertained everyone with accounts of his travels. At the conclusion of the "brilliant and companionable gathering," Nelson gave Buell his iron cot, and he went to sleep on the ground with a saddle for a pillow. His aide, Lt. Horace Fisher, instructed the night orderly to cancel Reveille at the headquarters and awake him at 4:00 A.M.[64]

Old Buster's ever-present energy had created a division that was second-to-none in the iron-fisted business of war. In that process, there was minimal regard for Stanley Matthew's sage advice to guard against an "uncontrolled or uncontrollable temper" that "sooner or later" might get him killed. Nelson also ignored how there might be repercussions from Mitchel's men seeing the occupation of Nashville as nothing more than gratuitous grandstanding that robbed them of the glory. Nor did he understand how the tragic execution of Michael Connell caused the men to resent how he made them participate in the "official murder" of a soldier. After the crossing of the Duck River, the young volunteers forgot that this "most odious" man could not "restrain his tongue or avoid showing contempt for those he disliked or had prejudices against." Now they had reached Savannah, what mattered most was the glory that would come from following their confounding leader into battle.[65]

Disputed Glory

April 6, 1862, was Palm Sunday, and the few members of the dislodged congregation of Shiloh Methodist Church who remained nearby felt uneasy as the first rays of light passed across the quiet fields. At 4:55 A.M., the advancing Confederate troops became engaged in a fight with the 250-man reconnaissance patrol from the Twenty-fifth Regiment Missouri Volunteer Infantry and the Twelfth Regiment Michigan Volunteer Infantry. The short, sharp, sounds of the musket fire were not heard in Savannah, and some twenty-five minutes later Lieutenant Fisher awoke Buell and Nelson with nothing to report.[1]

About 6:00 A.M., the commander of Grant's Third Division, Lew Wallace, sat down to breakfast with his staff aboard a steamboat at Crump's Landing. They soon heard the alarming boom of cannon fire and it seemed certain that would bring Grant forward at any moment. That hobbled commander had joined his staff for breakfast at the Cherry Mansion, and about 7:15 a private alerted them to the thunderous sound of artillery fire rolling down the Tennessee River. Grant realized the Confederates had seized the initiative, and before boarding the *Tigress*, he wrote one note to Buell and another to Nelson. The message to Buell said, "An attack has been made upon our most advanced positions. This necessitates my joining the forces up river instead of meeting to-day, as I had contemplated. I have directed General Nelson to move . . . opposite Pittsburg."[2]

Grant had departed before Nelson arrived at Cherry Mansion to inquire about the ominous sounds. Squire Walker, a local citizen, had assured Grant that two scouts were available, and his note to Nelson said there was a guide in town. A search for the man proved fruitless, and Capt. John Mills Kendrick went forward on reconnaissance with Capt. Robert Klein's Company I, Third Regiment Indiana Volunteer Cavalry. Buell and Nelson knew there were empty transports at Pittsburg Landing, and at 11:00 A.M. Colonel Ammen found them at the landing anxiously looking for any sign of those boats. Buell's sullenness and Nelson's impatience made Ammen uneasy, and he headed off to visit the ailing C. F. Smith. When word arrived for him to return to the landing, Ammen found that Buell had boarded a small transport and started for Pittsburg Landing just after 11:30.[3]

Elements of Braxton Bragg's Second Corps were hammering at the center of the Union position that stretched along a sunken farm road west to a stronghold that the Union troops called a "Hornet's Nest." Albert Sidney Johnston planned to drive Grant north of Pittsburg Landing and into the swamps of Snake Creek before reinforcements could come to Grant's aid. It was only a matter of time before Grant had to pull his troops back, and he sent a message by transport to the "Commanding Officer, advanced forces, near Pittsburg. . . . If you will get upon the field . . . it will . . . possibly save the day to us." Buell received that message midway between Savannah and Pittsburg Landing, and he forwarded it to Nelson with instructions to come forward without artillery and baggage.[4]

Over two decades later, Grant wrote Lew Wallace that he had personally instructed Nelson on Saturday to "march at an early hour the next morning; [but] that he did not start until 1 P.M." Grant further claimed it took an order from Buell to get Nelson to move forward. Those disingenuous words conflict with the messages left on Sunday, and they fail to explain why Nelson spent entire morning moving back and forth like a caged lion. Nelson was now the very picture of satisfaction and good humor as he rode down the line noting every detail. For the first three miles, the men found the "undulating, rolling ground easy to travel," but over the next mile, the path moved down into the sultry confines of dense undergrowth and slippery muck. The soldiers cheered wildly when they saw "Old Buster" ride to the front of the column and shout to Colonel Ammen, "I will take your guide; hurry on; you can follow our trail."[5]

About that same time, the Confederates were conducting a massive assault against the Federal line that stood in front of a flowering peach orchard. At 2:45 P.M., Albert Sidney Johnston, the master spirit of the Confederate army, lay dead and his army remained stalled near the center of the sunken road that ran through the orchard. Some fifteen minutes later, P. G. T. Beauregard assumed control of the Confederate army and Braxton Bragg took command of all the forces on the right. Grant ordered his chief scout, Capt. Irving W. Carson, across the river to find Nelson and deliver a verbal dispatch that said in effect, "Hurry up your command. . . . The boats will be in readiness to transport all troops of your command across the river. All looks well, but it is necessary for you to push forward as fast as possible." Colonel Ammen asked Carson, "How far to the river?" He answered, "A mile and a half or two miles through the swamp." Ammen then told Carson, "Return and tell the general we are coming."[6]

Grant had five 24-pound siege guns and three batteries that had not been committed to battle, and he ordered Chief of Staff Col. Joseph D. Webster to mount those twenty-two heavy guns in an arc along the road above the bluff facing south into Dill Branch. Capt. Relly Madison, Battery B, Second Illinois Light Artillery, commanded the siege guns, and he moved them one-quarter of a mile up the hill to a developing line of infantry and artillery that was falling back in such disorder that Grant's staff rode out to plead with them to stay in place.[7]

Brig. Gen. Daniel Ruggles commanded the center of the Confederate line that faced the Hornet's Nest, and now he assembled a line of about sixty artillery pieces some 450 yards southwest of that position. At 3:30 P.M., Ruggles's "battery" unleashed a horrendous barrage that prepared the way for the seventh assault of the day against the Hornet's Nest. The left flank of Brig. Gen. Stephen A. Hurlbut's Fourth Division was completely exposed, and he began a withdrawal toward the landing. By 4:30 P.M., the lines of W. H. L. Wallace and Benjamin M. Prentiss started to collapse under the strain of the Confederate assault.[8]

On the bluff above Pittsburg Landing, Hurlbut placed his Fourth Division in support of the artillery, and Grant ordered Lt. Col. Oscar Malmborg to assemble what was left of Stuart's Second Brigade into "a line of over 3,000 men." Grant then went down to the river to urge a terrified horde of battlefield refugees to return to their units. The panicked men paid no heed, and Grant then ordered a cavalry squadron to ride through the throng with their swords drawn. That broke up the mob, but by the time Grant reached the top of the bluff, the chaotic mass had returned.[9]

Bragg sensed that victory was within his grasp, and in his haste for glory, he overlooked the need for a reconnaissance that would have revealed the formidable obstacles his four thousand troops would face when he ordered them to drive Grant's troops into the Tennessee River. Colonel Webster had fifty-three guns in an arc facing the steep ravine and dense woods of Dill Branch that separated the forces. The Tennessee River served as a natural a barrier on the left flank, and Owl Creek protected the right. Grant was aware that this "terrible battle of the day" had depleted his army, and the men were "more or less shattered." He also knew that "five hundred yards from the river," Hurlbut's Fourth Division was in "intact" near the right of Webster's artillery line. On Hurlbut's right, the First Division under John A. McClernand held the center facing west. William T. Sherman's Fifth Division was on McClernand's right and Grant believed Lew Wallace's Third Division would arrive at any moment and go in on the right of Sherman.[10]

At 5:00 P.M., Grant and Buell pointed out to the troops on the bluff that just across the Tennessee River Nelson was marching through a field of soggy cornstalks at the head of the Fourth Division. Equally important, his "Gotohellsir" manner was no longer evident as he boarded a small sutler's boat with nine mounted officers and two hundred infantry under Lt. Col. O. H. P. Carey, Thirty-sixth Regiment Indiana Volunteer Infantry.[11]

Out in the middle of the river, the soldiers were shocked at the sight of battlefield refugees swimming toward the boat. Nelson ordered them to load their rifles, fix bayonets, and hold their fire. At the landing, the first company of the Thirty-sixth Regiment Indiana Volunteer Infantry moved down the gangplanks and into an unruly mob with their bayonets at the ready. The second company stood guard against the stragglers as Nelson and Bradford mounted their horses. The two men jumped over the gunwale. Nelson drew his sword, waved his plumed hat, and commanded, "Two aides on each side of me, other mounted officers (Adjutant Kendrick and Surgeon Irwin) second in line. . . . Gentlemen draw your sabers and trample these [bastards] into the mud! Charge!" The refugees froze in place, and Nelson yelled, "Damn your souls, if you won't fight, get out of the way, and let men come here who will!" The panic-stricken men cried back, "We are whipped! The battle is lost! It is no use to form! They're driving us into the river!"[12]

Buell reputedly told Nelson, "Here, General, is your opportunity. There is one hour left in which to decide the fight." The Thirty-sixth Regiment Indiana Volunteer Infantry started up the hill, and the embittered battlefield refugees yelled at them, "You will get it!" "You will come back!" "You will see!" Captain Madison W. Walden saw what was happening and encouraged the Sixth Regiment Iowa Volunteer Infantry to join the undaunted newcomers. Maj. William Belknap grabbed some fifteen to twenty men from the Fifteenth Regiment Iowa Volunteer Infantry, and they moved up the hill with about one hundred stragglers to a position near the Thirty-sixth Indiana Infantry. Companies A, F, and D, Sixth Regiment Ohio Volunteer Infantry arrived, and one of Grant's officers shouted, "Don't stop to form[,] colonel [Ammen] . . . we shall all be massacred if you do!" Buell told Ammen to put his men two hundred yards beyond the bluff, and as they moved across the top, they could hear regimental bands playing "Hail Columbia" and "Dixie." The sight of disciplined troops from Buell's army was a great boost to morale, and Nel-

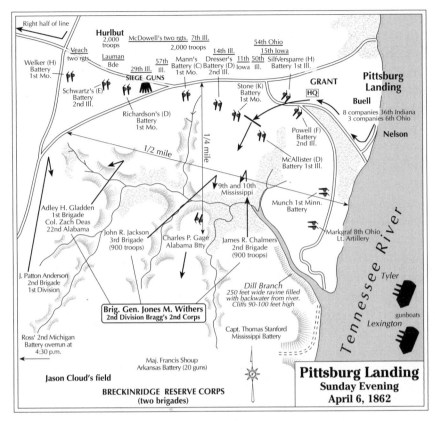

Map 6. Pittsburg Landing, Sunday Evening, April 6, 1862

son used the opportunity to smack the flat of his sword against his boot and holler in rhythmic cadence: "SHOUT BUELL, SHOUT BUELL, SHOUT BUELL."[13]

Buell and Nelson were at the front of Grant's log cabin headquarters, and Dill Branch was about one-quarter of a mile to their south. The gaping mouth of that deep crevice was about 250 yards wide and the cliffs along each side were about 90 feet high. Backwater extended west to near the center of the ravine, and near that point, Capt. Charles P. Gage had two 12-pound howitzers and two 3-inch rifles of his Alabama Battery on the rise of a 450-foot hill, 600 yards south of the Federal siege guns. On Gage's left, the western end of Dill Branch was dry and traversable ground.[14]

Shortly after 5:20 P.M., the three companies of the Sixth Regiment Ohio Volunteer Infantry reached the rear of the Thirty-sixth Regiment Indiana Volunteer Infantry. "Shells were whizzing overhead," and Pvt. George W. White, Company G, Thirty-sixth Regiment, was marching forward when a canister round tore off both of his legs and mortally wounded him. Ten feet behind Grant and Buell, Captain Carson could see that one of the field officers in the front was particularly nervous. As he started over to give encouragement, a six-pound shot took the front half of his head off, leaving a grotesque chin. The deadly missile barely missed Grant, and as it flew by Lieutenant Fisher, the ball stuck the cantle of Lt. William Preston Graves's saddle and broke the back of his horse. Graves got up and staggered over to Nelson with no coattails on his jacket. He saluted and asked permission to have his wounds treated. A staff surgeon gave Graves a quick look, congratulated him on his good fortune, and the young aide returned to the battle line.[15]

The ghastly episode caused the Thirty-sixth Regiment Indiana Volunteer Infantry to curve "a step or two back, but upon hearing [Colonel Grose command,] 'Straighten up that line,'" the men quickly aligned themselves. Buell directed Grose toward George H. Stone's Battery K, First Missouri Light Artillery, and Edward S. McAllister's Battery D, First Illinois Light Artillery. They were about 150 yards to the front, "firing and falling back by alternate sections." Some 300 to 400 hundred yards to the right of the Thirty-sixth Indiana Infantry there were five 24-pound siege guns ready to fire into the advancing Confederates. On the left side of those guns were six 30-pound Parrott Rifles and on the right, six 20-pound Parrott Rifles.[16]

Confederate Brig. Gen. Jones M. Withers seemed to be unaware of those guns when he ordered his men into action. Col. Zach C. Deas (Adley Gladden's First Brigade) advanced on the left. Jackson's Third Brigade went forward from the center, and Chalmers Second Brigade (Ninth and Tenth Regiments Mississippi Volunteer Infantry) moved across on the right. At 5:30 P.M., the Confederate units behind Withers surrounded the Union troops in the Hornet's Nest. Five minutes later, a force of 224 skirmishers from Deas's Twenty-second Regiment Alabama Volunteer Infantry advanced to within seven hundred yards of the defenders on the bluff above the landing. Using reduced charges in elevated guns, the naval gunboats *Lexington* and *Tyler* opened fire from the mouth of Dill Branch.[17]

Thirty-two rounds from the gunboats went directly into Gage's position as the Ninth and Tenth Regiments Mississippi Volunteer Infantry "struggled vainly to ascend the hill" to their front, which had "a whole line of batteries protected by infantry and assisted by shells from the gunboats." To their left, Jackson's men advanced with bayonets against the same "heavy fire." For ten minutes, they faced a situation every bit as terrible as the earlier demonstration against the Hornet's Nest. Gage ordered his Alabama Battery to limber their guns, and as they pulled back with three pieces, he told them to spike the fourth gun and roll it into the ravine.[18]

Maj. Francis Shoup had twelve guns from the Arkansas Battery plus an additional eight ready to replace Gage's. Capt. Thomas J. Stanford moved the 131 men of the Mississippi Battery in on the right of Shoup with two 12-pounder howitzers, three 6-pounders, and one 3-inch rifle. Brig. Gen. John C. Breckinridge supported Withers's right flank with two brigades, and some seven hundred yards across the way, his old friend Nelson sat on "Ned," a massive seventeen-hand stallion. As the Sixth Regiment Ohio Volunteer Infantry fixed bayonets, Nelson rode to the "front of the colors." He lifted his hat and, "with an expression of satisfaction and indomitable purpose," ordered the men to advance at trail arms—holding their weapons by the barrel and allowing the butt to trail along the ground while moving forward at a double quick—behind the four hundred men of the Thirty-sixth Regiment Indiana Volunteer Infantry. The foe opened fire from the other side of a small rise, and both sides fell back to reorganize. During the second charge, the "brave Duboese [Pvt. William W. Dubois] of Company C," lost his life. The firing stopped, and Captain Stone informed Colonel Grose that Battery K had to withdraw and resupply their ammunition.[19]

At 6:00 P.M., Major Shoup advised Breckinridge, "If you are going to charge, now is the time." In the next instant, a staff officer arrived to inform them, "The General [Beauregard] directs that the pursuit be stopped; the victory is sufficiently complete" for the day. That decision ended the fighting. One half-hour later, the Twenty-fourth Regiment Ohio Volunteer Infantry arrived on the bluff with news their transport had steered clear of the landing because the captain feared a desperate horde of stragglers would swamp the boat. Nelson sent the fresh arrivals forward a half-mile to investigate the intentions of the enemy, and he went to Grant's headquarters to speak with Buell about preparations for the night. At 7:00 P.M., "Wallace arrived with his division of five thousand effectives," and for Grant this meant "victory was assured."[20]

In Nelson's mind, the arrival of eleven companies of about 550 infantry at 5:20 P.M. "saved the day—10 minutes later—only ten minutes . . . [and Grant's] army was gone." That deluded misunderstanding gave no credit to the formidable nature of Grant's final line, the advent of darkness, or Beauregard's decision to cease fighting for the day. In a letter to Secretary Chase, Nelson incorrectly stated Grant was "unsupported by infantry," that Federal artillery on the left had been turned by the enemy, and the gunners were fleeing from their pieces. Nelson believed the entire situation arose "from the sheer stupidity of our Generals——." As for "the commander of this army Gen'l Grant I say x x x x x x x x Consider it said."[21]

Grant said "the firing had almost entirely ceased" before Nelson reached the landing. He acknowledged that a few enemy artillery shells did pass overhead (at 5:20 P.M.) but not "a single musket-ball" was heard when "General Buell [Nelson] marched several of his regiments part way down the hill, where they fired briskly for a few minutes [about 5:35 P.M.]." This was far from accurate, but on balance, Grant came much closer to expressing the reality of the situation.[22]

The much-criticized Grant also maintained that truthful reports about Shiloh did not appear until after judgments "had been erroneously formed." He particularly loathed accounts that said the troops in the Army of the Tennessee were surprised in their own beds and slaughtered. His good friend William Tecumseh Sherman believed the story originated with Buell and Nelson and that *Cincinnati Gazette* correspondent Whitelaw Reid gave it wide circulation. It further irritated Sherman that none of the three had "the manliness to admit *their* mistake."[23]

Nelson considered Sherman negligent for failing to put out pickets on Saturday, but he also believed that if it were not for his courageous actions during the first "eight hours" on Sunday, Grant's "army would have been captured or destroyed." Sherman said he appreciated "that Buell [Nelson] was there, because I knew his troops were older than ours and better systematized and drilled, and his [Nelson's] arrival made that certain, which was uncertain before." Decades later, Sherman informed Buell's adjutant, James B. Fry, that Grant and the officers of the Army of the Tennessee believed Buell was negligent in moving to Savannah and "Should have been there to help on the first day."[24]

Beauregard had remained isolated from the reality of the battlefield at the Shiloh Church headquarters, and this led him to misinform his superiors that "thanks be to the almighty," the Confederate army obtained "a complete victory, driving the enemy from every position." It was true the Federal army had paid a terrible price for Grant's misjudgment, but neither the troops nor their commander had lost the will to fight. As reinforcements from Buell's Army of the Ohio continued to arrive at a steady pace, Grant coolly announced the Confederates "can't force our lines around these batteries tonight. . . . Tomorrow we shall attack them with fresh troops and drive them" back to Corinth.[25]

At the landing, the surreal sounds of steamboat calliopes surrounded the Nineteenth and Twenty-second Brigades as they moved down bloodied gangplanks into a maddening mob of refugees. The suffocating smell of the wounded and dead sickened the men as they formed in columns of twos, took up torches, and marched up the hill to join an army "clothed with [the] music. . . . of 720 companies." A correspondent noted that Nelson "managed to lead his force over the sleeping soldiers in Hurlbut's division and was in the act of driving his horse over the body of the General" when he jerked the bridle of Nelson's horse. After a brief exchange of curses, both men went on about their business.[26]

At 10:00 P.M., Col. Sanders D. Bruce had the Twenty-second Kentucky in position, and Nelson went to the landing to speak with the naval officers of the gunboats about throwing 8-inch shells into the enemy every ten minutes. As he turned to leave, Nelson told his old friend, Lt. William Gwin, "Send me a bottle of wine and some cigars, I'll show you some man-of-war fighting to-morrow." Soon afterward, the *Tyler* began firing 5-, 10-, and 15-second delayed fuse shells into the right flank of the Confederates. In another three hours, Lt. James S. Shirk would take over the shelling with the *Lexington*.[27]

About midnight, McCook arrived in Savannah with the Second Division, and Crittenden started disembarking the Fifth Division at Pittsburg Landing. On the bluff, the horrendous noise from the navy gunboats caused some of Nelson's men to fantasize over how his death might rid them of his terrible temper. They also realized that under fire this warrior could be "cool as a cucumber." His "soldierly perceptions and instincts . . . [had] won him respect and, a strange sort of feeling that was almost affection." Their stern commander had forged them into well-disciplined soldiers who were "*unconsciously* alert, and emphatic in action." They could turn to him "with rare trust . . . [and were] proud of his oddities, and his obtrusive individuality." He "was a thorough soldier . . . terribly earnest; and they knew it." Here, of all places, was the time to forget past grievances and follow a special leader who would see them through the assaults and counterattacks that daylight would bring.[28]

Buell and Grant found they could not put aside their differences and confer with each other on a specific plan of battle. Nelson had no other instructions than to push the foe back, and at 3:00 A.M., he told Ammen they would go "find the enemy and whip him." One hour later, Lieutenant Fisher returned from duty as a temporary liaison with Grant. Nelson aroused Crittenden and advised he was about to go forward. Crittenden "supposed" that Nelson "had his orders" and that instructions from Buell were forthcoming.[29]

The river was beginning to reflect beams of light, and it must have pleased an opera lover like Nelson to hear a regimental band at the landing strike up a rousing tune from Giuseppe Verdi's *Il Trovatore* (The Troubadour). At 5:20 A.M., he had the Fourth Division on line at an oblique angle to Dill Branch. The guidons and flags went up, the men moved across the ravine to the beat of one hundred drums, and moments later the Sixth Regiment Kentucky Volunteer Infantry started across Jason Cloud's field. Confederate Nathan

Bedford Forrest sent a squadron from the Third Tennessee Cavalry forward. They fired one quick volley and pulled back to a wooded section 250 yards below Widow Wicker's field.[30]

Brig. Gen. James R. Chalmers had established the Confederate skirmish line just north of the bloody pond, and to oppose them, Col. William B. Hazen sent the Ninth Regiment Indiana Volunteer Infantry to a position behind a fence on the northern edge of Widow Wicker's field. The Sixth Regiment Kentucky Volunteer Infantry moved up on the left of the Ninth Indiana Regiment's position, and the Confederates withdrew to the peach orchard and commenced firing with three batteries. Nelson had no artillery, and Buell had no choice but to bring the Federal advance to a complete halt. To further complicate the situation, the right flank of Hazen's Nineteenth Brigade had no protection because Crittenden was not in position with the Fifth Division.[31]

Crittenden claimed that when he "heard the [enemy artillery] firing" he went to "the landing to find Gen. Buell," and Grant told him, "My division ought to be doing something . . . [so] I got my column in the road." The moment Buell saw Crittenden, he ordered him to send Capt. John Mendenhall's artillery up in support of Nelson. About the same time, Alexander McCook moved the Second Division up from the landing, into a position three-quarters of a mile west and on the right of the incoming Crittenden.[32]

William J. Hardee and John C. Breckinridge had five depleted infantry brigades and nine artillery batteries across Buell's front. That line extended from Col. David Stuart's old camp through the eastern edge of Sarah Bell's cotton field at the Hamburg-Savannah road. From there it ran westward to Daniel Davis's wheat field and the eastern Corinth road. The nearly thirteen thousand men under Buell were supported by a reserve force commanded by Col. John A McDowell (W. T. Sherman's Fifth Division, Army of the Tennessee) and Col. James M. Tuttle (H. L. Wallace's Second Division, Army of the Tennessee). At 8:00 A.M., Nelson received permission to resume the advance. Thick woods and rugged ravines made it hard for Buell to "anticipate the probable dispositions" of the enemy, and Nelson sent Colonel Whitaker's Sixth Regiment Kentucky Volunteer Infantry forward to reconnoiter the woods to the front. At the same time, he moved the Nineteenth and Twenty-second Brigades across the sunken road and into the peach orchard.[33]

At 9:00 A.M., Capt. John Mendenhall arrived with batteries H and M, Fourth U.S. Artillery. Those men unlimbered two 3-inch Rodman rifles and two 12-pound howitzers south of Wicker's field and west of the bloody pond. A half-hour later, the Sixth Regiment Kentucky Volunteer Infantry moved up to William Manse George's log cabin. Suddenly the front erupted into a "sheet

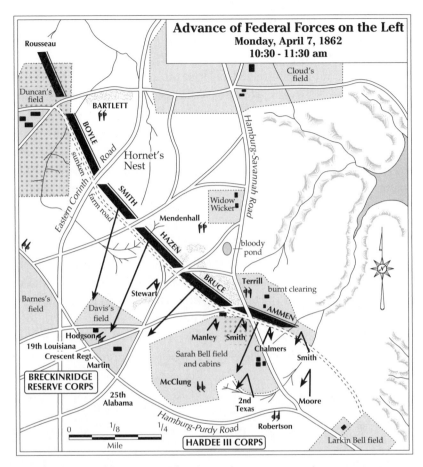

Map 7. Advance of Federal Forces on the Left, Monday Morning, April 7, 1862

of flame" as Irving Hodgson's Washington Artillery and Hugh McClung's Tennessee Battery enfiladed the right flank of Bruce's Twenty-second Brigade. Mendenhall sighted the enemy positions with his field glasses and had his guns alternately engage each of the enemy batteries. The Confederate infantry sought cover in a ravine filled with thick undergrowth, and the Second Regiment Kentucky Volunteer Infantry pushed them out of that thicket and seized several guns. Soon afterward, the Confederates launched a ferocious counterattack that forced the Second Kentucky Infantry back in disarray.[34]

That setback caused Bruce to withdraw the entire Twenty-second Brigade, and that exposed the left flank of the Nineteenth Brigade. Nelson advanced his line to cover that position, and when Capt. William R. Terrill's Battery H, Fifth U.S. Artillery, arrived at 10:00 A.M., he ordered Bruce to advance the Twenty-second Brigade back across the peach orchard and into Sarah Bell's old cotton field. Confederate John D. Martin thought this was the time to push his Second Brigade in between Walter Whitaker's Sixth Kentucky Infantry and Gideon C. Moody's Ninth Indiana Infantry.[35]

The Confederates were greeted by "Rise up, 41st [Ohio Infantry]"—"Fire, Fire." Then came, "Charge bayonets, 41st." Capt. Emerson Opdycke grabbed the colors from a fallen flag bearer and shouted again, "Forward, 41st, your flag is in advance of you." The men in Bruce's Twenty-second saw Confederates pulling back, and they shouted in amazement, "They run." The men in the Nineteenth Brigade looked over at Hazen, with his waxed mustache, broad-brimmed hat, and flying cape. He signaled for them to charge into the western edge of the peach orchard. With bayonets at the ready, they charged against the foe and drove them back through Sarah Bell's old cotton field to the Hamburg-Purdy road. There the Confederates made a determined stand that caused the Forty-first Regiment Ohio Volunteer Infantry to collapse. As Lt. Wickliffe Cooper and Colonel Bruce worked to reorganize that unit, Col. William Sooy Smith started the Fourteenth Brigade, Crittenden's Fifth Division, toward Daniel Davis's wheat field.[36]

On the Federal left, a hard attack against Ammen's Tenth Brigade caused Terrill to lose every man on one Napoleon gun and forced him to abandon

Fig. 7. "Gallant Charge of the 19th Brigade, commanded by Col. William B. Hazen, Gen. Nelson's division, on the field at Shiloh, Monday, April 7, 1862." Lithograph by Henry Mosler. Nelson is the large figure facing Buell and pointing to the front. The neatness of the line and general inaccuracy of the illustration made it the subject of great derision by other participants. Library of Congress

a caisson. Terrill then took charge of one gun, and Nelson dismounted and sighted another piece. When the firing had ended, "piles of mangled bodies" lay in front of the guns. Capt. Oliver D. Greene said, "Nothing could surpass the dash and enthusiasm . . . of Buell and Nelson; they seemed to be trying to outrival each other" with death-defying actions that led one officer to remark, "We like it."[37]

In the center on the line, Colonel Whitaker took control of the Forty-first Regiment Ohio Volunteer Infantry, and he gave Lt. Col. William Blake command of the Sixth Regiment Kentucky Volunteer Infantry. Mendenhall's artillery and the Ninth Regiment Indiana Volunteer Infantry unleashed a storm that drove the enemy back to Davis's wheat field, past the Washington Artillery, and across the Hamburg-Purdy road. The Ninth Indiana and Forty-first Ohio infantry raced forward and seized three guns. In the excitement of that moment, they ignored the cardinal rule of setting up a defensive perimeter and argued over which unit should take credit for the capture of the guns.[38]

That foolish bickering enabled the Crescent (Louisiana) Regiment, the Nineteenth Regiment Louisiana Volunteer Infantry, and First Regiment Missouri Volunteer Infantry to move back across the Hamburg-Purdy road with a strong counterattack. Bartlett's Battery G tried to help, but their misdirected fire struck the rear of the Nineteenth Brigade. In the ensuing panic, Hazen thought that thousands of Confederates had surrounded his men. He ordered the Nineteenth Brigade to pull "back as fast as it could go" and rode off on a lame horse through a field and into a wooded section. Hazen never reappeared, and when Lt. Charles J. Gaylord informed Nelson of the situation, he yelled, "For God's sake try and find him."[39]

While Gaylord sought to comply with that directive, Nelson rode over to the Ninth Regiment Indiana Volunteer Infantry and complimented them on their valiant actions. Old Buster had been at odds with them for foraging against his orders, and tears trickled down his cheeks as he told the troops "they were better men than he thought they were, and he hadn't calculated that a lot of thieves could fight so well." Nelson added, "Ah! volunteers *are* the men to fight after all. Believe me, my brave boys, I bear you no ill will." That brought loud shouts of "*Three cheers* for General Nelson!" He responded by telling the Hoosiers they would receive the finest colors that any regiment could be given, and the men gave him another hooray as he rode away toward another unit.[40]

The Confederates continued to pull back, and about 3:30 P.M., Grant was intent on pursuing them when he "saw a division of troops coming up in beautiful order, as if going on parade or review." Their commander, Alexander McCook, pleaded with Grant "not to send his men any further, saying they were worn out from [nonstop] marching and fighting." Grant said he no longer had "the heart to order men [into battle] who had fought desperately for two days," and that decision ended the fighting at Shiloh.[41]

About that same time, Nelson inquired again about the status of Hazen, who was now riding forward from Pittsburg Landing. Colonel Whitaker said, "We fear he is killed or wounded, none of us have seen him since the charge." Nelson offered a reward of $50 to six volunteers who were about to ride out and search for Hazen when he suddenly appeared at 4:00 P.M. The circumstances of his disappearance were carefully explained to Nelson, and he decided that this "was one of those unavoidable accidents that might fall to the lot of any man; there was no secret ever made of the matter; and it (his disappearance) was regarded as an accident."[42]

Word of Albert Sidney Johnston's death circulated among the troops, and late Monday evening they found a body dressed in a velvet suit. Nelson incorrectly identified the corpse as Johnston, and that mistake was confirmed by Brig. Gen. Lovell Rousseau, Capt. J. G. Chandler, and a wagon master from Johnston's Utah expedition. Nelson had the body dressed in one of his shirts and ordered a fence put around the grave. He later informed Secretary Chase that the fields were a "shocking sight, a heartrending sight. There were seven miles of dead and wounded in all conceivable postures suffering inconceivable agony—War is an emanation from Hell—to what perdition will the men who got up this thing be damned! Heads, legs, brains, seen strewn all along—My horses feet were red with human blood—."[43]

Of the 4,541 men in Nelson's Fourth Division, there were 93 killed, 603 wounded, and 20 missing. The largest battle in the Western hemisphere had failed to produce a conclusive victor, and for now, it represented the worse combat casualty rate ever seen on the North American continent.

	KILLED	WOUNDED	MISSING	TOTAL
Grant	1,513	6,601	2,830	10,944
Buell	241	1,807	55	2,103
Confederate	1,728	8,012	959	10,699
Total	3,482	16,420	3,844	23,746 [44]

The common soldier had to deal with the loss of friends, the burial of mangled remains, and the wretched burning of animal carcasses. Such heinous duty brought on depression and lackadaisical behavior, and this caused Nelson to resort to oppressive tactics intended to make the troops more alert.

Lt. Col. Nicholas Anderson quickly noted that his hero had become a tyrant; but rather than continue in that vein, Nelson began to exercise a more practical style of leadership by remitting court-martial sentences and praising the men for their gallant actions. Anderson welcomed this change, and he warned his men to be "careful in the future, and disgrace neither themselves or the regiment by unsoldierly conduct thereafter."[45]

News of Shiloh infuriated the Northern public, and the failure to pursue Beauregard at Corinth added fuel to that raging fire. For those reasons and more, when Henry W. Halleck arrived at Pittsburg Landing on Saturday, April 11, 1862, he intended to organize an enormous army that could not fail. Two weeks later, Nelson received orders to conduct a reconnaissance in force to Monterey (Pea Ridge), Tennessee. On April 26, his troops captured ten Rebels and returned to Stuart's old camp. A *New York Herald* correspondent noted that "the rebel general at Pea Ridge" declined to fight Nelson. But there would soon be an unprecedented slaughter between two armies numbering more than 250,000 men.[46]

On Thursday evening, May 1, 1862, Nelson informed his commanders the division would start forward in the morning. Eight companies from the First Regiment Michigan Engineers were to construct corduroy roads through the swamps, build defenses, and place siege guns in position. To further avoid any chance of replicating Shiloh, at the end of each daily advance, Halleck required the troops to construct breastworks of logs and dirt that were to be four feet high and four feet deep with rifle pits inside, ditching outside, and all underbrush cleared. The troops also learned that intense labor would not exempt them from guard detail or picket duty at night.[47]

Friday morning, May 2, Nelson marched the Fourth Division west along the "Bark Road." A torrential downpour kept him in place on Sunday, but at 5:00 A.M. Monday, he pushed the men forward on soggy ground that caused them to "go down—horse and rider—and perhaps have to pull both out." That evening, they were within five miles of Corinth when a hard-riding courier arrived with a message for Nelson to pull back to Monterey because the Rebels had burned the bridge at Chamber's Creek. John Pope showed no regard for maintaining flank integrity, and he continued to push the left wing forward. Confederate scouts could see that three miles of swampy jungle separated Pope from Nelson, and Beauregard ordered Brig. Gen. Earl Van Dorn to exploit that weakness.[48]

Throughout Tuesday, May 6, Nelson had the troops restore the Hamburg-Corinth road, and the following day orders arrived to pull back across the Tennessee line. Thursday he marched back into Mississippi, to Nichol's Ford on Seven Mile Creek. Early the next morning, Confederate Earl Van Dorn assaulted Pope's exposed right flank with twenty thousand troops. The poorly led attack soon plummeted into confusion , and Van Dorn withdrew before Nelson arrived later that morning. Nelson then returned to Nichol's Ford, and from May 13 to 16, his troops constructed roads across Seven Mile Creek.[49]

During this same time, Halleck tried to end rampant press speculation by banning all noncombatants from his headquarters. A short distance from there, newsman Franc Wilke was startled by a "bass voice of tremendous depth and power" that asked, "What are you doing there?" The befuddled Wilke said nothing, and the booming voice bellowed out again, "Who are you, you son of a bitch?" Wilke replied, "I am the correspondent for the New York Times." He was then told, "Go back from here, God damn you!" Wilke protested, "I have the authority of the Secretary of the War to pass anywhere with the lines." An officer checked his credentials, found them satisfactory, and the "burly brute with the boatswain's voice" rode off as if nothing had ever happened. Wilke, on the other hand, would never forget the "brutal manner" in which Nelson had addressed him.[50]

On Saturday, May 17, Halleck ordered a general advance, and Buell moved the Army of the Ohio across a one-and-three-quarter-mile-wide front with Nelson in the center. By the end of the day, Nelson had the Fourth Division two miles from the enemy defensive positions near Andrew Driver's house on the Monterey-Corinth road. Pope had reoccupied Farmington on the left of Nelson, and Sherman, who commanded a division on the extreme right of the Union's right wing (under George H. Thomas) held the high ground on the right, near the headwaters of Phillips and Bridge Creeks.[51]

On Sunday, ten draft horses pulled ten large siege guns forward, and the Sixth Regiment Ohio Volunteer Infantry started digging the first parallel. The Confederates responded by shelling the work parties, and Nelson ordered a section of artillery wheeled into position. Twenty-five rounds struck the Seventh Regiment Louisiana Volunteer Infantry, and that led three of the men to surrender with news that Beauregard had 110,000 men under guard to prevent desertion. On Wednesday, May 21, Nelson ordered Col. Thomas D. Sedgewick to conduct reconnaissance a mile from the Confederate fortifications. In the valley of Bridge Creek, near Widow Surratt's (or Seratt's) house, Sedgewick became engaged in a forty-five-minute fight that cost three men killed and twenty-six wounded.[52]

On Thursday, May 22, a second initiative by Beauregard failed when Van Dorn failed to get his men into position in time. Beauregard consulted with his officers and decided that the devastation caused by typhoid dysentery made the likelihood of bringing the fight to the Federal army improbable, and the time to evacuate had come. Halleck saw the tiny town as a prize equal to seizing the Confederate capital at Richmond, Virginia, and that created a wariness that made him ponder every painful inch of movement against "all hazards"—real or imagined.[53]

Caution in the face of the enemy enraged Nelson, and he stormed into Buell's headquarters to obtain permission to "take two commands in . . . the Fourth Division, and steal from . . . Corinth every Confederate soldier." Halleck wanted to keep bloodletting to a minimum, and he insisted that prudence take precedence over boldness. Over the next few days, the engineers and soldiers worked on gun positions. On Tuesday, May 27, Nelson, William B. Hazen, and James S. Jackson had little more to do than talk about how they were all born on the same day, September 27, and Nelson agreed to arrange a palatial dinner at the Galt House when they returned to Louisville.[54]

By Wednesday, May 28, the engineers had constructed two hundred miles of new road, and a telegraph wire ran to every commander. To protect against an enemy breakout, four lines of breastworks, ten miles long, would allow the huge Federal army to fall back and hold one line at a time. The 32-pound Rodman rifles were now firing from behind sod earthworks with bombproof magazines, and the moment those guns stopped, Nelson moved forward and seized the Bridge Creek crossing. The Confederates made three desperate attempts to regain the bridge and failed. Nelson sought permission to continue forward and attack Corinth, but Buell and Pope disagreed. They considered the Confederate fortifications too formidable to assault and worried that if the enemy should break out in force, Nelson would be overwhelmed.[55]

This left him with no other choice than to order the men to start a double line of rifle pits a mere thirteen hundred yards from the foe. Had the Federal commanders known the Confederates were critically short of water and plagued by unhealthy conditions, they might have allowed Nelson to go forward. They were also unaware that Maj. Robert Bailey Hurt, the Confederate military superintendent for the Memphis & Charlestown Railroad, had received a requisition that called "for as many cars and engines as could be furnished." On Thursday, May 29, the concurrent arrival of two trains brought mass confusion in Corinth. The "cars were ordered to different breastworks east of the town, others around the Y to the Mobile & Ohio road, and others to each of our own [Memphis & Charlestown] platforms."[56]

Nelson's troops were resting under tree-branch shelters that protected them from the hot sun, and at 4:00 P.M., the "hero of Piketon . . . [moved] along his lines to see that everything was in readiness for repelling any attack the rebels might choose to make." When darkness settled over Corinth, the Federal troops watched the glow of numerous enemy campfires. Bugles blared, train whistles blew, and men in the right wing of George H Thomas "could plainly hear the movement of trains . . . bands playing . . . rockets ascending in the air, signaling their out-posts, which clearly indicated that they were evacuating."[57]

At midnight, Friday, May 30, the loading of the "guns and carriages, which were at the defenses east of [Corinth]" remained unfinished, but the two troop trains were ready to leave. A half-hour later, Halleck informed Buell and Thomas the center and right wings should be ready for bitter resistance in the morning. At 1:30 A.M., Pope on the left wing informed Halleck "the enemy is re-enforcing heavily, by trains, in my front and on my left. The cars are running constantly, and the cheering is immense every time they unload in front of me. I have no doubt . . . that I shall be attacked in heavy force at daylight."[58]

At 2:00 A.M., the Confederates brought in the last of the guns, and by 3:30, they were on the Mobile & Ohio train. One half-hour later, Nelson ordered Mahlon D. Manson to take command of the Twenty-second Brigade and replace the embattled Sanders D. Bruce, who remained absent with an unexplained illness. At 4:30, the last Confederate train left Corinth, and a deserter rushed in with news that Beauregard had used twenty-six trains to move fifty-two miles south to Tupelo. Nelson was stunned to hear that only one small Confederate cavalry detachment remained, and he rushed all three brigades on line. In that haste, he failed to make up for the disadvantages of the terrain, and Buell ordered a halt. After Nelson completed the necessary adjustment, he was allowed to resume the advance at 6:00 A.M. Near the edge of town, a succession of loud explosions sent up a string of alarming black clouds. Soon after this, an old slave came out and announced, "Dey's gone, boss . . . You-uns can jess walk right into de town ef yer wants to!"[59]

Pope rushed forward and found Nelson in the middle of Corinth with the Seventh Regiment Kentucky Volunteer Infantry on his right and the Twenty-Forth Regiment Ohio Volunteer Infantry on the left. About 6:30 A.M., Nelson sent a messenger to inform Buell "the damned rascals" had left town. At 6:40, Pope wired Halleck that his troops had just placed the United States flag over the Tishomingo County courthouse. Nelson rode over to the Fifteenth Regiment Ohio Volunteer Infantry and ordered them to give way. Col. Moses R. Dickey firmly refused, and Nelson berated him with profane insults. The colonel then placed "his hand on his holster . . . [and] glared at General Nelson as if he intended to draw his pistol." Nelson shouted, "God damn you, don't you look at me that way." Nelson's aides quickly removed

Dickey to "the rear of the regiment," and that caused Pope to unleash a tirade of vulgar and demeaning insults that fouled the air with dishonor. Everyone expected a violent response from Nelson, but instead this veteran of brutal assaults showed such complete calm that Pope rode away in a huff. Brig. Gen. David. S. Stanley could not believe what he had just witnessed: two Union generals had disgraced their rank by arguing over who had been the first to enter this "miserable place."[60]

"B.C.T.," the correspondent for the *Philadelphia Press*, was a witness to the siege and occupation, and he noted, "Notwithstanding the multiplicity of faults easily discovered in General Nelson, he is truly a brave man. There is none braver in the service. He is shrewd, calculating, and ambitious. To do him justice, I will say that he barely arrived here before Pope. But the latter general was also on the alert, and immediately ordered the planting of the flag." Buell reported the Fourth Division had occupied Corinth a half-hour before any other Union troops, but because Sherman and Pope had promptly wired their accounts before him, they received the credit due Nelson. Buell said he had "no doubt myself the honor is due to Major-General Nelson. It is certain that he discovered the enemy had been evacuating when the others supposed instead that they were preparing to attack." Brig. Gen. Mahlon D. Manson's official report made a point of "congratulating the commander of the division [Nelson] on the masterly conduct of his troops in the approach to Corinth, and especially must congratulate the general commanding on being the first to enter and occupy that strong position."[61]

At 12:20 P.M., Nelson's escort troop found the enemy's rear guard about three and one-half miles south of Corinth. Twenty-five minutes later, Pope advised Halleck that his cavalry had found the enemy about eight miles from Corinth. Amid the excitement, Halleck wrongly informed the War Department that his army had captured ten thousand Rebels and a huge amount of supplies. Halleck viewed the taking of an abandoned objective as a superb triumph, and Horace Greeley's *New York Tribune* seemed to agree when it announced, "We shall be disappointed if the National flag is not flying over every considerable city of the South by the 4th of July."[62]

In a matter of months, the Federal army in the West had taken control of a vast amount of enemy real estate. The War Department paid no heed to the daunting nature of controlling that territory when it approved Halleck's plans for the reorganization of the Army of the Mississippi. Halleck wanted Buell to seize Chattanooga, move up to Knoxville, and take control of eastern Tennessee. At the same time, Old Brains also expected him to rebuild the Decatur railroad bridge and repair the dilapidated Memphis & Charleston

Railroad from Corinth to Bridgeport and Stevenson, Alabama.[63]

On Wednesday, June 11, Nelson dutifully marched the Fourth Division out of Smith's Crossroads and east along the Memphis & Charleston Railroad. That evening, he bivouacked at Iuka Mineral Springs, twenty-one miles from Corinth. The Fourth Division had seventy-five wagons for food and forage, and it was critical for Nelson to stay within five days' distance of rail supply. During the march to Tuscumbia on Tuesday, June 17, "the temperature reached 100 degrees" and the "dust [became] so thick you could taste it." There were not enough mules to pull the baggage trains, and one overburdened soldier spoke for many when he declared, "you have done the next thing to killing this man outright." Fast-moving Confederate cavalry added to their tribulations by striking the column at will, and on Wednesday, Nelson was within four miles of Alabama when he halted the march and ordered the division back to Iuka.[64]

The hot, dry weather had reduced the water level of the Tennessee River drastically, and that meant all forage and supplies would have to be unloaded at Eastport and hauled to Iuka, where they would go forward by rail. Halleck had refused a request for more wagons, locomotives, and cars, and Buell was anxious to have the use of 16 locomotives and 130 cars that were at Huntsville. The Rebels intended to circumvent that goal, and when the first train went forward from Iuka, they disabled the locomotive and tore up the track.[65]

Nelson spent all of Sunday, June 22, in Iuka fretting over bogus reports that indicated ten thousand Rebels would attack. He told Buell that should the Tenth Brigade have to fall "back [from Buzzard Roost] the railroad bridges all will be destroyed. If I leave here [Iuka] then Eastport [Mississippi] and the supplies will be lost. If [General] Wood and I both stand still we will both be beaten in detail. I solicit instructions." Buell told Nelson to move forward with the Tenth and Nineteenth Brigades and leave the Twenty-second at Iuka until Thomas arrived with the First Division. On Wednesday, Nelson marched the Nineteenth and Tenth Brigades through the "lovely town" of Tuscumbia, Alabama. The next morning, transports moved them across the Tennessee River to Florence, Alabama, and on July 3, 1862, the Fourth Division was camped at Athens, Alabama.[66]

Halleck's attempt to censure the press had taught them they no longer needed close associations with officers. In that maturation process, a growing number could also see that Buell's cautious implementation of an unsound strategy was giving the foe the opportunity to regain the initiative. Nelson's absurd behavior at Corinth had taken away all the celebratory glitter of Shiloh, and now he was about to be tossed into a briar patch the belonged to the enemy.

On July 4, 1862, black contrabands and a "poor class of [white] citizens" gathered at the Limestone County fairgrounds in Athens, Alabama, to see Nelson's troops conduct a traditional Independence Day parade. As those men marched through ankle-deep dust with 120 brass artillery pieces, it seemed like they were "scowled at from almost every [Rebel] house". Lt. Robert S. Dilworth, Twenty-first Regiment Ohio Volunteer Infantry, despised Nelson as much as he admired Ormsby M. Mitchel, and for him this parade was nothing more than a "selfish desire . . . of showing forth a little authority. . . . The poor fellows covered with dust and sweat. Parched with thirst and the heat of the sun and no permission to get a draught of water to cool their raging thirst, and still on the quick." Pvt. Amos Mount served in Walter Whitaker's Sixth Regiment Kentucky Volunteer Infantry, and for him it was "a vary prety site to see twelve redgiments on parade at wonce and to hear difrent bands playing [.] Thare was a great many citizens to see us some of them seemed to like it vary much and some looked rite sour."[1]

Twenty miles north of Athens, the soldiers in the Eighth Regiment Kentucky Volunteer Infantry were laboring to restore the rail bed of the Tennessee & Central Alabama Railroad. Nelson assisted the effort by sending the Sixth Ohio Infantry to work beside army engineers who were clearing a path through the Elk River tunnel to allow wagons to pass through while they replaced track. Brig. Gen. Jeremiah T. Boyle had become the commander of the Department of Kentucky at Louisville, and he advised that a two-thousand-man Confederate cavalry force (Morgan's Raiders) was now in Kentucky. At Nashville, military governor Andrew Johnson directed Capt. Oliver D. Greene to send one or two regiments to Boyle's aid. Buell's assistant adjutant general failed to respond with all due haste, and Johnson claimed that

Greene "refused to cooperate." He then wired Lincoln that Greene appeared to be "in complicity with the traitors here [Nashville] & shall therefore have him arrested & sent beyond the Influence of rebels and traitors if he is not immediately removed."[2]

Buell telegraphed Halleck on Friday, July 11, to inform him that Greene was no longer assigned to Nashville. Halleck was to report to the capital and take command as general-in-chief of all land forces, and he warned Buell the decision makers in Washington "have no conception of the length of our [the Army of the Ohio] lines of defense . . . [and] the disasters at Richmond [Virginia] have worked them up to the boiling point. . . . I will see that your movements are properly explained to the President."[3]

Earlier in the day, Brig. Gen. Thomas Turpin Crittenden assumed command at Murfreesboro, and later that evening, Nathan Bedford Forrest arrived in nearby McMinnville, Tennessee, with about fourteen hundred Rebel cavalry. Saturday, the repair of the Elk River tunnel was finished, and this opened the rail line between Nashville and Murfreesboro. At daylight Sunday, Crittenden had rations for the Chattanooga campaign ready to go forward from Murfreesboro to Stevenson, Alabama, when Forrest's cavalry assaulted the Third Battalion, Seventh Regiment Pennsylvania Volunteer Cavalry and six companies of the Ninth Michigan Infantry. About 3:30 P.M., the officers of the Third Regiment Minnesota Volunteer Infantry surrendered Murfreesboro to Forrest without any input from the enlisted ranks.[4]

Before leaving, Forrest destroyed the rail connection to Nashville and burned all the rations intended for the impending Federal advance from Stevenson to Chattanooga. This was a colossal setback for Buell. He wired Nelson, "You are to go in person . . . [and] move one of your brigades of infantry by forced march to Reynolds' Station [43 miles north of Athens and 12 miles south of Columbia, Tennessee], and there if possible take cars and move toward Nashville to any point which may be threatened."[5]

Late Sunday night, Nelson drove the bewildered men of the Tenth Brigade through the lines of the Twenty-first Regiment Ohio Volunteer Infantry. On Monday, the temperature soared to 100°. Sunstrokes and nosebleeds took an astounding toll, and at 9:00 P.M., Nelson called a halt fifteen miles north of Athens at the Tennessee state line. A telegraphed message from Buell said, "Use the train when it comes in and push with all energy." A second dispatch advised the train had broken down and urged, "don't wait for it." At 2:30 A.M. Tuesday, Nelson started the men on a horrendous nineteen-mile march. They forded the Elk River before sunrise and took a quick breakfast at Elkton. Hundreds fell out from heat exhaustion, and when the Tenth Brigade reached

Richland Creek in Pulaski, Tennessee, at 1:00 P.M., several were dead. The Sixth Ohio Infantry had only forty men, and Anderson privately pronounced Nelson "a fool" because it would take the rest of the day to bring the sick and feeble forward in ambulances. On Wednesday, Nelson had the men up at 2:00 A.M. and on the march at 3:30.[6]

Nelson arrived at Reynolds' Station four hours later and found a wire from Buell that directed him to put the troops "on the cars as soon as possible and proceed to [Nashville and then] Murfreesboro. . . . Take only one battery through with you, leave the other at Columbia." Buell feared a large enemy force might attack Federal troops at Battle Creek (Pittsburg, Tennessee). He cautioned Nelson, "If anything should come toward Nashville you must be prepared for it. If not, and the danger should come this way, I shall want you personally here [Huntsville]." Nelson advised that Federal troops "have been 7 miles beyond McMinnville" and it appeared the enemy had returned to Chattanooga. He then added, "The condition of affairs in Kentucky is very bad. I ask permission to march immediately to the relief of the State." Buell replied, "Neither you nor your division can be spared." Nelson then asked, "In case the enemy go into Kentucky what are your orders?"[7]

Buell gave no reply, and Nelson ordered the Second Regiment Kentucky Volunteer Infantry to guard the wagons and baggage while he headed for Nashville with his troops. Rebels had destroyed a water tank and burned a bridge, and during the first ten miles, Nelson stood beside an engineer in a single locomotive that scouted the way. Behind him, a train of platform and freight cars carried men from the Sixth and Twenty-fourth Regiments Ohio Volunteer Infantry and Mendenhall's battery. A second train carried the Thirty-sixth Regiment Indiana Volunteer Infantry and Twenty-third Regiment Kentucky Volunteer Infantry. About three miles from Columbia, an axle on the first train snapped and two cars in the rear went off the track. One of the cannons came off its mooring, struck Pvt. John Collins, and killed him. Another two men were severely injured. Nelson suspected the two engineers were guilty of sabotage. Without another thought, he struck one in the face, ordered their arrest, and threatened to hang them before sundown. Over the next three hours, the required repairs were completed, and the train started for Columbia with two experienced soldiers in charge. At the Duck River, Frank Wolford's First Kentucky Cavalry was guarding the trestle. They were delighted to see the man who had commanded them a year ago at Camp Dick Robinson and quite glad he "had become renowned and won his second star."[8]

On Thursday, July 17, John Hunt Morgan overwhelmed a motley group of Union defenders at Cynthiana, Kentucky, and Boyle wired Buell and

Nelson with excited demands for help. Halleck was about to leave Corinth for Washington, and he instructed Buell to "do all in your power to put down the Morgan raid [in Kentucky] even if the Chattanooga expedition should be delayed." That ill-considered change in priorities reached Buell about the same time that Brig. Gen. George W. Morgan advised that his wife's illness made it necessary for him to resign from the post at Cumberland Gap.[9]

Nelson reached Nashville about midnight, and his officers rushed into town to act "badly," while he continued to work at the telegraph office and keep an eye on the enlisted men who were fighting over twenty-five-cent pints of rotgut whiskey in the meadow near the penitentiary. Early Friday morning, July 18, the results of that drunken spree were seen in the black eyes and swollen faces of the men. At 8:00, Nelson had them on their way to Murfreesboro, thirty miles away. At noon, the troops jumped off the train a half-mile from town and Nelson formed them into a column that "marched up as if the place belonged to them, rung the [town] bell with quite an air." The flag was hoisted over the courthouse and pickets sent out in every direction. At the same time, other troops secured the deserted buildings fronting the public square, and they went through all the homes looking for the guns taken from T. T. Crittenden five days earlier.[10]

Nelson ran off nine of Mrs. Hagan's borders and "ordered her to get some mush and milk quick for his dinner or else she would see him in one of his tantrums." Resident Kate Carney was a diarist who relished every rumor, and she noted that someone said Nelson "threatened to cut a girl's throat if she did not let him call upon her." Late that afternoon, prisoners from the Third Minnesota arrived with orders to report directly to Nelson. He treated the men "as if" the disgraceful surrender of Murfreesboro "had been their fault," and those volunteers would not soon forget his rude remarks.[11]

That night Nelson had the entire command sleep on their arms, and at 3:00 A.M., Saturday, he had them go on line for battle. Later in the morning, he received a wire from Boyle that said, "I have no officers fit for the field . . . Can you come?" Adjutant of Kentucky Volunteers John W. Finnell also sought Nelson's services by telling him Morgan's men "are playing hell in all the Central Counties. Are beating our forces in detail. We have no one in the field worth a damn." Nelson informed Buell that Boyle "has lost his senses," and Buell replied, "We have an object in Tennessee of far greater importance to the Union and to Kentucky than driving Morgan out of Kentucky and you cannot be spared. I shall endeavor to be prepared for the time when you are more necessary there than here . . . there is no one to whom I would intrust the duty with more confidence."[12]

On Tuesday, July 22, Nelson had "about two hundred stout" slaves digging entrenchments around Murfreesboro when news arrived that Forrest had wrecked three bridges and part of the trestle five miles south of Nashville. Nelson drove his troops toward Nashville for twenty-two miles and then decided that Forrest must have doubled back to Murfreesboro. The townspeople there heard that Nelson was a prisoner of Forrest and that Beauregard had entered Kentucky. Nelson was in truth returning at a pace that caused one befuddled soldier to exclaim, "I bet, by God Damned, old Nelson or somebody's drunk." Lieutenant Colonel Anderson noted Nelson was "very considerate to me," but others felt quite differently. One man claimed Nelson beat a man over the head several times "because he was asleep & and didn't get out of his way soon enough." Another story said a lieutenant failed to "come as soon as he [Nelson] thought he ought to." Nelson ordered his arrest and stated that if there was any resistance he "was to be shot." Nelson was still highly agitated when he reached Murfreesboro at 7:00 P.M. Wednesday. He wired Buell, "Mr. Forrest shall have no rest. I will hunt him myself."[13]

On Thursday, July 24, there were rumors that thirty to forty thousand Confederates had started toward Nashville from Chattanooga and eight thousand would be in front of Murfreesboro by daylight. Throughout Friday, July 25, Nelson kept the main approaches to town secured with barricades and heavily armed details. Kate Carney recorded that "Gen. Nelson is to leave here for Louisville, Ky. He has gone out this afternoon to hunt Forrest." She said the soldiers "seemed quite freted with Genl. Nelson, for keeping them on horseback all [Friday] night & then [he] sent word to feed their horses & themselves by 8:00 A.M. [Saturday], & not a mouthful did they have for either horse or themselves." About 9:30 P.M. Sunday, it appeared the "cannons were fired in upon," the long roll sounded, and Nelson marched out the Lebanon Pike, convinced he would find the enemy.[14]

On Monday evening, July 28, he had the following order read before each regiment:

> Last night, the unexpected approach of a battalion of our own cavalry, on the Lebanon turnpike, created an alarm, which, if it served no other purpose, exposed the General, and the whole command, to the contemptible way in which the pickets on that road skulked their duty, and their poltroonery in running away from their posts when there was absolutely no enemy at all. Had there been enemy, it was their duty, acting as skirmishers to take advantage of fences and woodland, and to hold their ground till supported, ordered in, or compelled to give way

before a superior force, which should be done in an orderly manner, as becomes good soldiers. But, to the burning shame of our uniform, the pickets on the Lebanon pike ran away, like a pack of cowards, and could not be found by the General commanding when his staff, arrived on the field of fight. It is the intention of this order to hold them up to the scorn of the whole command.

Nelson ordered the men to turn in their arms, and he put them to work on fortifications as common laborers. These veterans had recently joined the Fourth Division, and like so many others, they would never forgive Nelson for dishonoring them in front of their peers.[15]

In Nashville, Andrew Johnson looked to Nelson, George H. Thomas, or ex-Tennessee governor William B. Campbell to replace Brig. Gen. George W. Morgan at Cumberland Gap. Johnson wrote to Nelson and asked, "can't you take command . . . redeem East Tennessee, and end your military career with . . . [what you] were first connected with, and which you should have commanded without interruption? . . . This is to be the crowning achievement in this War." Nelson said duty called him to protect Middle Tennessee, and it would be dishonorable to "quit this theater of action now." He allowed that should "circumstances warrant me leaving here I will notify you."[16]

Buell valued that loyalty, and he told Nelson, "I rely greatly on your judgment and energy." He wanted frequent communication and recommended that Nelson have one of the "staff officers learn the cipher from the [telegraph] operator, so that you can write and read in cipher." Nelson said "all sorts of vexations" had plagued his intent to go after Forrest, but he would continue that quest in the morning. He went on to say the officers in Nashville had disregarded his orders and made movements without his knowledge. Nelson warned, "The result will be the utter destruction of our commands." Buell curtly advised those forces had an existing role under his control, not Nelson's.[17]

On Wednesday, July 30, Kate Carney noted that Federal "soldiers were coming & going. . . . The Yankees that went to McMinnville are on their way back without accomplishing anything." Nelson had not pursued Forrest as promised, and he explained to Buell that without Brig. Gen. James S. Jackson's cavalry, it made no sense to march infantry directly against a foe on "race horses" that could easily entrap him. Nelson added the hot weather burdened the footsore soldiers, provisions remained critically short, and "neither troops nor officers have had a change of clothing or the shelter of a tent since we left Athens [two weeks ago]."[18]

Nelson would not allow those hardships to stand in the way of duty. At 5:00 A.M. Friday, August 1, his three brigades marched toward McMinnville with a large cavalry force and fourteen pieces of artillery. The Nashville & Chattanooga Railroad ended at this town, and Whitelaw Reid, the correspondent for the *Cincinnati Gazette*, surmised that this action indicated Nelson must have "some generalship mixed with his impetuosity."[19]

When Nelson arrived in McMinnville at dusk on Sunday, August 3, 1862, he blew up over how the advance had ransacked stores, raided gardens, and otherwise abused private property. On Monday, August 4, Nelson had the Sixth Regiment Ohio Volunteers remain in town as provost guard while he marched the rest of the troops toward Sparta. Early the next day, the 180-man detachment from the Seventh Regiment Pennsylvania Volunteer Cavalry encountered 700 enemy troops four miles below Sparta at Calf Killer Creek. When Buell learned about this, he feared that Nelson had encountered the vanguard for the main Confederate force at Chattanooga. He ordered Nelson back to McMinnville, and on the return march, suffocating heat overwhelmed the troops, their discipline collapsed, and the Rebel cavalry grabbed about one hundred stragglers.[20]

Col. Sidney M. Barnes commanded the Eighth Regiment Kentucky Volunteer Infantry, and the Estill County native told his wife, Elizabeth Mize:

> I have just returned from Sparta. Yesterday and last night we marched twenty miles. We rise at 2 ½ oclock in the morning and often dont get to bed till midnight. I have not had a nights sleep worth anything in three weeks. . . . It seems like our commanding General [Nelson] will never learn the utter folly of running infantry after cavalry in hot weather in mountain country. Our army . . . will come to ruin soon. . . . A few days perhaps will bring on a terrible battle. . . . We would rather fight and run the risk of death than be marched to death.[21]

Barnes obviously did not know that while Nelson shared the same thoughts, he also considered it his duty to follow Buell's instructions. What concerned Nelson most was how the men were allowing themselves to become prisoners in order to become noncombatants when paroled. His frustration with this problem caused him to resort to mindless punishment that failed to discourage the surrender of a foraging party from the Thirty-sixth Regiment Indiana Volunteer Infantry on Thursday. There had been no newspapers for weeks, and when they arrived later that same day, Nelson was delighted to learn that the longed-for navy pay-grade bill had passed. He then wrote to

Admiral David G. Farragut to say the April 29 victory at "New Orleans did it! . . . Your passage of the fort . . . and floating batteries is the finest thing in Naval History—I am happy to see that the rank that your genius and gallantry has conferred on the whole Navy is so worthy."[22]

On Friday, the captured foragers returned with instructions to report directly to their commander. Nelson told them to disregard the terms of their parole and return to duty. The Hoosiers saw this an affront to a long-standing custom, and they refused to comply. Nelson gave them a "terrible tongue lashing," sent them to the guardhouse, and ordered an immediate court-martial.[23]

In Washington, the cabinet was discussing the lack of progress by Buell, and Salmon P. Chase presented a letter from Nelson that defended the conciliation policy as "that which will put this rebellion down soonest." With great reluctance, the cabinet decided to give Buell one more chance to redeem himself when he pledged to concentrate his forces at Murfreesboro, McMinnville, or Sparta and move against Chattanooga without any further delay.[24]

Buell was convinced the Confederates would not move into Kentucky "without striking first at Nashville." He sent Nelson north to Smithville and learned that John Hunt Morgan had returned from Kentucky with the intent of moving to Gallatin, Tennessee, with four pieces of artillery. George W. Morgan had not resigned, and he now informed Buell it was "morally certain that the enemy has about 15,000 troops . . . extending from Bean's Station to Clinton [Tennessee]." This was near the Kentucky border, and Morgan ordered companies from the Third Regiment Tennessee Volunteer Infantry and Third Regiment Kentucky Volunteer Infantry to the Kentucky towns of Cumberland Ford, Barbourville, London, and Richmond.[25]

Early Tuesday morning, August 12, Col. John S. Scott started the nine hundred men in the First Louisiana Cavalry Regiment north toward Jamestown, Tennessee. Later in the day, John Hunt Morgan's cavalry captured the Federal garrison at Gallatin and collapsed the twin railroad tunnels that connected Nashville with Louisville The next morning Nelson informed Buell that he had "telegraphed several times" about being confined to McMinnville. "No notice has been taken of it," and he wanted to know why his division remained in place "regardless of [enemy] movement." Buell addressed this concern with a murky order for Nelson to continue to "cover Nashville and control as much of the country around you as possible."[26]

Thursday morning, August 14, Confederate Brig. Gen. Carter L. Stevenson advanced his division to a point just south of George W. Morgan at Cumberland Gap, and that opened the way for Maj. Gen. Edmund Kirby Smith to move ten thousand troops north from Knoxville. Seven miles west of that historic gateway, four Confederate brigades of some six thousand men marched through Rogers Gap while Kirby Smith brought the rest of his force up the wagon road toward Jellico, Tennessee, and Barbourville, Kentucky. Directly behind were the supply wagons, horse-drawn guns, and hundreds of horses, mules, and camp followers. Fifty wagons carried twenty-five thousand arms intended for recruits in Kentucky. Thirty miles west of Cumberland Gap, Brig. Gen. Henry Heth marched his four-thousand-man division through Big Gap Creek (LaFollette, Tennessee) just above Jacksboro.[27]

On Saturday, August 16, the Kentucky legislature enacted a measure that obligated Governor Magoffin to step aside because of his Southern sympathies. Later in the day, Colonel Scott arrived below Somerset with the First Louisiana Cavalry Regiment. Buell telegraphed Nelson, "It is of the highest importance for you to verify the report of Bragg's [Kirby Smith's] movement to Richmond [Kentucky]." It appeared to Buell that no one was as "suitable for the emergency as General Nelson." He ordered him "to proceed . . . to [Louisville] Kentucky and take command. Organize the old troops there and the new troops coming in from Ohio and Indiana; meet and drive them [the Confederate invaders] back. I will meet with you in Nashville to-morrow night."[28]

Before Nelson departed from McMinnville, he deemed it necessary to order the execution of three discharged Confederates who had the misfortune of being captured at the time of Brig. Gen. Robert McCook's shocking assassination near Winchester, Tennessee. At 4:00 A.M. Sunday morning, August 17, he started for Nashville with "1,500 infantry, 200 cavalry and 12 cannon." Stanley Matthews saw the sudden exodus as a response to reports of the enemy heading into Kentucky from Chattanooga. His intuition also sensed this "will deprive us of the General for some time to come, perhaps permanently." John Hunt Morgan supposed that Nelson was headed for Bowling Green to set up a defensive line that would block the intended advance of Bragg's army. Neither he nor Forrest had artillery, and prudence dictated they allow Nelson's better-armed escort to proceed unmolested.[29]

In London, Kentucky, Col. Leonidas C. Houk and five companies from the Third Regiment Tennessee Volunteer Infantry were waiting for a hospital train to arrive with ninety-eight convalescents. At 8:00 A.M. Sunday, Colonel Scott overwhelmed the three hundred Union defenders and headed for Barbourville to link up with Kirby Smith. Carter Stevenson had already blocked the southern entrance to the Cumberland Gap, and Scott's action closed access from the north. Buell told Boyle that any attempt to restore the line of communication with George W. Morgan would have to wait "until the greater evil of invasion is averted or removed." He further advised that the

Lebanon Depot and Nicholasville Depot were good points to operate from and recommended that a defensive force move to Danville for that reason.[30]

Nelson reached Nashville about midnight and found a dispatch from Buell that said he would not "see you to-night as I intended, nor perhaps is it necessary. . . . You have a great deal of work to accomplish and with little means." Nelson told Buell he planned to leave in the morning, and he suggested it would be useful for him to look into the situation at Nashville. His reasoning provided extraordinary insight that would soon take on striking significance. Nelson advised:

> My services in the army are too short to judge by my own experience, but I think that it cannot be right that the promptness of execution of the service required of any person should be relaxed to gratify the personal pretensions of any one. . . . I mention these things because I am sure that you wish the public service to go ahead, not to be stopped while this or that man ruffles his plumes. For my part, in my own limited vision, I estimate the value of an officer in the precise ratio of his zeal for the service, and if anything crosses him to still go on, and appeal to his superior.[31]

At 6:00 A.M., Monday, Nelson boarded a steamboat and headed down the Cumberland River to Clarksville. Good fortune was with him when the captain stopped to take on wood a few miles from that destination. A curious local man approached Nelson and asked if he had come to fight the Rebels. Nelson inquired, "How so, sir, what Rebels?" The man answered, "Why them that [Col. Rodney] Mason [of the Seventy-first Regiment Ohio Volunteer Infantry] got took by." The enemy presence clearly compromised his mission, and Nelson ordered the boat back to Nashville.[32]

At 9:10 P.M., that evening, Nelson wired Buell and asked, "What shall be done?" Early Wednesday morning, August 20, Buell provided Nelson with a regiment and two batteries that would enable him to march to Bowling Green and take the train from there to Louisville. Later that same day, Halleck shocked Buell with the news that Maj. Gen. Horatio G. Wright was to take command of Indiana, Ohio, Illinois, and key parts of Kentucky that included the Cumberland Gap. Old Brains expected Buell to "continue [the] general direction of affairs in that State until General Wright arrives [in Louisville]." Buell's response to that insult was to ask that he be relieved of all duties.[33]

Nelson marched into Bowling Green at 11:15 P.M., Friday, and he immediately telegraphed the Louisville headquarters to expect him early Saturday. When Nelson arrived, a correspondent from the *Cincinnati Commercial* saw him enter the Galt House. It appeared that the Kentuckian was "hale and hearty, and shows no signs of fatigue, although he has been constantly at work for months." It surprised Nelson to learn that Wright had orders to take command of the Department of the Ohio. He outranked Wright by several days, and the Senate had not confirmed Wright's promotion to major general. There were also questions about the command abilities of an engineering officer who was a bureaucratic clone of Halleck. At 10:00 A.M., Wright officially assumed command, and at 11:10 A.M., Nelson wired Halleck to inquire about returning to Tennessee. Halleck instructed Nelson to remain in Kentucky. Wright then ordered him to relieve Lew Wallace at Lexington and complete the organization of the Army of Kentucky.[34]

Wright telegraphed Wallace that Nelson would relieve him of command within the next twenty-four hours, and no new actions were to be undertaken in that interim. That directive did not arrive in time to stop Colonel Metcalfe from completing his assigned duty of escorting twenty-seven wagonloads of supplies fifteen miles south of Richmond to the crest of Big Hill. That striking seven-hundred-foot mountain overlooked the outer edge of the Bluegrass Region, and Lt. Col. John C. Chiles had come forward from the Cumberland Gap with the Third Regiment Tennessee Volunteer Infantry to make the exchange near there. In the midst of that transaction, Scott's First Louisiana Cavalry Regiment attacked both units and drove them back to Richmond. Scott demanded the surrender of the town, but he elected to withdraw after the arrival of Federal reinforcements early Sunday morning. That afternoon, Nelson arrived in Lexington with three general officers and a staff of regular army officers.[35]

Mahlon D. Manson had been with Nelson since Corinth. He was an accomplished Indiana politician who enjoyed a close relationship with Governor Morton. Nelson gave him command of the First Infantry Brigade. The Second Brigade went to Charles Cruft, a lawyer from Terre Haute who was well acquainted with Thomas H. Nelson. Former Kentucky congressman James S. Jackson was a Mexican War veteran and good friend of Nelson. He was to replace the ailing Brig. Gen. Green Clay Smith, a man who was better suited for politics than command of a cavalry brigade. Nelson had no previous acquaintance with Brig. Gen. Ebenezer Dumont, a former Indiana state legislator with a reputed drinking problem. Dumont was already protecting the all-important L&N rail depot at Lebanon, and his command became the Third Brigade.[36]

Nelson informed Manson and Cruft that Wright was opposed to the use of raw levies unless success appeared certain. If the enemy engaged them,

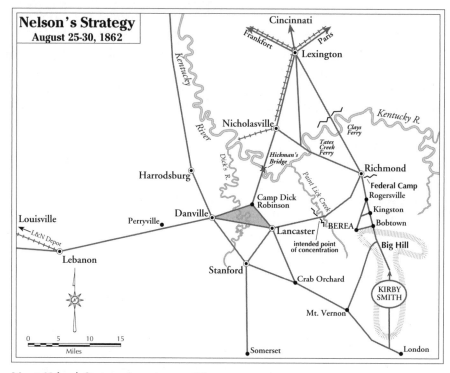

Map 8. Nelson's Strategy, August 25–30, 1862

Wright preferred that they *fall back to a defensive position*. Hickman's Bridge represented the only span across the Kentucky River above Frankfort, and Nelson wanted incoming levies to become part of a defensive configuration between Camp Dick Robinson, Lancaster, and Danville. Once the level of incoming troops reached twenty-five thousand, he could extend the base of that triangle north to Nicholasville or south to Crab Orchard, as needed. If the enemy moved against the two untrained brigades at Richmond, they could withdraw to Paint Lick and become the point for a force of thirty thousand troops on the left flank of the enemy. James S. Jackson was to take command of Col. Richard T. Jacob's Ninth Regiment Kentucky Volunteer Cavalry and Col. Edward S. Williams's Ninth Regiment Pennsylvania Volunteer Cavalry. Once Jackson reached Crab Orchard, he was to send scouts to observe Big Hill, Mount Vernon, and London. Should Kirby Smith advance, Jackson was to threaten the rear of his column. Metcalfe's Seventh Regiment Kentucky Volunteer Cavalry was to scout for enemy activity south of Richmond.[37]

When Nelson arrived at Richmond on Tuesday, he found the troops had no tents to shade them from the hot sun, food distribution was haphazard, and the men were feeding themselves with stolen goods or taking meals at private homes. He ordered the soldiers back to their camps two miles below town and informed Governor Robinson that the situation gave him "lively apprehensions for the morale of the troops." Nelson added, "Men who rob and steal won't fight . . . and a regiment without discipline cannot be depended on, no matter how gallantly led. . . . I shall endeavor to put this army in the same condition as the splendid division I left in Tennessee."[38]

On Wednesday, August 27, the *Frankfort Commonwealth* informed its readers that Nelson "is, we believe, thoroughly the right man in the right place. . . . He has what we all feel and want—skill, zeal, tact, and what is worth them all—vim. He is a severe officer, but a remarkable just one. . . . He does not believe in regiments squatting on the ground in camp until they become rooted there . . . things will begin to move in this State . . . and inside of a week there will be news to tell—glorious news, we hope, to make amends for the past." Had that writer spoken directly to officers in the field, his understanding would have been quite different. Acting Lt. Col. James B. Armstrong believed that Col. William L. McMillan, Ninety-fifth Regiment Ohio Volunteer Infantry, suffered from

> ill-starred anxiety for distinction, which caused him . . . [to go along with Lew] Wallace's order . . . to meet the enemy at Richmond, when not one half of the men hardly knew each other by sight, and the regiment never had battalion drill; the inhumanity to the sick—the brutality to the well—such as knocking men down with his fist, striking them with his sword, drawing pistols on them, and coming [at] it à la Nelson generally, winding up arresting the whole Quartermaster's Department at once; . . . putting the officer of the day and other officers under arrest—for these and other reasons, to be held in general execration, his men are utterly demoralized, and lost to the service under his command.

General Cruft said he hated to contemplate the fate of raw levies "in a trial at arms with experienced troops." General Manson found that a majority did not know what a "line of battle was." He was equally disturbed to see that Wallace had forwarded artillery from Lexington with no "caissons or a proper supply of . . . fuses and friction-primers."[39]

Mistaken intelligence reports indicated the sole intent of the enemy was to isolate the Federal forces at Cumberland Gap, and that suggested there was no interest in moving beyond Big Hill. Nelson wrongly surmised that Kirby Smith was "a much smaller potato than I took him for," and he saw no pressing need to remain in the field. Before leaving, Nelson wanted to tell

Manson he was to make no troop movements without his approval. Manson was unavailable, and Nelson left it up to the adjutant to see that Manson received those orders. Late Wednesday afternoon, the soldiers joked among themselves that Nelson must have run out of whiskey and gone to Lexington to imbibe without them. What he really wanted was direct access to the telegraph. At 6:10 P.M., Nelson informed Halleck and Wright he had just read a wire from Buell that advised "the most momentous consequences depend on . . . opening our communications with Louisville." Nelson told Wright that he would order Manson and Cruft to move from Richmond to Paint Lick, where "I will direct that the telegraph wire be extended to the different camps."[40]

On Thursday, August 28, Nelson asked permission from Wright to assemble regiments at Louisville that would join with those at Bowling Green and march to Gallatin, Tennessee, in relief of Buell. He said this would "not require more than a week of active exertion," and in his stead, a staff officer could direct the arrival of incoming troops at Lexington to the camps below Richmond. Wright told Halleck that he agreed the "opening [of] communication with General Buell is the most important." He then added, "Nelson don't like serving in the department; it would be well to relieve him as soon as he can be replaced. In many respects, he is a good officer, too changeable however, being influenced too much by every report [of Buell] that reaches him. This could all be overlooked if it were not for the rank and his consequent dissatisfaction." Wright stated it was unreasonable to expect anyone to form an army in one week's time, and he concluded that if the untrained levies were committed to battle, "I shall not expect success except by chance."[41]

Nelson answered to the will of two masters who were disinclined to communicate with each other. His original orders from Buell called for him to reopen the line of communication between Louisville and Nashville. Wright had given him an added mission that was akin to a fool's errand. On Friday, August 29, 1862, Nelson was convinced Braxton Bragg intended to attack Buell in the left and rear. He thought the nascent Army of Kentucky should be between Kirby Smith's veterans in southeastern Kentucky and Bragg's experienced troops in middle Tennessee. Captain Gilbert headed for Cincinnati to explain that Nelson wanted Charles Anderson's Ninety-third Ohio to move to Lancaster while Manson and Cruft took up a blocking position at Paintsville. Brig. Gen. Ebenezer Dumont was to move to Danville, and the entire force would obtain supplies from Louisville by way of the Lebanon branch of the L&N Railroad.[42]

Manson did not tell Nelson that earlier that morning he sent Lt. Col. Reuben J. Munday south of Richmond with a battalion-sized detachment of the Sixth Regiment Kentucky Volunteer Cavalry. Below Kingston, Munday encountered Scott's First Louisiana Cavalry Regiment coming forward with several 6-pound howitzers drawn by single mules. Directly behind Scott, Patrick Cleburne's Fourth Infantry Division was coming across Big Hill with four to five thousand men. Munday sent that astonishing information back to Manson's headquarters with a courier who arrived about 11:00 A.M. Manson made two copies for Nelson: one went to Lancaster and the other to Lexington by way of Reverend McCray of Bloomington, Indiana.[43]

By 2:00 P.M., Metcalfe, Munday, and four companies of the Sixteenth Regiment Indiana Volunteer Infantry were retreating to Richmond as fast as possible. Manson gave no thought to the primary directive that called for withdrawal. He believed "the only question for me to determine was whether I should allow the enemy to attack me in my camp or whether I should advance and meet him. It did not take a moment to decide." Manson advanced three-quarters of a mile and fired several rounds of artillery into the First Louisiana Cavalry Regiment. Scott withdrew and purposely left behind "an old brass cannon" for the Federals to "capture." Manson advanced another mile and formed a battle line facing south across a dominant ridgeline along each side of Old Richmond Road (Rt. 421). The Confederates skirmished for one hour and withdrew. Manson moved forward another mile and went into bivouac, convinced his completely untrained troops would achieve a great victory in the morning.[44]

About 2:30 A.M., Saturday, August 30, Manson's courier arrived in Lexington with the startling news that four to five thousand enemy troops had come across Big Hill at 11:00 A.M. Friday. Charles Gilbert said Nelson could not accept that "a concentration of all the [Federal] forces at Danville would [not] cover Louisville and the [L&N] railroad, and at the same time protect Cincinnati." He ordered a courier to Richmond to tell Manson to pull back to Paint Lick using the Lancaster road. Nelson placed Col. Daniel McCook in command of Lexington, and he ordered two companies of the Ninth Regiment Kentucky Volunteer Cavalry to escort the headquarters staff to Richmond.[45]

About 3:30 A.M., Nelson came out of the Phoenix Hotel wearing white duck pants and a blue blouse. He tied a sword around his waist, climbed into a waiting buggy, and rode off to Lancaster with one aide. Several hours later, Kirby Smith was moving through Kingston, and Manson sent word for Cruft to bring his brigade forward "as quickly as possible." At 9:30 A.M., the rumble of artillery fire from Richmond greeted Nelson as he rode into Lancaster. Nelson and his aide obtained fresh horses and started toward Richmond on "by-paths" that would enable them to avoid the "enemy's cavalry."[46]

On the battlefield, Cpl. Richard M. Hunt watched in horror as Manson charged into the rear of the Sixty-ninth Regiment Indiana Volunteer Infantry. Hunt thought he heard Lt. Oran Perry say Manson appeared "drunk as a lord and crazy as a loon." It seemed to others that Manson was "scarcely able to maintain his seat in the saddle," and rather than follow a "howling drunkard," the soldiers believed there was "nothing left to do but break and run."[47]

Cruft and Manson overcame that mayhem and re-formed the men about two miles north of Rogersville. Manson claimed that as it neared 12:30 P.M. the courier Nelson sent at 3:30 A.M. arrived with a message to avoid a fight that had been going on for five hours. Moments later, the newly invigorated Federal line unleashed a barrage of fire. There was no return fire from the hidden enemy and that lured the naïve Federal officers into ordering their troops forward. Once the gullible volunteers were fully exposed, their determined adversary made them suffer terribly for this foolish mistake.[48]

Nelson had come through Richmond about 2:00 P.M., and now he was riding toward a mass of Union soldiers who looked upon him as the one person who could "bring order out of chaos." After Nelson conferred with Manson, he decided to keep the enemy "in check until night and then resume the retreat." Over the next half-hour, he exposed himself to extraordinary danger while directing the execution of more movement than the two previous stands.[49]

A half-hour later, Kirby Smith rode forward with William R. Boggs, expecting to see the entire Federal army in full retreat. Much to their surprise, they found the unwavering Nelson assembling troops in front of a cemetery. They had no way on knowing that four of the Federal artillery pieces lacked munitions or that the two remaining 6-pound guns had a mere twenty-seven rounds between them. Lt. Byron Paddock put one of those guns with the Sixty-ninth Regiment Indiana Volunteer Infantry, and Nelson shouted, "Wait till the rebels get within short range and give them hell." On the right of the Sixty-ninth Indiana stood the Sixteenth and Twelfth Indiana and two companies of the Seventy-First Regiment Indiana Volunteer Infantry. The Sixth-sixth Indiana was directly in front of the cemetery.[50]

Nelson, Manson, and Cruft moved among the exhausted troops to keep them from wandering off looking for water or falling asleep. Nelson assured the green volunteers he would show them "how to whip the scamps," and about 3:45 P.M., the Confederates gave him that opportunity. Over the next hour, they drove into the Federal position with an especially fierce resolve. Three determined volleys from the defenders punished the enemy severely, but it failed to stop them. The Confederates pushed through the thicket on the right, and Nelson shouted to the Sixth-ninth Indiana, "Reinforcements will be here right away." The desperate Hoosiers wanted to believe that twenty thousand men would magically appear in fifteen minutes. Nelson yelled again, "Keep it up men—the rebels are running. That's it. Let them have it. Fire low. Take good aim. We'll whip them yet." The thirty men in Company B, Seventy-first Indiana Infantry did their best to hold the edge of the cornfield, but fifteen minutes later nine had fallen.[51]

Nelson resorted to the old ploy used at Ivy Mountain and yelled, "Boys, if they can't hit something as big as I am, they can't hit anything!" In the next instant, a sizzling musket ball penetrated his upper thigh. Frightened officers told their men to run for their lives and suddenly the "whole line broke in wild confusion. . . . Both officers and men became reckless . . . and rushed pell-mell to the rear. . . . Every effort possible was made [by Nelson] to rally the men behind . . . the few shots . . . [left in] the howitzers, to make our way to the rear. [However, the] Officers, or men . . . deliberately refused to render any assistance or respond to any order." Colonel Link lay on the ground with a shattered thigh, Lieutenant Paddock stood behind the lone 6-pound gun firing the very last rounds, and Cruft pleaded with his men, "Remember Indiana."[52]

Nelson suddenly caught sight of men throwing their guns to the ground and it sent him into a berserker rage. He rode forward "hatless, his long hair streaming in the wind, his eyes glaring and bloodshot." It seemed that at least six Union soldiers were hit by his sword, "inflicting terrible wounds [that left two] . . . victims lying by the roadside unable to speak or move." Within moments, Nelson was the only one on the field. Maj. Green Clay Smith rode out and seized the bridle of his horse, and as they rode back, Nelson learned the First Louisiana Cavalry Regiment was in "our rear, and . . . it was a sheer impossibility to do anything."[53]

About 4:45 P.M., the "excoriating pain [in his thigh] finally obliged him [Nelson] to seek refuge in the fence corner of a cornfield." Captain Irwin and the staff moved out under a flag of truce and offered to become prisoners so they could treat the wounded. The intentional distraction allowed an ambulance detail to remove Nelson to Richmond, where he told Lieutenant Paddock, "the artillery had done extremely well and had the infantry done half as well, we could have whipped them." Governor Morton's private secretary, Col. William R. Holloway, took charge of the ambulance and proceeded toward the home of Cassius Clay. The entourage then went across the Kentucky River, and about 7:00 P.M., they encountered Col. Daniel McCook as he was coming forward from Lexington with four regiments. Nelson told him, "Colonel we are whipped and whipped like hell. Use your judgment and do the best you can." Nelson made sure that a wire went forward to Wright that informed him of how Manson had disregarded instructions not to attack the enemy, and hours later, surgeons in Lexington were removing the painful Minnie ball from his thigh.[54]

Earlier in the week Nelson had commented on how the "bad and the worthless will make a clamor" about severe discipline practices. He also declared, "War *is* war, and nothing will make one man march to certain death at the bidding of another *but discipline*; and without *that* we cannot whip the enemy on one hand, or protect our citizens on the other." It was that pronouncement that led "Pontiac" to say Nelson would put a "stop to inexcusable surrenders and surprises" that had plagued the lethargic advance against Chattanooga and encouraged the Confederate invasion of Kentucky.[55]

That observation overlooked how the dutiful and loyal Nelson ended up in a position where he tried to serve two masters. Out of concern for Buell's situation, Nelson wanted to be at the telegraph in Lexington. That mistake in judgment and Manson's injudicious action involved Nelson in the *most conclusive defeat for its size in the Civil War.* That decision to leave the field had resulted in the capture, wounding, or death of 82 percent of the sixty-five-hundred-man Army of Kentucky, which was comprised of "seven and a half regiments of Indiana, one of Ohio, one of Kentucky."[56]

"Pontiac" had noted that Nelson "may not be without faults of manner and conduct, which, especially in his new position, he might do well to guard against." In his desire to be of maximum service to his superiors, Nelson failed to show proper respect for a public that had become exasperated by the numerous failures of the national army. That angry citizenry blamed those debacles on the conceit of Federal military commanders and Nelson wrongly assumed that his pitiless style of leadership would be "sustained by everyman who has the welfare of Kentucky and the army at heart." At Pittsburg Landing, unabashed public patriotism endured the use of violent force to save good men from the uncontrolled behavior of panicked men. At Richmond, the exhausted and enraged Nelson forgot that a "regiment [of raw levies] without discipline cannot be depended on, no matter how gallantly led." Now he had to overcome the outrage produced by the terrible loss, and that meant keeping the focus on Manson and off his fateful lapse in judgment.[57]

Fatal Conceit [10]

Late Saturday and early Sunday morning, the city of Lexington was overcome by "chaotic masses of men, horses and wagons, cursing and swearing officers who had deserted their regiments; stragglers who wanted to be captured; refugees who wanted to get away." At the depot, the implacable drone of the "grapevine telegraph" bedeviled frightened civilians who anxiously awaited the first available train to Louisville or Covington. One rumor said that Washington had fallen; another indicated the Rebels occupied Glasgow, and that made it seem to many that Kentucky would be under Confederate control within two weeks.[1]

The state legislature was on its way to Louisville, and in Indianapolis, Governor Morton ordered additional troops sent to Kentucky while the press whipped the city into frenzy with slanted half-truths: "Nelson made no preparation . . . didn't believe there would be a fight. . . . had only six pieces of artillery, manned by raw hands." The wounded Nelson arrived in Covington at 8:00 P.M. Sunday, and Larz Anderson brought him to his home in Cincinnati. By midnight, Lexington had regained a sense of security through the presence of eight to ten thousand Federal troops in and around the city.[2]

On Monday, September 1, 1862, the press assailed Nelson with a pack of unproven stories. A deserter from the Ninety-fifth Regiment Ohio Volunteer Infantry claimed he had slashed one Union man with his sword and shot two others. Another account said Nelson struck at least six of his own men with his sword and possibly killed some others. The *Philadelphia Inquirer* announced, "All accounts agree that General Nelson's conduct in his attempt to rally our troops was not only unbecoming and unnecessary, but absolutely brutal and barbarous [treatment of]. . . . [Federal] soldiers who were worn out with eight hours of fighting." The *Cincinnati Gazette* reported that Nelson used vulgar, profane, and abusive language with gallant officers and boasted of shooting two or three Union soldiers who tried to escape to the rear.[3]

The *New Albany (Ind.) Daily Ledger* countered the scurrilous allegations by saying:

> A soldier. . . . states that . . . General Nelson did pound some with [the flat of] his sword . . . milder treatment . . . could not rally the men. . . . [Those who know war realize] nothing but force can cause them to fight. General Nelson was said to have cut a frightful gash in the head of one soldier, but when the facts are known, it is found that a slight bruise is the only trace . . . showing that the stroke must have been very light. We are also told that he struck a soldier . . . [that] was engaged in leading a wounded man from the field . . . it [now] appears that same wounded man was one of the first to arrive in this city . . . without a scratch. We are of the opinion that many of the men who were so barbarously murdered by the general, will be found at home, as healthy and able to fight as any soldier.[4]

Cincinnati Commercial correspondent, Joseph B. McCullagh, admitted it was impossible to say "with certainty" that Nelson "killed one or two [Union] men and wounded three others," but one of his sources claimed it was true. In a direct interview with that paper, Nelson asserted that Manson ignored a preemptory order to fall back and avoid a fight. He was particularly interested in making the public aware of his deep admiration for the spirit and courage of volunteers who were "unsteady simply for the want of instruction" and discipline.[5]

Horatio Wright was now in Lexington seeking a replacement for Nelson, and after two better-qualified men turned down the offer, Capt. Charles C. Gilbert agreed to take command of the Army of Kentucky. Before Wright boarded the 5:00 P.M train for Louisville, he advised Gilbert to withdraw to Covington or Louisville because it would be "madness to attempt the defense of Lexington." By 8:00, the tumultuous sounds of Gilbert's departure had faded into the west. Three hours later, "the last company of Federal troops left town," and a long line of civilian carriages began moving up the pike for Cincinnati.[6]

Tuesday, September 2, advance troops from Kirby Smith's army rode in Lexington at 8:30 A.M. Garrett Davis was in Cincinnati, and he wired Halleck to "suggest that you send . . . 30,000 disciplined troops into Kentucky. Generals Wallace and Nelson approve it." It was important for Kirby Smith to maintain the advantage gained, and he ordered Henry Heth to march the Confederate Second Division into the hills overlooking Cincinnati. That afternoon, Dr.

Irwin found Nelson working on a plan to organize a new army that would prevent the occupation of those hills. In conjunction with that effort, Lew Wallace ordered the Cincinnati police to round up some seven hundred African Americans and put them to work on batteries at Fort Mitchell and Fort Wright.[7]

Wednesday morning, September 3, Col. John S. Scott reached the southeastern edge of Frankfort, and Gilbert ordered his troops to march away from the foe. That decision offended many of the men, and their resentment grew deeper during a merciless march that caused some of those who fell behind to claim "Nelson's staff" tied them to battery wagons or beat them with the flats of their swords. In Louisville, it appeared to the state legislature they were no longer safe, and most of them were in Cincinnati when Manson arrived on Thursday afternoon. To his "utter astonishment," Manson discovered a letter from Nelson in the *Cincinnati Gazette* that said he disregarded standing orders to avoid battle. Nelson then requested that Manson meet with him in private. Whatever transpired between them is unknown, but sixteen years later, the highly political Manson would wrongly lay all the blame on Nelson's grave.[8]

On Friday, September 5, a published order in the *Louisville Journal* called for "all loyal, able bodied citizens between the ages of eighteen and forty-five" to report to "Capt. Thos. W. Gibson, commanding State forces in this [Louisville] district." Gibson was the acting inspector general for the Kentucky State Guard, and he warned that anyone caught avoiding military duty would end up working beside the slaves. Late that afternoon, Gilbert's eight thousand troops arrived in the city looking more like "a prison gang" than a glorious band of soldiers. Still suffering from the shock of Richmond, these young volunteers were merged with seventeen thousand infantrymen and two thousand cavalry troops, who taunted them with malicious gossip of how Nelson called them cowards who would not stand up to the enemy.[9]

Adding to that insult, the Indiana soldiers found they had to camp in a "filthy place" along Bear Grass Creek. Oliver Perry Morton, the "grandest and noblest Governor of all the land," learned of their plight, and he sent Asahel Stone, the commissary general, to their rescue. Stone spoke with Gilbert and asked that the men return to their homes. Gilbert supposedly screamed back, "Your Indiana men acted and fought like God Damned cowards, as they are—all of them—and deserve no mercy. I have them under guard, and (with a cruel oath) I will keep them there till they rot." Stone contacted Morton, who wired Wright in Cincinnati. That resulted in the aggrieved men moving across the river where they could ruminate over the seeming disrespect shown them in the past few weeks.[10]

Manson returned to Indianapolis on Tuesday, September 9, and he found the *Indianapolis Journal* denouncing Nelson as a "brutal and barbarous" general who should never again hold command. Manson completed his official battle report on Wednesday, and in the conclusion he simply said, "Allow me to express a wish that the wound which you [Nelson] received in the last action at Richmond may speedily heal and that you may soon be able to take to the field again."[11]

Across from Louisville, the *New Albany (Ind.) Ledger* spoke in support of Acting Major General Gilbert by noting the problem with "the loafing of Federal officers about the saloons and hotels of Louisville" had disappeared because of his orders. Merchants were pleased about the removal of trade restrictions and the "pass system," which was bringing commerce back to a level that existed before the crisis. The paper wrongly declared the emergency associated with the Confederate invasion had ended, and Buell would likely remain in Nashville. It then noted, "among the distinguished officers at Louisville today [September 10] was Brigadier General Jeff. C. Davis of Fort Sumter fame. A general desire is expressed in military circles that this distinguished officer be assigned a command in Kentucky."[12]

Nelson was continuing his recuperation in Cincinnati, and he now met with Philip H. Sheridan and others to discuss how to drive Henry Heth's 6,000 Confederates back from the northern Kentucky hills. Wright had redeployed 50,000 troops from Louisville to Cincinnati, and Wallace's morning report showed 72,000 men present for duty. This left Louisville with an effective force of 20,730, and it appeared that Braxton Bragg would reach there before Buell could arrive with reinforcements. There were no fortified positions, and George D. Prentice noted the city was dependent on the "masses of brave but undisciplined Indianans . . . who are fresh from the harvest field. . . . Let the work commence immediately."[13]

On Wednesday, September 17, Col. John Wilder, the commander of a vastly outnumbered Federal garrison at Munfordville, Kentucky, agreed to terms of surrender from Braxton Bragg. The *Cincinnati Commercial* was unaware of that development when it noted the pleasure of seeing "Major General Nelson on the street. His wound, which was severe and dangerous, has healed with surprising rapidity, he will be fit for service in a few days." Before Nelson left to resume command in Louisville, he told his uncle by marriage, William H. Rainy, that if he should die prematurely to have the remains buried at Camp Dick Robinson. Soon after his arrival, Nelson called for a thousand laborers to work additional hours by candlelight to complete the defensive entrenchment. Any Negroes "found at large in the streets . . . were [to be] seized and put to work."[14]

As the Army of the Ohio was approaching Cave City on Thursday, September 18, the paroled Union troops from Munfordville joined them about 10:00 P.M. A mere ten miles separated the two forces, and both opposing commanders were reluctant engage each other at this point. Buell believed it made more sense to march toward the reinforcements and supplies at Louisville, and Bragg preferred to join forces with Kirby Smith at Bardstown. At Louisville, Governor James F. Robinson, Garrett Davis, and John J. Crittenden wanted to stop a clandestine effort to remove Nelson. They informed Halleck "the fate of Kentucky is hanging in the balance . . . Nelson comprehends the whole matter . . . He can render greatly more service here than he can upon any other theater. Do not order him away." Shortly after this, Acting Maj. Gen. Charles C. Gilbert headed for Cincinnati.[15]

George D. Prentice remarked in the *Louisville Journal* that while Nelson did not appear "fully recovered," he would "soon be up in the saddle." "Pontiac" remained an avid supporter, and he reported in the *New York Times* that Nelson "will make fur fly. . . . His time will not be wasted by dilly-dallying, palavering, listening to everybody's complaints and grievances and quibbles on 'constitutional issues' . . . it won't be his fault if the foe is not pushed out of the State pell-mell. . . . the people have an abiding confidence in Gen. Nelson. Let him be fully sustained and all will be well."[16]

Wright feared Bragg would attack Louisville before Buell could arrive with reinforcements, and he ordered Nelson to take up a position on Muldraugh's Hill with six untrained/ill-disciplined divisions and a brigade of cavalry. Wright telegraphed Buell, "Nelson has orders . . . to retard enemy as far as he can and to form junction with you, if desirable. . . . We ought to whip Bragg, and . . . be able to protect Louisville till movements [of additional troops] can be arranged." Nelson asked Wright to send "all the troops you can at once; it is of the most momentous consequence." Wright responded by ordering Brig. Gen. Andrew J. Smith at Fort Mitchell to send "eight or ten regiments of your command to Louisville," and he advised Nelson to expect fifteen Illinois regiments in the coming week.[17]

On Sunday, September 21, Phil Sheridan arrived at the Galt House, and Nelson greeted him with "the bluff and hearty fashion of a sailor." Jefferson C. Davis and other general officers were in the process of endorsing a recommendation for Dr. Irwin to become medical director of the Army of the Southwest and it appeared to Nelson that Davis was ideally suited for the temporary task of organizing the Home Guard brigade. When this regular army officer arrived at the city council room of the courthouse, he was appalled to find the command consisted of nothing more than a motley group of young boys, old men, and fat officials with no experience.[18]

At 1:00 A.M. Monday morning, Nelson received an alarming wire from Buell. It said Bragg might "attack Louisville, or . . . he may halt at Elizabethtown . . . and fight me there. The latter I think the most probable considering that I am so close on him." Buell warned Nelson not to "attempt a defense of Louisville unless you are strongly intrenched; under no circumstances should you make a fight with his [Bragg's] whole or main force. The alternative would be to cross the [Ohio] river or march to this [Kentucky] side to the mouth of the Salt River and bridge it, so as to form a junction with me." Buell added, "so much depends on circumstances that I must leave this question to your discretion." In any case, Nelson was to put aside one million rations, have a pontoon bridge ready to be put across the Salt River, and hold the transports under steam on the Indiana shore opposite Brandenburg, Kentucky.[19]

Louisville was extraordinarily important to the Union cause, and Nelson intended "to resist to the last extremity." He proclaimed, "Let every man feel the importance of the occasion, and do his duty." From 12:00 P.M., Monday, until further notice, Nelson ordered the Jeffersonville (Ind.) Ferry restricted to military purposes, and only persons on foot could pass as usual. Should the enemy advance on Louisville, he would put "all women and children and Southern sympathizers" across the river on one hour's notice. The defense would continue "as long as possible, then he would set fire to the city and withdraw . . . to the Indiana shore . . . turn his guns on Louisville and reduce it to rubble."[20]

While that pronouncement "created a terrible flurry" among the citizenry, it also put Bragg on notice there would be a dreadful price attached to every inch of ground. "Pontiac" confirmed that if Louisville could not be held, Nelson would "lay it in ashes." He added, "We are willing to sacrifice our city and ourselves to the cause of Union, but not to [Buell's] military imbecility, ignorance and cowardice." "Pontiac" grudgingly acknowledged that the arrival of "that notorious military sluggard" was important, and he trusted that if everyone obeyed Nelson's orders, all would be well.[21]

Merchant John F. Jefferson suspected that Nelson did this "for effect," but he soon learned that was not the case. Nelson ordered the placement of batteries at Jeffersonville, had two coal barges converted to pontoon bridges, and announced that all "the women and children" would go across the river "without delay." As mobs of civilians tried "to get out; thousands of government teams and droves of mules crowded the river banks at every available point of crossing . . . some of the mules were swimming the river . . . [with] people . . . in every kind of vessel, skiff, flat, ferry, and steam boats." Once they reached New Albany and Jeffersonville, the refugees camped in the nearby woods and fields.[22]

The soldiers who remained behind desperately needed shoes and uniforms, and it shocked them when they saw the first of many loads of equipment and supplies start across the Ohio River. Prentice's *Louisville Journal* declared the enemy might take the ground "but never occupy the city." Mayor Delph proclaimed, "All citizens are hereby directed to close their places of business within the city. The Provost Marshall has been instructed to assist the Mayor in carrying out this order. The citizens are called upon to assemble [under Brig. Gen. Jefferson C. Davis] at the Courthouse this day [Monday] at 4 o'clock P.M., for organization of such citizens as are willing to defend the city." Cpl. L. G. Bennett and Chaplain William M. Haigh served in Sheridan's division, and they characterized that citizen brigade as an "unimportant command over raw and insubordinate home-guards, who were constantly vibrating between their homes and commands, and it was extremely difficult for . . . [Davis] to tell at a given time who he could depend on in case of an emergency."[23]

Cuthbert Bullitt, the self-important son of a city founder, informed President Lincoln that Nelson's proclamation seemed "like that of Genl Butler [at New Orleans], unfortunately worded. The men women and children are wild with panic, & and there is not conveyance enough to take them away." The *New York Times* asked what should we "expect when fools and madmen are permitted thus to hold the destiny of States and nations in their hands?" The paper surmised that the threat of an assault on Louisville within forty-eight hours had caused Nelson "to commit the most phrenzied and absurd actions." The writer noted that throughout history, military leaders seldom resorted to such "cruel and irrational" acts. He asked why it was necessary to remove the women and children so Nelson could "batter down [the city] as soon as he [Bragg] reached it?" Traditional warfare practices dictated that women and children be given the opportunity to leave, and the writer felt certain Bragg would do the same. That second-guessing was concluded with the comment that the "opaque, dense headed" Nelson simply showed a lack of "coolness, sagacity and courage" by his failure to fell trees across the roads and delay Bragg in a way that would allow Buell to catch up and engage him.[24]

The *Brooklyn Eagle* reported that Nelson was certain the enemy could be whipped and refused to surrender to Bragg. The *New York Herald* announced that Buell's "troops are being pushed into the interior, and an animating and encouraging vigor seems suddenly to have been put into this army by the presence of Major General Nelson." The paper predicted the intensity of those actions could cause Kirby Smith to "halt or delay for several days" and thereby prevent a junction with Bragg, which would halt the advance against Louisville. The *Herald* went on to say Nelson had ordered Brig. Gen. Gordon Granger to replace Indiana general Ebenezer Dumont for having abandoned supplies in the face of the enemy. Granger appeared ideally suited to command under Nelson because he was a "rude, rough, and tough soldier" with a thoroughly indifferent attitude toward "the dangers of battle." The most honest assessment of the situation came from the *New York Tribune* reporter who simply stated, "Between the tide of rumors and the ebb of facts, your correspondent floats like a craft without a wheel."[25]

Nelson was not going to let his ship go adrift, and late Monday afternoon he asked Capt. James H. Cole about the status of the Home Guard brigade. That staff officer said Davis loathed drilling a "rabble of citizens" and devoted most of his time to gossiping about Nelson. There was an urgent need to prepare all available troops, and that apparent disrespect for the situation sent Nelson into a whirl. Cole was told to have Davis report to the Galt House immediately, and when Davis learned of this about 4:00 P.M., he "jumped quickly from the heater upon which he was sitting and went to the headquarters." Nelson immediately inquired about the Home Guard brigade, and Davis said there about twenty-five hundred men who needed arms. The cavalier tone of voice further irritated Nelson, and he supposedly shouted back, "About! Damn your 'abouts'! Any God Damned regular army officer should know precisely how many men." How many regiments? Companies?" The contempt stunned Davis, and he dryly replied, "I don't know." Nelson jumped up and yelled, "You are not fit to command."[26]

Davis somberly declared, "I am a Regular soldier, and I demand the treatment due me as a general officer." A young ordnance officer, Lt. Ben F. Horton, served as an aide to Nelson, and he said most generally agreed that Davis "had done nothing toward organizing the citizens." Horton could hear the two, and it seemed to him that Davis "must have raised his finger at Gen. Nelson as the latter in great threatening language told him not to raise his finger at him." Davis stepped into the hall and asked Captain Irwin "to be a witness to this conversation." Nelson agreed. "Yes, doctor, I want you to remember this."[27]

Irwin watched as Davis once again asked Nelson to show him the courtesy due his rank. Nelson told Davis, "I will treat you as you deserve; you have disappointed me; you have been unfaithful to the trust reposed in you, and I shall relieve you at once." He ordered Davis to leave at once and report to

Wright in Cincinnati for further assignment in the Department of the Ohio. Davis said Nelson did not have authority to order him away, and Nelson informed Captain Kendrick that if Davis had not departed from Louisville by 9:00 P.M., the provost marshal should then escort him across the river to Jeffersonville, Indiana. Davis stormed off, and Nelson turned his attention back to the threat against Louisville. He telegraphed Wright, "The advance of the enemy [Bragg] was at Bardstown yesterday. . . . The troops are in the best of spirits possible, and I shall make good the defense." Nelson then asked Cmdr. Alexander M. Pennock, the fleet commander at Cairo, Illinois, to send two light-draft gunboats up to New Albany, Indiana, because "an attack is expected here Wednesday night by overwhelming force."[28]

In the course of all the confusion, Brig. Gen. Stephen Gano Burbridge had incurred the wrath of Nelson. Many Kentuckians would come to revile this Scott County native as a butcher, but on Tuesday morning, no one took notice when he joined Davis on the train to Cincinnati. Wright informed Davis that while he investigated the incident with Nelson, to report to Brig. Gen. Andrew J. Smith at one of the fortifications behind Covington. In Washington, officials kept their decision to replace Buell with Maj. Gen. George H. Thomas a secret. At Louisville, Nelson had to deal with the just announced Preliminary Emancipation Proclamation, and to curb the fear of loyal slaveholders, he urged them to wait for the disclosure of the full truth that would come through "the stern logic of events."[29]

Governor Morton arrived in Louisville with the supposed purpose of inspecting defensive positions. At Indianapolis, his friends at the *Journal* announced that the removal of Lew Wallace, Ebenezer Dumont, and Jeff. C. Davis was "too significant" to think they were not premeditated. The paper took particular note of how Indiana had "more men in Kentucky and more blood on her soil" than any other state, but remained "hindmost where there is honor." George D. Prentice genuinely respected the contributions made by that state, but for the moment he was far more worried over how the streets were about to become "reddened with blood."[30]

At dawn Wednesday, September 24, a disparate mix of apprehensive defenders looked for a ravaging horde of Rebels to attack any moment. At the Galt House, Nelson met with Governor Morton and assured him he would "wipe out any stain which may be slanderously imputed to Indiana troops on account of the recent disasters." Twenty-three Indiana regiments (approximately twenty-five thousand men) were in Louisville, and Nelson confidently declared, "With one hundred thousand Indianans he could end the rebellion." The dreaded enemy failed to appear as the day wore on, and the sense of alarm faded with the falling sun. At 5:00 P.M., there was a collective sigh of relief when the vanguard of Buell's staff arrived at the Galt House. More than twelve thousand Federal troops had reached the north side of the Salt River with six batteries of artillery, and Nelson telegraphed Wright to say, "We can destroy Bragg with whatever force he may bring against us." He then wired Buell, "I have 35,000 men. I am intrenched and believe that I can hold the city. . . . When you have brought Bragg to bay then I will attack him." When Buell arrived at the Galt House about midnight, the need for such action made no sense with Bragg still in Bardstown studying his next move.[31]

Wright believed he should confer with Buell immediately, and before leaving Cincinnati, he directed Burbridge to remain there. Davis was told to put the welfare of the nation first, return to his old command at Louisville, and forget the quarrel with Nelson. Wright added it would be wise to stay away from Nelson, avoid gossipmongers, and keep opinions about superiors to himself. At the Galt House, Nelson penned a letter of introduction to President Lincoln on behalf of Morgan Vance, a strong Union supporter. That Thursday evening, city councilman George Herbert wrote to his parents that "the excitement is over and those who went a short distance from the City are returning. Gen. Nelson ordered business to be resumed and once more the hum of industry is resounding in our streets." Herbert was equally pleased to find that "the Citizens can pass without being molested or called upon to show their passes."[32]

In one week, Nelson had done a stellar job of seeing the defenses at Louisville were completed. To complement the earthworks there was a "semi-circle of rifle-pits, eight miles in length—beginning at the river above the city, and terminating at the river below the city." Those positions protected all the roads that led into Louisville from the south side. Beyond the rifle-pits, another shorter entrenchment extended from the L&N railroad to the old turnpike than ran parallel to it. On Friday, the pontoon bridge between New Albany and Louisville was completed and the other to Jeffersonville under construction.[33]

Knowing that Buell was about to be relieved by Thomas, Halleck granted him permission to form three distinct commands. Alexander McCook received command of the First Corps, Thomas L. Crittenden the Second Corps, and Nelson the Third Corps. The seven divisions of the Army of the Ohio absorbed the eighteen regiments in the Army of Kentucky. Buell and his staff looked down on them as a "motley mess of about twenty thousand officers and men." The morning reports suggested that forty thousand of the fifty-eight thousand troops in Louisville were fit for duty, but Buell knew better than to rely on that information. He ordered all officers under the rank of brigadier general to remain in camp and establish firm control while guards combed the city for wayward soldiers and returned them to their command.[34]

The *Indianapolis Journal* now complained the "affair of Gen. Dumont's gets uglier the more we learn of it." The paper pointed out that during the evacuation of forces from Lebanon "another Indiana general was suspended for nothing. It is . . . time this sort of thing was ended. . . . By a letter from Louisville we [also] learn that the cause of the removal [Jeff. C. Davis] was rather less that no cause at all." The *Journal* asserted that Davis formed the Home Guard brigade as ordered, and when he requested about twenty-five hundred arms, Nelson blew up and relieved him.[35]

Brig. Gen. Richard W. Johnson contended that Governor Morton viewed "Nelson's conduct towards Davis . . . [as] an insult to Indiana" that would be addressed when he came to Louisville with Davis on Saturday, September 27. That afternoon the two men checked into the Galt House, and Davis made no effort to report to Buell for further assignment. Nelson had completed arrangements for the elegant birthday party that had been conceived in front of Corinth. William B. Hazen was turning thirty-two, James S. Jackson thirty-seven, and Nelson thirty-eight. They were a unique threesome. Jackson and Nelson had almost come to blows at Camp Wickliffe, and at various times enlisted men had threatened to kill them. Hazen's "missionary efforts were directed against the spiritual darkness of his superiors in rank," and some saw him as "a synonym of insubordination."[36]

Halleck wanted to ensure that Col. Joseph C. McKibbin did not serve the orders that would relieve Buell, and he wired instructions to withhold delivery. Buell stayed away from the dinner because of the severe criticism that surrounded him, and John J. Crittenden took advantage of that absence to make a shameless toast to the health of "General McCook, the coming leader of the Army of the Ohio." Hazen viewed that tasteless gesture as a sign some terrible misfortune would befall the command. Nelson continued to play the role of the congenial host, and he did not allow this slur against his relationship with Buell to disturb the gathering. Crittenden's son Thomas saw Nelson as someone who was often "misunderstood. . . . [and he believed] no man was more lovely or considerate of those whom he liked." Nelson demonstrated that nature by congratulating Dr. Irwin on his becoming a full surgeon and wishing him the very best on his upcoming assignment as the medical director for the Army of the Southwest. Irwin thanked his good friend and said he planned to leave for Arkansas in the morning, and Nelson promised they would ride again in the future.[37]

On Sunday, September 28, the *Louisville Journal* commended Nelson for the energetic leadership that provided the city with a solid defense. George D. Prentice was equally grateful for the merciful supply of Indiana regiments by Governor Morton. *New York Herald* correspondent W. F. G. Shanks stayed true to form. He felt the management of the invasion "exceeds all praise . . . [and it] has been fraught with no mistakes. In no single instance has . . . [Buell] been outgeneraled. . . . The danger to the city was from the excited populace, not the approaching enemy." Shanks praised Nelson's use of patrols that arrested any civilian caught on the streets without a pass and the orders that sent soldiers into "Houses of known skulkers" to march them "away to duty in the trenches." Shanks concluded his tribute by saying that Buell should place Nelson in command of the field and order him to dash out and strike the enemy from "from three directions."[38]

Lieutenant Colonel Anderson's mother arrived for a visit, and he noted the city seemed oddly quiet. At the Galt House, Joseph Crawford entered the lobby to mail a letter and this gave him "the pleasure of seeing Gen. Nelson . . . a fine looking very large man." Nelson was sending a recommendation to Governor Robinson that asked for the promotion of Sgt. George H. McFadden, Company B, Second Regiment of Kentucky Volunteer Infantry, to second lieutenant. Another letter writer, Cpl. Bliss Morse, Company D, One Hundred Fifth Ohio Volunteer Infantry, informed his mother "the boys rather dislike him [Brig. Gen. William R. Terrill] since that *review* down to Louisville. Some of them swore they would take his life."[39]

Hundreds of miles away at Peoria, Illinois, U.S. Senator Orville Browning finalized plans to board an early train. At 5:00 A.M., Monday, September 29, 1862, Browning sat beside Maj. George D. Wright, and they talked about how Nelson had saved the Army of the Tennessee from total destruction. At the Galt House, Colonel Whittaker informed Lt. Anderson N. Ellis that during the night he overheard someone say they intended to provoke Nelson into an ugly confrontation that would justify taking his life. Nelson's aide brushed the improbable news aside, thinking it could wait until they met at 8:00 A.M.[40]

At breakfast, Nelson told Governor Morton he might sue and/or give *Indianapolis Journal* editor Berry R. Sulgrove "a good thrashing" if the paper continued to defame his character with unverified stories about Richmond. As it neared 8:00 A.M., Captain Cole headed back to Nelson's office, and Nelson went over to the clerk's desk to inquire if Buell had taken breakfast yet. Nelson then lit a huge cigar and leaned back against the counter. Jeff. C. Davis was now coming across the room with his "heavy black beard, and coarse, wiry hair, starting up into a sort of pyramid on the top of his head." Within moments the five-foot seven-inch, 125-pound Hoosier was standing directly in front of the six-foot four-inch, 300-pound Nelson. Davis declared, "Sir, you seemed to take advantage of your authority the other day. I want to know why you disgraced me by placing me under arrest." Nelson cupped his hand to his ear and asked, "Speak louder, I don't hear very well." Davis repeated in a loud voice that he wanted an apology. Nelson had no regrets to offer. Rather than meet "Davis's request with dignity or consideration," he yelled, "Do you know who you are talking to, sir?" That brought Governor Morton over, which encouraged Davis to badger Nelson harder than ever. Nelson glared at his antagonist and shouted, "Go away you God Damned puppy, I don't want anything to do with you!"[41]

The pasty-faced Davis started twisting a hotel calling card into a tight little ball. The wad fit neatly between his thumb and forefinger, and in the next instant, it sailed directly into the face of his huge tormentor. Nelson instinctively slapped Davis on the side of the head with the back of his hand, and Davis clenched his fist. Nelson mocked that gesture and belittled Davis as a "cowardly son of a bitch" who would not dare try to hit him. Davis took that affront as a challenge to his honor, and he grimly advised, "This is not the last of it; you will hear from me again." The confounded Nelson looked at Morton and asked, "Did you come here, sir, to see me insulted?" The governor replied, "General Nelson, you astonish me. I was standing here and Davis asked me to hear what he had to say to you." Alf Burnett entered the lobby as Nelson continued his protest with confused onlookers. Nelson glanced over at Burnett and asked, "Did you hear that God Damned insolent scoundrel insult me, Sir? I suppose he don't know me, Sir. I'll teach him a lesson, Sir."[42]

Nelson turned about, headed for his office, and Burnett supposed that "Old Buster" probably intended to pick up a revolver. James B. Merriwether supported that idea when he said it appeared to Davis that "Nelson had gone to arm himself." Moments later, Nelson reappeared at the top of the stairway to the main floor. Capt. Thomas Ware (Weir) Gibson was a lawyer and friend of Davis who commanded the State Guard troops. He had just advised Davis, "I always carry an article," and handed that gun to him, thinking he "would receive an apology, or trouble would ensue." Davis started away and Gibson reminded him, "It is a Tranter trigger—be careful."[43]

Capt. William T. Hoblitzell, an aide to Alexander McCook, sensed trouble, and as Davis moved toward the stairway, he rushed after him. Nelson was now at the top of landing, and Davis ordered him to halt about ten steps away. The warning went unheeded, and Davis called out a second time, "General Nelson, take care of yourself." The pistol went off, Nelson's arms went up in the air, and he yelled, "I am shot." Nelson fell into the arms of Captain Hoblitzell, and John J. Crittenden shouted to his son, "General Davis has just shot General Nelson!" Tom rushed over, kneeled down, and asked, "Are you seriously hurt?" His mortally wounded friend answered, "Tom, I am murdered." William B. Hazen rushed out of his office and "met Davis," whom he "had never seen before. He was in shirtsleeves, without a hat, and greatly agitated." Hazen started to grab Davis, but he realized Captain Fry and another officer were placing him under arrest.[44]

Nelson slowly and deliberately started up the stairs to find Buell, and Alf Burnett rushed off to telegraph the *Cincinnati Times* that Davis had just mortally wounded Nelson and "everybody who witnessed the affair justifies Davis." Colonel Anderson agreed, "Davis [was] not generally blamed." Nelson collapsed on reaching the second floor and John Allen Crittenden, nephew of John J. Crittenden, Lieutenant Ellis, and Col. George T. Cotton took him to the room of Lt. Col. Thomas C. James. The latter had recently received "the best apology that such a brute could make." Dr. D. C. Cummins started to treat Nelson, and aides rushed to get Dr. Robert Murray from a nearby hotel.[45]

Fig. 8. Nelson's assassin, Jefferson Columbus Davis (1828–79). Library of Congress

Fig. 9. Tranter pistol used to kill Nelson. Courtesy of Frederick Schneider and Mrs. Bromby Earle

Tom Crittenden and Captain Fry came in the room, and Nelson asked the hotel proprietor, Silas F. Miller, to summon a clergyman. Nelson wanted to hear "words of compassion, charity and forgiveness, rather than revenge, retribution, and vengeance." Dr. Jeremiah J. Talbot, chaplain for the Fifteenth Regiment Kentucky Volunteer Infantry, rushed from the dining room and invited his "old friend" to accept Jesus Christ as his savior and forgive everyone who had ever harmed him. Talbot said a short prayer, recited the Apostle's Creed, and asked Nelson if he should baptize him in the Episcopal faith. Nelson replied, "Baptize me in that faith, quick! Now! for I am going!" Talbot "sprinkled drops of the bright new birth" and asked God to "give the warrior forgiveness, rest. . . . His repentance was as deep and fervent, his contrition as overwhelming, as I ever saw, and his last audible sounds were a prayer for the forgiveness of his sins." Doctor Murray arrived at 8:25 A.M., and he found Nelson "insensible, with stentorous breathing, and evidently dying from hemorrhage." Further investigation revealed a small ball had entered just over the heart and severed the large vessels connected to it. At 8:30 A.M., Nelson's inner spirit shed the cloak of the dreaded outer man and sailed off to be at eternal peace with his God.[46]

Adjutant William H. Spencer and Captain Fry had Davis under arrest in his room on the upper floor of the Galt House. Fry considered Nelson a warm, personal friend. He had also served with Davis in the First Regiment U.S. Artillery and viewed him likewise. Davis appeared to have control of his emotions, and he wanted to explain the events while they remained fresh in his mind. He had ignored Wright's advice to stay away from Nelson and had not attempted to use regular army protocol for righting a grievance. Davis said he did "not come to the hotel that morning with murder in mind." His only intent was to publicly confront Nelson, obtain an apology, and thereby reclaim his image. If that failed, he would then "insult" Nelson and leave it to him to handle it as he saw fit. Nelson refused to apologize and insulted Davis instead. Without realizing it, Davis flicked a wadded calling card off his fingers into Nelson's face. Nelson struck him in the face and called him a coward. Desperate to save his honor, Davis obtained a pistol and approached Nelson with the intent of forcing an apology. In the heat of that moment, the pistol went off and killed Nelson. Fry considered what he had just heard and concluded the homicide was the unintended consequence of a verbal altercation that went horribly wrong.[47]

Buell ordered the provost guard to keep order among the "very bitter" friends of Nelson. The Eighty-fifth Regiment Illinois Volunteer Infantry rushed a detachment of guards forward from their post at Eighteenth and Broadway, and on reaching the corner of First and Main Streets, they found Generals James S. Jackson and William R. Terrill causing a commotion in front of the Galt House. Terrill wanted Davis "hanged on the spot." Others saw Morton as "an accessory to the killing . . . [because] it was through his intrigues that the quarrel had taken place." Jerry Boyle struggled to speak with the harried Hoosier as he tried to leave the hotel, and when aides pushed the paunchy Boyle aside, he abruptly threw a punch. It seemed certain there would be a huge brawl, and General McCook prevented it by sternly announcing his men would remove everyone to the guardhouse if cooler heads did not prevail.[48]

At the Fourth Division camp on Goose Island, the soldiers in Colonel Whittaker's Sixth Regiment Kentucky Volunteer Infantry made a secret pledge "to kill Jeff Davis on sight." The Ninth Regiment Indiana Volunteer Infantry did not know that Nelson had planned to visit their camp after breakfast and present them with the stand of colors promised at Shiloh. Thomas Prickett belonged to that unit, and while he mourned the loss of a good "fighting man," it seemed that Nelson's notorious temper "probably gave Davis sufficient cause" to kill him.[49]

The Eighth Regiment Kentucky Volunteer Infantry had served under Nelson at Murfreesboro and McMinnville for a very short time, and their historian later held they were glad that "a tyrant of the 'first water' had been killed" for the abusive language he heaped on others. *New York Times* correspondent Franc Wilke had not forgotten the brief encounter at Corinth, and he believed the killing was probably not "without justifiable cause." Wilke considered Nelson "a brave soldier and fairly good leader . . . [but in this instance the] overbearing brute . . . found a man whom he could not insult with impunity." The One Hundred Fifth Regiment Ohio Volunteers had marched to the relief of the troops at Richmond, and they had no firsthand knowledge of Nelson when they let out boisterous cheers that conferred a voice of approval for that *every man* who had ever resented taking orders from a military tyrant.[50]

Ａt 9:00 A.M., Monday, September 29, 1862, the U.S. Military Telegraph
Service informed authorities in Washington that Brig. Gen. Jeff. C. Davis
had killed Maj. Gen. William Nelson and would be brought before a local
police court judge. Halleck's messenger, Colonel McKibbin, had not received
the wire to hold delivery, and one half-hour after Nelson's death, that overeager
courier handed Buell the orders that relieved him of command. It was nearing
noon when George H. Thomas tactfully informed Halleck it would be wrong
for him to assume command because he did not know enough about Buell's
preparations. Buell and Thomas waited patiently for additional instructions
from the War Department, and at 2:30 P.M., Buell advised he would leave for
Indianapolis as instructed. That brought an immediate reply from Halleck.
He professed to have no authority to rescind Buell's removal and requested
that both men consider the matter suspended until further notice.[1]

Due to the uncertainty of his situation, Buell made no effort to order a
general court-martial, appoint an investigator, or ask for written statements.
He did issue general orders that praised Nelson. Buell made no mention of
the circumstances surrounding the murder, but he noted no shortcoming offended Nelson more than the "disobedience or neglect of public duty." Years
later, Buell stated that while the iniquitous assassination deeply upset him, it
was simply impossible for him to defend Nelson's odious outbursts. Adjutant
James B. Fry considered Nelson's loss "the greatest the Army of the West
had yet received. He was everything himself—his staff were very young and
inexperienced but all gentlemen; he seemed to care more for that than any
knowledge they might have." Those officers needed Nelson more than ever,
and Buell selfishly replaced that warrior with Charles C. Gilbert, a insensitive
martinet who had lost the respect of the officers and men. Buell had originally

intended to move the twenty-five brigades of the Army of the Ohio in a three-column advance against Braxton Bragg in the morning. Now that would have to wait until Wednesday. At 9:00 P.M., he informed his corps commanders that Tuesday, September 30, would be devoted to memorializing Nelson.[2]

The next morning, friends of Nelson took one last look at his remains in the Grand Hall of the Galt House. At 3:00 P.M., the visitation ended. A military band and tolling church bells accompanied the solemn procession that moved the body over to Calvary Episcopal Church. Soldiers quietly arranged bouquets of flowers around a rich mahogany coffin with massive silver mountings. They placed Nelson's sword on the flag-draped casket, the music ended, and the crowd grew somber as Rev. Messrs. Newell and Lange began to read the Episcopal burial service.[3]

Dr. Talbot then spoke of how "Justice was . . . [Nelson's] distinctive characteristic. Ever ready to accord praise and promotion to the officer who did his duty, he fell like a thunderbolt on imbecility. Careful to a fault of the soldiers in his command, he lashed unsparingly at the official cause of their miseries. Indifferent to the praise or censure of those who surrounded him he marked out his course and he followed it despite every obstacle. Independent in the extreme, he sought the advice of a few, and would tolerate the interference of none." Talbot concluded by saying, "The General is dead! Let us remember his virtues and emulate them. Let us forget his faults and bury them . . . let us deal kindly with his memory."[4]

The *Indianapolis Journal* found it difficult to follow the last admonition. The paper noted that while Nelson "was a man of considerable ability," the basis for his fatal encounter with Davis arose from "language that no decent man will use to a dog." The *Louisville Democrat* said very little about Nelson other than "His loss at this time is very serious." The *New York Times* admired Nelson's "virtue and loyalty, and courage" and it deeply regretted that his "rude and offensive personal deportment" would very likely "exempt . . . his killing from the usual regrets and sympathies." The *Times* added that condemnation of Nelson's disrespectful behavior did not justify the terrible crime of murder, and Davis therefore "must meet a swift and relentless penalty."[5]

The *Cincinnati Times* disagreed. The paper believed Davis was right in killing an unqualified tyrant who had contributed nothing to the war effort. It supported that morally unsuitable position by stating:

> military power must be exercised in the same spirit as the principles upon which our government is based. The constitution guarantees the political equality of the citizen; an idea so deeply imprinted in the

minds of the people that they will not allow themselves to be subjected to the ways of a despotic power. When a citizen of the United States becomes a soldier, he willingly surrenders some of that freedom. It is essential for the manner in which an army must operate, but by no means does it make him a mere dog in the hands of superiors.

It is disgraceful that so many West Point officers suffer from a self-important *sense of aristocracy.* They [Nelson's superiors] have seriously compromised the effectiveness of the national army by sustaining the dignity of those who have a known record of misusing the power of command. *The General at Louisville* had no pressing need to defend his position, nor did the immediate situation [defense of the city] require him to protect the honor of soldiers who served under him.

The homicide at Louisville shows that hatred between merciless military aristocrats has reached the point where one general is willing to kill another. A review of Nelson's record shows why the public should have no sympathy for him. He did nothing to justify his promotion from a mere lieutenant in the navy to Major General of Volunteers. For no reason at all, this tyrant disgraced a subordinate officer simply because he enjoyed exercising power over him. When Davis sought an apology a week later, he received the answer in the form of insults that no man should have to take. Several slaps in the face forced Davis to engage in justifiable homicide to defend his honor. Under civil law, an intelligent and honorable judge would agree that the shooting was reasonable under the circumstances. However, if the final military decree should prove different, it will not overcome public sentiment for a man wrongly pushed beyond his endurance.[6]

At Louisville, mourners were waiting outside the church, and an African American man looked up at "a passing cloud [that] obscured the rays of the sun." He added his own rebuke of Nelson by noting how "De Lord am done gone and hid His face from the one who kicks the cullered folks and break dar bones." Major Generals Thomas L. Crittenden, Alexander McCook, and Gordon Granger were assisting Brigadier Generals James S. Jackson and Richard W. Johnson in placing the coffin in an elegant hearse decked with white plumes and drawn by four white horses. Jackson looked at Johnson and somberly asked, "Dick, who will be the next one?" Before he could answer, the "chief mourners," Maj. Charles H. Buford, Captains Cole, F. P. Gross, Martin, and Jones joined Chief of Staff Walworth Jenkins. Lieutenant Colonel Anderson led twelve companies of 101 men from the Ninth Regiment Indiana

Volunteer Infantry, the Sixth Regiment Ohio Volunteer Infantry, and the Twenty-fourth Regiment Ohio Volunteer Infantry. Captains Otis and Crittenden commanded two companies of the Fourth U.S. Cavalry, joined by Captain Mendenhall's Fourth U.S. Light Artillery Battery.[7]

The solemn sound of muffled drums started the procession slowly down Second Street. Captain John B. Davis, Second Regiment Minnesota Volunteer Infantry, a foster brother and the only family member present, joined Colonels Whitaker and Cotton behind a black servant who led a large gray warhorse with two swords draped over a saddle with boots reversed and fastened in the stirrups with crape. At Cave Hill Cemetery, the coffin was placed in a receiving vault that would hold the remains for eventual removal to Camp Dick Robinson. A squad of soldiers from the Sixth Ohio Infantry gave a twenty-one-gun salute, after which the men returned to prepare for the advance in the morning.[8]

At 6:00 A.M., Wednesday, Buell was about to order the Army of the Ohio forward when a messenger arrived with a note from Jeff. C. Davis. Captain J. M. Wright went to Davis's room and found him in a morbid state with nothing to say. The next day, Davis complained to Horatio Wright that "since my arrest [two days ago] I have confined myself to my room & find my health is somewhat failing by it."[9]

Governor Morton was in Indianapolis finalizing plans to leave for Washington, and his friends at the *Indianapolis Journal* sought to calm heated emotions by noting:

> some of our Indiana soldiers, to whom Nelson has always been especially odious, are foolish enough to express their satisfaction that he was shot by an Indiana man, and that some Kentuckians are foolish enough to try and turn these senseless boastings into a cause for State jealousy and dislike. Probably there is some secret secession feeling [Copperhead conspiracy] at the bottom of this attempt [of Indiana and Kentucky dissidents] to create ill will between the two States. But whether it starts in malice or mere folly, no sensible or true man can lend a moment's countenance to either side of the insane quarrel. There must be no State jealousy. . . . The death of Nelson was the result of a private difficulty in which there is no shade of State feeling, and nothing but wildness or madness can manufacture such feeling out of it. . . . General Boyle has always been one of Governor Morton's warmest friends, and one of the best friends to Indiana . . . [And while] General Buell . . . has few admirers in his own State [of Indiana]. . . . There is every reason . . . why all

attempts to create such [ill] feeling out of the death of General Nelson should be crushed, and none, not the shadow of one, for its continuance.[10]

On Friday, October 5, Buell was advancing his army toward the enemy when he telegraphed Halleck to ask that Davis be tried "by court martial or military commission . . . [in] Washington." The following Monday, Morton arrived there believing that Copperheads and Peace Democrats would stop at nothing to get rid of him. A highly publicized trial of Davis could play into the hands of those enemies, and the ardent politician called on all of his Republican friends to elicit support against a general court-martial. Powerful men like Halleck and Stanton were particularly sympathetic to those pleadings because they did not want to see anything get in the way of Morton's ability to supply troops.[11]

Tuesday afternoon, Buell reached the western outskirts of Perryville, Kentucky with no idea that his request for a court-martial of Davis had become ensnared in a web of intrigue. By noon Wednesday, Buell was engaged in serious fight with the enemy, but he decided against making a full assault until "all would . . . be ready" on Thursday. Two hours later, the Confederates pushed the Federal army back about one mile. John Marshall Harlan noted that "if Nelson had . . . been in command . . . he would not have awaited orders [from Buell], but would have regarded the [fighting] . . . as sufficient order . . . [to] 'go in' and assist in defeating the enemy." Nelson's good friends James S. Jackson and William R. Terrill were on the left, and shortly after 3:00 P.M., enemy fire struck and killed Jackson. Terrill met a similar fate when he tried to rally his brigade at 3:55. Three hours later, the bloodiest battle of the Civil War in Kentucky was over. Buell made no effort to go after Bragg, and to make matters worse, he waited until Friday, October 10, 1862, to start a half-hearted pursuit.[12]

After the bloody fighting at Perryville, the ill will between the troops loyal to Nelson and those loyal to Davis began to wane, and Horatio Wright released Davis from close arrest on October 13, 1862. With no explanation for his reasons, Wright also concluded that Davis killed Nelson in self-defense. He then dismissed the matter because there were no specifications and charges against Davis. That decision suggests he knew nothing about Buell's request to hold a trial in Washington and it insinuates that Wright was under the unseen influence of powerful men who sympathized with Davis.[13]

The press suspected that President Lincoln would not push for a military court-martial because that would go against a public who loathed military tyrants. The fourth estate also supposed a civilian court would call the killing of Nelson justified. That reasoning encouraged the *Indianapolis Journal* to state the best way for military authorities to avoid responsibility for the tragedy was to allow civilian authorities in Jefferson County, Kentucky, to proceed with the case. On Tuesday, October 21, 1862, many of the papers simply announced, "Gen. Jeff. C. Davis, who killed Gen. Nelson, has been released from arrest, and ordered to report for duty at Cincinnati." The next day, Department of the Ohio Special Orders No. 78 assigned "the gallant Indianan" to succeed the hard-edged Gordon Granger as commander of the Army of Kentucky in Covington, Kentucky.[14]

Secretary Chase was appalled by this, and on Thursday, October 23, 1862, he wrote President Lincoln:

> Under no circumstances whatever, in my judgment, can personal violence by one officer to another—much less the killing of one officer by another,—be passed over without the arrest and trial of the offender, except at the cost of serious detriment to the service & serious injury to the respect due you as Commander in Chief. . . . The published facts . . . do not seem to warrant it. . . . These circumstances, I think, imperatively demand a Court Martial. Under the Common Law the act is murder; under our law manslaughter; under both, a crime. Nelson was the superior officer of Davis . . . Nelson was imperious, overbearing, arrogant, insulting . . . [but, those faults should] not be received as grounds for dispensing with a trial . . . should it not be remembered how generous, patriotic & brave a man was killed? You cannot have forgotten—I never shall—how disinterestedly he left his proper sphere of service . . . in our darkest day . . . [and] saved the state from rebel intimidation & probably from secession. . . . I do not exaggerate it or its value. . . . Can it be that . . . the affair is to be passed over . . . as an ordinary & insignificant occurrence?[15]

The shooting of the unarmed Nelson belonged under the jurisdiction of Article 9 of the Uniform Code of Military Justice, and the *Cincinnati Gazette* wrongly attacked the victim by saying he intentionally misused that statute to intimidate those below him. An honest examination would have revealed the military has an obligation to make soldiers aware of those offenses that call for the death penalty. The code states, "any officer or soldier who shall strike his superior officer, or draw or lift up any weapon, or offer any violence against him, being in the execution of his office, on any pretense whatsoever, or shall disobey any lawful command of this superior officer, shall suffer death, or such punishment as shall according to the nature of the offense, be inflicted upon him by the sentence of court-martial." A ruling by the president of the court required a concurrence by two-thirds of the court, a final review, and approval by the department commander.[16]

Incredibly, the murder of an unarmed superior officer by a subordinate officer was in the hands of the Jefferson County grand jury. This was clearly a matter for the Federal government to decide, and at a Friday cabinet meeting Salmon P. Chase and Montgomery Blair recommended military involvement. Secretary Seward and Secretary of the Navy Gideon Wells believed that at the minimum there should be a court of inquiry. Morton's friend and Halleck's superior, Secretary of War Stanton, suggested that maybe a government inquiry would be appropriate if needed. On Monday, October 27, 1862, nothing had been decided when the Jefferson County grand jury issued an indictment for manslaughter. Thomas W. Gibson and his noted law partner, William P. Thomasson, became securities on a $5,000 bond that released Davis. On Wednesday, October 29, Special Orders No. 90 called for Davis to join the newly formed Army of the Cumberland.[17]

Weeks later, Mary Bryson Nelson penned a letter to a friend in Terre Haute that described her life as the daughter of a foreign minister in Santiago, Chile. Mary further explained, "Although I am so far away from the battle field . . . I feel for the men that fall as much as you possibly can who are so near. . . . I look forward with trembling heart for the news that is to come in an hour . . . [and] hope that none of my dear Uncles have fallen or any of my friends." Later in the day, Mary added a postscript about her "dear uncle William's death. We have not heard how it occured, the despach only says, that he was killed by J. C. Davis. O' I shall hate that man and all connected with him from this day until the end."[18]

Nothing short of swift and sure victory could console the public, and Mary would find her deceased uncle was an ideal scapegoat for a press that felt duty-bound to attack the conceited behavior of officers who trampled on the basic dignity of volunteers. The *Evening Bulletin* in St. Louis declared, "Opinion of the Press on Gen. Nelson's Homicide—'Served him Right.'" In New York, the *World* wrongly informed its audience that Nelson was a despot who had "no friends to mourn" him, and his passing "can barely atone for the wrong and injury he has inflicted."[19]

Those who served with Nelson did not forsake him. On Christmas Day, 1862, Col. James P. Fyffe presented the men of the Fifty-ninth Regiment Ohio Volunteer Infantry with a "beautiful stand of colors" that had "Ivy Creek, Shiloh, Corinth, Perryville, [and] Crab Orchard [emblazoned] upon its shining folds." The former commander remarked how "our hearts grow sad when we remember Nelson." During the following week, the Army of the Cumberland defeated the Confederates in a series of hard-fought battles at Murfreesboro (Stones River). The Fourth Division had become the Second Division under John M. Palmer, and he noted that those men bore Nelson's spirit and determination in their actions. Murfreesboro/Stones River also inspired Maj. Gen. William S. Rosecrans to recommend that Jefferson C. Davis, Charles Cruft, John M. Palmer, and others become "major-generals in our service."[20]

The Emancipation Proclamation was to go into effect on January 1, 1863, and some feared that when the General Assembly convened on that date, Kentucky slaveholders would lead the commonwealth into an alliance with the states that were in rebellion. Union men made sure that did not happen. During the second week of the session, they also noted that just before the planned offensive into the Chaplin Hills (Perryville), Maj. Gen. William Nelson had "repeatedly expressed his earnest desire that should he fall in battle, he wanted to be buried at Camp Dick Robinson." In addition to his uncle-in-law, he had asked Brig. Gen. John S. Jackson, Maj. Gen. Thomas L. Crittenden, and Richard Henry Crittenden to honor that request. On January 11, Jeremiah T. Boyle presented a letter to Joshua F. Bell in the Kentucky House of Representatives. It called Nelson a "great man, and a noble self-sacrificing patriot, of whom the state was justly proud." Boyle added that Richard "Dick" Robinson had offered to donate one acre and $1,000 to erect an appropriate monument. On January 14, John W. Finnell presented a joint resolution that called for a committee of two from the Senate and three from the House to arrange for the removal of the remains from Cave Hill Cemetery to Camp Dick Robinson.[21]

In February, Capt. Oliver D. Greene commented to Admiral Samuel Du Pont that "if it were not for Nelson," Kentucky would now be the same battleground as Tennessee. The Department of the Ohio was in serious disarray under Horatio G. Wright, and Lincoln trusted that while Maj. Gen. Ambrose E. Burnside had failed miserably as McClellan's replacement, he could instill new life in that department. The Senate refused to confirm Wright's promotion, he reverted to brigadier general, and on March 25, 1863, Burnside relieved him of command. Lincoln then ordered a massive reorganization of the Federal army, and Wright became one of many who benefited from that action. Rosecrans used the occasion to inform Lincoln that the "brave and true" Jeff. C. Davis had been "in fifteen successful battles since Sumter" and deserved the rank of major general. The president said nothing about the fact that Davis remained under indictment, and he simply advised there were not enough positions available to promote everyone.[22]

Plans to reinstitute the long-delayed advance against Knoxville were underway, and to support that initiative a large depot was under construction five miles south of Nicholasville, Kentucky. Brig. Gen. Speed S. Fry had established a camp just north of Hickman Bridge, and Burnside intended to move the Cincinnati headquarters of the Department of the Ohio to that locale on June 4. The *Louisville Journal* reported, "Recruiting officers are busily engaged in raising squads, companies and battalions all have orders to report promptly to Camp Speed Fry." It was also noted there were plans to re-inter Nelson's remains at Camp Dick Robinson on June 14.[23]

The intent to honor those wishes conflicted with the immediate circumstances, and a curiously veiled conscience saw that Camp Speed Fry became a memorial to Nelson on June 12, 1863. General Orders No. 99 declared, "In honor of the memory of Major General William Nelson, the Headquarters' Camp near Hickman's Bridge, Ky will be called Camp Nelson." The press remained strangely quiet until they learned the Federal government planned to arm and train African American soldiers at this facility. The shock of that development took precedence over news that "General Jefferson C. Davis . . . was let off without punishment by a Military Court of Inquiry . . . [but will] be tried for manslaughter at the next term of the Louisville Circuit Court."[24]

Kentuckians were far more alarmed over the prospect that African Americans were being empowered by Federal government actions. In the midst of the growing turmoil, Nelson cohorts Thomas E. Bramlette and Richard T. Jacob were elected governor and lieutenant governor on August 3, 1863. Several weeks later, Burnside started the long-sought advance into East Tennessee, and that cleared the way to re-inter Nelson's remains at Camp Dick Robinson. When the cortège arrived in Frankfort on August 20, the train paused before an adoring crowd while "the bells in the city were tolled—minute guns were fired from an adjoining hill, and every demonstration of respect shown, with the shortness of time allowed." An admiring observer remarked that history would put "a proper and very high estimate upon his [Nelson's] service and his noble exertions to preserve and defend the honor and loyalty of his State."[25]

At 11:00 A.M. Thursday, a special gun salute greeted the train as it pulled into Lexington. A committee of citizens headed by Dr. Robert Peter and Benjamin Gratz greeted the accompanying lawmakers, John W. Finnell, Joshua Fry Bell, Joshua Tevis, Thornton F. Marshall, and George Denny. The First Regiment Ohio Volunteer Infantry and Forty-eighth Regiment Pennsylvania Volunteer Infantry led the grand procession to the outskirts of town, where a two-hundred-man detail from the Twentieth Regiment Michigan Volunteer Infantry took control of the hearse. Those new troops had come up from Nicholasville with a complement of men from other regiments, and on Friday, August 21, they crossed Hickman's Bridge and proceeded to Camp Dick Robinson. The 11:00 A.M. memorial service turned out to be "the largest concourse ever assembled in Garrard County." Georgetown College president Duncan Robertson Campbell reminded the crowd, "Only those who knew Nelson well can have any idea of the grasp and varied power of his great intellect, or of his vast and well-digested stores of knowledge on almost every subject of interest."[26]

That fall, John Fitch, the former provost judge of the Army of the Cumberland, published the *Annals of the Army of the Cumberland*. The first three editions of this popular work attributed the authorship to "an officer" who was eager to clothe his subjects with honor and respectability. It was a combination unit history and souvenir book filled with biographies. The piece on Jefferson C. Davis said he had "an unfortunate personal difficulty . . . which resulted in the death of" Nelson. It said nothing about the indictment against Davis that continued to go on and off the docket of the Jefferson County Circuit Court until May 24, 1864. At that time, James Speed asked for removal with leave to reinstate, and that ended the matter for all time.[27]

That October, John M. Stockton corresponded with President Lincoln on behalf of his wife, "the only sister" of Nelson. He stated Matilda Stockton wanted to settle the William Nelson estate, and she "would not trouble you—knowing that every moment of your time is occupied—but, that, she has been unable after repeated applications" to have his account with the government audited. On November 3, 1864, E. B. French of the Second Auditors Office endorsed the query. He stated that in December 1863 (eleven months prior), the third auditor and the commissary general found Nelson indebted to the United States for $482,234.43 in supplies and equipment, and nothing would be done until there was a resolution.[28]

There was still no progress in the matter when Robert E. Lee surrendered to Ulysses S. Grant at Appomattox Court House on April 9, 1865. Governmental indecision also prevented Richard Robinson from receiving reimbursement for the use of his property, and that precluded him from erecting the promised flagpole at Nelson's gravesite. Officials now found a way to provide a 130-foot staff, and on July 4, Nelson's friends and family gathered at Camp Dick Robinson to watch "Old Glory" hoisted up the grand pole. Kentuckians were seething over Federal policies, and the following spring, workers at Camp Nelson started dismantling the buildings and leveling the fortifications. The next year an anonymous band of citizens gave notice they would cut down the national flag beside Nelson's grave. That group followed through with the threat on the night of June 18, 1867. At Lexington, the *Kentucky Statesman* declared that such actions would doom the commonwealth "to be ruled by men who will lay" the honor of the state "in the dust by insulting the grave of a son you delighted in." When Camp Nelson became a national cemetery the following year, no one suggested that a small corner of that divisive spot become the final resting place for the man who "saved Kentucky from the vortex of rebellion."[29]

In Washington, the commissary general and quartermaster general continued to look for answers to "certain inquiries" about Nelson's debt. Eventually, Charles H. Brown of the Second Auditor's Office resolved the matter, and Matilda Stockton turned her attention to the isolated burial plot at Camp Dick Robinson. At the end of February 1872, she had her brother's remains exhumed, and on Friday morning, March 8, 1872, the family plot at Maysville Cemetery became the final resting place for William Nelson.[30]

Five years later, Kentucky legislators passed a $10,000 appropriation to erect a monument to John C. Breckinridge. Cassius Marcellus Clay caustically noted how an earlier resolution for a similar sum to honor Nelson had been "voted down with contempt and indignation!" Clay believed it was wrong to bestow honor on "those who . . . failed in the admitted duties of civilized society." However, this veteran of several notorious fights said nothing about the failure to prosecute Davis for killing Nelson in cold blood.[31]

Clay and the many like him accepted the underlying premise behind honor killings. They fully understood what Davis meant when he told James Merriwether he "had to do it." Davis said that for a member of "the regular army . . . not to resent an insult of that kind would make me . . . be as [low as] the dog that sleeps under my father's floor." Likewise, an aide to Governor Morton had informed Alf Burnett that if Davis had not taken the action, he "would have deserved to be shot himself." William Tecumseh Sherman shared with his wife, "I cannot justify the act [of murder], but do not condemn it." James Steedman had no ax to grind with either man, and he indicated there was universal sorrow "that Nelson was killed, but . . . Davis could not do anything else." If Davis had accepted being struck in the face, "he would have been disgraced and compelled to leave the army." Those comments and others like them led historian Nathaniel Southgate Shaler to conclude that Davis's "brother soldiers generally approved" of the cold-blooded assassination because "in war the personal dignity of officers and men must be preserved. It cannot be kept without such cruel customs."[32]

In his memoirs, Phil Sheridan said he considered the Nelson-Davis affair a mystery shrouded by "a hundred conflicting stories." Sheridan then went to the heart of the problem by saying, "It now appears . . . Davis threw a small paper ball . . . into Nelson's face and this insult was returned by Nelson slapping Davis in the face." Two-decades had gone by before James B. Fry finally revealed that vital detail in *Killed by a Brother Soldier*. In *Military Miscellanies*, he further noted that Shaler's "cruel customs" argument was wrong because soldiers have "little excuse for resorting to the pistol or bowie-knife. . . . They are not only protected by the civil code, but the more stringent military code, to which they are pledged by the oath of office, and by duty to their country." Richard W. Johnson employed that same reasoning when he stated:

> Military law, as he [Davis] well knew, offered prompt and ample re-dress for all the wrong Nelson had done to him at their first meeting [September 22]. But he [Davis] made no appeal to law. On the contrary, he deliberately took all law into his own hands. Whether he [Davis] proceeded solely on his own judgment or was advised and incited by others is not positively known, but I do not doubt that Morton, and perhaps others without foreseeing the fatal consequences, encouraged Davis to insult Nelson publicly for the wrong done in an official in-terview. One step led to another in the attempt to place and fix insult, until the end was Nelson's violent death [a week later].[33]

Buell believed the "fine Italian hand of Morton" sowed the "seeds of mis-chief" that undermined the "authority of the general government." He sur-mised the shameful disregard for prosecuting Davis was "made virtually, if not actually, at his [Morton's] direction." Supreme Court Justice John Marshall Harlan supported that position when he later noted, "Strenuous efforts were made by Gov. Morton of Indiana for his [Davis's] protection."[34]

Morton was a biased politician, but he did not engage in a plot to kill Nelson. He and his allies saw an urgent need to defend against the intrigues of Southern sympathizers who wanted him removed from office. There is no record of what occurred with Washington officials. They were under assault by a public that had come to loath the arrogant style of military leadership that Nelson represented. Buell was under enormous pressure to defeat the Confederate invaders, and he rightfully handed the matter of a trial over to Halleck in Washington. The case went to Wright, who dismissed everything. Davis treated that undeserved reprieve like someone who thought he should be exempt from any regrets that normally come with taking the life of another. If it were not for Congress and the unseen guardians of justice in the War

Department, Davis might have attained what he coveted most: an appointment to major general before he died on November 30, 1879, at age fifty-one.[35]

At the turn of the twentieth century the *Boston Globe's* daily lesson in history correctly noted that the failure to prosecute Davis was an aberration that did not represent the true nature of our "civil institutions." The writer did not know the whole story, and it was wrongly surmised that the reason the matter went unpunished was "public opinion" in Kentucky tolerated murderous "*affairs of honor.*"[36]

That misunderstanding was just one of many that gave us a meager appreciation for the true nature of a tragic event with no parallel in American military history. Worse yet, those incomplete pieces provided a poor understanding of Nelson's temperament, skills, and contributions. This was "a man of real culture, great strength of character, and many endurable traits." Abraham Lincoln and other Washington leaders believed Nelson had the pedigree and native intelligence, the experience and daring that would keep his native state loyal to the Union. Salmon P. Chase said he could never forget how fairly Nelson "left his proper sphere of service. . . . [to] save the state [of Kentucky] from rebel intimidation & probably from secession. . . . I do not exaggerate it or its value." Selflessness was an extraordinarily important factor in his becoming a Civil War general. Admiral Daniel Ammen said that Nelson simply wanted "to be useful to his country rather than great." Longtime aide Lt. Ben F. Horton declared, "No man ever had more at heart the good of the country."[37]

As a young man, Nelson possessed the uncommon courage, aptitude, and character to go from "ship to ship" and remain at sea. His tireless conduct made his men second to none in the iron-fisted business of war, and after death, it was still apparent they had "caught a large part of his heroic and unconquerable spirit." Adjutant Oliver D. Greene was a regular army officer who was truly impressed with the way this bold, resolute commander threw "himself into every enterprise." Lieutenant Horton admired the "energetic, industrious" way in which Nelson superintended the men and insisted they be extraordinarily alert and ready for action. Horton was among the novices that Nelson chose for their impeccable manners, and it astounded West Point–trained James B. Fry to see a former navy lieutenant make up for the shortcomings of those aides by taking on the entire workload.[38]

Nelson's exposure to the republican principles espoused by the Young Americans and his involvement with European revolutionary Louis Kossuth led him to embrace the Democratic Party. Duty to his country took precedence over any political feelings, and in the daring process of arming loyal Kentuckians and establishing Camp Dick Robinson, this brash navy lieutenant earned the admiration and respect of Abraham Lincoln, Salmon P. Chase, and various other national leaders. Because Nelson's accomplishments spoke louder than the negativity of his detractors, those men endorsed his appointments to brigadier general and major general.

Over the course of the next year, this callous veteran of the Old Navy failed to master the art of grace under pressure, an attribute seen in those who attain the mantle of greatness. Stanley Matthews despised his brut manner, but he came to admire how the high-spirited Nelson turned the Fourth Division into a supremely confident fighting machine. Historian Nathaniel S. Shaler was close to Lew Wallace, and he characterized Nelson as "able but erratic" and therefore unqualified for the frenzied nature of independent command. Regular army officer Charles C. Gilbert served with Nelson, and he declared this was someone who was well suited "for the exercise of separate command." Buell stated, "No [other] man seemed . . . so suitable for the emergency" when the Confederates invaded Kentucky. Captain Greene declared that Nelson's military skills were "a source of wonder to us West Point gentlemen." Likewise, William B. Hazen said there was no equal to Nelson when it came to the "quick perception and industry, so necessary for a commander in the field." James B. Fry summed it up when he said the loss of this former navy lieutenant was "the greatest the Army of the West had yet received."[39]

In our nation's journey to achieve the noble aspirations of the founding fathers, a hot-blooded quarterdeck general and other imperfect patriots triumphed over the temporary obstructions of violence, discord, and injustice. With Nelson, the reality often found in the middle of opposing extremes succumbed to the intense loathing aimed at military tyrants in general. The foregoing biography has removed that problem, and it allows us to reach useful conclusions that honor our heritage with dignity and respect.

Abbreviations / Notes / Bibliography / Index

Abbreviations

ALP/LOC Abraham Lincoln Papers at the Library of Congress, Series 1, General Correspondence, 1833–1916, Washington, D.C.

Ammen Diary Diary of Jacob Ammen, *OR*, Series 1, 10 (1): 329-37.

CINHS Cincinnati Historical Society.

DANFS *Dictionary of American Naval Fighting Ships.* 9 vols. Washington, D.C.: United States Naval History Division, 1959–91.

FCHQ *Filson Club History Quarterly*, Filson Historical Society, Louisville, Kentucky.

FHS Filson Historical Society, Louisville, Kentucky.

KDLSA Kentucky Department of Libraries and State Archives, Frankfort.

KHS Kentucky Historical Society, Frankfort.

LOC Library of Congress, Washington, D.C.

NA National Archives.

NAB National Archives Building, Washington, D.C.

NNR-MAW *Nile's National Register*, "The Mexican-American War and the Media, 1845–48." Digital online project of Virginia Tech, Blacksburg.

OR United States War Department, *The War of the Rebellion: A Compilation of the Records of the Union and Confederate Armies*, series 1–3, 70 vols., 128 serials. Washington, D.C.: GPO, 1880–1901. Citation by series, volume, part, and page.

ORN United States War Department, *Official Records of the Union and Confederate Navies in the War of the Rebellion*, series 1, vols. 1–27, series 2, vols. 1–3. Washington, D.C.: GPO, 1894–1922. Citation by series, volume, part, and page.

RKHS *Register of the Kentucky Historical Society*, Kentucky Historical Society, Frankfort.

SOR *Supplement to the Official Records of the Union and Confederate Armies*, edited by Janet B. Hewett et al., 100 vols. Wilmington, N.C.: Broadfoot Pub. Co., 1994–2006.

UK-SC University of Kentucky Special Collections, King Library, Lexington.

Notes

PREFACE

1. Robert M. Kelly, "Holding Kentucky for the Union," in *Battles and Leaders of the Civil War*, ed. Robert Underwood Johnson and Clarence C. Buel (New York, 1886), 1:375 (first two quotations); E. Hannaford, *The Story of a Regiment: A History of the Campaigns and Association in the Field of the Sixth Regiment Ohio Volunteer Infantry* (Cincinnati, 1868), 367 (second two quotations); Peter Cozzens and Robert I. Girardi, eds., *The Military Memoirs of General John Pope* (Chapel Hill, 1998), 102 (last two quotations).

2. Alf Burnett, *Incidents of the War: Humorous, Pathetic, and Descriptive* (Cincinnati, 1863), 28 ("noble, warm-hearted"); Daniel Stevenson, "General Nelson, Kentucky, and Lincoln Guns," *Magazine of American History* 10 (August 1883): 138 ("extraordinary character"); *Biographical Encyclopedia of Kentucky* (Cincinnati, 1878), 67 ("absolutely fearless"); "Coming Up at Shiloh," *Continental Monthly* 6 (October 1864): 400 ("the very foremost of Kentucky's loyal sons"); William H. Perrin, ed., *History of Bourbon, Scott, Harrison, and Nicholas Counties, Kentucky* (Chicago, 1882), 240 ("too recent").

3. John H. Fahey, M.D., "The 'Fighting Doctor': Bernard John Dowling Irwin in the Civil War," *North & South* 9 (March 2006): 46 (quotation); James B. Fry in *Military Miscellanies* (New York, 1889), 501, referred to this February 23, 1885, newspaper account when he said it was "one of the latest [inaccurate stories from] . . . the Philadelphia Press." A reprint from the *Toledo Blade* quoted Gen. James B. Steedman as saying he saw Gov. Oliver P. Morton hand the gun to Davis.

4. *National Tribune*, December 4, 1913 (quotation).

5. *Cincinnati Commercial*, November 18, 1861 (quotation); Jack T. Hutchinson, "Bluegrass and Mountain Laurel: The Story of Kentucky in the Civil War," *Cincinnati Civil War Round Table* (2000), 14–15.

1. THE ROOTS OF IMPERFECTION

1. Henry Villard, *The Memoirs of Henry Villard: Journalist and Financier, 1835–1900*, 2 vols. (New York, 1969), 1:205; Cozzens and Girardi, *Military Memoirs of General John Pope*, 102; *Brooklyn Eagle*, April 26, 1862 (last quotation).

2. Burnett, *Incidents*, 32–35 (quotations).

3. Ibid., 36 (first quotation); Dr. [M. F.] Adamson, "Anderson Doniphan, M.D.," *Mason County Genealogical Society* 9 (1991); Doniphan Vertical File, KHS (second quotation); Frances Frazee Hamilton, *Ancestral Lines of the Doniphan, Frazee and Hamilton Families* (Greenfield, Ind., 1928), 516 (third quotation).

4. W. D. Frazee, *Reminiscences and Sermons* (Nashville, 1898); Doniphan Vertical File, KHS; Hamilton, *Ancestral Lines*, 511–13, 517.

5. Frazee, *Reminiscences*; Rosemarie Bonwell Pell, *Bracken County, Kentucky, Tax Lists, 1797–1826*, 2 vols. (Brooksville, 2002), 1:79; *Pennsylvania Correspondent and*

Farmer's Almanac, July 16, 1805; Bracken County Deed Books B: 98 and D: 105, Brooksville, Ky., KDLSA; Augusta Town Council, Minute Books, 2 vols., Municipal Offices, Augusta, Ky, 1:7; Caroline R. Miller, *African-American Records: Bracken County, Kentucky, 1797–1999*, 2 vols. (Brooksville, Ky., 1999), 1:133.

6. Walter R. Borneman, *1812: The War That Forged a Nation* (New York, 2004), 57, 158–61; Anderson C. Quisenberry, *Kentucky in the War of 1812* (Frankfort, 1915), 86–87, 98–99, 188.

7. Bracken County Deed Book E: 300 (first quotation), 336, KDLSA; Pell, *Bracken County Tax Lists*, 2:332, 362; Augusta Town Council, Minute Book 1:72; Sherry Sawyers et al., *Mason County, Kentucky, Marriage Bonds and Permissive Notes*, 8 vols. (N.p., 199?), 2:112 (second quotation).

8. Hamilton, *Ancestral Lines*, 33 (quotation); Sawyers et al., *Mason County Marriage Bonds*, 3:7; Karen Mauer Green, *The Kentucky Gazette, 1801–1820* (Baltimore, 1985), 286, 301; Annella Louise Rose, *Fayette County Census, 1820–1850* (Utica, 1982), 28, 166.

9. Richard H. Collins and Lewis Collins, *History of Kentucky*, 2 vols., 1874 (reprint, Berea, 1976) 2:547; *Maysville Eagle*, May 27, 1827 (quotation); Mason County Will Book H: 96, KDLSA. An especially bright blue church steeple led to the name of the Presbyterian church. It burned to the ground during a devastating fire that destroyed much of Second Street in April 1850. The Opera House at 116 West Second Street replaced the building.

10. *Lexington (Ky.) Reporter*, April 11, 1827.

11. Benjamin Drake and E. D. Mansfield, *Cincinnati in 1826* (Cincinnati, 1827), 96 (first quotation). The South did not have a state military school until the founding of Virginia Military Institute in March 1839.

12. A. N. Ellis, "Sketch of the Life of William Nelson," in *The Biographical Cyclopedia and Portrait Gallery with a Historical Sketch of the State of Ohio* (Cincinnati, 1894), 5:1290–1301. Also see the 37-page extract at CINHS; and Dr. A. M. [N] Ellis, "Major General William Nelson," *RKHS* 7 (May 1906), 56 (quotation); App. #247 Anderson D. Nelson, U.S. Military Academy Cadet Application Papers, 1805–66, Publication No. 000119677, M688, Roll 106, RG 94, NAB; George W. Cullum, *Biographical Register of the Officers and Cadets of the United States Military Academy at West Point from Its Establishment in 1802 to 1890, with the Early History of the Untied States Military Academy*, 3rd ed., 3 vols. (New York, 1891), 1:69–70.

13. Collins and Collins, *History of Kentucky*, 2:581 (first quotation); Ellis, "Major General William Nelson," 56–58 (second and third quotations); Mason County Court Order Book M: 514. During that same 1836–37 school year, 14-year-old Hiram Ulysses Grant also attended the academy; see Ulysses S. Grant, *Personal Memoirs of U. S. Grant*, 2 vols. (New York, 1885–86), 1:17.

14. *Catalogue of the Officers and Students of Norwich University for the Academic Year 1836–37* (Montpelier, 1837), 6, 12–14, Kreitzberg Library Special Collections, Norwich University. Under criminal law, hazing is called assault and battery and/or the intent to inflict emotional distress. This serious national issue is an ongoing problem at Norwich University; see "Despite Efforts by Norwich University, Hazing Persists," *Barre-Montpelier (Vt.) Times Argus*, September 22, 2008; also see

Brueckner v. Norwich University (97–3960): 169 Vt. 118: 730. A. 2d 1086. Hazing was well entrenched in our military schools, and it would be a gross injustice to this story to ignore the practice because of a lack of specific records. The comments on bullying come from the study of a variety of sources that have delved into the psychology of this peculiar rite of passage. In addition, the author is personally acquainted with fraternity and military hazing in some of its worse forms.

15. N. L. Sheldon, "Norwich University," *New England Magazine* n.s. 20 (March 1899): 77; Harry Sholk, *Drumbeats in the Valley: A Story of Life at Norwich University in the Early Nineteenth Century* (Haverford, Pa., 2004), 37.

16. Sholk, *Drumbeats in the Valley*, 43 (lecture quotations), 67; *Catalogue of the Officers and Cadets of Norwich University for the Academic Years 1838–41* (Hanover, N.H., 1841), 16 (drill quotation), Kreitzberg Library Special Collections, Norwich University.

17. *Catalogue, Norwich University, 1838–41*, 14; Abstracts of Service Records of Naval Officers 1798–1893, 1, July 1840–December 1845, Microfilm Publication No. 330, Roll 6, RG 45, NAB; Letters Received Accepting Appointments as Commissioned and Warrant Officers, April 20, 1812–October 1864, entry 125, RG 45, NAB.

18. Misc. Records, U.S. Navy, 1789–1925, Appointments, Orders, and Resignations, Microfilm Publication T829, entry 385, roll 394, Oct. 20, 1838–Oct. 12, 1840, v. 17:3, 418½; entry 386, roll 395, Oct. 12, 1840–Feb. 13, 1842, v. 18:70, RG 45, NAB; Colyer Meriwether, *Raphael Semmes* (Philadelphia, 1913), 15 (quotation).

19. Herman Melville, *White-Jacket, or The World in a Man-of-War* (Boston, 1850), 206–7; Frederick Marryat, *Peter Simple and the Three Cutters* (London, 1834), 148 (quotations). The latter is a novel about a British midshipman in the Napoleonic Wars.

20. *DANFS*, 8:530.

21. James E. Valle, *Rocks and Shoals: Naval Discipline in the Age of Fighting Sail* (Annapolis, 1980), 14–16, 18; Melville, *White-Jacket*, 322–23, 326; Walter Colton, *Deck and Port; or, Incidents of a Cruise in the United States Frigate Congress to California. With sketches of Rio Janeiro, Valparaiso, Lima, Honolulu, and San Francisco*(New York, 1850; reprint, Michigan Historical Reprint Series, 2005), 191–92 (grog quotation); Richard LeRoy Parker, "Cruizing under the 'Stars and Stripes': Being the Private Journal of Richard LeRoy Parker, 1842–1861," 36 (last quotation), Accession 1962–00112R, Rare Books and Manuscripts, Special Collections Library, Pennsylvania State University.

22. *DANFS*, 8:530; *Yorktown* Log Book No. 1 (January 1, 1842–March 5, 1843), Records of the Bureau of Naval Personnel 1798–1991, Logs of U.S. Naval Ships and Stations, 1801–1946, RG 24, NAB (hereafter cited by name of ship, log book number if available, dates, RG 24, NAB); *Yorktown* (Sloop of War), Vertical Files, U.S. Naval Academy, Annapolis, Md.; *Madisonian* (Washington, D.C.), February 26, 1842 (quotations).

23. Allen Johnson and Dumas Malone, eds., *Dictionary of American Biography* (New York: Charles Scribner's Sons, 1964), 6:90–91; Arthur A. Griese, "A Louisville Tragedy: 1862," *FCHQ* 26 (April 1952), 151; Robert Erwin Johnson, *Thence Round Cape Horn: The Story of United States Naval Forces on Pacific Station, 1818–1923* (Annapolis, 1963), 59–65.

24. R. E. Johnson, *Thence Round Cape Horn*, 225–28; R. H. Dana Jr., *Two Years before the Mast* (New York, 1909), 35–36 (first quotation); Melville, *White-Jacket*, 64–65, 136, 352 (second and fourth quotations); Valle, *Rocks and Shoals*, 3–4, 28 (third quotation), 29.

25. Valle, *Rocks and Shoals*, 108–10; Wikipedia, s.v. "USS *Somers*," <http://www.google.com/search?hl=en&client=firefox-a&rls=org.mozilla%3Aen-US%3-Aofficial&channel=s&> (accessed June 14, 2010). Herman Melville served as a seaman aboard the *United States* in 1843–44. His familiarity with flogging abuses ended up in *White-Jacket*, a politically charged novel that was supplied to members of the U.S. Congress for the express purpose of having flogging outlawed.

26. Griese, "A Louisville Tragedy," 151; *Shark* (Schooner), Vertical Files, U.S. Naval Academy, Annapolis, Md.; R. E. Johnson *Thence Round Cape Horn*, 67; Wikipedia, s.v. "Thomas ap Jones," <http://www.google.com/search?hl=en&client=firefox-a&rls=org.mozilla%3Aen-US%3Aofficial&channel=s&q=Commodore+Thomas+Ap+Jones&btnG=Search&aq=f&aqi=&aql=&oq=&gs_rfai=>. Accessed June 14, 2010. A court-martial found Jones guilty of charges relating to the oppression of junior officers and relieved him of command for two and a half years. That conviction of a tyrant gave notice to those who were reluctant to change that they would have to answer for their actions if they remained the same.

27. *Erie* Log Book No. 18 (April 6, 1844–August 26, 1845), RG 24, NAB (quotation); *DANFS*, 2:363, 387–88; William Maxwell Wood, "The Late Commodore Dallas," *Southern Literary Magazine* 11 (January 1845): 22–23; Griese, "A Louisville Tragedy," 151.

28. Griese, "A Louisville Tragedy," 151. Polk was the country's first Young America president. That vaguely defined movement was championed by John L. O'Sullivan and other literati who were interested in promoting a progressive Democratic Party. In the July–August 1845 issue of the *Democratic Review*, O'Sullivan declared it was "our manifest destiny to overspread the continent." The idea gained wide attention when O'Sullivan used it again to address the boundary dispute over the Oregon territory in the *New York Morning News* on December 27, 1845; see Wikipedia, s.v. "John L. O'Sullivan," <http://en.wikipedia.org/wiki/John_L._O%27Sullivan>.

29. Griese, "A Louisville Tragedy," 151; Mason County Cemetery Records, Mason County Historical Society, Maysville, Ky.; Johnson and Malone, *Dictionary of American Biography*, 1:566, 2:206; *Southern Patriot* (Charleston, S.C.), July 24, 1845; James C. Bradford, ed., *Captains of the Old Steam Navy: Makers of the American Naval Tradition, 1840–1880* (Annapolis, 1986), 94, 96 (quotation).

30. James Russell Soley, *Historical Sketch of the United States Naval Academy* (Washington, 1876), 69–70 (school quotations), 81, 124; Charles Todorich, *The Spirited Years: A History of the Antebellum Naval Academy* (Annapolis, 1984), 32–33, 44; Jack Sweetman, *The U.S. Naval Academy: An Illustrated History*, 2nd ed. (Annapolis, 1979), 26; William Harwar Parker, *Recollections of a Naval Officer, 1846–1865* (New York, 1883), 121 ("Bully"); "This Month in Our History—The Death of William Nelson," *Shipmate Magazine* 20 (September 1957): 18 ("Gas House" quotation); *New York Times*, October 5, 1895; Valle, *Rocks and Shoals*, 90–93.

31. Justin H. Smith, *The War with Mexico*, 2 vols. (New York, 1919), 1:150 (first quotation); Frederick Merk, *The Monroe Doctrine and American Expansionism, 1843–1849* (New York, 1966), 159 (quotation).

32. Alvin P. Stauffer, "Supply of the First American Overseas Expeditionary Force: The Quartermaster's Department and the Mexican War," *Quartermaster Review* (May–June 1950), <http://www.qmfound.com/quartermaster_department_mexican_war.htm>.

33. George L. Rives, *The United States and Mexico, 1821–1848* (New York, 1913), 126; Todorich, *Spirited Years*, 41–42; Soley, *Historical Sketch of the Naval Academy*, 81. Nelson was the twelfth graduate, and his journals have long since disappeared; see U.S. Naval Academy Alumni Association, *Register of Alumni*, Book 1: Classes of 1846–1917 (Annapolis, 1996). Final grades posted on July 11, 1846, indicate Nelson ranked 19th out of 50 in Math and Navigation, 21st out of 50 in Gunnery and Steerage, 14th out of 50 in Natural Philosophy, and 10th out of 50 in Chemistry. Also see Student Records, Academic Board of Records, Class of 1846, 44, 128–31: RG 405, NA at Annapolis.

34. *Baltimore Sun*, July 6, 1846.

35. Charles Benedict Davenport, *Naval Officers, Their Heredity and Development* (1919; reprint, Whitefish, Mont., 2008), 4; Collins and Collins, *History of Kentucky*, 2:581 (first quotation); Valle, *Rocks and Shoals*, 29 (second quotation).

2. A TASTE OF WAR

1. Justin H. Smith, *War with Mexico*, 1:202–3, 216–19.

2. Doris Kearns Goodwin, *Team of Rivals: The Political Genius of Abraham Lincoln* (New York, 2005), 123 (quotation).

3. Richard D. Morris, ed., *Encyclopedia of American History* (New York, 1998), 243; Paul C. Clark Jr. and Edward H. Moseley, "D-Day Veracruz, 1847: A Grand Design," *Joint Force Quarterly* 10 (Winter, 1995–96): 107–8; Brig. Gen. William A. Mitchell, *Outlines of the World's Military History* (Harrisburg, 1931); 453; Stauffer, "Supply."

4. John S. Jenkins, *History of the War between the United States and Mexico, from the Commencement of Hostilities to the Ratification of the Treaty of Peace* (Auburn, 1850), 196; *Brooklyn Eagle*, September 18, 1846 (quotation); Donald Frazier, ed., *The United States and Mexico at War* (New York, 1997), 11, 288.

5. Clark and Moseley, "D-Day Veracruz," 108; John W. Chambers, *The Oxford Companion to American History* (New York, 1999), 433–34; NNR-MAW, 72.021, .035, .059; William H. Parker, *Recollections*, 91 (quotation); Justin H. Smith, *War with Mexico*, 2:18.

6. John Frost, *Pictorial History of the Mexican War* (Philadelphia, 1849), 469–70; NNR-MAW, 72.032, .035; Clark and Moseley, "D-Day Veracruz," 110; J. Jacob Oswandel, *Notes of the Mexican War, 1846–47–48* (Philadelphia, 1885), 67 (first three quotations).

7. William H. Parker, *Recollections*, 93 (quotation). Future Confederate Civil War generals Simon Bolivar Buckner and Edmund Kirby Smith were also part of the Sixth Regiment. Don Carlos Buell served in the Third Regiment. He would become commander of the Army of the Ohio, and William Nelson would serve under

him. Also see K. Jack Bauer, *The Mexican War* (New York, 1974), 240–44; 245–48; "The British Press and the Mexican-American War," *Living Age* 14 (July 3, 1847), 41.

8. *The Mexican War and Its Heroes*, 2 vols. (Philadelphia, 1860), 2:28; Joseph Whee-lan, *Invading Mexico: America's Continental Dream and the Mexican War, 1846–1848* (New York, 2007), 315. Conner suffered from *tic douloureux*. For this reason, it had been agreed earlier that Perry would assume the rigors of this command as soon as he returned from Norfolk.

9. Patrick H. Roth, "Sailors as Infantry in the U.S. Navy/Sailors Operating Ashore as Artillerymen in the U.S. Navy," *Navy Historical Center* (October 2005), 1; John H. Schroeder, *Matthew Calbraith Perry: Antebellum Sailor and Diplomat* (Annapolis, 2001), 138 (first quotation); William Elliot Griffis, *Matthew Calbraith Perry: A Typical American Naval Officer* (Boston, 1887), 227; Oswandel, *Notes of the Mexican War*, 89 (second quotation).

10. Frazier, *The United States and Mexico at War*, 460; Justin H. Smith, *War with Mexico*, 2:29–30, n23: 338–39; William H. Parker, *Recollections*, 102–6; John S. Jenkins, *History of the War*, 259; Edgar S. Maclay and Roy C. Smith, *A History of the United States Navy from 1775 to 1902* (New York, 1902), 182–83

11. *NNR-MAW*, 72.110–.111.

12. *Appleton's Annual Cyclopedia and Register of Important Events of the Year 1880* (New York, 1885), n.s. 5: 588; Alden Hatch, *Heroes of Annapolis* (New York, 1943), 81 (Shubrick); Sweetman, *U.S. Naval Academy*, 31 (Shubrick); Douglas Southhall Freeman, *R. E. Lee: A Biography*, 4 vols. (New York, 1934) 1:229–30. Shubrick was the son of Capt. Irvine Shubrick.

13. Wheelan, *Invading Mexico*, 315 (first and second quotations), 316; Byron A. Lee, *Naval Warrior: The Life of Commodore Isaac Mayo* (Linthicum, Md., 2002), 121; *NNR-MAW*, 72.110–.11.

14. William H. Parker, *Recollections*, 106; *NNR-MAW*, 72.100; Cadmus M. Wilcox and Mary Rachel Wilcox, eds., *History of the Mexican War* (Washington, D.C., 1892), 258 (first quotation); Henry B. Dawson, *Battles of the United States, by Sea and Land* (New York, 1858), 501 (second quotation); Clark and Moseley, "D-Day Veracruz," 113; Bauer, *Mexican War*, 251; *National Era* (Washington, D.C.), April 15, 1847.

15. William H. Parker, *Recollections*, 111, 192; Bauer, *Mexican War*, 252–53; *NNR-MAW*, 72.081, .114, .131, .332; NNR-MAW, "The Taking of Tabasco: News of a successful military campaign and the capture of the city of Tabasco, July 20, 1847," RE47v44n23c1p4; Edward D. Mansfield, *The Mexican War* (New York, 1848), 192; K. Jack Bauer, *Surfboats and Horse Marines: U.S. Naval Operations in the Mexican War, 1846–48* (Annapolis, 1969), 111–12.

16. Roth, "Sailors as Infantry," 1 (quotation); Justin H. Smith, *War with Mexico*, 2:204; John S. Jenkins, *History of the War*, 448–49. Raritan Log Book (April 1– July 25, 1847), RG 24, NAB; Bauer, *Surfboats*, 114–15; "The Taking of Tabasco," *NNR-MAW*; *Ascending Tabasco River at Devils Bend*, by Henry Walke (1847), U.S. Naval Academy Museum (second quotation), <http://www.aztecclub.com/art/tabasco002a. htm>. Robert E. Lee's brother, Lt. Samuel P. Lee, commanded the *Washington*. Lt. Henry H. Walke was second in command of the *Vesuvius*. The quotations from his sketch of the action are found at

<http://www.aztecclub.com/art/tabasco002b.htm>,
<http://www.aztecclub.com/art/tabasco004.htm>, and
<http://www.aztecclub.com/art/tabasco006.htm>.

17. Bauer, *Surfboats*, 116 (first quotation); William H. Parker, *Recollections*, 121 (second and third quotations); Naval Historical Center, Online Library of Selected Images: People—United States—Gustavus V. Fox (1821–83), <http://www.history.navy.mil/branches/org11-2.htm>.

18. Bauer, *Surfboats*, 116; Frazier, *The United States and Mexico at War*, 397; "The Taking of Tabasco," *NNR-MAW* ; Rev. Fitch W. Taylor, *The Broad Pennant; or, A Cruise in the United States Flag Ship of the Gulf Squadron during the Mexican Difficulties together with Sketches of the Mexican War* (New York, 1848), 400; John S. Jenkins, *History of the War*, 450; William H. Parker, *Recollections*, 124; Griffis, *Matthew Calbraith Perry*, 245 (quotation).

19. Bauer, *Surfboats*, 117–18 (quotation).

20. Ibid., 119–20; William H. Parker, *Recollections*, 124 (first quotation), 125 (second quotation).

21. John S. Jenkins, *History of the War*, 451–53; Bauer, *Mexican War*, 342; *Raritan* Log Book (April 1–July 25, 1847) RG 24, NAB; William H. Parker, *Recollections*, 110–11, 127; Taylor, *Broad Pennant*, 401; *DANFS*, 6:35–36, 388; Griese, "A Louisville Tragedy," 151–52.

22. *Baltimore Sun*, February 13, 1847; Ellis, extract from "Sketch of the Life of William Nelson," 4 ; *Scourge* Log Book (February 16, 1847–February 20, 1848), RG 24, NAB (quotations).

23. J. G. Randall and David Donald, *The Civil War and Reconstruction*, 2nd ed. (Boston, 1961), 83.

3. WORLDLY AFFAIRS

1. Griese, "A Louisville Tragedy," 152; *DANFS*, 4:350; *Michigan* Log Book No. 3 (July 11, 1848–December 31, 1849), RG 24, NAB; James Morton Callahan, *Cuba and International Relations: A Historical Study in American Diplomacy* (Baltimore, 1899), 201, 206, 240.

2. Maysville Cemetery Records, Mason County Historical Society, Maysville, Ky.; G. Glenn Clift, *Kentucky Obituaries, 1787–1854* (reprint, Baltimore, 1977), 180; Second Presbyterian Church (Lexington, Ky.) Records 1818–1979, M585, reel 1, UK-SC; *DANFS* 3:424–25; Griese, "A Louisville Tragedy," 152; *Milwaukee Sentinel and Gazette*, March 7, 1851; "Reminiscences of Washington," *Atlantic Monthly* 47 (April 1881): 541; Edmund Flagg, *Venice: The City of the Sea, from the Invasion by Napoleon in 1797 to the Capitulation to Radetzky, in 1849; with a Contemporaneous View of the Peninsula* (New York, 1853), 143, 250.

3. William Oscar Scroggs, "William Walker and the Steamship Corporation in Nicaragua," *American Historical Review* 10 (July 1905): 792–93; Robert G. Caldwell, *The Lopez Expeditions to Cuba, 1848–1851* (Princeton University Press, 1915), 57; Louis N. Feipel, "The Navy and Filibustering in the Fifties," *United States Naval Institute Proceedings* 44 (April 1918), 769. López was an aristocratic native of Venezuela and former officer in the Spanish military.

4. *National Era*, January 22, 1852; *Boston Daily Evening Transcript*, November 11, 1852; *DANFS*, 4:388; *Journal of the United States Senate* (Monday, December 29, 1851), 85; Donald S. Spencer, *Louis Kossuth and Young America: A Study in Sectionalism and Foreign Policy, 1848-1852* (Columbia, Mo., 1977), 2; *United States Gazette* (Philadelphia), May 5, 1851; *Savannah Republican*, June 9, 1851.

5. Fiepel, "The Navy and Filibustering," 1009; Collins and Collins, *History of Kentucky*, 1:62; Anderson C. Quisenberry, *Lopez's Expeditions to Cuba, 1850 and 1851* (Louisville, 1906), 34, 38, 70-72, 76. John Thomas Pickett (1823-1884) was a native of Maysville, Ky., who was acquainted with William Nelson. Pickett attended Transylvania University and studied for a career in law. On April 9, 1840, Linn Boyd (1800-1859), a Western Kentucky congressman, wrote to J. K. Paulding seeking a warrant for Pickett in the U.S. Navy; see Collection of Select Letters from American Political Figures, 1788-1949, MS 91-12, Box 1, FF 6, Special Collections and University Archives, Wichita State University Libraries. Pickett received an appointment to West Point in 1841, and Lt. Richardson Hardy noted, "He had too wild and erratic [a] disposition to remain long enough to graduate." Pickett resigned to accept a post as consul to the Turks Islands in the West Indies and he became involved with the efforts of Narciso López to "liberate" Cuba from Spain. See Richardson Hardy, *The History and Adventures of the Cuban Expedition, from the First Movements down to the Dispersion of the Army at Key West, and the Arrest of General Lopez. Also: An Account of the Ten Deserters at Isla de Murgeres* (Cincinnati: Lorenzo Statton, 1850), 21-22.

6. Eric Foner and John A. Garraty, eds., *The Readers Companion to American History* (Boston, 1991), 183; Randall and Donald, *Civil War*, 82-88; Mary Truedley, "The United States and Santo Domingo, 1789-1866," *Journal of Race Development* 7 (October 1916): 238-40, 244.

7. Randall and Donald, *Civil War*, 89-90.

8. Caldwell, *The Lopez Expeditions*, 83-84, 86; Fry, *Military Miscellanies*, 497. William Logan Crittenden, a nephew of John J. Crittenden, and Gen. John Pragay were among those executed. Albin F. Schoepf avoided a similar fate. He fled to America in 1851 became a protégé of Joseph Holt, and served under Nelson at Richmond and Louisville.

9. *National Era*, January 22, 1852 ("Acting Lieutenant"); Spencer, *Louis Kossuth*, 3 (Marsh quotation).

10. John H. Komlós, *Louis Kossuth in America, 1851-1852* (Buffalo, 1973), 46, 53 (quotation), 54-56; "Kossuth and His Mission," Hungarian Territorial Integrity League, 1919, pamphlet at University of Michigan (digitized June 19, 2008), 2-8. Original source: the *United States Congressional Set,* 32nd Cong. 1853.

11. Komlós, *Kossuth in America*, 57-58.

12. Spencer, *Louis Kossuth*, 3; *Covington Journal*, March 13, 1852; Komlós, *Kossuth in America*, 59 (first quotation). *National Era*, January 22, 29, 1852 (second quotation).

13. Griese, "A Louisville Tragedy," 152; Komlós, *Kossuth in America*, 62; Spencer, *Louis Kossuth*, 8; *New York Times*, November 17, 1851, February 10, 1852.

14. Stephen Beszedits, "The Nation's Guest: Lajos Kossuth in America, December 1851-July 1852," 1-4 (quotation), <http://www.hungarianamerica.com/harc/pa-

pers.asp>; Francis Pulszky and Theresa Pulszky, "White, Red, Black: Sketches of American Society," *Living Age* 37 (April 9, 1853): 97–98 (quotation). Count Francis Pulszky was the secretary of state for Kossuth.

15. Pulszky and Pulszky, "White, Red, Black," 99 (quotations); *Report of the Special Committee Appointed by the Common Council of the City of New York to Make Arrangements for the Reception of Gov. Louis Kossuth the Distinguished Hungarian Patriot* (New York, 1852), 119.

16. Komlós, *Kossuth in America*, 91, 160–62. George Nicholas Sanders (1812–73) was the son of Lewis Nicholas, a noted horse breeder, and the grandson of Col. George Nicholas, the inspiration for the Kentucky Resolutions.

17. *Baltimore Sun*, December 30, 185; Komlós, *Kossuth in America*, 92–93; Beszedits, "The Nation's Guest," 1–4; "Reminiscences of Washington," 541–42 (first quotation); Alexander DeConde et al., eds., *Encyclopedia of American Foreign Policy*, 2nd ed. (New York, 2002), 2:319–20 (second quotation).

18. *(Columbus) Ohio Statesman*, April 6, 1852; Stephen Sisa, *The Spirit of Hungary: A Panorama of Hungarian History and Culture* (Ontario, 1995), 158–61. Henningsen (1815–77) married a southern widow, invested in Nicaragua, and became involved in the Walker filibustering of 1856–57. He later served in the Confederacy during the Civil War. See *The National Cyclopedia of American Biography*, vol. 9 (New York., 1924), 236–37; also see Steven Béla Várdy, "Kossuth's Effort to Enlist America into the Hungarian Cause," in *Hungarian Studies* 16 (Budapest, 2002), 242.

19. Charles T. Greve, *Centennial History of Cincinnati* (Chicago, 1904), 725–29; Pulszky and Pulszky, *White, Red, Black: Sketches of Society in the United States* (New York, 1853) 288–95; John W. Oliver, "Louis Kossuth's Appeal to the Middle West—1852," *Mississippi Valley Historical Review* 14 (March 1928), 481-95; Beszedits, "The Nation's Guest," 1–4.

20. "Reminiscences of Washington," 541–42.

21. Komlós, *Kossuth in America*, 124–25.

22. Ibid., 130–31, 134–35.

23. Ibid., 160–62; Mr. Greenough, "Kossuth and Hayti, 1852," *Massachusetts Historical Society Proceedings* 44 (November 1910), 212–13. In 1851, Zachary Taylor appointed newspaperman James Watson Webb to become minister to Austria. Webb became bitter when the Senate failed to confirm the appointment and that led him to advise Daniel Webster of Kossuth's letter.

24. *Congressional Globe*, 32nd Cong., 2nd sess. (1853), 280. On January 1, 1852, Nelson served in a U.S. Navy that had 68 captains, 97 commanders, 327 lieutenants, 232 passed midshipman, and 171 midshipmen; see *Debow's Review* 13 (December 1852): 614.

25. Thomas Kabdebo, *Diplomat in Exile: Francis Pulszky's Political Activities in England, 1849–1860* (New York, 1979), 88–91; Komlós, *Kossuth in America*, 169–70.

26. *Baltimore Sun*, February 15, 1853; Griese, "A Louisville Tragedy," 151–52; *DANFS*, 4:388.

27. *Princeton* Log Book No. 4 (June 27, 1853–July 6, 1854), RG 24, NAB; *Portsmouth Journal*, September 3, 1853; Maclay and Smith, *History of the United States Navy*, 211; Susan F. Cooper, "Rear-Admiral William Branford Shubrick," *Harper's New Monthly Magazine* 53 (August 1876), 405-6.

28. Ellis, extract from "Sketch of the Life of William Nelson," 5; "The Death of William Nelson," *Shipmate* 20 (September 1957): 18; Thomas Kabdebo, *Diplomat in Exile*, 88–91; Komlós, *Kossuth in America*, 169–71.

29. Griese, "A Louisville Tragedy," 151–52; Ellis, extract from "Sketch of the Life of William Nelson," 5; *Independence* Log Book No. 16 (September, 4, 1854–September 9, 1855), Log Book No. 17 (September 10, 1855–September 15, 1856) RG 24, NAB; *DANFS*, 3:425.

30. U.S. Congress, S. Report No. 277, 36th. Cong., 1st sess. (1860).

31. [Benjamín Vicuña Mackenna], "The Editor's Drawer," *Harper's New Monthly Magazine* 28 (April 1864): 714 (quotation); Edmundo Murray, "Benjamín Vicuña Mackenna (1831–1886)," *Dictionary of Irish Latin American Biography*, <http://www.irlandeses.org/dilab_vicuna.htm>; Benjamín Vicuña Mackenna, "General William Nelson," in *La Voz de Chile* (New York /Santiago, November 20, 1862), republished in the *Frankfort Commonwealth*, January 23, 1863; William L. Langer, ed., *An Encyclopedia of World History* (New York, 1940), 809, 813.

32. *Harper's New Monthly Magazine* 28 (April 1864): 714 (quotations).

33. Ibid.

34. Ibid., 714–15 (quotation).

35. U.S. Congress, *Senate Exec. Journal*, 35th Cong., 1st sess., April 8, 1858 (first quotation); John Von Sonntag Haviland, "The Gwin Fancy-Dress Ball (1858)," *Magazine of History with Notes and Queries*, Extra No. 23 (October 1913): 362, 379 ("huge Falstaff" quotation); Margaret Leech, *Reveille in Washington, 1860–1865* (New York, 1941), 17; *New York Times*, April 13, 17, 1858 (lances quotation). When Nelson called on "Miss Ready" at Murfreesboro in August 1862, she was engaged to marry John Hunt Morgan. They married on December 14, 1862. Mallory became secretary of the navy for the Confederacy.

36. Griese, "A Louisville Tragedy," 152; *DANFS*, 5:81; *The Public Statutes at Large of the United States of America*, vols. 1–8 (Boston, 1845–67): "An act to prohibit the carrying on of the Slave Trade from the United States to any foreign place or country," vol. 2, May 10, 1808, sections 2–3, 70–71; vol. 3, April 20, 1818, "An Act to prohibit the introduction (importation) of slaves into any part or place within the jurisdiction of the United States, from and after the first day of January, the year of our Lord one thousand eight hundred and eight," sections 2–8, 450–53; vol. 3, March 3, 1819, "An Act in addition to the Acts prohibiting the slave trade," sections 2–7, 532–33. Also see Glenn Williams, "The Crowning Time: The International Slave Trade," <http://www.constellation.org/history/articlecrime.html>; *New York Times*, September 1, 1862. Lt. John N. Maffit commanded the *Dolphin* and later served in the Confederacy.

37. *New York Times*, September 1, 6, 1862 (quotations); Allen Nevins, *The Emergence of Abraham Lincoln* (New York, 1950), 1:434–35; *Niagara* Log Book (September 10, 1858–December 17, 1858), RG 24, NAB; U.S. Congress, *Senate Exec. Journal*, 35th Cong., 2nd sess., December 6, 1858; Samuel S. Cox, *Eight Years in Congress, 1857 to 1865* (New York, 1865), 252; Randall and Donald, *Civil War*, 547; James P. Jones, "Jefferson C. Davis in Blue: The Military Career, 1846–1866, of General Jefferson C. Davis, USA," masters thesis, University of Florida, 1954, 31–32.

38. *Niagara* Log Book, RG 24, NAB; *New York Times*, December 13, May 18, 1858; Jones, "Jefferson C. Davis in Blue," 31–32 (quotation).

39. *Niagara* Log Book, RG 24, NAB; *New York Times*, December 13, 1858; Richard LeRoy Parker, "Cruizing under the 'Stars and Stripes,'" 85–86; *Baltimore Sun*, September 24, 1858 (quotation). Richard Leroy Parker (1828–62) kept a detailed diary of this voyage. He was the nephew of William Harwar Parker, who referred to Nelson as "Bully" in *Recollections of a Naval Officer*.

40. *Niagara* Log Book, RG 24, NAB; *New York Times*, December 13, 1858; Richard L. Parker, "Cruizing under the 'Stars and Stripes,'" 86–87 (quotations).

41. *Niagara* Log Book, RG 24, NAB; *New York Times*, December 13, 1858; Richard L. Parker, "Cruizing under the 'Stars and Stripes,'" 86–87 (quotations).

42. Richard L. Parker, "Cruizing under the 'Stars and Stripes,'" 87–89, 99 (quotations); *Niagara* Log Book), RG 24, NAB.

43. Richard L. Parker, "Cruizing under the 'Stars and Stripes,'" 89–91; *Niagara* Log Book, RG 24, NAB

44. Richard L. Parker, "Cruizing under the 'Stars and Stripes,'" 91–93 (quotations); *Niagara* Log Book, RG 24, NAB. Nelson referred to them as "Krumen."

45. Richard L. Parker, "Cruizing under the 'Stars and Stripes,'" 93 (quotations), 95, 99; *Niagara* Log Book, RG 24, NAB; *New York Times*, December 13, 1858.

46. Richard L. Parker, "Cruizing under the 'Stars and Stripes,'" 93–95, 96–98 (quotation), 102; *Niagara* Log Book, RG 24, NAB; *DANFS*, 5:81; *Harper's New Monthly Magazine* 18 (January 1859): 257; *New York Times*, December 13, 1858. The *New York Herald* catered to those with financial interests in the South. That audience likewise sympathized with the slaveholders.

47. Griese, "A Louisville Tragedy," 152; Richard L. Parker, "Cruizing under the 'Stars and Stripes,'" 120 (quotation); *Congressional Globe*, 36th Cong., 2nd sess., 22 (1860); on George Hunneus and Emanuel Montt, see Virtual American Biographies, <http://www.famousamericans.net/georgehunneus> and <http://famousamericans.net/manuelmontt/>.

48. Hutchinson, "Bluegrass and Mountain Laurel," 4; J. Blaine Hudson, *Fugitive Slaves and the Underground Railroad in the Kentucky Borderland* (Jefferson, N.C., 2002), 50 (quotation); Randall and Donald, *Civil War*, 125.

49. "The Time of the Lincolns," *American Experience*, PBS/WGBH-Boston, Primary Sources, Reponses to John Brown's Raid at Harper's Ferry, <http://www.pbs.org/wgbh/amex/lincolns/filmmore/ps_brown.html> (quotations). The *Cincinnati Enquirer* appealed to an audience that traded with the agrarian South.

50. Griese, "A Louisville Tragedy," 152; U.S. Congress, S. Report No. 277, S. Bill 508, 36th Cong., 1st sess. (1860).

51. *Harper's New Monthly Magazine* 46 (December 1872): 94 (first quotation); Melville, *White-Jacket*, 208 (second quotation).

52. H. C. Bradsby, *History of Vigo County, Indiana, with Biographical Selections* (Chicago, 1891), 879; Peter Scott Campbell, "The Civil War Reminiscences of John Marshall Harlan," *Journal of Supreme Court History* 32 (November 2007): 256.

4. MEASURING THE POLITICAL CURRENTS

1. Taylor Peck, *Round Shot to Rockets: A History of the Washington Navy Yard* (Annapolis, 1949), 110–11; John B. Ellis, *The Sights and Secrets of the National Capital* (New York, 1869), 331–34.

2. Joseph F. Stevens, *1863: The Rebirth of a Nation* (New York, 2001), 1–3; *Louisville Journal*, November 1, 1860; Randall and Donald, *Civil War*, 133–34.

3. *Maysville Eagle*, November 8, 10, 1860 (first quotation); *Frankfort Commonwealth*, November 9, 1860 (second quotation); Lowell H. Harrison, *The Civil War in Kentucky* (Lexington, 1975), 4–5.

4. James Mason Hoppin, *Life of Andrew Hull Foote* (New York, 1874), 147–48 (quotations).

5. Harrison, *Civil War*, 4–5; Collins and Collins, *History of Kentucky*, 1:84–85; *Maysville Eagle*, November 22, 29, 1860; Senate, 36th Cong., 1st sess. (1860), Mr. Mallory, from the Committee on Naval Affairs, report No. 277 accompanied by S. 508, "A Bill for the Relief of William Nelson," June 14, 1860; John E. Kleber, editor-in-chief, *The Kentucky Encyclopedia* (Lexington, 1992), 241; Kenneth M. Stampp, "Kentucky's Influence upon Indiana," *Indiana Magazine of History* 39 (September 1943): 265.

6. *Charleston (S.C.) Mercury*, December 20, 1861; Henry B. Hibben, *Navy-Yard, Washington: History from Organization, 1799 to Present Date* (Washington, 1890), 93 (first quotation), 94 (third quotation); Peck, *Round Shot*, 115 (second quotation).

7. E. Merton Coulter, *The Civil War and Readjustment in Kentucky* (Gloucester, Mass., 1966), 30 (Davis quotation); Collins and Collins, *History of Kentucky*, 1:86 (remaining quotations); Thomas B. Van Horne, *Army of the Cumberland: Its Organization, Campaigns, Battles; Written at the Request of General George H. Thomas* (1875; reprint, New York, 1996), 7; *Covington Journal*, February 16, 1861; Kelly, "Holding Kentucky for the Union," 1:373.

8. *Covington Journal*, January 26, 1861.

9. Henry S. Foote, *War of the Rebellion; or, Scylla and Charybdis* (New York, 1866), 236–38 (quotations).

10. Peck, *Round Shot*, 115; *ORN*, Series 1, 4:413 (orders quotation).

11. C. F. Mitchell to Abraham Lincoln, Sunday, January 27, 1861, ALP/LOC. This staunch antislavery Quaker first wrote Lincoln just after the Republican Convention on May 23, 1860, and again after the November victory.

12. *Daily Gazette* (Janesville, Wisc.), February 13, 1861; *Louisville Democrat*, February 15, 1861.

13. David H. Donald, *Lincoln* (New York, 1995), 273; Villard, *Memoirs*, 1:150–51; Roy P. Basler, ed., *The Collected Works of Abraham Lincoln*, 11 vols. (New Brunswick, 1953–55), 4:197–203 (quotation); *New York Herald*, February 14, 1861; *Cincinnati Commercial*, February 13, 1861; *Daily Gazette* (Janesville, Wisc.), February 13, 1861.

14. Donald W. Zacharias, "John J. Crittenden Crusades for the Union and Neutrality in Kentucky," *FCHQ* 38 (July 1964): 194; William S. Dudley, *Going South: U.S. Navy Officer Resignations and Dismissals on the Eve of the Civil War* (Washington, 1981), 6 (first and second quotations); Charles P. Stone, "Washington on the Eve of the War," *Century Magazine* 26 (July 1883): 466; *Cincinnati Commercial*, November 18, 1861; Joseph F. Paull, "A Most Unusual Alumnus," *Shipmate Magazine* 36 (September 1973): 15; Gideon Wells, *The Diary of Gideon Wells*, 3 vols. (Cambridge,

Mass., 1911), 1:5; Ellis, extract from "Sketch of the Life of William Nelson," 6 (last quotation).

15. Villard, *Memoirs*, 1:156–57 (second quotation), 205 (first quotation); Paull, "A Most Unusual Alumnus," 15 (third quotation).

16. E. W. Emerson and Waldo E. Forbes, eds., *Ralph Waldo Emerson: Essays and Journal* (Garden City, 1968), 667 ("Here I am"); Ellis, extract from "Sketch of the Life of William Nelson," 6 (last quotes).

17. *Lexington Statesman*, March 19, 1861 (quotations); Gayla Koerting, "For Law and Order: Joseph Holt, the Civil War, and the Judge Advocate General's Department," *RKHS* 97 (Winter 1999): 8–9; Kleber, *Kentucky Encyclopedia*, 438; Rev. Roger J. Bartman, "Joseph Holt and Kentucky in the Civil War," *FCHQ* 40 (April 1966): 106; Salmon P. Chase to Abraham Lincoln, March 25, 1861, ALP/LOC. Adams (1812–84) was a lawyer, state representative, circuit court judge, U.S. congressman, and chief clerk of the U.S. House of Representatives.

18. William H. Russell to Mary Todd Lincoln, March 28, 1861, ALP/LOC; William Howard Russell, *My Diary North and South*, 2 vols. (1863; reprint, Baton Rouge, 2001) 1:30, (260-pound), 52–53 (first quotation); John D. Hayes, "Civil War Naval Officers—Southern Born," *Shipmate Magazine* 24 (March 1961): 61 (second quotation); Horace Gooch Scrapbook, FHS, 14; *Louisville Journal*, October 2, 1862; on Gustavus V. Fox, see Naval History Center, <http://www.history.navy.mil/branches/org11-2.htm>.

19. Russell, *Diary*, 1:54–55; Robert V. Bruce, *Lincoln and the Tools of War* (Indianapolis, 1956), 8–9; Lowell H. Harrison and James C. Klotter, *New History of Kentucky* (Lexington, 1997), 187 (quotation); Collins and Collins, *History of Kentucky*, 1:87.

20. Thomas H. Nelson to Abraham Lincoln, April 8, 1861, ALP/LOC; Peck, *Round Shot*, 117; Leech, *Reveille in Washington*, 55; Winfield Scott to Abraham Lincoln, April 13, 1861, ALP/LOC.

21. *Covington Journal*, May 4, 1861 (second and third quotations); Elizabeth Rhea Babcock, "Unionist Activity in Louisville, Kentucky: Nov. 1860–Sept. 1861 inclusive," typescript, April 1975, 17–18 (fourth and fifth quotations), FHS; Robert Peter in William H. Perrin, ed., *History of Fayette County, Kentucky* (Chicago, 1882), 452 (sixth quotation); *Dallas Herald*, May 1, 1861 (seventh and eighth quotations).

22. *Louisville Democrat*, April 17, 1861 (quotations); Timothy McKnight Russell, "Neutrality and Ideological Conflict in Kentucky during the First Year of the American Civil War," Ph.D diss., University of New Mexico (1989), 170–73.

23. Francis F. Brown, *The Every-Day Life of Abraham Lincoln* (reprint, Lincoln, Neb., 1995), 437–38 (first quotation); John G. Nicolay and John Hay, "Abraham Lincoln: A History; The Border States," *Century Magazine* 36 (May 1888): 72 (second quotations).

24. John S. C. Abbott, *The History of the Civil War in America . . . Touching Scenes in the Field, the Camp, the Hospital, and the Cabin,* 2 vols. (Springfield, Mass., 1877 [first published 1863], 2: 177 (first quotation); George M. Jackson and Will T. Hanly operated the *National Union*. See A. C. Quisenberry, "Kentucky's 'Neutrality' in 1861," *RKHS* 15 (May 1917): 17. See also William Nelson to John B. S. Todd, April 18, 1861, ALP/LOC (second quotation). Union recruits signed up at Eighth and

Main Streets before they went across the Ohio River to Indiana. On April 20, two companies of Confederate volunteers went by steamboat to New Orleans. Five days later, three more companies went to Nashville on the L&N. Colonel Blanton Duncan had engaged men throughout the state to raise Confederate troops, and he took a regiment of 480 men to Harper's Ferry by way of Nashville. One of Joe Desha's men told a friend, "Be sure and vote for Crittenden [Union candidate for the Border State Convention] and keep Kentucky out of the fuss. We are going to Virginia on a little frolic and will be back in three months." Collins and Collins, *History of Kentucky*, 1:90; Kelly, "Holding Kentucky for the Union," 375.

25. Coulter, *Civil War and Readjustment*, 49; Thomas Speed, *The Union Cause in Kentucky, 1860–1865* (New York, 1907), 123 9 (first quotation); *Kentucky Statesman*, April 19, 1861 (second quotation); *The Rail Splitter: A Journal for the Lincoln Collector. Civil War Broadsides, Ephemera, Philately, Currency and Relics*, no. 700, "To Arms!! Protect Your Home and Freedom.," <http://www.railsplitter.com/sale11/cw-bdsides.html >.

26. William Nelson to John B. S. Todd, April 22, 1861, ALP/LOC (Nelson quotations).

27. Unknown, Memorandum to Abraham Lincoln, April 1861, ALP/LOC (quotations).

28. Peck, *Round Shot*, 118; Edward J. Marolda, *The Washington Navy Yard: An Illustrated History* (Washington, 1999), 21–22; Brown, *The Every-Day Life of Abraham Lincoln*, 425; OR Series 1, 51 (1): 335 (quotation); *ORN*, Series 1, 4:421. In 1861, the Navy experienced 259 desertions and dismissals; see Hoppin, *Life of Andrew Hull Foote*, 147.

29. *Louisville Commercial*, September 11, 1895; William Cassius Goodloe, *Address on Kentucky Unionists in 1861: Read before the Society of Ex-Army and Navy Officers in Cincinnati, Ohio, April 10, 1884* (Cincinnati, 1884), 13 (quotations).

30. Robert L. Kinkaid, "Joshua Fry Speed, Lincoln's Confidential Agent in Kentucky," *RKHS* 52 (April 1954): 102–3; *OR*, Series 1, 52 (1): 137–39.

31. Bruce, *Lincoln*, 44–45; Theodore Calvin Pease and James G. Randall, eds., *The Diary of Orville Hickman Browning*, 2 vols. (1925; reprint, Whitefish, Mont., 2007), 2:598–99; David Donald, ed., *Inside Lincoln's Cabinet: The Civil War Diaries of Salmon P. Chase* (New York, 1954), 12–13 (first quotation); John Niven, *Salmon P. Chase: A Biography* (New York, 1995), 253 (remaining quotations).

32. Michael Burlingame, *Lincoln's Journalist: John Hay's Anonymous Writings for the Press, 1860–1864* (Carbondale, Ill., 1999), 276 (Hay quotation); Paul M. Angle and Earl Schenck Miers, eds., *Fire the Salute: Murat Halstead Report of the Republican National Convention in Chicago, May 16–18, 1860* (Kingsport, Tenn., 1945), 48–49 ("last lingering relic"). Murat Halstead became a force in the newspaper industry after he acquired an ownership interest in the *Cincinnati Commercial*. See also Cassius Marcellus Clay, *The Life of Cassius Marcellus Clay: Memoirs, Writings, and Speeches Showing His Conduct in the Overthrow of American Slavery, the Salvation of the Union, and the Restoration of the Autonomy of the States*, 2 vols. (Cincinnati, 1886), 1:312 ("piercing voice"). Lincoln saw to it that Clay stayed out of trouble by making him minister to Russia.

33. *OR*, Series 1, 52(1): 137; Collins and Collins, *History of Kentucky*, 1:89; *Wisconsin Patriot*, May 11, 1861 (quotation).

34. Speed, *The Union Cause in Kentucky*, 99 (first quotation); Bruce, *Lincoln*, 45–46; Nicolay and Hay, "The Border States," 72; Daniel Stevenson, "General Nelson," 118 (second quotation).

5. "NEUTRALITY WITH A VENGEANCE"

1. Robert L. Kinkaid, "Joshua Speed, Lincoln's Most Intimate Friend," *FCHQ* 17 (April 1943), 77–78; Daniel Stevenson, "General Nelson," 119–21 (quotation); Kinkaid, "Joshua Fry Speed," 103; Speed, *Union Cause*, 100.

2. *Western Citizen* (Paris, Ky.), May 31, 1861; Daniel Stevenson, "General Nelson," 122. The *New York Times*, May 27, 1861, published a summary of testimony before a legislative committee that refused to hear from Davis how he came to distribute 1,500 arms.

3. Robert J. Wimberg, *Cincinnati and the Civil War: Off to Battle* (Cincinnati, 1992), 68 (first quotation); *Western Citizen*, May 31, 1861; Cincinnati Home Guards, Minutes of the Central Committee of the Home Guards of Cincinnati, , April 17, 1861–July 8, 1862, Mss qH765g RMV, CINHS; John E. Burns, "A History of Covington, Kentucky through 1865" (manuscript, 6 vols.), 5:1099–1100, Kenton County Public Library, Covington, Ky; Daniel Stevenson, "General Nelson," 123–25.

4. Burns, "History of Covington," 5:1097; Wimberg, *Cincinnati*, 73–74; *Frankfort (Ky.) Yeoman*, May 16, 1861; Speed, *Union Cause*, 101.

5. Daniel Stevenson, "General Nelson," 124–25; R. H. Stevenson to T. B. Stevenson, May 18, 1861, Thomas B. Stevenson Letters and Correspondence (1807–81), Mss, s847, 2:131 (quotation), CINHS. Thomas B. Stevenson was a Whig friend of Henry Clay and publisher of the *Maysville Eagle*. His younger brother, Dr. Benjamin Franklin Stevenson, served in the Twenty-second Kentucky Infantry Regiment as a surgeon. The letters were donated by him.

6. *Western Citizen*, May 31, 1861 (quotations).

7. Daniel Stevenson, "General Nelson," 125–26; William H. Perrin, J. H. Battle, and G. C. Kniffin, eds., *Kentucky: A History of the State* (Louisville, 1887), 351; Collins and Collins, *History of Kentucky*, 1: 90–91 (first quotation); Abbott, *The History of the Civil War in America*, 1:79; *Western Citizen*, May 31, 1861 (second quotation).

8. Kelly, "Holding Kentucky for the Union," 373; W. F. G. Shanks, "Recollections of General Rousseau," *Harper's New Monthly Magazine* 31 (November 1865): 764; *Covington Journal*, June 15, 1861; *Louisville Commercial*, September 11, 1895.

9. Allan A. Burton to William H. Seward, May 24, 1861, ALP/LOC (quotations).

10. Abbot, *History of the Civil War*, 1:177–78 (quotation).

11. Edward Conrad Smith, *The Borderland in the Civil War* (New York, 1927), 278–80; Charles A. Wickliffe et al. to Abraham Lincoln, May 28, 1861, ALP/LOC. The report had the signatures of Charles A. Wickliffe, Garrett Davis, J. H. Garrard, James Harlan, James Speed, Thornton F. Marshall, J. F. Robinson, W. B. Horton, J. K. Goodloe, J. B. Bruner, and Joshua F. Speed. See Joshua F. Speed to Abraham Lincoln, May 29, 1861, ALP/LOC (quotations). The muskets appear to have come through the efforts of Schuyler Colfax and Thomas H. Nelson. See *OR*, Series 3, 1:243–44.

12. Kinkaid, "Joshua Fry Speed," 102; George B. McClellan to Abraham Lincoln, May 30, 1861, ALP/LOC (quotations).
13. *OR*, Series 1, 2:677–78 (Davis quotation); *Louisville Journal*, August 20, 1861; Coulter, *Civil War and Readjustment*, 88; Russell, "Neutrality and Ideological Conflict in Kentucky," 182–83 (Holt quotations); Bartman, "Joseph Holt and Kentucky," 110–11 (Nelson quotations).
14. *OR*, Series 1, 52 (1): 160–61 (quotations). Officers were mustered in for service in West Virginia on May 17. The two controversial brigades officially entered service on June 9–10. Also see Van Horne, *Army of the Cumberland*, 14.
15. *Covington Journal*, June 22, October 26, 1861 (first and second quotations); *OR*, Series 1, 52 (2): 116 (third quotation).
16. Jacob W. Schuckers, *The Life and Public Services of Salmon Portland Chase* (1874; reprint, New York, 1970), 427–28; Richard N. Current, *Lincoln's Loyalists: Union Soldiers from the Confederacy* (Boston, 1992), 29 (first quotation); *OR*, Series 1, 4:251–52 (second quotation); Daniel Stevenson, "General Nelson," 132–33; Kenneth A. Hafendorfer, *The Battle of Wild Cat Mountain* (Louisville, 2003), 279. Judge Allan A. Burton of Lancaster, Garrard Co., Ky., served as a delegate-at-large to the 1860 Republican National Convention that nominated Lincoln.
17. *Louisville Courier*, July 11, 1861 (quotations); *Kentucky Statesman*, July 11, 1861 (quotations).
18. Kinkaid, "Joshua Fry Speed," 111; Collins and Collins, *History of Kentucky*, 1: 92; Garrett Davis to Hon. Simon Cameron, July 15, 1861 (quotations), Metcalfe Collection, 89M02, KHS-SC.
19. "Biographical Sketch of Samuel Powhatan Carter, 1882," Microfilm 16,791–1P: 2, Manuscripts Division, LOC, Washington, D.C.; Collins and Collins, *History of Kentucky*, 1: 92; Maj. J. A. Brents, *The Sufferings of the Patriots; Also the Experiences of the Author as an Officer in the Union Army, including Sketches of Notes on Guerrillas and Distinguished Patriots* (New York, 1863) 91–93; Current, *Loyalists*, 31–32 (quotations); John Niven, ed., *The Salmon P. Chase Papers*, 5 vols. (Kent, 1993), 3:77–78 (last quotation).
20. Hambleton Tapp and James C. Klotter, eds., *The Union, The Civil War, and John W. Tuttle: A Kentucky Captain's Account* (Frankfort, 1980), 42 ("old Bryant tavern"); *OR*, Series 1, 4:252–53 (all other quotations).
21. Wm. Nelson to Metcalfe [mid-July 1861], Metcalfe Collection, 89M02, KHS-SC (first quotation); Harrison, *Civil War in Kentucky*, 111–12 (second quotation); Susan Lyons Hughes, *Camp Dick Robinson: Holding Kentucky for the Union in 1861* (Frankfort, 1990), 2–3. U.S. Congress, S. Report No. 130, 41st Cong., 2nd sess. (1870), clears up the mistaken idea that Robinson provided 3,200 acres.
22. Byron A. Dunn, *General Nelson's Scout*, 7th ed. (Chicago, 1909), 30 (quotation); Speed, *Union Cause*, 111. Col. Ambrose Burnside, Col. William T. Sherman, and Lt. Oliver D. Greene served in the Federal army at First Bull Run. In early September, the latter two regular army officers would become part of the Army of the Cumberland at Louisville. Burnside would come to Kentucky in 1863; see Wikipedia, s.v. "First Bull Run Union Order of Battle."
23. "Biographical Sketch of Carter," 2–4, 6, Manuscripts Division, LOC; Bruce, *Lincoln*, 56–57; Perrin, Battle, and Kniffin, *Kentucky*, 372, 355 (quotation).

24. Niven, *Chase Papers*, 3:82 (Adams and Mellon quotations); William B. Carter to Abraham Lincoln, August 1, 1861, ALP/LOC (Carter quotation); Garrett Davis to Abraham Lincoln August 4, 1861, ALP/LOC (Davis quotation).

25. Goodloe, *Kentucky Unionists of 1861*, 15; "Two Noted Civil War Recruiting Camps: A Look at Camp Dick Robinson and Camp Nelson," *Kentucky Explorer* (March 2000): 60–63; *Covington Journal*, August 17, 1861 (Adams quotations and "making efforts"); John J. Crittenden Papers, MSS 26, 5347-48, LOC (Prentice quotation); *Chicago Tribune*, August 22, 1861 (last quotation).

26. *New York Times*, August 11, 1861; *Philadelphia Sunday Transcript*, August 11, 1861; Perrin, Battle, and Kniffin, *Kentucky*, 361; Eastham Tarrant, *The Wild Riders of the First Kentucky Cavalry* (Louisville, 1894), 24 (second and third quotations).

27. Richard Miller Devens [pseud. Frazar Kirkland], *The Pictorial Book of Anecdotes and Incidents of the War of the Rebellion* (Hartford, 1867), 402 (first quotation); Tapp and Klotter, *Union, Civil War, and Tuttle:*, 42–43 (remaining quotations). A year later, the *Gettysburg Republican Compiler* printed an article from the *Ironton (Ohio) Register* entitled *General Nelson Made to Mark Time*. That article wrongly placed the incident at Camp Joe Holt and said Nelson had begun to enjoy the humor in the situation when the corporal of the guard arrived.

28. Tarrant, *Wild Riders*, 24–25 (first quotations), 61 (second quotation); Brents, *Sufferings of the Patriots*, 87.

29. Perrin, Battle, and Kniffin, *Kentucky*, 361 (first quotations); Tapp and Klotter, *Union, Civil War, and Tuttle*, 43–44 (last quotation).

30. Thomas Edward Pickett, *The Quest for a Lost Race: Presenting the Theory of Paul B. DuChaillu, . . .* (Louisville, 1907), 72–73 (quotations); Dunn, *General Nelson's Scout*, 23. Colonel Owens is probably the same Sam W. Owens who served as an aide to William H. Wadsworth during the Confederate invasion of 1862.

31. U.S. Congress, H. Report No. 83, 42nd Cong., 3rd sess. (1873); W. F. G. Shanks, "Recollections of Sherman," *Harpers's New Monthly Magazine* 30 (April 1865), 641 (first quotation); *OR*, Series 1, 4:186; Gerald J. Prokopowicz, *All for the Regiment: The Army of the Ohio, 1861–1862* (Chapel Hill, 2001), 13 (second quotation); David Stephen Heidler and Jeane T. Heidler, eds., *Encyclopedia of the American Civil War: A Political, Social, and Military History* (New York:, 2002), 1681; *Harpers Weekly*, November 9, 1861.

32. Perrin, Battle, and Kniffin, *Kentucky*, 368; *Louisville Courier*, August 13, 14, 17, 1861; *Covington Journal*, August 24, 1861; William A. Penn, *Rattling Spurs and Broad-Brimmed Hats: The Civil War in Cynthiana and Harrison County, Kentucky* (Cynthiana, 1995), 2–3.

33. *Western Citizen*, August 16, 1861 (quotations); "Two Noted Civil War Recruiting Camps," 63–64.

34. *Western Citizen*, August 16, 1861 (quotations); *Covington Journal*, August 17, 1861 (quotation).

35. *OR*, Series 2, 2:1522–524 (quotations). Buford (1820–84) graduated from the USMA in 1841 with Anderson D. Nelson, Don Carlos Buell, and Horatio G. Wright; also see Thomas P. Kettell, *History of the Great Rebellion: . . . Embellished with over 125 engravings, including 80 portraits of Prominent Statesmen, Military and Naval Officers* (Cincinnati, 1865), 162.

36. Tapp and Klotter, *Union, Civil War, and Tuttle*, 52; Brents, *Sufferings of the Patriots*, 96.

37. Brents, *Sufferings of the Patriots*, 10–11 (first and second quotations); Perrin, Battle, and Kniffin, *Kentucky*, 362; "Biographical Sketch of Samuel Powhatan Carter, 1882" 8 (third quotation), Manuscripts Division, LOC; *New York Times*, August 26, 28, 1861.

38. Daniel Stevenson, "General Nelson," 136–37; Speed, *Union Cause*, 114–15, 120–21; Rev. F. Senour, *Morgan and His Captors* (Cincinnati, 1865), 43; Tarrant, *Wild Riders*, 27–29 (quotation).

39. Coulter, *The Civil War,* 102–3; William Nelson to Garrett Davis, March 5, 1862, ALP/LOC (Nelson quotation); Niven, *Chase Papers*, 3:85–86, 88–89 (Chase quotations).

40. *New York Times*, September 2, 1861; "The Secession Conspiracy in Kentucky, and Its Overthrow; with the Relations of Both to the General Revolt," *Danville Review* 3 (September 1862): 371–95.

41. Niven, *Chase Papers*, 3:90 (Chases quotations); Ephraim Otis, "Recollections of the Kentucky Campaign of 1862," in *Campaigns in Kentucky and Tennessee, including the Battle of Chickamauga, 1862–1864,* Papers of the Military Historical Society of Massachusetts (Boston, 1908), 7:246 ("control" quotation).

6. "A SHOWMAN'S CARAVAN"

1. Daniel Stevenson, "General Nelson," 136; John Coburn, "General Recalls Civil War Experiences In Kentucky during 1861–1862: Action at Louisville, Frankfort, Wildcat Hill, and Cumberland Gap," *Kentucky Explorer* 12 (June 1997): 46 (second quotation); *Covington Journal*, September 7, 14, 1861, (first and third quotations).

2. Jim Miles, *Piercing the Heartland* (Nashville, 1991), introduction.

3. Niven, *Chase Papers*, 3:95–97 (first three quotations); Leslie Combs to Abraham Lincoln, September 6, 1861, ALP/LOC (fourth quotation).

4. *OR*, Series 1, 4:257 (quotation); Basler, *Collected Works* 4:531–32 (quotation); *Harper's Weekly*, September 28, 1861 (General Assembly resolutions).

5. Robert Means Thompson and Richard Wainwright, eds., *Confidential Correspondence of Gustavus Vasa Fox, Assistant Secretary of the Navy, 1861–1865* (New York, 1918), 1:379–80; Thomas Bramlette to Wm. Nelson, September 15, 1861 (quotations), Nelson Papers, FHS ; Perrin, Battle, and Kniffin, *Kentucky*, 369 (last quotation).

6. *Wisconsin Patriot*, September 21, 1861; Thompson and Wainwright, *Confidential Correspondence*, 1:379–80 (quotations); *OR*, Series 1, 52 (1):188.

7. Daniel Ammen, *The Old Navy and the New* (Philadelphia, 1891), 340 (first four quotations); "Biographical Sketch of Carter," 9–10, Manuscripts Division, LOC.

8. Robert Anderson to Abraham Lincoln, September 20, 1861 ALC/LOC; Glenn G. Cliff, *History of Maysville and Mason County* (Lexington, 1936), 218; *Wisconsin Patriot*, September 21, 1861; Alexander K. Marshall invoice, Nelson Papers, FHS.

9. *OR*, Series 1, 4:316–17 ("energetic and pushing"); *Harper's Weekly*, May 3, 1862 ("old friends"); Cliff, *History of Maysville*, 219–20; Nathaniel Southgate Shaler, *Kentucky, A Pioneer Commonwealth* (Boston, 1897), 273 (third quotation).

10. W. T. Lafferty, ed., "The Civil War Reminiscences of John Acker Lafferty," *RKHS* 59 (January 1961): 1–4; Thomas W. Parsons and Frank F. Mathias, eds., *Incidents and Experiences in the Life of Thomas W. Parsons from 1826 to 1900* (Lexington, 1975), 77; William Thacker Beatty, Journal No. 1, *Buffalo County Beacon* (Gibbon, Neb.), February 9, 1883; James P. Fyffe, to William Dennison. W[illiam] Nelson, to [J. P. Fyffe] at Ripley, Ohio, October 2, 1861, Correspondence to the Governor and Adjutant General, 1861–66, Series 147, 14:44, Ohio Historical Society, Columbus; James Perry Fyffe to Dear Willa, October 9, 1861, James Perry Fyffe Letters, MS 220, Chattanooga Public Library; Van Horne, *Army of the Cumberland*, 60.

11. *OR*, Series 1, 4:298 (first quotation), 302–4 (second quotation); Rev. Edward O. Guerrant, "Marshall and Garfield in Eastern Kentucky," in *Battles and Leaders of the Civil War*, ed. Robert U. Johnson and Clarence C. Buel (New York, 1887), 1:394–95. John Mills Kendrick was quartermaster for the Thirty-third Regiment Ohio Volunteer Infantry, and he became a key member of Nelson's staff.

12. Guerrant, "Marshall and Garfield," 394–95; *Covington Journal*, October 19, 1861 (quotation).

13. *OR*, Series 2, 2:106 (quotation); *Lexington Observer & Reporter*, October 19, 1861. Colonel Leonard A. Harris issued a similar order to the people of Bath and the adjoining counties.

14. Parsons and Mathias, *Incidents and Experiences*, 78; *OR*, Series 1, 4:309.

15. Henry P. Scalf, "The Battle of Ivy Mountain," *RKHS* 56 (January 1958): 12–13. John Acker Lafferty indicated that McCormick's Gap later became Frenchburg. Thomas K. Parsons noted that some called Frenchburg the "Head of the Beaver"; see Parsons and Mathias, *Incidents and Experiences* 87. Hazel Green is actually 15 miles from West Liberty and 5 miles from Rt. 460. Nelson reported it as 18 miles east from McCormick's Gap and 45 miles west of Paris on the Old State Road. See also Everett A. Nichol and Marie Nichol, *Battered Destinies* (Pasadena, Tex., 1996), 12–13. This is an edited reprint of Samuel Cordell Frey et al., *A Military Record of Battery D, First Ohio Veteran Volunteer Light Artillery, Its Military History 1861–1865* (Oil City, Pa., 1906–8).

16. Nichol and Nichol, *Battered Destinies*, 16–17; *OR*, Series 1, 4:309–10; Ara C. Spafford, 1st Sergeant, C Company, Twenty-first Regiment Ohio Volunteer Infantry, Letter to *Perrysburg (Ohio) Journal*, November 14, 1861 (first quotation); George Scheets, "Memoir of Adjutant George Scheets, C Company, 21st Ohio Volunteer Infantry; A Special Report: War Reminiscences," paper read at the regular meeting of Ford Post, East Toledo, Ohio, December 1883 (second quotation); Winchester Byron Rudy, Civil War Diary, October 17, 1861–June 17,1864, UK-SC; Beatty, Journal No. 2; Schuckers *Life and Public Services*, 431–32. "Pontiac" reported in the November 4, 1861, issue of the *New York Times* that Garrett Davis raised 500 mounted men to operate against Rebels in Floyd and Pike Counties. Levi McCormac's hotel and the Laurel Spring Church were on the Dry Ridge near Camp Garrett Davis. See

Parsons and Mathias, *Incidents and Experiences*, 87. James Laughlin served as an escort before William McLaughlin. See *SOR,* Serial 61:564–65.

17. *OR,* Series 1, 4:316–17; Van Horne, *Army of the Cumberland,* 60; Beatty, Journal No. 2; Nichol and Nichol, *Battered Destinies,* 17; Kentucky Climate Center, "Weather during the Civil War, Battle of Camp Wildcat."

18. Loyal B. Wort to Dear Susan, October 28, 1861, Loyal B. Wort Correspondence, 1861–64, MS 700, Bowling Green State University, Center for Archival Collections, Bowling Green, Ohio; Hannaford, *Story of a Regiment,* 366 (quotation). Bradford lived in neighboring Augusta, Ky. He became Nelson's personal physician and the acting brigade surgeon.

19. Scalf, "Battle of Ivy Mountain," 12, 14–15; Collins and Collins, *History of Kentucky,* 1:96.

20. Robert H. Caldwell to Dear folks at home, October 24, 1861, Robert H. Caldwell Papers, 1861–63, MS 623 ("Noah's ark"), Bowling Green State University, Center for Archival Collections, Bowling Green, Ohio; Parsons and Mathias, *Incidents and Experiences,* 81; *Covington Journal,* November 9, 1861 (re: Ficklin); *SOR,* Serial 61:565; Frank Moore, ed., *The Rebellion Record: A Diary of American Events,* 12 vols. (New York, 1861–68), 3:55, 231–33.

21. Collins and Collins, *History of Kentucky,* 1: 96; *Western Citizen,* November 1, 1861.

22. *OR,* Series 1, 4:214 (first quotation); *Western Citizen,* November 1, 1861 (second quotation); *Macon Daily Telegraph,* November 21, 1861.

23. S. S. Canfield, *History of the 21st Ohio Volunteer Regiment* (Toledo, 1893), 22–23, 26, 32–33 ("closed up"); Prokopowicz, *All for the Regiment,* 44 (second quotation);

24. Benjamin J. Lossing, *Pictorial History of the Civil War in the United States* (Hartford, 1868), 2:90 (quotation).

25. *Philadelphia Press,* November 22, 1861; Nichol and Nichol, *Battered Destinies,* 17; *OR,* Series 1, 4:225; *SOR,* Serial 1: 290–91 (quotations); *Cincinnati Gazette,* November 16, 1861. On November 10, 1861, the morning report, Department of the Cumberland, carried 49,586 men. Nelson had an *estimated* 3,500 men. See *OR,* Series 1, 4:349. About 1,600 Union troops fought at Ivy Mountain. Joshua Sill had similar amount at Johns Creek. The combined total for the units deployed was about 5,600.

26. Canfield, *History of the 21st Ohio,* 25.

27. *Philadelphia Press,* November 22, 1861; *SOR,* Serial 1:290–91 (quotation); *Cincinnati Gazette,* November 16, 1861; *New York Times,* November 26, 1861; Scalf, "The Battle of Ivy Mountain," 14–15; Lafferty, "Reminiscences," 1–4; Robert Perry, *Jack May's War* (Johnson City, Tenn., 1998), 1–7; Canfield, *History of the 21st Ohio,* 25.

28. *SOR,* Serial 1:292 (quotations).

29. *OR,* Series 1, 4:225–30; *Philadelphia Press,* November 22, 1861 (quotation); John E. Hayes, ed., *Samuel Francis Du Pont: A Selection of His Civil War Letters,* 3 vols. (Ithaca, N.Y., 1969), 2:383 (Greene quotations).

30. Scheets, "Memoir" (quotations).

31. James Perry Fyffe to Dear Willa, November 10, 1861, Fyffe Letters, Chattanooga Public Library.

32. Descendents of Wilson T. Johnson, <http://familytreemaker.genealogy.com/ users/c/a/1 /Noreen-Callahan/GENE4-0002.html>; Scalf, "The Battle of Ivy Mountain," 14–16;

33. Lafferty, "Reminiscences," 1–4; Canfield, *History of the 21st Regiment,* 26 (quotation). A Committee of Investigation looked into foraging abuses and concluded that Nelson had "strictly prohibited any depredations upon the property of citizens by his troops." See the *Philadelphia Christian Recorder,* December 14, 1861 (quotation).

34. Kentucky Climate Center, "The Battle of Ivy Mountain"; Scalf, "The Battle of Ivy Mountain," 16–17; Canfield, *History of the 21st Regiment,* 26; *Cincinnati Gazette,* November 18, 1861; *OR,* Series 1, 4:225–26 (quotation).

35. John David Preston, *The Civil War in the Big Sandy Valley of Kentucky* (Baltimore, 1984), 28–29; *OR,* Series 1, 4:228–30 (first quotation); *Charleston (S.C.) Mercury,* November 20, 1861 (second quotation). In October 1862, Hawes would become the second Confederate governor of Kentucky.

36. *Macon Daily Telegraph,* November 21 (Piketon quotes), December 7, 1861 (Moore quotes); *Charleston (S.C.) Mercury,* November 20, 1861 ("frightful").

37. *New York Times,* November 13, 1861("brilliant event"); *Cincinnati Commercial,* November 14, 1861 (quotations); *OR,* Series 1, 6:66 (McClellan quotation).

38. *Cincinnati Gazette,* November 16 ("reduced"), December 2, 1861 ("caravan"); *Covington Journal,* November16, ("universal proneness"), 23 (Finnell), 1861; *New York Times,* November 17, 1861 ("Hoax"); *Cincinnati Gazette,* November 19, ("exaggerated"). The *Covington Journal* named Dr. B. P. Drake as a source and noted he had relied on a Mr. Hurst and Calvin Brock, the editor pro tem of the *Mount Sterling Whig.* Thomas Turner, an aide to Nelson, informed that same paper the Federal loss at Ivy Creek was 6 killed and 24 wounded. Confederate losses were 10 killed, 15 wounded, and 40 missing. As a point of comparison, the Federal losses at the Battle of Wildcat Mountain were 5 killed and 20 wounded. The Confederates there had 11 killed and 42 wounded.

39. *New York Times,* November 25, 1861 (first quotation); Stanley Matthews to Dear Minnie, November 25, 1861 (second quotation), Stanley Matthews Collection, Mss qM442, CINHS; Charles C. Gilbert, "Bragg's Invasion of Kentucky," *Southern Bivouac* n.s. 1 (1885–86): 218, 339 ("crudest"); *OR,* Series 1, 7:451 ("absurdly"). Capt. Walworth Jenkins served as inspector general and chief of staff to Buell at Louisville; see *New York Herald,* September 22, 1862.

7. "MARCH OF THEIR LIFE"

1. *Covington Journal,* December 14, 1861.

2. *Cincinnati Gazette,* November 16, 1861.

3. Stephen D. Engle, *Don Carlos Buell: Most Promising of All* (Chapel Hill, 1999), 117, 120; Hannaford, *Story of a Regiment,* 172–73; Stanley Matthews to Dear Minnie, December 14, 1861 (quotation), Matthews Collection, CINHS; Benjamin F. Wade to William B. Hazen, January 27, 1862, Correspondence to the Governor and Adjutant General, 1861–66, Series 147, 28:23–24, Ohio Historical Society, Columbus.

4. Joseph R. Reinhart, *A History of the 6th Kentucky Volunteer Infantry: The Boys Who Feared No Noise* (Louisville, 2000), 31 (first quotation); Frank Elliot Myers, "Died for Discipline," *Overland Monthly* 29 (March 1897): 303–4. The author of this version used the name Burkhardt to hide the true name of Pvt. Michael Connell who served in Co. E, Twenty-fourth Regiment, Ohio Volunteer Infantry (the Buckeye Guards recruited from Dayton, Montgomery Co., Ohio). Pocock (1841–1914) served in Company K, and he became regimental quartermaster sergeant on February 15, 1863.

5. Van Horne, *Army of the Cumberland*, 49, 53; *OR*, Series 1, 7:496 (first quotation); *Cincinnati Commercial*, January 7, 1862 (second quotation); Hannaford, *Story of a Regiment*, 175. Camp Wickliffe was two miles north of the town of Buffalo in present-day Larue County, Kentucky. See Hannaford, *Story of a Regiment*, 173, 548.

6. Stanley Matthews to Dear Minnie, December 14, February 19, 1861 ("so far" and "my opinion" quotations), Matthews Collection, CINHS; William B. Hazen, *A Narrative of Military Service* (Boston, 1885), 57–60 (advice quotation).

7. Mark Hoffman, *My Brave Mechanics: The First Michigan Engineers and Their Civil War* (Detroit, 2007), 44–45; Stanley Matthews to Dear Minnie, December 19, 22, 1861, Matthews Collection, CINHS; Hannaford, *Story of a Regiment*, 554 (second quotation).

8. *Cincinnati Commercial*, January 7, 1862 (Burnett quotations); Hannaford, *Story of a Regiment*, 181–82 (second and third quotations), 364 (first quotation), 367 (fourth quotation).

9. Isabel Anderson, ed., *The Letters and Journals of General Nicholas Longworth Anderson: Harvard, Civil War, Washington, 1854–1892* (New York, 1942), 150 (first quotation); Myers, "Died for Discipline," 303.

10. *Cincinnati Commercial*, January 6, 7, 21, 1862 (quotations); Burnett, *Incidents*, 24–26; Joshua Taylor Bradford, Diary (1862), January 7–8, Manuscripts Division, LOC.

11. *Cincinnati Commercial*, January 11, (first and second quotations), 13, 1862 (third quotation); Garrett Davis to Abraham Lincoln, January 7, 1862, ALP/LOC (last quotations).

12. Joshua T. Bradford Diary, January 9, 10, 12, 1862 (first three quotations), LOC; Anderson, *Letters and Journals*, 137, 150 (fourth through sixth quotations).

13. Joshua T. Bradford Diary, January 9, 10, 12 (quotation), LOC; *Covington Journal*, January 18, 1862 (Blackman quotation); *Philadelphia Press*, January 10, 1862 (Von Treba quotation).

14. *Cincinnati Commercial*, January 13, 21, 1862 (first quotation); Anderson, *Letters and Journals*, 138 (second quotation); William Nelson to J. B. Fry, RG 393, Part 2, Entry 843:22, NAB (third quotation).

15. *Cincinnati Commercial*, January 21, 1862; Hayes, *Du Pont Letters* (New York, 1969), 2:383–84 (Greene quotations); Prokopowicz, *All for the Regiment*, 50; Robert E. Best, Diary/Letters, January 22, 1862, the Genealogy Center, <http://www.genealogycenter.info/military/civilwar/search_bestdiary.php>.

16. Joshua T. Bradford Diary, January 29–31, LOC; W. Stephen McBride, *The Union Occupation of Munfordville, 1861–1865* (Munfordville, 1999), 10; Hannaford, *Story of a Regiment*, 190; Thomas L. Connelly, *Army of the Heartland: Army of Tennessee*

(Baton Rouge, 1967), 18–20; William Farrar Smith, "The Campaign of 1861–1862 in Kentucky Unfolded through the Correspondence of Its Leaders," *Magazine of American History* 14 (July–December 1885): 480.

17. *Cincinnati Commercial*, February 4, 11, 1862; Engle, *Buell*, 163–65; Anderson, *Letters and Journals*, 139; Joshua T. Bradford Diary, February 4–9, LOC; Robert L. Kimberly and Ephraim S. Holloway, *The Forty-first Ohio Veteran Volunteer Infantry in the War of the Rebellion, 1861–1865* (Cleveland, 1897), 119 (quotation).

18. Engle, *Buell*, 166; Reinhart, *History of the 6th Kentucky*, 42–44; *OR*, Series 1, 7:603; Miles, *Piercing the Heartland*, 26–27; Hannaford, *Story of a Regiment*, 195; Joshua T. Bradford Diary, February 13, LOC; Best Diary, February 15, Genealogy Center.

19. *Philadelphia Press*, March 6, 1862; Joshua T. Bradford Diary, February 16–17, LOC; Anderson, *Letters and Journals*, 140.

20. Anderson, *Letters and Journals*, 140; Hoffman, *My Brave Mechanics*, 49.

21. *OR*, Series 1, 7:610 (quotations); Joshua T. Bradford Diary, February 17, LOC; Ellis, extract from "Sketch of the Life of William Nelson," 9, 14–15; William Grose, *The Story of the Marches, Battles and Incidents of the 36th Regiment Indiana Volunteer Infantry* (New Castle, Ind., 1891), 95–96; Reinhart, *History of the 6th Kentucky*, 44.

22. Engle, *Buell*, 170, 174, 176; *OR*, Series 1, 7:651; Kimberly and Holloway, *The Forty-first Ohio*, 15; *Pittsfield (Mass.) Sun*, February 27, 1861; Jean Edward Smith, *Grant* (New York, 2001), 169–70 (quotation).

23. *OR*, Series 1, 22:631; Jean Smith, *Grant*, 169–70 (quotation); Stanley Matthews to Dear Millie, February 19, 1862, Matthews Collection, CINHS.

24. *Philadelphia Press*, March 25, 1862; *OR*, Series 1, 7:662 (quotation).

25. *OR*, Series 1, 7:660–61 (quotation).

26. Horace Cecil Fisher, *A Staff Officer's Story: The Personal Experiences of Colonel Horace Newton Fisher in the Civil War* (Boston, 1960), 3–4; Stephen D. Engle, *Struggle for the Heartland: The Campaign from Fort Henry to Corinth* (Lincoln, Neb., 2001), 97–98 (first quotation); *New York Daily Tribune*, March 6, 1862; Stanley Matthews to Dear Millie, February 26, 1862, Matthews Collection, CINHS.

27. Grose, *Story of the Marches*, 96; *Pittsfield (Mass.) Sun*, February 27, 1862; Jean Smith, *Grant*, 170–77; Annie M. Sehon to My dear sister, Atlanta, March 10, 1862, Kimberly Family, Personal Correspondence, 1862–64, Manuscripts Dept., Southern Historical Collection, University of North Carolina, Wilson Library, Chapel Hill ("behaved cowardly"); *SOR*, Serial 10:480; *Philadelphia Press*, March 6, 1862.

28. Grose, *Story of the Marches*, 96–97; William N. Pickerill, *History of the Third Indiana Cavalry* (Indianapolis, 1906), 42. Klein first joined Nelson at Paducah.

29. Lucy Virginia (Smith) French, War Journal, October 7, 1862, Tennessee State Library and Archives, Nashville. In her journal, French stated the story might have been a "fib."

30. Clifton R. Hall, *Andrew Johnson: Military Governor of Tennessee* (Princeton, N.J., 1916), 69 (Johnson quotations); Engle, *Buell*, 190–92 (Nelson quotation).

31. *OR*, Series 1, 7:675 (first quotation); David G. Martin, *The Shiloh Campaign: March–April 1862*, rev. ed. (Conshohocken, 1996), 44 (second quotation), 57; John Y. Simon, ed., *The Papers of Ulysses S. Grant*, vol. 31: *January 1, 1883–July 23, 1885* (Carbondale, 2009), 299–300.

32. Glenn V. Longacre and John E. Hass, eds., *To Battle for God and the Right: The Civil War Letter Books of Emerson Opdycke* (Champaign, 2003), 18 (first quotation); Kimberly and Holloway, *Forty-first Ohio*, 19 (second and third quotations); Hannaford, *Story of a Regiment*, 216–17 (fourth quotation), 555–56; L. P. Brockett, *The Camp, the Battlefield, and the Hospital* (Philadelphia, 1866), 140–41(fifth quotation).

33. *Burlington (Iowa) Weekly Hawkeye*, March 22, 1862; Myers, "Died for Discipline," 304–6; Anderson, *Letters and Journals*, 141, 150; Hannaford, *Story of a Regiment*, 555–57.

34. *Burlington (Iowa) Weekly Hawkeye*, March 22, 1862; Myers, "Died for Discipline," 304–6; Anderson, *Letters and Journals*, 141, 150; Hannaford, *Story of a Regiment*, 555–57. Matthews would go on to become an associate justice of the Supreme Court. A year later at Covington, Ky., a military court ruled that a "superior officer" had to be a commissioned officer. Had that decision come earlier, it would have made the Connell case defective and illegal; see Thomas P. Lowry, *Don't Shoot That Boy! Abraham Lincoln and Military Justice* (Mason City, 1999), 160. The Federal army executed 267 men; see Burke Davis, *The Civil War: Strange and Fascinating Facts* (New York, 1982); Philip Katcher, *The American Civil War Source Book* (London, 1998); Kimberly and Holloway, *Forty-first Ohio*, 19 (last two quotations).

35. Prokopowicz, *All for the Regiment*, 95; Edwin C. Bearss, "General Nelson Saves the Day at Shiloh," *RKHS* 63 (January 1965): 39–43.

36. Grose, *Story of the Marches*, 98–99; , Log Book 2, George W. Baum Papers (1855–91), Indiana Historical Society, William Smith Library, Indianapolis; Anderson, *Letters and Journals*, 141, 151; "The Old Flag over Jackson's Grave," *Scientific American*, n.s. 6 (April 19, 1862), 242; Kimberly and Holloway, *Forty-first Ohio*, 19–20 (quotations); Simon, *Grant Papers,* 300.

37. Engle, *Buell*, 213; *OR*, Series 1, 10 (2): 38 (first and third quotations), 71 (second quotation), and 52 (1): 223.

38. *OR*, Series 1, 10 (2): 38 (first and second quotations), 48; William Sumner Dodge, *History of the Old Second Division, Army of the Cumberland, Commanders M'Cook, Sill, and Johnson* (Chicago, 1864), 165–66.

39. Bearss, "General Nelson Saves the Day," 39–43; Harry J. Carman, ed., "Diary of Amos Glover," *Ohio Archeological and Historical Quarterly* 44 (April 1935): 265 (quotation). Col. Moses Dickey commanded the Fifteenth Regiment Ohio Volunteer Infantry. Col. W. H. Gibson commanded the Sixth Brigade, and Brig. Gen. Alexander McCook commanded the Second Division.

40. Hannaford, *Story of a Regiment*, 231 ("whipped"); *New York Times*, April 9, 1876 (remaining quotations).

41. Villard, *Memoirs* 1:238 (first and third quotations); Hayes, *Samuel Francis Du Pont Letters*, 2: 384 (fourth quotation); Hannaford, *Story of a Regiment*, 232 (fifth quotation); Ammen Diary, 330 (last quotation).

42. Longacre and Hass, *To Battle for God*, 24 (quotation).

43. Ammen Diary, 330; Joshua T. Bradford Diary, March 28, 1862 ("march of their life"), LOC. The crookedness referred to the oblique angles of the rock bottom.

44. Robert I. Girardi, ed., *Campaigning with Uncle Billy: The Civil War Memoir of Lyman S. Widney* (Victoria, B.C., 2008), 62 ("astonished," "passing"); *New York Times*, April 9, 1876 ("queerest").

45. Prokopowicz, *All for the Regiment*, 98 ("sport for us"); Hannaford, *Story of a Regiment*, 233; Villard, *Memoirs*, 1:238.

46. Larry J. Daniel, *Shiloh: The Battle That Changed the Civil War* (New York, 1998), 114; Grose, *Story of the Marches*, 101; Hannaford, *Story of a Regiment*, 233.

47. Ammen Diary, 330 (first quotation); Girardi, *Campaigning with Uncle Billy*, 63 (second quotation); Longacre and Hass, *To Battle for God*, 25 (third quotation); Anderson, *Letters and Journals*, 143; Hannaford, *Story of a Regiment*, 233.

48. Girardi, *Campaigning with Uncle Billy* (first quotation), 63; Charles C. Briant, *History of the Sixth Regiment Indiana Volunteer Infantry of both the three months' and three years' services* (Indianapolis, 1891); 98 (bridge quotations); Villard, *Memoirs*, 1:239 ("exploit," "bravado"); Prokopowicz, *All for the Regiment*, 98 ("tyrant").

49. Simon, *Papers of U.S. Grant*, 31:300 (first and second quotations); Hannaford, *Story of a Regiment*, 233–34 (third and fourth quotations); Ammen Diary, 330; Villard, *Memoirs*, 1:239. The saving of that bridge meant the Army of the Ohio would arrive in time to help Grant at Shiloh.

50. Personal communication, Maury County, Tenn., archivist Robert A. Duncan to the author, November 12, 2008.

51. Dodge, *Second Division*, 171–73 (quotation). The phosphate in that yellow soil would prove to be a boon during the Reconstruction period.

52. Hannaford, *Story of a Regiment*, 234; Villard, *Memoirs*, 1:239 (first and second quotations); Reinhart, *History of the 6th Kentucky*, 55 (third quotation); Ellis, extract from "Sketch of the Life of William Nelson," 9 (fourth quotation); Bearss, "Nelson Saves the Day," 49.

53. Ammen Diary, 330; "General Nelson Was Noted for His Temper and Bad Talk," *Kentucky Explorer* 14 (September 1999): 10 (quotations).

54. Joshua T. Bradford Diary, April 1–2 (quotation), LOC.

55. Hannaford, *Story of a Regiment*, 234–35; Ammen Diary, 330; Villard, *Memoirs*, 1:239.

56. *OR*, Series 1, 10 (2): 89; *Chicago Tribune*, April 14, 1862.

57. *OR*, Series 1, 10 (2): 387 (first quotation); Simon, *Grant Papers*, 300–301 (second quotation).

58. *OR*, Series 1, 10 (1): 90–91; Bearss, "Nelson Saves the Day," 49–51; James R. Arnold, *Shiloh 1862: The Death of Innocence* (Oxford, 1998), 28.

59. *OR*, Series 1, 10 (1): 89 (quotation); Simon, *Grant Papers*, 300–301; Hannaford, *Story of a Regiment*, 236.

60. Joshua T. Bradford Diary, April 5, LOC; Grose, *Story of the Marches*, 101 (first quotation).

61. Fisher, *Staff Officer*, 10 (first quotation); Bearss, "Nelson Saves the Day," 51–52 (second and third quotations); Simon, *Grant Papers*, 201, 301. Grant made this unsupported statement well after the fact. The orders issued to Nelson on Sunday further detract from this claim.

62. *OR*, Series 1, 10 (1): 89 (Grant quotations).

63. Ammen Diary, 330–31 (quotation).

64. "Coming Up at Shiloh," 401–10; Don Carlos Buell, "Shiloh Reviewed," *Century Magazine* 31 (March 1886): 753; Don Carlos Buell, "A Contradicted Famous Saying," *Century Magazine* 30 (October 1885): 956; Ellis, extract from "Sketch of the Life of William Nelson," 18–19 (first and second quotations); Ammen Diary, 331; Fisher, *Staff Officer*, 10.

65. Ephraim A. Otis, "Recollections of the Kentucky Campaign of 1862" in Military Historical Society of Massachusetts, 7:247 (first two quotations).

8. DISPUTED GLORY

1. John William Draper, *History of the American Civil War*, 3 vol. (New York, 1867–70), 1: 291; Fisher, *Staff Officer*, 11

2. Royal Cortissoz, *The Life of Whitelaw Reid* (London, 1921), 1:85; O. Edward Cunningham, Gary D. Joiner, and Timothy B. Smith, eds., *Shiloh and the Western Campaign of 1862* (New York, 2007), 156–57 (quotations).

3. Hannaford, *Story of a Regiment*, 241–42 (quotation), 247–49, 280–81; Fisher, *Staff Officer*, 11; Daniel, *Shiloh*, 174.

4. *OR*, Series 1, 10 (2): 95–96 (first quotation); Buell, "Shiloh Reviewed," 753; Hannaford, *Story of a Regiment*, 250, 562.

5. Simon, *Grant Papers*, 213, 201, 301; Fisher, *Staff Officer*, 11; Grose, *Story of the Marches*, 102 (first quotation); Ammen Diary, 332 (second quotation).

6. Hannaford, *Story of a Regiment*, 251–52; *OR*, Series 1, 10 (2): 95–96 (Carson dispatch); Stacy D. Allen, "Shiloh!" A Visitors Guide, *Blue & Gray Magazine* (1997), 30–32; Ammen Diary, 330 (quotations).

7. *OR*, Series 1, 10 (1): 259, 261; Allen, "Shiloh!" 34.

8. *OR*, Series 1, 10 (1): 204–5, 245, 259, 261; Cunningham, Joiner, and Smith, *Shiloh and the Western Campaign*, 309.

9. James Lee McDonough, *War in Kentucky: From Shiloh to Perryville* (Knoxville, 1994), 169–70; *OR*, Series 1, 10(1): 204–5 (Hurlbut), 259 (Stuart), 261(Mason).

10. Ulysses S. Grant, "The Battle of Shiloh," *Century Magazine* 29 (February 1885): 601–2; Buell, "Shiloh Reviewed," 760 ("five-hundred yards"); Allen, "Shiloh!" 36. The bluff was leveled when the National Cemetery was built in 1866.

11. *New York Times*, April 9, 1876 (quotation).

12. Fisher, *Staff Officer*, 12–13 (first quotation); John A. Cockerill, "A Boy at Shiloh," in *Under Both Flags: A Panorama of the Great Civil War as Represented in Story, Anecdote, Adventure, and the Romance of Reality* (Chicago, 1896), 369 (second quotation); Ralph P. Buckland, "Description of the Battle of Shiloh," in *Report of the Proceedings of the Society of the Army of the Cumberland at the Fourteenth Annual Meeting Held at Cincinnati, Ohio April 6th and 7th, 1881* (Cincinnati, 1885), 60–62 (last quotes).

13. Hannaford, *Story of a Regiment*, 256 (Buell quotation), 257 ("don't stop"); 258, 577–78; Moore, *Rebellion Record*, 11:68 (admonitions); *OR*, Series 1, 10 (1): 204–5; Abbott, *Civil War*, 2:209; Fisher, *Staff Officer*, 13 (last quotation), 14; M. F. Force, *Campaigns of the Civil War*, vol. 2: *From Fort Henry to Corinth*, 1881 (reprint, Edison, N.J., 2002), 158.

14. Cunningham, Joiner, and Smith, *Shiloh and the Western Campaign*, 313, 323.

15. Grose, *Story of the Marches*, 103–04, 246; Fisher, *Staff Officer*, 13–14; Orville J. Victor, *Incidents and Anecdotes of the War* (New York, 1862), 360; Hannaford, *Story of a Regiment*, 257, 577 ("shells"); Lloyd Lewis, *Sherman: Fighting Prophet* (New York, 1932), 228; Moore, *Rebellion Record*, 11:68; Buckland, "Description of the Battle of Shiloh," 60–62.

16. Grose, *Story of the Marches*, 103–4, 246.

17. Buell, "Shiloh Reviewed," 760; Cunningham, Joiner, and Smith, *Shiloh and the Western Campaign*, 313, 323.

18. *OR*, Series 1, 10 (1): 550–51 (Chalmers report), 555 (Jackson report); Allen, "Shiloh!" 36.

19. Daniel, *Shiloh*, 254; "Coming Up at Shiloh," 407 (Nelson quotes); Hannaford, *Story of a Regiment*, 257–58; Grose, *Story of the Marches*, 103–4 (Dubois); Moore, *Rebellion Record*, 11:68.

20. Daniel, *Shiloh* (first and second quotations), 254; Hannaford, *Story of a Regiment*, 261; Simon, *Grant Papers*, 308 (last quotation).

21. *OR*, Series 1, 10 (1): 323 (Nelson report); Niven, *Chase Papers*, 3:167–70 (quotations).

22. Grant, "The Battle of Shiloh," 601–2 (quotations).

23. Simon, *Papers of U. S. Grant*, 31:318 (first quotation), 202 (second quotation).

24. Lewis, *Sherman*, 232 (quotations); Engle, *Buell*, 236–38 (quotation); Simon, *Papers of U. S. Grant*, 31:203 (last quotation). Sherman also took great offense at an article by Ebenezer Hannaford in the *Philadelphia Times* and *Louisville Courier-Journal* that declared the timely arrival of Nelson saved the day. Sherman called on every commander who commanded troops at Shiloh to provide statements that would protect their men from such "untruthful assaults." See Buckland, "Description of the Battle of Shiloh," 60–62.

25. Arnold, *Shiloh*, 72; *OR*, Series 1, 10 (1): 384 (first quotation); Shelby Foote, *The Civil War, A Narrative: Fort Donelson to Memphis* (Alexandria, 1998), 2:213 (second quotation).

26. Bearss, "Nelson Saves the Day," 68–69; *SOR*, Serial 1:645–50; Force, *From Fort Henry to Corinth*, 180 ("music"); *Philadelphia Press*, June 16, 1862. Force noted that after Shiloh, the Federal army restricted the number of bands to one per regiment.

27. Hannaford, *Story of a Regiment*, 263, (quotation); Martin, *Shiloh*, 163–64. Lieutenant Fisher disliked Bruce and viewed him as "real Kentucky-Colonel type [who] kept a barrel of whiskey on tap." See Prokopowicz, *All for the Regiment*, 104 (quotation). Larry J. Daniel, *Days of Glory: The Army of the Cumberland, 1861–1865* (Baton Rouge, 2004), noted "Bruce, who always kept a flask of whiskey by his side, had been in and out of arrest by Nelson, the officers detesting each other," 82; Benjamin F. Buckner (1836–1901) said Bruce "did not do his duty at Shiloh." See Benjamin Forsythe Buckner Papers (1785–1918), UK-SC.

28. Prokopowicz, *All for the Regiment*, 102–3 (first quotation); W. F. G. Shanks, "Gossip about Our Generals," *Harper's New Monthly Magazine* 35 (July 1867): 215 (second quotation); *New York Times*, April 9, 1876 (third quotation).

29. Ammen Diary, 335 (first quotation); Fisher, *Staff Officer*, 15; *New York Times*, April 15, 1879 (remaining quotations).

30. Cockerill, "A Boy at Shiloh," 370; Hannaford, *Story of a Regiment,* 368; Reinhart, *History of the 6th Kentucky,* 61; Thomas Jordan and J. P. Pryor, *The Campaigns of Lieut.-Gen. N. B. Forrest, and Forrest's Cavalry* (New Orleans, 1868), 140.
31. Martin, *Shiloh,* 168.
32. *New York Times,* March 14, April 15, 19, 1879 ("heard the firing"); OR, Series 1, 10 (1): 324, 340–41; 52 (1): 308; Cunningham, Joiner, and Smith, *Shiloh and the Western Campaign,* 346.
33. Mark Grimsley and Steven E. Woodworth, *Shiloh: A Battlefield Guide* (Lincoln, Neb., 2006), 115; OR, Series 1, 10 (1): 292–94 ("anticipate"); Martin, *Shiloh,* 169,172; Cunningham, Joiner, and Smith, *Shiloh and the Western Campaign,* 346–48; Reinhart, *History of the 6th Kentucky,* 62–64.
34. Cunningham, Joiner, and Smith, *Shiloh and the Western Campaign,* 347–48; OR, Series 1, 10 (1): 325 ("sheet of flame"); Martin, *Shiloh,* 172–73; Arnold, *Shiloh,* 80;
35. Cunningham, Joiner, and Smith, *Shiloh and the Western Campaign,* 347–48.
36. Longacre and Haas, *To Battle for God,* 27–28 ("Rise up 41st,"etc); Arnold, *Shiloh,* 80 ("they run"); Reinhart, *History of the 6th Kentucky,* 64–65; OR, Series 1, 10 (1): 340–44, 348–49, 351–55.
37. OR, Series 1, 10 (1): 302, 322–26, 351–53, 583- 84; Cunningham, Joiner, and Smith, *Shiloh and the Western Campaign,* 348; Daniel, *Shiloh,* 274 ("piles"); Arnold, *Shiloh,* 80–81; Ellis, extract from "Sketch of the Life of William Nelson," 4; Hayes, *Du Pont Civil War Letters,* 2:383 (Greene quotations).
38. OR, Series 1, 10 (1): 492, 524, 556, 564 (Moore); Reinhart, *History of the 6th Kentucky,* 67; Martin, *Shiloh,* 172–173; Cunningham, Joiner, and Smith, *Shiloh and the Western Campaign,* 357.
39. Hazen, *Narrative,* 28–29; *New York Times,* May 3 (Hazen quotes), April 19, 26, 27 (Gaylord), 1879.
40. *New York Times,* April 19, 1879 ("lot of thieves" quotation); Washington Davis, *Camp Fire Chats* (Boston, 1890), 224–25 ("volunteers" quotation).
41. Simon, *Papers of U. S. Grant,* 31:310–11 (quotations). For inexplicable reasons, Grant thought Nelson had done all the fighting on the left and he was therefore unsure of what role Crittenden and McCook played; ibid., 172.
42. Martin, *Shiloh,* 40–42, 180–81; Longacre and Haas, *To Battle for God,* 28; OR, Series 1, 10 (1): 345–46; Edward S. Cooper, *William Babcock Hazen: The Best Hated Man* (Madison, N.J., 2005), 48; *New York Times,* May 3, April 22, 1879. Decades later it would be said that Hazen socialized with artists and historians so he could curry favor from them. Sketch artist Henry Mosler was a close friend of Maj. William H. Blake. Both were frequent visitors to Hazen's headquarters. Captain Suman despised the lithograph picture produced for *Harper's* and he stated vehemently, "Gen. Hazen did not lead." Colonel Moody viewed the picture as a fraud intended to please Hazen. Buell had Moody mustered out for drunkenness at Shiloh, and before he departed, everyone sat around Charles Cruft's headquarters at Murfreesboro expressing their disdain for the picture. Captain Emerson Opdyke said he could not look at it "without feeling very indignant"; see *New York Times,* April 19, 27, 1879.
43. Hannaford, *Story of a Regiment,* 288; Anderson, *Letters and Journals,* 143–44; *Baltimore Sun,* April 21, 1862; Niven, *Chase Papers* 3:167–70 (quotations). Albert

Sidney Johnston and Thomas W. Nelson attended Transylvania University in 1819. Dr. Nelson also rented the Johnston home in the 1830s. About the same time William Nelson returned to Maysville, Ky., on sick leave, in the spring of 1860, Bvt. Brig. Gen. Albert Sidney Johnston was residing in Louisville and Mason County, and it seems likely this is when the two became acquainted with each other.

44. Cunningham, Joiner, and Smith, *Shiloh and the Western Campaign*, 422–24.

45. Anderson, *Letters and Journals*, 144 (first quotation), 152–53 (second quotation).

46. Van Horne, *Army of the Cumberland*, 101–2; *New York Herald*, April 28, 1862 (quotation).

47. Joshua T. Bradford Diary, May 1, LOC; Charles Sligh, *History of the Services of the First Regiment Michigan Engineers and Mechanics during the Civil War, 1861–1865* (Grand Rapids, 1921), 12; Grose, *Story of the Marches*, 114.

48. Joshua T. Bradford Diary, May 4–5 (quotations), LOC; Anderson, *Letters and Journals*, 145; Foote, *Civil War*, 259; Engle, *Struggle*, 177.

49. *OR*, Series 1, 10 (1): 682, (2): 625; Anderson, *Letters and Journals*, 145; Stacy D. Allen, "Crossroads of the Western Confederacy, Corinth," A Visitors Guide, *Blue & Gray Magazine* (2002), 24–25.

50. Franc Bangs Wilke, *Pen and Powder* (Boston, 1888), 174–77.

51. Allen, "Crossroads of the Western Confederacy," 25–27.

52. Joshua T. Bradford Diary, May 18, LOC; Anderson, *Letters and Journals*, 146; *New York Herald*, June 5, 1862; Van Horne, *Army of the Cumberland*, 103; *OR*, Series 1, 10, (1): 346, 674–75, 702.

53. Allen, "Crossroads of the Western Confederacy," 25 (quotation), 29.

54. Nichol and Nichol, *Battered Destinies*, 31 (quotation); Hazen, *Narrative*, 54–55.

55. Brayton Harris, *Blue and Gray in Black and White: Newspapers in the Civil War* (Washington, 1999), 160; *Davenport (Iowa) Daily Gazette*, June 7, 1862; Reinhart, *History of the 6th Kentucky*, 85; Villard, *Memoirs*, 1:274–75.

56. *OR*, Series 1, 10 (1): 871 (quotations).

57. Reinhart, *History of the 6th Kentucky*, 85; *New York Herald*, June 4, 1862 (first quotation); John A. Bering and Thomas Montgomery, *History of the Forty-eighth Ohio Vet. Vol. Inf.* (Hillsboro, Ohio), 1880, (second quotation).

58. Villard, *Memoirs*, 1:274–75; *OR*, Series 1, 10 (1): 675, 871 (first quotation) (2), 225 (second quotation).

59. Reinhart, *History of the 6th Kentucky*, 90; Anderson, *Letters and Journals*, 153 (first quotation); Gilbert, "Bragg's Invasion," 339; *OR*, Series 1, 10 (1): 680, 692, 872, (2): 226–25; Cunningham, Joiner, and Smith, *Shiloh and the Western Campaign*, 395 (second quotation). Ammen and Hazen were on sick leave. Bruce had been gone since April 18, 1862, because he had suffered a paralyzing stroke on his left side and returned to Kentucky. A week after the siege of Corinth, Maj. Benjamin F. Buckner, a staff officer in the Second Brigade, told his wife Helen that Bruce had returned to Pittsburg Landing seeking revenge against those who said he did not do his duty at Shiloh. See Benjamin F. Buckner to Helen, June 5, 1862, Benjamin Forsythe Buckner Papers, UK-SC.

60. Alexis Cope, *The Fifteenth Ohio Volunteers and Its Campaign, War of 1861–65* (Columbus, 1916), 153 (first quotation). The Fifteenth Ohio was part of Rousseau's

Sixth Brigade, McCook's Second Division. Dickey resigned his commission on October 24, 1862; see Peter Cozzens, *General John Pope: A Life for the Nation* (Chicago, 2000), 70 (second quotation); Cozzens and Girardi, *Military Memoirs of General John Pope*, 102, 265–66. While Pope detested Nelson's temper, he also considered him a valuable officer who had the capacity for greater distinction.

61. *Philadelphia Press*, June 16, 1862 (first quotation); *OR*, Series 1, 10 (1): 681, 676 (second quotation), 693 (third quotation).

62. Villard, *Memoirs*, 1:275; *OR*, Series 1, 10 (1): 683, (2): 227; Grose, *Story of the Marches*, 116; Engle, *Buell*, 251; *New York Tribune*, June 5, 1862 (quotations).

63. Engle, *Buell*, 258–60; Prokopowicz, *All for the Regiment*, 121; Van Horne, *Army of the Cumberland*, 116–17.

64. *OR*, Series 1, 16 (1): 281, (2): 15, 25; Engle, *Buell*, 258 (first quotation); Prokopowicz, *All for the Regiment*, 119 (second quotation); Reinhart, *History of the 6th Kentucky*, 90; Grose, *Story of the Marches*, 119.

65. Lenette S. Taylor, *"The Supply for Tomorrow Must Not Fail": The Civil War of Captain Simon Perkins, Jr., a Union Quartermaster* (Kent, Ohio, 2004), 50–52, 55. Prior to movement, Nelson requisitioned a huge amount of stationery paraphernalia. The 37,000 sheets of paper, 6,000 steel pens, 50,000 envelopes, 1,000 ounces of sealing wax, 3,000 pieces of office tape, and 600 papers of ink powder could have supplied the entire Army of the Ohio, but in actuality he received one-fourth those amounts.

66. Daniel, *Days of Glory*, 91; *OR*, Series 1, 16 (2): 48 (quotation), 49; Reinhart, *History of the 6th Kentucky*, 90.

9. THE ROAD TO CALAMITY

1. Robert H. Dilworth Papers, Bowling Green State University, Center for Archival Collections. Bowling Green, Ohio, MS 623, July 4, 1862 (Dilworth quotations); Grose, *Story of the Marches*, 121 ("scowled at," "poor class"); Amos G. Mount to Aunt, July 5, 1862, item 33 (Mount quotation), Oldham County Historical Society, LaGrange, Ky. The aggregate total for the Fourth Division on July 10 was 12,349. Those present for duty totaled 7,282 and that consisted of 328 officers and 6,954 men with 597 being cavalry; see *OR*, Series 1, 16 (2): 120.

2. Capt. T. J. Wright, *History of the Eighth Regiment Kentucky Vol. Inf. U.S.A. during Its Three Years of Campaigns* (St. Joseph, Mo., 1880), 44; Andrew Johnson to Abraham Lincoln, July 10, 1862, ALP/ LOC (first and second quotations). Oliver Davis Greene (1833–1904) became a lieutenant colonel and chief of staff for the Sixth Army Corps. In 1893, he received the Medal of Honor for heroism at Antietam. Greene incurred the ire of Johnston when he directed the provost marshal to remove the family of a man who served as an officer of Johnston's guard. See Hall, *Andrew Johnston*, 69–70.

3. *OR*, Series 1, 11 (2): 371 (first quotation); Clement A. Evans, ed., *Confederate Military History*, 13 vols. (Secaucus, N.J., 1997), 9: 108; *OR*, Series 1, 16 (2): 127–28 (second and third quotations).

4. William Lochren and the Minnesota Board of Commissioners, *Minnesota in the Civil Wars, 1861–1865* (St. Paul, 1891), 150–53; *OR*, Series 1, 16 (2): 127, 129–30, 134; Grose, *Story of the Marches*, 121.

5. *OR,* Series 1, 16 (1): 35, (2): 197 (first quotation), 139 (second quotation); Series 2, 4: 174–77; Engle, *Buell,* 275–76; Grose, *Story of the Marches,* 121–23; Anderson, *Letters and Journals,* 155.

6. Dilworth Papers, July 13, 1862, Archives and Special Collections, Bowling Green State University; *OR,* Series 1, 16 (2): 144 (first and second quotations); Anderson, *Letters and Journals,* 155 (third and fourth quotations); Grose, *Story of the Marches,* 122.

7. *OR,* Series 1, 16 (2): 151, 169–70 (quotations). Buell did not receive that communication until July 19. Battle Creek empties into the Sequatchee River just above the confluence with the Tennessee River. It was 20 miles from the Confederate forces at Chattanooga.

8. Grose, *Story of the Marches,* 123; Anderson, *Letters and Journals,* 170; Tarrant, *Wild Riders,* 98–100 (quotation); U.S. Congress, *Senate Exec. Journal,* 37th Cong., 2nd sess., July 15, 1862. The official date of promotion to major general is July 17, 1862. On July 14, Secretary of War Stanton recommended to Lincoln that Nelson become a major general in the volunteer forces. Dr. Anderson Nelson Ellis indicated that the commission carried the date of Independence Day, July 4, 1862. Ellis said it contained "a neat autobiographical letter from President Lincoln, saying that he had watched over the career of his young naval friend with many emotions of pride, and that his achievements had more than come up to his most sanguine expectations." Lincoln told Nelson to look onward and upward to greater honors and successes. Nelson also received a promotion to lieutenant commander because he intended to eventually return to the navy; see Ellis, extract from "Sketch of the Life of William Nelson," 22.

9. *OR,* Series 1, 16 (1): 741–42, (2): 143 (quotation); Collins and Collins, *History of Kentucky,* 1: 104.

10. Grose, *Story of the Marches,* 123–24; Anderson, *Letters and Journals,* 155.

11. Kate Carney Diary, No. 139 (April 15, 1861–July 31, 1862), entries for July 18, 21, 1862 (Carney quotations), Manuscripts Dept., Southern Historical Collection, University of North Carolina, Chapel Hill; Lochren et al., *Minnesota in the Civil and Indian Wars,* 157 ("their fault").

12. Grose, *Story of the Marches* 124; Harrison, *Civil War,* 38 ("can you come" and "are playing hell"); *OR,* Series 1, 16 (2): 176, 179 (Buell "We have"), 183 (Nelson "senses"), 747. Green Clay Smith, G. T. Ward, and Leonidas Metcalfe were available, but considered unqualified.

13. *OR,* Series 1, 16 (1): 815–17; John Beatty, *The Citizen Soldier; or, Memoirs of a Volunteer, 1861–1863* (Cincinnati, 1879), 155 (first quotation); Wright, *Eighth Regiment,* 47–48 (second quotation); also see William Mark Eames Papers 1862–1864, Microfilm No. 1306, p. 5, Tennessee State Library Archives; Kenneth A. Hafendorfer, *They Died by Twos and Tens: The Confederate Cavalry in the Kentucky Campaign of 1862* (Louisville, 1995), 145–48; *OR,* Series 1, 16 (1): 816 (third quotation); Anderson, *Letters and Journals,* July 24, 1862, 156 (fourth quotation); Carney Diary, July 23, 1862 (fifth quotation), July 24, 1862 (sixth quotation).

14. Carney Diary, July 25, 1862 (first quotation), July 26, 27, 1862 (second quotation); Hannaford, *Story of a Regiment,* 327.

15. Hannaford, *Story of a Regiment,* 327–28. Hannaford did not identify the unit as the Eighth Kentucky, but the attitude of that regiment makes it an ideal candidate.

16. *OR,* Series 1, 16 (2): 216; Leroy P. Graf and Ralph W. Haskins, eds., *The Papers of Andrew Johnson,* vol. 5: *1862–1864* (Knoxville, 1983), 575 (quotations).

17. *OR,* Series 1, 16 (2): 217 (first four quotations); Engle, *Buell,* 277; *OR,* Series 1, 16 (2): 226 (last two quotations).

18. Carney Diary, July 30, 1862 (first quotation); *OR,* Series 1, 16 (2): 234 (quotations).

19. Grose, *Story of the Marches,* 125–26; Stanley Matthews to Dear Millie, July 31, August 7, 1862, Matthews Collection, CINHS; *Philadelphia Inquirer,* August 13, 1862 (quotation).

20. Anderson, *Letters and Journals,* 156–57; Grose, *Story of the Marches,* 126–27; *Nashville Daily Union,* August 10, 1862.

21. Maude Barnes Miller, *Dear Wife Letters from a Union Colonel* (Ravenna, Ky., 2001), 44–45.

22. Anderson, *Letters and Journals,* 157; W. Nelson to Admiral Farragut, August 7, 1862, Civil War Documents, 1860–66, ID 1/6/MSS 004, Morris Library Special Collections Research Center, Southern Illinois University, Carbondale.

23. Hannaford, *Story of a Regiment,* 336.

24. Prokopowicz, *All for the Regiment,* 133; Engle, *Buell,* 278 (quotations).

25. Anderson, *Letters and Journals,* 157; *OR,* Series 1, 16 (2): 304 (Buell quotation), 310, 312–13 (Morgan quotation), 321–22.

26. Evans, *Confederate Military History,* 110–11; *OR,* Series 1, 16 (2): 321–23, 328 (Nelson), 335 (Buell).

27. A. C. Quisenberry, "The Battle of Richmond, Kentucky, September 1862," *RKHS* 16 (September 1918): 10; B. F. Stevenson, "Cumberland Gap," in *Sketches of War History, 1861–1865* (Cincinnati, 1888); *Jellico (Tenn.) Advance Sentinel,* May 19, 1999.

28. *OR,* Series 1, 16 (2): 341 (first quotation), 348 (third quotation); Hannaford, *Story of a Regiment,* 365 (second quotation); Kenneth A. Hafendorfer, *Battle of Richmond, Kentucky, August 30, 1862* (Louisville, 2006), 22–23; Collins and Collins, *History of Kentucky,* 108.

29. *Macon (Ga.) Weekly Telegraph,* August 22, 1862; Confederate States of America, War Department, *Southern History of the War: Official Reports of Battles, as Published by Order of the Confederate Congress at Richmond* (New York, 1864), 546 (first quotation); Stanley Matthews to Dear Millie, August 17, 1862 (second quotation), Stanley Matthews Collection, CINHS.

30. *OR,* Series 1, 16 (1): 860, 937–38, (2): 352, 357–58 (quotation); Hafendorfer, *Battle of Richmond,* 22–23.

31. *OR,* Series 1, 16 (2): 357 (Buell quotation), 362–64 (Nelson quotations).

32. *Philadelphia Inquirer,* August 28, 1862.

33. *OR,* Series 1, 16 (2): 360–61, 369 (first quotation), 375 (second quotation), 379.

34. *OR,* Series 1, 16 (2): 394, 405; *Philadelphia Inquirer,* August 28, 1862 (quotation).

35. Hafendorfer, *Battle of Richmond,* 47–49, 62; *OR,* Series 1, 16 (1): 884, (2): 405–6, 886; *Cincinnati Commercial,* August 26, 1862; *Cincinnati Gazette,* August 28, 1862.

36. William J. Kann, "Mahlon D. Manson and the Civil War in Kentucky: The Politics of Martial Glory," *RKHS* 96 (Summer 1998): 237–46; Hafendorfer, *Twos and Tens,* 227–28. The namesake for Manson was Mahlon Dickerson, secretary of the navy under Martin Van Buren (1834–38).

37. *OR,* Series 1, 16 (1): 908 (first quotation), 909; Nelson to Editor, *Cincinnati Gazette,* September 5, 1862.

38. Hafendorfer, *Battle of Richmond,* 72; *OR,* Series 1, 16 (2): 435; *Frankfort Commonwealth,* August 27, 29, 1862 (quotations).

39. *Frankfort Commonwealth,* August 27, 1862 (first quotation); Moore, *Rebellion Record,* 5:413 (Armstrong quotation); *OR,* Series 1, 16 (1): 915, 919 (Cruft and Manson quotations); D. Warren Lambert, "The Decisive Battle of Richmond" in *The Civil War in Kentucky: Battle for the Bluegrass State,* ed. Kent Masterson Brown (Mason City, 2000), 113; McDonough, *War,* 121. The Sixty-sixth Regiment Indiana Volunteer Infantry went into service at New Albany, Ind., on August 19, 1862.

40. *OR,* Series 1, 16 (2): 434–35 (quotations); *Jamestown (N.Y.) Journal,* October 15, 1862; Lambert, "Decisive Battle of Richmond," 114.

41. *OR,* Series 1, 16 (1): 440 (Nelson quotation), (2): 447–48 (Wright quotation).

42. Gilbert, "Bragg's Invasion," 219; *OR,* Series 1, 16 (2): 449 (quotation).

43. *OR,* Series 1, 16 (1): 911 (Manson report to Nelson); Hafendorfer, *Richmond,* 82–84,

44. *OR,* Series 1, 16 (1): 911 (Manson quotation); Grace Aye Howard to Indiana Historical Society, February 24, 1962, SC 0034, containing letter of Civil War service of Henry H. Aye extracted from *Soldiers' and Citizens' Album of Military Service and Civil Record* (Chicago, 1891) ("brass cannon"); Hafendorfer, *Battle of Richmond,* 82–84, 380; Moore, *Rebellion Record,* 5:416.

45. *Cincinnati Commercial,* September 1, 1862; Gilbert, "Bragg's Invasion," 339 (second quotation); Hafendorfer, *Battle of Richmond,* 108; *OR,* Series 1, 16 (1): 909, 913 (first quotation) (2): 467; Moore, *Rebellion Record,* 5:11; Quisenberry, "The Battle of Richmond," 13; Fahey, "The 'Fighting Doctor,'" using letter Irwin submitted to the Board of Officers for Recommendations of Brevets, April 6, 1866, Irwin Family Papers (Private Collection), Doylestown, Pa.

46. Hafendorfer, *Battle of Richmond,* 108; *OR,* Series 1, 16 (1): 909, 912 (quotation).

47. *Jamestown (N.Y.) Journal,* October 15, 1862 ("scarcely"); Hafendorfer, *Battle of Richmond,* 148, 166, 169 ("drunk as a lord," "howling drunkard," "break and run").

48. *OR,* Series 1, 16 (1): 912–13 (quotation); Moore, *Rebellion Record,* 5:418. Moore is using here the account of Jim R. S. Cox in the *Indianapolis Journal,* September 20, 1862.

49. *Rebellion Record,* 5: 418 (first quotation); *Cincinnati Gazette,* September 1, 1862. See also *OR,* Series 1, 16 (1): 909 (second quotation); Nelson traveled 30 miles south to Lancaster and arrived there at 9:30 A.M. (6 hours). He went 20 miles east to Richmond and 2 miles south to the battlefield, arriving there at 2:00 P.M. (4 ½ hours). The 52-mile journey computes to 5 miles per hour.

50. William Robertson Boggs, *Military Reminiscences of Gen. Wm. R. Boggs, C.S.A.* (Durham, N.C., 1913), 38–39; electronic edition, University of North Carolina, Documenting the American South <http://docsouth.unc.edu/fpn/boggs/boggs. html >; *Indianapolis Journal,* September 20, 1862; Hafendorfer, *Battle of Richmond,* 241–42 (quotation).

51. Hafendorfer, *Battle of Richmond,* 245–46 (first quotation); John W. Barber and Henry Howe, *The Loyal West in the Times of the Rebellion* (Cincinnati, 1865), 121 (second and third quotations); D. Warren Lambert, *When the Ripe Pears Fell: The*

Battle of Richmond (Richmond, 1995), 136 (fourth quotation); *Cincinnati Commercial*, September 1, 1862; *Indianapolis Journal*, September 20, 1862.

52. McDonough, *War*, 143 ("boys"); *Indianapolis Journal*, September 6, 1862; *Cincinnati Commercial*, September 1, 1862 ("wild confusion"); Lambert, "The Decisive Battle of Richmond," 128 ("Remember Indiana"). Noted newsman Joseph B. McCullagh served as a correspondent for the *Cincinnati Commercial*. He witnessed much of the final stage and suspected it was a round from the rifle of a Union soldier that struck Nelson.

53. Quisenberry, "The Battle of Richmond," 13 ("hatless"); *Indianapolis Journal*, September 6, 1862 ("inflicting terrible wounds"); OR, Series 1, 16 (1): 909, 921 ("sheer impossibility"), 931.

54. *Cincinnati Commercial*, September 1, 1862 (first quotation); Hafendorfer, *Battle of Richmond*, 278 (Paddock quotation), 292, 323–24 (McCook quotation); OR, Series 1, 16 (2): 467.

55. *Frankfort Commonwealth*, August 27, 1862 (Nelson quotations); *New York Times*, August 22, 30, 1862 ("Pontiac" quotations).

56. *Cincinnati Commercial*, September 1, 1862 (first quotation); Lambert, *Ripe Pears*, 143–44.

57. *New York Times*, August 22, 30, 1862 ("Pontiac" quotations); *Frankfort Commonwealth*, August 27, 1862 (Nelson quotations).

10. FATAL CONCEIT

1. *Cincinnati Commercial*, September 2, 1862; Perrin, *History of Fayette County*, 459 (first quotation); John David Smith and William Cooper Jr., eds., *A Union Woman in Civil War Kentucky: The Diary of Frances Peter* (Lexington, 2000), 28–29 (second quotation).

2. *Milwaukee Daily Sentinel*, September 2, 1862 (quotation); *Cincinnati Gazette*, September 5, 1862; Hafendorfer, *Battle of Richmond*, 339–40, 356–57.

3. *Philadelphia Inquirer*, September 15, 1862 (quotation); *Cincinnati Gazette*, September 5, 1862; Lambert, *Ripe Pears*, 143–44, 189.

4. Hafendorfer, *Battle of Richmond*, 272–73; *New Albany (Ind.) Daily Ledger*, September 18, 1862.

5. *Cincinnati Commercial*, September 2, 1862 (quotations).

6. Gilbert, "Bragg's Invasion," 221; OR, Series 1, 16 (1): 907 (first quotation); *Cincinnati Commercial*, September 2, 1862 (second quotation).

7. OR, Series 1, 16 (2): 471 (first quotation), 472 (fourth quotation); Perrin, *History of Fayette County*, 459–60 (second quotation); Fahey, "The 'Fighting Doctor,'" 44; T. B. Read, "The Siege of Cincinnati," *Atlantic Monthly* 11 (February 1863): 232; Peter H. Clark, *The Black Brigade of Cincinnati . . . with Various Orders, Speeches, etc.* (Cincinnati, 1864), 16; Earl J. Hess, *Banners to the Breeze: The Kentucky Campaign, Corinth, and Stones River* (Lincoln, Neb., 2001), 45.

8. Hafendorfer, *Twos and Tens*, 321–22; Kenneth Noe, *Perryville: This Grand Havoc of Battle* (Lexington, 2001), 84; Susan G. Hall, *Appalachian Ohio and the Civil War, 1862–1863* (Jefferson, N.C., 2000), 48; McDonough, *War*, 150–51 (quotation); *Cincinnati Gazette*, Sept. 5, 1862. The same letter was published in the *New York*

Times on September 7. Manson enjoyed a distinguished career in Indiana politics, and sixteen years after the meeting, he did his best to lay the curse of defeat on Nelson's grave:

> I think, under the circumstances, that I may be pardoned for saying that General Nelson made a great mistake. First, in relieving General Lewis Wallace, who had sent these troops across the Kentucky river for a temporary purpose only, of his command. Second—in not promptly ordering troops back from Richmond if he did not wish to risk raw troops in an engagement. Third—In not promptly responding to the information I gave him Friday in relation to the advance of the enemy. Fourth—in not ordering a retreat when he came upon the ground, instead of making a stand near Richmond. And lastly—In publishing in the papers that I had fought the battle contrary to his orders; for I here reiterate, in the most positive manner, that I received no orders, verbal or written, either from General Wright or Nelson, to fall back or avoid an engagement, and that the order I received was the verbal order through his adjutant to remain at my camp until he returned, except the one I received after the battle had been raging for five hours or more.

Lambert, *Ripe Pears*, 189–90, using an article from the *Louisville Courier Journal*, April 6, 1878.

9. Nathaniel Cheairs Hughes and Gordon D. Whitney, *Jefferson Davis in Blue: The Life of Sherman's Relentless Warrior* (Baton Rouge, 2002), 4–5, 11, 105 (quotation); Noe, *Perryville*, 85; Charles K. Messmer, "Louisville and the Confederate Invasion of 1862," *RKHS* 55 (October 1957): 301–2; Hall, *Appalachian Ohio*, 48 (second quotation); Capt. Thomas Ware Gibson (1815–76) was a protégé and lifelong friend of Jefferson C. Davis. He had been dismissed from the U.S. Military Academy as a troublemaker and resigned from the navy because of a duel with a fellow midshipman. As a civilian, he served as second in a number of duels.

10. Carolyn Sue Bridge, *These Men Were Heroes Once: The Sixty-ninth Indiana Volunteer Infantry* (West Lafayette, Ind., 2005), 54 ("noblest"), 55–56 (Stone/Gilbert) 111.

11. *Indianapolis Journal*, September 9, 1862 (first quotation); *OR*, Series 1, 16 (1): 915 (second quotation).

12. *Philadelphia Inquirer*, September 15, 1862.

13. Fahey, "The 'Fighting Doctor,'" 45; *OR*, Series 1, 16 (2): 510 (quotation); Messmer, "Louisville and the Confederate Invasion," 302–3; Engle, *Buell*, 288–89; *Louisville Journal*, September 16, 1862. J. Edward Stacy reported 18,250 infantry, 1,930 cavalry, and 550 artillerymen at Louisville on September 15, 1862. See *OR*, Series 1, 16 (2): 520.

14. *Cincinnati Commercial*, September 18, 1862 (first quotation); Daniel Stevenson, "General Nelson," 138; *Louisville Journal*, September 17, 1862; *Bradford (Pa.) Era*, August 27, 1887 (second quotation).

15. Hess, *Banners*, 68; Harrison, *The Civil War in Kentucky*, 46; Anderson, *Letters and Journals*, 160; Engle, *Buell*, 290–91; *OR*, Series 1, 16 (2): 529 (quotation); Gilbert, "Bragg's Invasion," 299.

16. *Louisville Journal*, September 19, 1862 (quotations); *New York Times*, September 28, 1862 (quotation).

17. *OR*, Series 1, 16 (2): 526 (first quotation), 527–30 (second and third quotations).

18. Philip Henry Sheridan, *Personal Memoirs of P. H. Sheridan, General, United States Army*, 2 vols. (London, 1888), 1:146 (first quotation); Fahey, "The 'Fighting Doctor,'" 45; Hambleton Tapp, "The Assassination of General William Nelson, September 29, 1862, and Its Ramifications," *FCHQ* 19 (October 1945): 197, 200.

19. Anderson, *Letters and Journals*, 160; *OR*, Series 1, 16, (2): 533–34 (quotations).

20. Gilbert, "Bragg's Invasion, 336 (first quotation); Messmer, "Louisville and the Confederate Invasion," 304 (second quotation); McDonough, *War*, 191–92 (third quotation).

21. *Harper's Weekly*, October 11, 1862 (quotation); *New York Times*, September 28, 1862 (quotation).

22. John F. Jefferson, September 22, 1862, John F. Jefferson Papers (1849–1925), FHS (first quotation); *Philadelphia Christian Recorder*, October 21, 1862 (second quotation).

23. Messmer, "Louisville and the Confederate Invasion," 304–5; *Louisville Journal*, September 22, 1862 (quotations); Noe, *Perryville*, 88; L. G. Bennett and William M. Haigh, *History of the Thirty-sixth Illinois Volunteers during the War of the Rebellion* (Aurora, Ill., 1876), 238 (last quotation).

24. Cuthbert Bullitt to Abraham Lincoln, September 22, 1862, ALP/LOC (first quotation); *New York Times*, September 23, 1862 (quotations).

25. *New York Herald*, September 22, 1862 (quotations); Shanks, "Personal Recollections," 268 (Granger quotation); J. Cutler Andrews, *The North Reports the Civil War* (Pittsburgh, Pa., 1955), 293 (*Tribune* quotation); *Brooklyn Eagle*, September 23, 1862.

26. Gilbert, "Bragg's Invasion," 338. Davis probably arrived on Saturday and had Sunday and part of Monday to organize troops; see also James B. Fry to Dr. B. J .D Irwin, March 28, 1885, Irwin Family Papers; Tapp, "The Assassination of General William Nelson," 200; Robert E. McDowell, *Louisville and the Civil War, 1861–1865* (Louisville, 1962), 93 (dialogue quotations); *Indianapolis Journal*, September 26, 1862; *Dawson's Times and Union* (Fort Wayne, Ind.), October 3, 1862; Devens, *Pictorial Book of Anecdote*, 413; William Dudley Foulke, *Life of Oliver P. Morton, including His Important Speeches* (Indianapolis, 1899), 194 ("about" quotations). Foulke's account is problematic. For better insight on the request for arms, etc., see The *History of the Thirty-sixth Illinois*, the *Indianapolis Journal*, and *Dawson's Times*.

27. Ben F. Horton to Alphonso Taft, September 29, 1862, William Howard Taft Papers, entry 925, LOC (first quotation); Tapp, "The Assassination of General William Nelson," 200–201 (dialogue quotations).

28. McDowell, *Louisville and the Civil War*, 93–94; Dr. B. J. D. Irwin to James B. Fry, April 27, 1885, Irwin Family Papers; James B. Fry, *Killed by a Brother Soldier* (New York, 1885), 4–5; *OR*, Series 1, 16 (2): 537–38 (Wright quotation); 52 (1): 284; *ORN*, Series 1, 23:373 (Pennock quotation).

29. Ellis, "Major General William Nelson," 59 (first quotation); Randall and Donald, *Civil War*, 379–84; George W. Herbert Papers (1854–71), Johnson W. Culp Diary (1862–63), FHS.

30. Messmer, "Louisville and the Confederate Invasion," 306 (Prentice quotation); *Indianapolis Journal*, September 23, 1862 (quotations).

31. *New Albany (Ind.) Ledger* September 26, 1862 (first and second quotations); *Portland (Maine) Daily Advertiser*, September 25, 1862; Gilbert, "Bragg's Invasion," 337; Almon F. Rockwell Papers, LOC; McDowell, *Louisville and the Civil War*, 89; OR, Series 1, 16 (2): 539–40 (third quotation), 541 (fourth quotation); *Scientific American 7* (October 1, 1862), 227.

32. OR, Series 1, 16 (2): 541 and 52 (1): 284; Ellis, "Major General William Nelson," 60–61; William Nelson to Abraham Lincoln, September 25, 1862, ALP/LOC. This last correspondence with the president arrived just days after his murder. See George W. Herbert Papers, FHS. Morgan Vance allowed Union troops to use his farm at "Pralltown" on the Nicholasville road across from the fairgrounds in Lexington, Ky.

33. *New York Times*, October 5, 1862 (quotation); *New Albany Ledger*, September 26, 1862.

34. Engle, *Buell*, 295–96; Messmer, "Louisville and the Confederate Invasion," 308 (quotation), 309, 311–12.

35. *Indianapolis Journal*, September 26, 1862; *Dawson's Times and Union* (Fort Wayne, Ind.), October 3, 1862; *Louisville Journal*, September 23, 1862; Tapp, "The Assassination of General William Nelson," 201.

36. Richard W. Johnson, *A Soldier's Reminiscences in Peace and War* (Philadelphia, 1866), 256 (Morton quotation); *Indianapolis Journal*, October 2, 1862; Ambrose Bierce, *The Collected Works of Ambrose Bierce* (New York, 1909), 1:284 (Hazen quotations).

37. Ellis, "Major General William Nelson," 62; Grose, *Story of the Marches*, 134; Anderson, *Letters and Journals*, 160; Joseph P. Fried, "How One Union General Murdered Another," *Civil War Times Illustrated* 1 (June 1962): 15; Hazen, *Narrative*, 54 (first quotation), 55; Campbell, "John Marshall Harlan," 264 (second quotation); Fahey, "The 'Fighting Doctor,'" 45; OR, Series 1, 16 (2): 549.

38. *Louisville Journal*, September 28, 1862; *New York Herald*, September 28, 1862 (quotations).

39. Anderson, *Letters and Journals*, 161; Diary of Joseph C. "Kit" King, 1862–63, LH-MISC MSS (quotation), Rutherford B. Hayes Presidential Center; Robinson Papers, William Nelson to Governor James F. Robinson, September 28, 1862 R2–188, KDLSA; Loren J. Morse, ed., *Civil War Diaries and Letters of Bliss Morse* (Wagoner, Okla., 1985), 29. Terrill's friend, James S. Jackson, also had men who threatened to murder him the first time they came under fire; see Noe, *Perryville*, 85.

40. Pease and Randall, *Diary of Orville Hickman Browning*, 1:575; Ellis, "Major General William Nelson," 62; Reinhart, *History of the 6th Kentucky*, 112–13, 355. Whittaker enjoyed "ardent spirits" and in his later years had to be confined to a mental hospital.

41. Foulke, *Life of Oliver P. Morton*, 194 ("a good thrashing"); James R. Gilmore, *Down in Tennessee and Back by Way of Richmond* [by Edmund Kirke, pseud.] (New York, 1864), 207 ("heavy black beard"); Devens, *Anecdotes*, 414 (dialogue quotes); Fry, *Killed*, 5–6; Hughes and Whitney, *Jefferson Davis in Blue*, 112; Otis, "Recollections of the Kentucky Campaign," 246 ("dignity or consideration").

42. *New York Times*, September 30, 1862 ("son of a bitch") from a special dispatch to a morning paper in Philadelphia; Horace Gooch Scrapbook, FHS (second quotation); Fry, *Killed*, 5-6 (third quotation); Foulke, *Life of Oliver P. Morton*, 195 (fourth quotation); Burnett, *Incidents*, 28 (fifth quotation). This is confirmed again in Andrews, *The North Reports the War*, 292.

43. Burnett, *Incidents*, 27-28. Gibson knew Nelson, liked him socially, but thought he deserved to be shot; see Hughes and Whitney, *Jefferson Davis in Blue*, 113-14 including notes; "Killing of Gen. Nelson: Some Facts Exonerating Gov. Morton and Capt. Gibson," J. B. Weirwether interview with Col. James B. Merriweather, "Olden Times Review," *Evening News*, 1880, clipping in the Thomas Ware Gibson Papers, property of Mrs. Robert A. Earle, Richmond, Va. (third quotation). The Tranter had a unique cocking mechanism. At the bottom of the trigger guard, a second triggerlike device cocked the hammer and rotated the cylinder. This arming device also allowed a firmer grip and better aim. It was the trigger within the guard that released the hammer. Famed detective Allan Pinkerton encouraged his agents to use this weapon during the Civil War; see Jeff Kinard, *Pistols: An Illustrated History of Their Impact* (Santa Barbara, 2003), 77-78.

44. *Indiana (Pa.) Messenger*, October 15, 1862 (Hoblitzell account); *Indianapolis State Sentinel*, February 23, 1882; Devens, *Anecdotes*, 414 (first quotation); *Cincinnati Commercial*, October 2, 1862 (sixth quotation); Fry, *Killed*, 3 (second and third quotations), 6; *Syracuse Evening Herald*, June 26, 1890; Cooper, *William Babcock Hazen*, 58 (Hazen quotes).

45. *Cincinnati Times*, September 30, 1862 (first quotation); Anderson, *Letters and Journals*, 161 (second quotation); McDonough, *War*, 195 (third quotation); Horace Gooch Scrapbook, 11, FHS; Howard H. Peckham, "I Have Been Basely Murdered," *American Heritage* 14 (August 1963): 91; Gilbert, "Bragg's Invasion," 338; *Indiana (Pa.) Messenger*, October 15, 1862.

46. James C. Klotter, *Kentucky Justice, Southern Honor and American Manhood* (Baton Rouge, 2003), 63 (first quotation); *Philadelphia Christian Recorder*, November 15, 1862; *Baltimore Sun*, October 2, 1862 (second through fifth quotations); Ellis, "Major General William Nelson," 63 (sixth and seventh quotations); Tarrant, *Wild Riders*, 100; Fry, *Killed*, 6 (eighth quotation); McDonough, *War*, 195; Burnett, *Incidents*, 29-30. The congregation of Cavalry Episcopal Church openly sympathized with the South, and Talbot found it necessary to resign in December 1862; see *New York Times*, December 21, 1862.

47. Fry, *Killed*, 7-8; Tapp and Klotter, *Union, Civil War, and Tuttle*, 49; Anderson, *Letters and Journals*, 161 (first quotation); Sheridan, *Memoirs*, 1:147 (second and third quotations).

48. Foulke, *Life of Oliver P. Morton*, 195 (first and second quotations); Hughes and Whitney, *Jefferson Davis in Blue*, 116 (third quotation); Henry J. Aten, *History of the Eighty-fifth Regiment, Illinois Volunteer Infantry* (Hiawatha, Kans., 1901), 30; McDowell, *Louisville in the Civil War*, 103; *Madison (Ind.) Evening Courier*, September 30, 1862.

49. Reinhart, *History of the 6th Kentucky*, 112-13 (first quotation); *Cincinnati Commercial*, October 2, 1862; Prokopowicz, *All for the Regiment*, 154 (second and third quotations), 155.

50. Wright, *Eighth Regiment*, 66 (first quotation); Wilke, *Pen and Powder*, 176–77 (second quotation); John H. Tilford Papers (1862–66), FHS.

11. A MARTYR TO POLITICAL EXPEDIENCY

1. Hannaford, *Story of a Regiment*, 358; *OR*, Series 1, 16 (2): 554–55, 557–58, Series 2, 2:576; Shanks, "Gossip about Our Generals," 212.

2. *OR*, Series 1, 16 (2): 558 (General Orders 47a); Hazen, *Narrative*, 57; Hayes, *Du Pont Civil War Letters*, 2:383 (Fry quotation); Henry Stone, "The Operations of General Buell in Kentucky and Tennessee in 1862," in *Campaigns in Kentucky and Tennessee, including the battle of Chickamauga, 1862–1864: Papers of the Military Historical Society of Massachusetts* (Boston, 1908), 7:279; Engle, *Buell*, 297; *OR*, Series 1, 16 (2): 558, 887.

3. Burnett, *Incidents*, 31–32; *New York Times*, September 30, 1862.

4. Ellis, "Major General William Nelson," 64 (quotation); Kirk C. Jenkins, "A Shooting at the Galt House: The Death of General William Nelson," *Civil War History* 43 (June 1997): 111–12 (quotations); *Baltimore Sun*, October 2, 1862 (complete sermon).

5. *Indianapolis Journal*, September 30, 1862; *New York Times*, September 30, 1862; *Louisville Democrat*, September 30, 1862.

6. *Cincinnati Times*, September 30, 1862.

7. Messmer, "Louisville and the Confederate Invasion," 312 (first quotation); Richard W. Johnson, *A Soldier's Reminiscences*, 257 (second quotation); Ellis, "Major General William Nelson," 64; *New York Times*, October 6, 1862; *Milwaukee Daily Sentinel*, October 7, 1862.

8. Burnett, *Incidents*, 32; McDowell, *Louisville in the Civil War*, 105; Anderson, *Letters and Journals*, 161.

9. J. M. Wright, "A Glimpse of Perryville," *Southern Bivouac* n.s. 1 (1885–86): 129; Jefferson Columbus Davis to H. G. Wright, October 2, 1862, Letters Received, Department of the Ohio, RG 98, NAB (quotation).

10. *Indianapolis Journal*, October 2, 1862.

11. *OR*, Series 1, 16 (2): 567 (first quotation); *Philadelphia Public Ledger*, October 7, 11, 1862.

12. Campbell, "John Marshall Harlan," 265; James Street Jr. and Time-Life Books, *The Struggle for Tennessee: Tupelo to Stones River* (Alexandria, Va., 1985), 61, 67; Harrison, *Civil War*, 53.

13. Foulke, *Life of Oliver P. Morton*, 195; Messmer, "Louisville and the Confederate Invasion," 316; Hughes and Whitney, *Jefferson Davis in Blue*, 120.

14. Griese, "A. Louisville Tragedy," 144; *St. Louis Daily Evening Bulletin*, October 24, 27, 1862; *New York Times*, October 22, 1862 (first quotation); Jones, "Jefferson Davis in Blue," 73; *OR*, Series 1, 52 (1): 294; *Indianapolis Journal*, October 25, 1862 ("gallant Indianan").

15. Salmon P. Chase to Abraham Lincoln, October 23, 1862, ALP/LOC (quotations). Salmon P. Chase was well aware of the faults of this valued protégé. He wrote in his journal that Nelson "died as a fool dieth—how sad . . . [his actions] compelled my admiration . . . [but] his cruelty & passion & tyranny especially when excited by drink often excited my indignation." Robert B. Warden, *An Account of the Private Life and Public Services of Salmon Portland Chase* (Cincinnati, 1874), 496.

16. *Baltimore Sun*, October 3, 1862 (Article 9); *St. Louis Daily Evening Bulletin*, October 27, 1862 (*Cincinnati Gazette*).

17. Wells, *The Diary of Gideon Wells*, 178–79; Engle, *Buell*, 314 (quotation), 315; Donald, *Lincoln* (New York, 1995), 389; *OR*, Series 1, 16 (2): 642; Fry, *Killed*, 9; Jefferson County (Ky.), Circuit Court Order Book, October Term, 1862: 313, 335, January Term, 1863: 357, KDLSA; Hughes and Whitney, *Jefferson Davis in Blue*, 120–21 n 81; *OR*, Series 1, 52 (1): 297.

18. Mary Bryson Nelson to Margaret Preston, November 14, 1862, Thomas Henry Nelson Papers, Special Collections, Vigo County Public Library, Terre Haute, Ind.

19. *St. Louis Daily Evening Bulletin*, October 27, 1862 (quotations).

20. *Nashville Daily Union*, January 11, 1863 (quotations). Fyffe said the original "frayed and stained emblem of the 'Old Glory' [that came from] . . . the fair ladies of Maysville, Kentucky, by the hands of your honorary and honored member, Mr. Hamilton Gray [in October 1861], will be carefully preserved"; see also *OR*, Series 1, 20 (1): 198 (second quotation), 518, (2): 282. Charles Cruft had the First Brigade, William Hazen the Second Brigade, and William Grose the Third Brigade, which included Col. Nicholas L. Anderson and the Sixth Ohio.

21. *Frankfort Commonwealth*, January 17, 1863 (first and second quotations); *Journal of the House of Representatives of the Commonwealth of Kentucky* (Frankfort, 1861–63), 2:1155, 1177.

22. Hayes, *Du Pont Civil War Letters*, 2:383 (first quotation); Harris, *Blue and Gray in Black and White*, 207; John A. Garraty and Mark Carnes, eds., *American National Biography* (New York: Oxford University Press, 1999), 24:29–30; William S. Rosecrans to Abraham Lincoln, March 24, 1863, ALP/LOC (second quotation); Basler, *Collected Works*, 6:148.

23. "Two Noted Civil War Camps," 64–65; *New York Times*, May 31, June 1, June 5, 1863; *Louisville Journal*, June 4, 1863 (quotation).

24. General, Special, and other Orders, Department of the Ohio, General Orders August 1862—February 1864, Part 1, Para. 2, Entry 3493, General Order # 99, RG 393, NAB; *OR*, Series 3, 3:416–18, 4:467–68; *Milwaukee Daily Journal*, June 6, 1862 (quotation). This reference to a military inquiry appears to be another example of the confusion that existed over the "prosecution" of Davis.

25. Collins and Collins, *History of Kentucky*, 1:127; Kleber, *Kentucky Encyclopedia*, 240; *Frankfort Commonwealth*, August 21, 1863 (first and second quotations);

26. *Frankfort Commonwealth*, August 21, 1863; Wm. H. Fosdick Diary, Bodley Family Papers, 1773–1939, FHS; Eliza A. Herring, "The Hoskins of Kentucky," *RKHS* 15 (May 1917): 11 (first quotation); Byron M. Cutcheon, comp., *The Story of the Twentieth Michigan Infantry* (Lansing, 1904), 64–65; *Journal of the House of Representatives of the Commonwealth of Kentucky* (Frankfort, 1861–63), 2:1155, 1177; John William Finnell, Kentucky General Assembly, *Funeral Obsequies of Major General William Nelson* (Frankfort, 1863); Hannaford, *Story of a Regiment*, 358–69 (last quotation). Hannaford relied on Campbell for information, and he failed to make the connection to Nelson.

27. Bert Barnett, Review of John Fitch, *Annals of the Army of the Cumberland*, H-CivWar, H-Net Reviews (August 2004), < http://www.h-net.org/reviews/showrev.

php?id=11084>; Tapp, "The Assassination of General William Nelson," 205–6.

28. John M. Stockton to Abraham Lincoln, October 24, 1864, ALP/LOC; *Records of the Office of the Second Auditor, 1776–1920*, Register of Settled Accounts, vol. 1 of 1 (1861–73), Entry 454: 281, RG 217, NA, College Park, Md. (first and second quotations).

29. *Rally 'Round Camp Nelson Newsletter* 5 (Spring 2001): 3, (Winter 2001): 2; *Lexington Kentucky Statesman*, June 28, 1867 (quotation).

30. *Records of the Office of the Third Auditor, 1775–1923*, Letters Sent by the Quartermaster and Collection Divisions, Vol. 2 of 19 (December, 13, 1869–October 7, 1870), Entry 595: 105, RG 217, NA, College Park, Md.; John M. Stockton to Abraham Lincoln, October 24, 1864, ALP/LOC; *Register of Accounts and Claims Reported by the Second Auditor*, Vol. 48 of 69 (March 15, 1817–July 30, 1894), Entry 197, No. 9525, RG 217, NA, College Park, Md. (quotations); *Maysville(Ky.)Bulletin*, March 9, 1872; Nelson is buried in Section 8, Lot #137, next to the Stockton family plot.

31. *Lexington Herald-Leader*, January 13, 2002. By 2002, the statue had an accumulated trust balance of over $200,000; also see Clay, *The Life of Cassius Clay*, 1:220–21 (first and second quotations).

32. Statement of James B. Merriweather in unidentified news clipping, c. 1880, Jefferson Columbus Davis Collection, William Smith Library, Indiana Historical Society, Indianapolis. This conflicts slightly with the J. B. Merriweather interview ("Killing of Gen. Nelson"), which ends with "made me shunned by all brother officers"; see Frederick Schneider, "Civil War Murder Weapon," *North South Trader's Civil War* 26 (1999): 25; Burnett, *Incidents*, 29 (aide quotation); Brooks D. Simpson and Jean V. Berlin, eds., *Sherman's Civil War: Selected Correspondence of William T. Sherman, 1860–1865* (Chapel Hill, 1999), 314 (quotation taken from letter of W. T. Sherman to Ellen E. Sherman, October 4, 1862); Fry, *Military Miscellanies*, 501–5 (Shaler quotes); *Philadelphia Press*, February 23, 1885 (Steedman quotation). Shaler served as captain of the Fifth Battery of Kentucky Volunteers under Maj. Gen. Lew Wallace, a man who held a deep resentment over being relieved of command at Lexington.

33. Sheridan, *Memoirs*, 1:147 (quotations); Fry, *Military Miscellanies*, 501–5 ("little excuse"); Richard W. Johnson, *A Soldier's Reminiscences*, 255 (first and third quotations); Richard W. Johnson, "War Memories," *Military Order of the Loyal Legion of the United States*, comp. William Marvel (Wilmington, N.C.: Broadfoot Pub. Co., 1997), 26:14 (second quotation).

34. Fry, *Killed*, 7–8 (Buell quotations); Campbell, "John Marshall Harlan," 264 (Harlan quotation)

35. Hughes and Whitney, *Jefferson Davis in Blue*, 423, 424–25, 425n.

36. *Boston Globe*, September 29, 1904.

37. *Biographical Encyclopedia of Kentucky*, 67 (first quotation); Salmon P. Chase to Abraham Lincoln, October 23, 1862, ALP/LOC (second quotation); Ammen, *Old Navy*, 340 (third quotation); Ben F. Horton to Alphonso Taft, September 29, 1862, Manuscript Collection, LOC (fourth and last quotation).

38. Melville, *White Jacket*, 208 (first quotation); *OR*, Series 1, 20 (1): 518 (second quotation); Hayes, *Du Pont Civil War Letters*, 2:383 (Green/Fry quotations); Ben F.

Horton to Alphonso Taft, September 29, 1862, LOC (Horton quotation); Bierce, *Collected Works*, 1:284.

39. Shaler, *Kentucky*, 291 (first quotation); Gilbert, "Bragg's Invasion," 219, 239 (second quotation); ; Hannaford, *Story of a Regiment*, 365 (third quotation); Hayes, *Du Pont Civil War Letters*, 2:383 (fourth quotation, last quatation); Hazen, *Narrative*, 55 (fifth quotation).

Bibliography

PRIMARY SOURCES

Manuscripts, Diaries, Collections, Papers, Pictures, Public Documents

Augusta (Kentucky) Town Council, Municipal Offices
  Minute Books, 1: 1798–1841, 2: 1841–61

Barkley-Brannen Papers.
  Private Collection of Mrs. Nancy Brannen, Maysville, Ky.

Bowling Green (Ohio) State University, Center for Archival Collections
  Robert H. Caldwell Papers, 1861–63. MS 623
  Robert S. Dilworth Papers. MS 800
  Loyal B. Wort Correspondence, 1861–64. MS 700

Chattanooga (Tennessee) Public Library
  James Perry Fyffe Letters (Civil War) MS 220

Cincinnati (Ohio) Historical Society
  Sarah Wilson Bullock Papers 1861–62
  Cincinnati Home Guards. Minutes of the Central Committee of the Home Guards of Cincinnati, April 17, 1861–July 8, 1862. Mss qH76g RMV.
  Stanley Matthews Collection. Mss qM442
  Thomas B. Stevenson Letters and Correspondence, 1807–81. Mss s847

Crown Hill Cemetery, Indianapolis, Indiana
  Jefferson C. Davis Records
  Oliver P. Morton Records

Filson Historical Society, Louisville, Kentucky.
  Journal of John Daeuble, 6th Kentucky Volunteer Infantry Regiment U.S. Part 1: December 30, 1861–September 4, 1862; Part 2, September 5–November 15, 1862. Translated by Joseph R. Reinhart.
  Horace Gooch Scrapbook. News Clippings. Louisville and the Civil War, 1859–74.

Don Carlos Buell Papers, 1813–61 and 1843–98

Johnson W. Culp Diary, 1862–63

Garrett Davis Miscellaneous Papers, 1844–68

George W. Herbert Papers, 1854–71

John F. Jefferson Papers, 1849–1925

William Nelson Papers, 1861–62

John H. Tilford Papers, 1862–66

Thomas Ware [Weir] Gibson Papers (Private Collection of Mrs. Robert A. Earle), Richmond, Va.

"Killing of Gen. Nelson: Some Facts Exonerating Gov. Morton and Capt. Gibson, J. B. Weirwether interview with Col. James B. Merriweather, Olden Times Review, *Evening News*, 1880

Rutherford B. Hayes Presidential Center, Fremont, Ohio

Diary of Joseph C. "Kit" King, 1862–63, LH-MISC MSS

Indiana Historical Society, William Smith Library, Indianapolis

George W. Baum Papers (1855–91)

Jefferson Columbus Davis Collection (1847–80)

Indiana State Library and Archives, Indianapolis

Oliver P. Morton Papers

Oliver P. Morton Register of Telegrams

Irwin Family Papers (Private Collection), Doylestown, Pennsylvania.

Kentucky Department of Libraries and State Archives, Frankfort

Bracken County Census, Court Order Books, Deeds, Wills

John J. Crittenden Letters

Jefferson County Records, Circuit Court Order Books 1862–64

Fayette County Census, Tax Records, Deeds, Wills

Mason County Census, Tax Records, Deeds, Wills

James F. Robinson Papers

Thomas E. Bramlette Papers

Kentucky Historical Society, Frankfort

Special Collections

John Finnell Letter Book

Metcalfe Collection. 89M02

Todd Collections

Vertical Family Files

> *Doniphan*
>
> *Nelson*

Library of Congress, Washington, D.C.

U.S. Congressional Documents and Debates, <http://memory.loc.gov/ammem/amlaw>

Manuscripts Division

> *Joshua Taylor Bradford Diary, 1862*
>
> *Biographical Sketch of Samuel Powhatan Carter, 1882. Microfilm 16,791-P*
>
> *John J. Crittenden Papers (1782–1888)*
>
> *Almon F. Rockwell Papers*
>
> *William Howard Taft Papers*

Mason County (Kentucky) Historical Society, Maysville

Maysville Cemetery Records

Nelson Files

Maury County (Tennessee) Archives, Columbia

National Archives and Records Administration, Washington, D.C.

Record Group 24. Records of the Bureau of Naval Personnel, 1798–1991

> *Logs of U.S. Naval Ships and Stations, 1801–1946*
>
> *Records Relating to Naval Officers. Commissions and Warrants, 1844–1936. Book One*

Record Group 45. Naval Records Collection of the Office of Naval Records and Library

> *Abstracts of Service Records of Naval Officers, 1798–1893. Vol. 1. July 1840 to December 1845. Microfilm Publication 330, Roll 6*
>
> *African Squadron Letters Received by the Secretary of the Navy from the Commanding Officers of the Squadron, 1853, no. 36*
>
> *Misc. Records U.S. Navy, 1789–1925. Appointments, Orders, and Resignations. Microfilm Publication T829. Entry 385*
>
> *Microfilm 394. October 20, 1838, to October 12, 1840. v. 17: 3, 418½: Entry 386*
>
> *Microfilm 395. october 12, 1840, to February 13, 1842. v. 18: 70*
>
> *Letters Received Accepting Appointments as Commissioned and Warrant Officers, April 20, 1812, to October 1864. Entry 125*

Record Group 92. Office of the Quartermaster General

Record Group 94. Letters Received by the Appointment, Commission and Personnel Branch, Adjutant General's office

Joshua Taylor Bradford 2916 ACP 1887, 9W3/19/33/5 Box No. 1091

Medical Officer Files 7W2/23/8/1 Box 64. CMSR— J.T. Bradford 7W3/1/22/5 Box 9

Anderson D. Nelson 7 ACP 1886. United States Military Academy. Cadet Application Papers. 1805–66. Microcopy No. 688. Roll 106. File 247

William Nelson 1921 ACP 1885. Fiche 00051. National Archives Microfiche Publication M-1395. Item B 574

Record Group 98. Records of United States Army Commands (Geographical).

Letters Sent Department of the Tennessee

Letters Received Department of the Ohio

Record Group 107. Records of the Secretary of War

Letters Received

Orders and Endorsements Sent by the Secretary of War 1846–70

Record Group 108. Records of the Headquarters of the Army

Letters Sent, 1828–1903

Letters Received, 1828–1903

Record Group 192. Office of the Commissary General. College Park, Maryland

Record Group 217. Records of the Accounting Officers of Department of Treasury, 1775–1927. College Park, Maryland

Records of the Office of the Second Auditor, 1776–1920

Register of Accounts and Claims Reported by the Second Auditor, March 5, 1817–July 30, 1894, Vol. 48 of 69, Entry 197, No. 9525

Register of Settled Accounts, 1861–73, Entry 454

Volume 1 of 1. Records of the Office of the Third Auditor, 1775–1923

Letters Sent by the Quartermaster and Collection Divisions, December, 13, 1869–October 7, 1870, Vol. 2 of 19, Entry 595: 105.

Record Group 393. Records of United States Army Continental Commands, 1821–1920 Parts 1 and 2

Records of Named Departments

General, Special, and other Orders. Dept. of the Ohio General Orders August 1862–February 1864

Register of Letters Received

Register of Letters Sent

Register of Telegrams Sent

Norwich University, Kreitzberg Library Special Collections, Norwich, Vermont

Catalogue of the Officers and Students of Norwich University for the Academic Year 1836–37, Montpelier, Vt., 1837

Catalogue of the Officers and Cadets of Norwich University for the Academic Years 1838–41, Hanover, N.H.: E. A. Allen, 1841

Oldham County Historical Society. LaGrange, Kentucky

Civil War Letters and Correspondence of Amos G. Mount

Pennsylvania State Library, Special Collections Library, Rare Books and Manuscripts, University Station

Richard LeRoy Parker, "Cruizing under the 'Stars and Stripes': Being the Private Journal of Richard Leroy Parker, 1842–1861," Accession 1962–0012R

Shiloh National Park, Shiloh, Tennessee

Horace N. Fisher. "Memorandum of Sept. 5, 1904: Buell's Army at Shiloh, Apr. 6 and 7, 1862."

Southern Illinois University, Morris Library Special Collections Research Center, Carbondale

Civil War Documents, 1860–66

Tennessee State Library and Archives, Nashville

William Mark Eames Papers 1862–64, Microfilm No. 1306

Lucy Virginia (Smith) French Papers. War Journal

Transylvania University, Lexington, Kentucky, Special Collection Archives

William A. Leavy Papers, 1812–1955 (bulk 1873–1877) MSC 17

Transylvania Medical Student Dissertations

University of Kentucky Libraries, Lexington

King Library, Special Collections and Archives
  Benjamin F. Buckner Papers, 1785–1918
  Winchester Byron Rudy Civil War Diary
  Second Presbyterian Church (Lexington) Records, 1818– 1979, Microfilm No. 64M–584, reel 1 of 3.
W. T. Young Library

University of North Carolina, Southern Historical Collection, Wilson Library, Chapel Hill

Southern Historical Collection, Manuscripts Dept.
  Kate Carney Diary: April 15, 1861– July 31, 1862
  Kimberly Family. Personal Correspondence. 1862–64

U.S. Military Academy, West Point, New York

USMA Library Archives/Special Collections

> *Record Group 404. Records of the United States Military Academy*
> *Cadet Applications*

U.S. Naval Academy, Annapolis, Maryland

Nimitz Library, Special Collections and Archives Division.
William W. Jeffies Memorial Archives

> *Record Group 405. Records of the United States Naval Academy*
> *Academic Board of Records Class of 1846*
> *Student Records and Grades, 1840–46*
> *Vertical Files*
> > *Delaware* (Ship of the Line)
> > *Shark* (Schooner)
> > *Yorktown* (Sloop of War)

Vigo County (Indiana) Library, Special Collections and Archives, Terre Haute

> *Thomas Henry Nelson Papers*

Federal and State Publications

Confederate States of America. War Department. *Southern History of the War: Official Reports of Battles.* New York, 1864.

Finnell, John William. Kentucky General Assembly. *Funeral Obsequies of Major General William Nelson.* Frankfort, Ky., 1863.

Heitman, Francis B. *Historical Register and Dictionary of the United States Army, 1789–1903.* 2 vols. Washington, 1903.

Hibben, Henry B. *Navy-Yard, Washington. History from Organization, 1799, to Present Date.* Washington, 1890.

Journal of the House of Representatives of the Commonwealth of Kentucky. Frankfort, 1861–62–63.

Lochren, William, and the Minnesota Board of Commissioners. *Minnesota in the Civil and Indian Wars, 1861–1865.* 2 vols. St. Paul, 1890–93.

National Park Service. Shiloh National Military Park Commission. D. W. Reed, comp. *The Battle of Shiloh and the Organizations Engaged.* Washington, D.C.: GPO, 1903. Revised 1909. Reprint 1913.

Soley, James Russell. *Historical Sketch of the United States Naval Academy.* Washington, 1876.

United States Military Academy. *Official Register of the Officers and Cadets of the U.S. Military Academy.* West Point, N.Y., 1838–41.

———. *Seventeenth Annual Reunion of the Association of Graduates of the United State Military Academy at West Point, New York, June the 10th, 1886.* East Saginaw. 1886.

United States Naval History Division. *Dictionary of American Naval Fighting Ships*. 9 vols. Washington. 1959–81.

United States Naval War Records Office. *Official Records of the Union and Confederate Navies in the War of the Rebellion*. Series 1, vols. 1–27. Series 2, vols. 1–3. Washington, D.C.: GPO, 1894–1922.

United States Statutes at Large, Treaties, and Proclamations of the United States of America, 12 vols. Boston: Little, Brown and Co., 1845–66.

United States War Department. *The War of the Rebellion: A Compilation of the Official Records of the Union and Confederate Armies*. Series 1–3. 70 vols. 128 serials. Washington, D.C.: GPO, 1880–1901.

Newspapers

Adams Sentinel (Gettysburg, Pa.)
Arkansas True Democrat
Baltimore Sun
Barre-Montpelier (Vt.) Times Argus
Boston Daily Evening Transcript
Bradford (Pa.) Era
Brooklyn (N.Y.) Eagle
Burlington (Iowa) Weekly Hawkeye
Cairo City (Ill.) Weekly News
Chicago Tribune
Cincinnati Commercial
Cincinnati Enquirer
Cincinnati Gazette
Cincinnati Press
Cincinnati Times
Clarksville (Tenn.) Chronicle
Columbia (Pa.) Spy
Covington (Ky.) Journal
Covington (Ky.) Licking Valley Register
Fort Wayne (Ind.) Daily Times and Union
Dallas Herald
Danville (Ky.) Tribune
Davenport (Iowa) Daily Gazette
Dawson's Times and Union (Fort Wayne, Ind.)
Dubuque (Iowa) Herald
Edwardsville (Ill.) Speculator
Farmers Repository (Wheeling, W.Va.)
Flemingsburg Kentuckian
Frankfort (Ky.) Commonwealth
Frankfort (Ky.) Yeoman
Frank Leslie's Illustrated (New York, N.Y.)
Goshen (Ind.) Times
Harper's Weekly (New York, N.Y.).

Illustrated London News
Indiana (Pa.) Messenger
Indianapolis Daily Journal
Indianapolis Democrat
Indianapolis State Sentinel
Ironton (Ohio) Register
Jamestown (N.Y.) Journal
Janesville (Wisc.) Daily Gazette/Weekly Gazette
Jellico (Tenn.) Advance Sentinel
Kentucky Statesman (Lexington)
La Voz de Chile (New York/Santiago)
Lexington (Ky.) Gazette
Lexington (Ky.) Herald
Lexington (Ky.) Herald-Leader
Lexington (Ky.) Observer & Reporter
Lexington (Ky.) Reporter
Louisville (Ky.) Anzeiger
Louisville (Ky.) Courier
Louisville (Ky.) Democrat
Louisville (Ky.) Evening News
Louisville (Ky.) Journal
Louisville (Ky.) Times
Macon (Ga.) Telegraph
Madison (Ind.) Evening Courier
Madisonian (Washington, D.C.)
Maysville (Ky.) Dollar Weekly Bulletin
Maysville (Ky.) Eagle
Maysville (Ky.) Independent
Maysville (Ky.) Ledger-Independent
Memphis Avalanche
Memphis Daily Appeal
Milwaukee Daily Sentinel
Mobile (Ala.) Daily Advertiser and Register
Nashville (Tenn.) Union
Nashville (Tenn.) Union and American
National Era (Washington, D.C.)
National Intelligence (Washington, D.C.)
National Tribune (Washington, D.C.)
National Union (Winchester, Ky.)
New Albany (Ind.) Ledger
New-England Palladium (Boston, Ma.).
New Hampshire Patriot and State Gazette (Concord)
New York Evening Post
New York Herald
New York Sun

New York Times
New York Tribune
New York World
Ohio Statesman (Columbus)
Pennsylvania Correspondent and Farmer's Almanac (Philadelphia)
Perrysburg (Ohio) Journal
Philadelphia Christian Recorder
Philadelphia Inquirer
Philadelphia Press
Philadelphia Public Ledger
Philadelphia Sunday Transcript
Pittsfield (Mass.) Sun
Portland (Maine) Daily Advertiser
Portsmouth (N.H.) Journal
Republican Compiler (Gettysburg, Pa.)
Richmond (Va.) Examiner
Ripley (Ohio) Bee
Savannah (Ga.) Republican
Semi-Weekly Raleigh (N.C.) Register
Southern Patriot (Charleston, S.C.)
Staunton (Va.) Speculator
(St. Louis) *Daily Evening Bulletin*
(St. Louis) *Missouri Republican*
St. Paul (Minn.) Pioneer Press
Syracuse (N.Y.) Evening Herald
Terre Haute (Ind.) Daily Wabash Express
Terre Haute (Ind.) Gazette
Terre Haute (Ind.) Tribune-Star
Toledo (Ohio) Blade
Topeka (Kans.) Weekly Capital
United States Gazette (Philadelphia)
Washington Times
Wellsboro (Pa.) Agitator
Winchester (Va.) National Union
Wisconsin Patriot (Madison*)*

Published Diaries, Personal Papers, Reminiscences, Memoirs, Speeches, and Other Orginal Narratives

Adamson, Dr. [M. F.] "Anderson Doniphan, M.D." *Mason County Genealogical Society* 9 (1991). Kentucky Historical Society, Frankfort.

Ammen, Daniel B. *The Old Navy and New.* Philadelphia: J. P. Lippincott & Co., 1891.

Anderson, Isabel., ed. *The Letters and Journals of General Nicholas Longworth Anderson: Harvard, Civil War, Washington, 1854–1892.* New York: Fleming H. Revell Co., 1942.

Angle, Paul M., and Earl Schenck Miers, eds. *Fire the Salute: Murat Halstead Report of the Republican National Convention in Chicago* [May 16, 17, & 18, 1860]. Kingsport, Tenn.: Kingsport Press, 1960.

Barber, John W., and Henry Howe. *The Loyal West in the Times of the Rebellion.* 1865. Reprint, Whitefish, Mont.: Kessinger Pub. Co., 2007.

———. *Our Whole Country.* 2 vols. New York: George F. Tuttle and Henry M'Cauley, 1861.

Basler, Roy P., ed. *The Collected Works of Abraham Lincoln.* 11 vols. New Brunswick: Rutgers University Press, 1953–55.

Beatty, John. *The Citizen Soldier; or, Memoirs of a Volunteer, 1861–1863.* Cincinnati: Wilstach, Baldwin & Co., 1879.

Beatty, William Thacker. "William Thacker Beatty, Journals 1–4." *Buffalo County Beacon* (Gibbon, Neb.), February 9, 1883, <http://homepages.rootsweb.ancestry.com/~bp2000/WilliamThackerBeatty/WTBeatty.htm>.

Best, Robert E. Diary/Letters. The Genealogy Center, <http://www.genealogycenter.info/military/civilwar/search_bestdiary.php>.

Bierce, Ambrose. *The Collected Works of Ambrose Bierce.* Vol. 1. New York: Neale, 1909.

Boggs, William Robertson. *Military Reminiscences of Gen. Wm. R. Boggs, C. S. A.* Electronic Edition, University of North Carolina, Documenting the American South, <http://docsouth.unc.edu/fpn/boggs/boggs.html>.

Brents, Maj. J. A. *The Sufferings of the Patriots: Also the Experiences of the Author as an Officer in the Union Army Including Sketches of Notes on Guerrillas and Distinguished Patriots.* New York: J. A. Brents, 1863.

"The British Press and the Mexican-American War." *Living Age* 14 (July 3, 1847): 41.

Brockett, L. P. *The Camp, the Battlefield, and the Hospital.* Philadelphia: National Pub., 1866.

Brown, Francis F. *The Every-Day Life of Abraham Lincoln.* Lincoln: University of Nebraska Press, 1995.

Buckland, Ralph P. "Description of the Battle of Shiloh." In *Report of the Proceedings of the Society of the Army of the Cumberland at the Fourteenth Annual Meeting Held at Cincinnati, Ohio, April 6th and 7th, 1881.* Cincinnati: F. W. Freeman, 1885: 58–88.

Buell, Don Carlos. "A Contradicted Famous Saying." *Century Magazine* 30 (October 1885): 956.

———. "Shiloh Reviewed." *Century Magazine* 31 (March 1886): 749–81.

Burnett, Alf[red]. *Incidents of the War: Humorous, Pathetic, and Descriptive.* Cincinnati: Rickey & Carroll, 1863.

Clark, Peter H. *The Black Brigade of Cincinnati: Being a Report of Its Labors and Muster Roll of Its Members together with Various Orders, Speeches, etc.* Cincinnati: J. B. Boyd, 1864.

Clay, Cassius Marcellus. *The Life of Cassius Marcellus Clay. Memoirs, Writings, and Speeches Showing His Conduct in the Overthrow of American Slavery, the Salvation of the Union, and the Restoration of the Autonomy of the States.* 2 vols. [1 volume published]. Cincinnati: J. Fletcher Brennan & Co., 1886.

Cockerill, John A. "A Boy at Shiloh." In *Under Both Flags: A Panorama of the Great Civil War as Represented in Story, Anecdote, Adventure, and the Romance of Reality.* Chicago: National Book Concern, 1896.

Colton, Walter. *Deck and Port; or, Incidents of a Cruise in the United States Frigate Congress to California. With sketches of Rio Janeiro, Valparaiso, Lima, Honolulu, and San Francisco.* 1850. Michigan Historical Reprint Series, 2005.

"Coming Up at Shiloh." *Continental Monthly* 6 (October 1864): 399–408.

Cox, Samuel S. *Eight Years in Congress—1857 to 1865.* New York: D. Appleton & Co., 1865.

Cozzens, Peter, and Robert I. Girardi, eds. *The Military Memoirs of General John Pope.* Chapel Hill: University of North Carolina Press, 1998.

Davis, Washington. *Camp Fire Chats.* Boston: B. B. Russell, 1890.

Devens, Richard Miller [pseud. Frazar Kirkland]. *The Pictorial Book of Anecdotes and Incidents of the War of the Rebellion.* Hartford, Conn.: Hartford Pub., 1867.

Donald, David Herbert, ed. *Inside Lincoln's Cabinet: The Civil War Diaries of Salmon P. Chase.* New York: Longmans, Green & Co., 1954.

Drake, Benjamin, and E. D. Mansfield. *Cincinnati in 1826.* Cincinnati: Morgan, Lodge, and Fisher, 1827.

Ellis, A[nderson]. N[elson]. "Sketch of the Life of William Nelson, Maj.-Gen. U.S.A." In *The Biographical Cyclopaedia and Portrait Gallery with a Historical Sketch of the State of Ohio.* Vol. 5. Cincinnati: Western Biographical Pub. Co., 1883–95. (Printed 37-page extract at the Cincinnati Historical Society)

Ellis, Dr. A. M. [N]. "Major General William Nelson." *Register of the Kentucky Historical Society* 7 (May 1906): 56–64.

Ellis, John B. *The Sights and Secrets of the National Capital.* New York: United States Pub. Co., 1869.

Emerson, E. W., and Waldo E. Forbes, eds. *The Journals of Ralph Waldo Emerson.* In *Ralph Waldo Emerson: Essays and Journal.* Garden City: Nelson Doubleday, 1968.

Fisher, Horace Cecil. *A Staff Officer's Story: The Personal Experiences of Colonel Horace Newton Fisher in the Civil War.* Boston: Thomas Todd Co., 1960.

[Fitch, John]. "An Officer." *Annals of the Army of the Cumberland. Comprising Biographies, Descriptions of Departments, Accounts of Expeditions, Skirmishes, and Battles.* Philadelphia: J. B. Lippincott & Co., 1863.

Flagg, Edmund. *Venice: The City of the Sea, from the Invasion by Napoleon in 1797 to the Capitulation to Radetzky, in 1849; with a Contemporaneous View of the Peninsula.* New York: Charles Scribner, 1853.

Foote, Henry S. *War of the Rebellion; or, Scylla and Charybdis.* New York: Harper & Brothers, 1866.

Force, M. F. *Campaigns of the Civil War. Vol. 2: From Fort Henry to Corinth.* 1881. Reprint, Edison, N.J.: Castle Books, 2002.

Frazee, W. D. *Reminiscences and Sermons*. Nashville: Gospel Advocate Pub. Co., 1898.

Fry, James B. *Killed by a Brother Soldier*. New York: G. P. Putnam's Sons, 1885.

———. *Military Miscellanies*. New York: Brentanno's, 1889.

———. *Operations of the Army under Buell*. New York: D. Van Nostrand, 1884.

Gilbert, Charles C. "Bragg's Invasion of Kentucky." *Southern Bivouac*. 6 vols. 1882–1887 (September 1883–84) 2: 87–88.

———. "Bragg's Invasion of Kentucky." *Southern Bivouac* n.s. 1 (June 1885–May 1886): Chapters 1: 217–22, 2: 296–301, 3: 336–42, 4: 430–36.

Gilmore, James R. [pseud. Edmund Kirke]. *Down in Tennessee and Back by Way of Richmond*. New York: Carleton, 1864.

Girardi, Robert I., ed. *Campaigning with Uncle Billy: The Civil War Memoir of Lyman S. Widney*. Victoria, B.C.: Trafford Pub., 2008.

Glover, Amos. "Diary of Amos Glover." Edited by Harry J. Carman. *Ohio Archeological and Historical Quarterly* 44 (April 1935): 258–72.

Goodloe, William Cassius. *Address on Kentucky Unionists in 1861: Read before the Society of Ex-Army and Navy Officers in Cincinnati, Ohio, April 10, 1884*. Cincinnati: Peter G. Thompson, 1884: 1–27.

Graf, Leroy P., and Ralph W. Haskins, eds. *The Papers of Andrew Johnson*. 16 vols. Knoxville: University of Tennessee Press, 1967–2000.

Grant, Ulysses S. "The Battle of Shiloh." *Century Magazine* 29 (February 1885): 593–614.

———. *Personal Memoirs of U. S. Grant*. 2 vols. New York: C. L. Webster & Co., 1885–86.

Green, Karen Mauer. *The Kentucky Gazette, 1801–1820*. Baltimore: Gateway Press, 1985.

Greenough, Mr. "Kossuth and Hayti, 1852."*Massachusetts Historical Society Proceedings* 44 (November 1910): 212–13.

Guerrant, Rev. Edward O. "Marshall and Garfield in Eastern Kentucky." In *Battles and Leaders of the Civil War*, edited by Robert U. Johnson and Clarence C. Buel., 1:393–97. New York: Century Co., 1887.

Hardy, Richardson. *The History and Adventures of the Cuban Expedition, from the First Movements down to the Dispersion of the Army at Key West, and the Arrest of General Lopez. Also: An Account of the Ten Deserters at Isla de Murgeres*. Cincinnati: Lorenzo Statton, 1850.

Hayes, John D., ed. *Samuel Francis Du Pont: A Selection from His Civil War Letters*. 3 vols. Ithaca, N.Y.: Cornell University Press, 1969.

Hazen, William B. *A Narrative of Military Service*. Boston: Ticknor & Co., 1885.

Johnson, Richard W. *A Soldier's Reminiscences in Peace and War*. Philadelphia: J. P. Lippincott & Co., 1886.

———. "War Memories." In *Military Order of the Loyal Legion of the United States*, compiled by William Marvel. 70 vols. Wilmington, N.C.: Broadfoot Pub. Co., 1991–97. 26:14.

Jordan, Thomas, and J. P. Pryor. *The Campaigns of Lieut. -Gen. N. B. Forrest, and Forrest's Cavalry*. New Orleans.1868. Reprint, New York: Da Capo Press, 1996.

Kell, John McIntosh. *Recollections of a Naval Life*. Washington, D.C.: Neale Co., 1900.

Kelly, Robert M. "Holding Kentucky for the Union." In *Battles and Leaders of the Civil War*, edited by Robert Underwood Johnson and Clarence C. Buel, 1:73–91. New York: Century Co., 1887.

Knox, Thomas Wallace. *Camp-fire and Cotton-field: Southern Adventure in Time of War*. New York, 1865. Reprint, Whitefish, Mont.: Kessinger Pub., 2004.

Longacre, Glenn V., and John E. Hass, eds. *To Battle for God and the Right: The Civil War Letter Books of Emerson Opdycke*. Champaign: University of Illinois Press, 2003.

Lossing, Benjamin J. *Pictorial History of the Civil War in the United States*. Hartford, Conn.: T. Belnap, 1868.

MacCabe, Julius P. Bolivar. *Directory of the City of Lexington and County of Fayette for 1838 and '39*. Lexington, Ky.: J. C. Noble, 1838.

Mackenna, Benjamín Vicuña. "Editor's Drawer." *Harper's New Monthly Magazine* 28 (April 1864): 714–17.

———. "General William Nelson." *La Voz de Chile* [NewYork/Santiago], November 20, 1862. Reprinted in the *Frankfort (Ky.) Commonwealth*, January 23, 1863.

Mansfield, Edward D. *The Mexican War*. New York: A. S. Barnes & Co., 1848.

Mathias, Frank F., ed. *Incidents and Experiences in the Life of Thomas W. Parsons from 1826 to 1900*. Lexington: University Press of Kentucky, 1975.

McPherson, James B. Letters. Battle of Shiloh. April 30, 1862. Sandusky County Scrap Book, <http://www.sandusky-county-scrapbook.net/McPherson/Letters3.htm#shiloh>.

"The Merchant Fleets and Navies of the World. " *DeBow's Review* 6 (October–November 1848): 327.

The Mexican War and Its Heroes: Being a Complete History of the Mexican War, Embracing all the Operations under Generals Taylor and Scott, with a Biography of the Officers. Also, an account of the conquests of California and New Mexico. 2 vols. Philadelphia: G. G. Evans, 1860.

Military Historical Society of Massachusetts. *Campaigns in Kentucky and Tennessee, including the battle of Chickamauga, 1862–1864: Papers of the Military Historical Society of Massachusetts*. Vol. 7. Boston: Military Historical Society of Massachusetts, 1908.

Miller, Maude Barnes. *Dear Wife Letters from a Union Colonel*. Ravenna, Ky.: Estill County Historical and Genealogical Society, 2001.

"Monthly Record of Current Events" *Harper's New Monthly Magazine* 18 (January 1859): 254–58.

Moore, Frank. ed. *The Rebellion Record: A Diary of American Events with Documents, Illustrative Incidents, Poetry, etc*. 12 vols. New York. G. P. Putnam, 1861–68.

Morse, Loren J., ed. *Civil War Diaries and Letters of Bliss Morse.* Wagoner, Okla.: L. J. Morse, 1985.

Nicolay, John G., and John Hay. "Abraham Lincoln: A History. The Border States." *Century Magazine* 36 (May 1888) : 56–78.

———. "Abraham Lincoln: A History. Tennessee and Kentucky." *Century Magazine* 36 (August 1888): 562–83.

———. "Abraham Lincoln: A History. The Mississippi and Shiloh." *Century Magazine* 36 (September 1888): 658–79.

Niven, John, ed. *The Salmon P. Chase Papers.* 5 vols. Akron: Kent State University Press, 1993.

"Notes and Military Affairs." *Scientific American* n.s. 7 (October 11, 1862): 227.

"Notes on Military and Navy Affairs, the Victory in Kentucky." *Scientific American* n.s. 5 (November 23, 1861): 322.

"The Old Flag over Jackson's Grave." *Scientific American* n.s. 6 (April 19, 1862): 242.

Oswandel, J. Jacob. *Notes of the Mexican War 1846–47–48.* Philadelphia: N. P., 1885.

Otis, Ephraim A. "Recollections of the Kentucky Campaign of 1862." In *Papers of the Military Historical Society of Massachusetts.* Boston, 1908, 7:227–54.

"Our Mission-Diplomacy and Navy." *United States Democratic Review* 31 (July 1852): 33–44.

"Our Navy." *Scientific American* n.s. 4 (March 30, 1861): 198.

Parker, William Harwar. *Recollections of a Naval Officer, 1846–1865.* New York. 1883. Reprint, Whitefish, Mont.: Kessinger Pub., 2008.

Pease, Theodore Calvin, and James G. Randall, eds. *The Diary of Orville Hickman Browning.* 2 vols. Springfield, Ill., 1925. Reprint, Whitefish, Mont.: Kessinger Pub. 2007.

Pulszky, Francis, and Theresa Pulszky. "White, Red, Black: Sketches of American Society." *Living Age* 37 (April 9, 1853): 97–104. [Originally published in the *New York Tribune*]

Read, T. B. "The Siege of Cincinnati." *Atlantic Monthly* 11 (February 1863): 229–35.

"Recollections of an Old Stager." *Harper's New Monthly Magazine* 46 (December 1872): 92–97.

Reed, Maj. David W. "Review of Villard's Memoirs and John Codman Ropes' Story of the Civil War, Especially the Chapters on 'Shiloh.'" In *Report of the Proceedings of the Society of the Army of the Tennessee at the Thirty-Sixth Meeting Held at Council Bluffs, Iowa, November 8–9, 1906* (Cincinnati: Charles O. Ebel, 1907).

"Reminiscences of Washington." *Atlantic Monthly* 47 (April 1881): 538–47.

Report of the Special Committee Appointed by the Common Council of the City of New York to Make Arrangements for the Reception of Gov. Louis Kossuth the Distinguished Hungarian Patriot. New York, 1852.

Richardson, Albert D. *The Secret Service, the Field, the Dungeon, and the Escape.* Hartford, Conn.: American Pub., 1865.

Russell, William Howard. *My Dairy North and South*. 2 vols. 1863. Reprint, edited by Eugene H. Bewanger, Baton Rouge: Louisiana State University Press, 2001.

Scheets, George. "Memoir of Adjutant George Scheets, C Company, 21st Ohio Volunteer Infantry; A Special Report: War Reminiscences. A Paper Read at the Regular Meeting of Ford Post. East Toledo, Ohio, December 1883.

Schuckers, Jacob W. *The Life and Public Services of Salmon Portland Chase*. 1874. Reprint, New York: Da Capo Press, 1970.

"The Secession Conspiracy in Kentucky, and Its Overthrow: With the Relations of Both to the General Revolt." *Danville Review* 3 (September 1862): 371–96.

Senour, Rev. F. *Morgan and His Captors*. Cincinnati: C. V. Vent, 1865.

Shanks, W. F. G. "Gossip about Our Generals." *Harper's New Monthly Magazine* 35 (July 1867): 210–16.

———. "Recollections of General Rousseau." *Harper's New Monthly Magazine* 31(November 1865): 764.

———. "Recollections of Sherman." *Harper's New Monthly Magazine* 30 (April 1865): 640–46.

Sheridan, Philip H. *Personal Memoirs of P. H. Sheridan, General, United States Army*. 2 vols. London. 1888.

Simpson, Brooks D., and Jean V. Berlin, eds. *Sherman's Civil War: Selected Correspondence of William T. Sherman, 1860–1865*. Chapel Hill: University of North Carolina Press, 1999.

Smith, John David, and William Cooper Jr. *A Union Woman in Civil War Kentucky: The Dairy of Frances Peter*. Lexington: University Press of Kentucky, 2000.

Spafford., Ara C., 1st. Sergeant, C Company, 21st Ohio Volunteer Infantry. Letter to the *Perrysburg* (Ohio) *Journal*, November 14, 1861.

Stevenson, B. F. "Cumberland Gap." In *Sketches of War History, 1861–1865: Papers Read before the Commandery of the State of Ohio, Military Order of the Loyal Legion of the United States, 1883–1886*. Cincinnati: Robert Clarke & Co., 1888.1:329–57, <http://suvcw.org/mollus/warpapers/OHv1p329.htm>.

Stevenson, Daniel. "General Nelson, Kentucky, and Lincoln Guns." *Magazine of American History* 10 (August 1883): 115–39.

Stone, Charles P. "Washington on the Eve of War." *Century Magazine* 26 (July 1883): 458–67.

Stone, Henry. "The Battle of Shiloh." *Papers of the Military Historical Society of Massachusetts*. Boston, 1908, 7:31–100.

———. "The Operations of General Buell in Kentucky and Tennessee in 1862." *Papers of the Military Historical Society of Massachusetts*. Boston, 1908, 7:255–92.

Tapp, Hambleton, and James C. Klotter, eds. *The Union, the Civil War, and John W. Tuttle: A Kentucky Captain's Account*. Frankfort: Kentucky Historical Society, 1980.

Taylor, Rev. Fitch W., A.M., U.S.N. *The Broad Pennant; or, A Cruise in the United States Flag Ship of the Gulf Squadron during the Mexican Difficulties together with Sketches of the Mexican War.* New York: Leavitt & Tron Co., 1848.

Thompson, Robert Means, and Richard Wainwright, eds. *Confidential Correspondence of Gustavus Vasa Fox, Assistant Secretary of the Navy, 1861–1865.* Vol. 1. New York: De Vinne Press, 1918.

Victor, Orville J. *Incidents and Anecdotes of the War.* New York: J. D. Torrey, 1862.

"U. S. Navy, 1st January, 1852." *Debow's Review* 13 (December 1852): 614.

Villard, Henry. *Lincoln on the Eve of '61.* Edited by Harold G. and Oswald Garrison Villard. New York: Alfred E. Knopf, 1941.

———. *The Memoirs of Henry Villard: Journalist and Financier, 1835–1900.* 2 vols. 1904. Reprint, New York: Da Capo Press, 1969.

Wallace, Lew. *Lew Wallace: An Autobiography.* 2 vols. New York: Harper and Brothers, 1906.

Warden, Robert B. *An Account of the Private Life and Public Services of Salmon Portland Chase.* Cincinnati: Wilstach, Baldwin and Co., 1874.

Wells, Gideon. *The Diary of Gideon Wells.* 3 vols. Cambridge, Mass.: Houghton Mifflin, 1911.

Wilcox, Cadmus M., and Mary Rachel Wilcox, eds. *History of the Mexican War.* Washington, D.C.: Church News Pub. Co., 1892.

Wood, William Maxwell. "The Late Commodore Dallas." *Southern Literary Magazine* 11 (January 1845): 22–23.

Wright, J. M. "A Glimpse of Perryville." *Southern Bivouac* 1 (1885–86): 149-54.

Regimental Histories

Aten, Henry J. *History of the Eighty-fifth Regiment, Illinois Volunteer Infantry.* Hiawatha, Kans.: The Association, 1901.

Bennett, L. G., and William M. Haigh. *History of the Thirty-Sixth Illinois Volunteers during the War of the Rebellion.* Aurora, Ill.: Knickerbocker & Hodder, 1876.

Bering, John A., and Thomas Montgomery. *History of the Forty-Eighth Ohio Vet. Vol. Inf.* Hillsboro, Ohio. Highland News Office, 1880, <http://www.48ovvi.org>.

Blackburn, John. *A Hundred Miles, a Hundred Heartbreaks.* N.p.: Reed Printing, 1972.

Briant, Charles C. *History of the Sixth Regiment Indiana Volunteer Infantry of Both the Three Months' and Three Years' Services.* Indianapolis: W. B. Burford, 1891.

Bridge, Carolyn Sue. *These Men Were Heroes Once: The Sixty-Ninth Indiana Volunteer Infantry.* West Lafayette, Ind.: Twin Publications, 2005.

Canfield, S. S. *History of the 21st Regiment Ohio Volunteer Infantry.* Toledo: Vrooman, Sanders & Bateman, 1893.

Conner, Philip Syng. *The Home Squadron under Commodore Conner in the War with Mexico: Being a Synopis of Its Services (With an Addendum Con-*

taining Admiral Temple's Memoir of the Landing of Our Army at Vera Cruz in 1847), 1846–1847. Philadelphia. 1896. Reprint, Whitefish, Mont.: Kessinger Pub., 2007.

Cope, Alexis. *The Fifteenth Ohio Volunteers and Its Campaign, War of 1861–65.* Columbus, Ohio, 1916.

Cutcheon, Byron M., comp. *The Story of the Twentieth Michigan Infantry.* Lansing, Mich.: R. Smith Printing Co., 1904.

Dodge, Wm. Sumner. *History of the Old Second Division, Army of the Cumberland, Commanders M'Cook, Sill, and Johnson.* Chicago: Church & Goodman, 1864.

Grose, William. *The Story of the Marches, Battles and Incidents of the 36th Regiment Indiana Volunteer Infantry.* New Castle, Ind.: Courier Co., 1891.

Hannaford, E. *The Story of a Regiment: A History of the Campaigns and Association in the Field of the Sixth Regiment of Ohio Volunteer Infantry.* Cincinnati. Privately printed, 1868.

Hoffman, Mark. *My Brave Mechanic: The First Michigan Engineers and Their Civil War.* Detroit: Wayne State University Press, 2007.

Kimberly, Robert L., and Ephraim S. Holloway. *The Forty-first Ohio Veteran Volunteer Infantry in the War of the Rebellion, 1861–1865.* Cleveland: W. R. Smellie, 1897.

Nichol, Everett A., and Marie Nichol. *Battered Destinies.* Pasadena, Tex. : Infotrans Press, 1996. Edited reprint of Samuel Cordell Frey et al., *A Military Record of Battery D, First Ohio Veteran Volunteer Light Artillery: Its Military History, 1861–1865.* Oil City, Pa.: Derrick Pub., 1908.

Pickerill, William N. *History of the Third Indiana Cavalry.* Indianapolis: Aetna Printing, 1906.

Prokopowicz, Gerald J. *All for the Regiment: The Army of the Ohio, 1861–1862.* Chapel Hill: University of North Carolina Press, 2001.

Reinhart, Joseph R. *A History of the 6th Kentucky Volunteer Infantry: The Boys Who Feared No Noise.* Louisville, Ky.: Beargrass Press, 2000.

Sligh, Charles R. *History of the Services of the First Regiment Michigan Engineers and Mechanics during the Civil War, 1861–1865.* Grand Rapids: White Printing,1921.

Speed, Thomas, R. M. Kelly, and Alfred Pirtle. *The Union Regiments of Kentucky.* Louisville, Ky.: *Courier-Journal,* 1897.

Tarrant, Eastham. *The Wild Riders of the First Kentucky Cavalry.* Louisville, Ky.: R. H. Carothers, 1894.

Van Horne, Thomas B. *History of the Army of the Cumberland: Its Organization, Campaigns, Battles, Written at the Request of General George H. Thomas.* 1875. Reprint, New York: Smithmark, 1996.

Wright, T. J., Capt. *History of the Eighth Regiment Kentucky Vol. Inf. U.S.A., during Its Three Years of Campaigns.* St. Joseph, Mo.: St. Joseph Steam Printing, 1880.

SECONDARY SOURCES

Books Consulted

Abbott, John S. C. *The History of the Civil War in America: Comprising a Full and Impartial Account of the Origin and Progress of the Rebellion, of the Various Naval and Military Engagements, of the Heroic Deeds Performed by Armies and Individuals, Touching Scenes in the Field, the Camp, the Hospital, and the Cabin.* 2 vols. Springfield, Mass.: C. A. Nichols & Co., 1877. Originally published in 1863.

Andrews, J. Cutler. *The North Reports the Civil War.* Pittsburgh, Pa.: University of Pittsburgh Press, 1955.

———. *The South Reports the Civil War.* Princeton, N.J.: Princeton University Press, 1970.

Appleton's Annual Cyclopedia and Register of Important Events of the Year: 1880. N.s. 5. New York: D. Appleton & Co., 1885.

Arnold, James R. *Shiloh 1862: The Death of Innocence.* Oxford: Osprey Pub., 1998.

Bauer, K. Jack. *The Mexican War, 1846–1848.* New York: Macmillan & Co., 1974.

———. *Surfboats and Horse Marines: U.S. Naval Operations in the Mexican War, 1846–48.* Annapolis: U.S. Naval Institute Press, 1969.

Béla Várdy, Steven. "Kossuth's Effort to Enlist America into the Hungarian Cause." *Hungarian Studies*, vol. 16. Budapest, 2002.

Biographical Encyclopedia of Kentucky. Cincinnati: J. M. Armstrong & Co., 1878. Reprint, Easely, S.C.: Southern Historical Press, 1980.

Boatner, Mark M., III. *The Civil War Dictionary.* New York: Davis McKay, 1959.

Borneman, Walter R. *1812: The War That Forged a Nation.* New York: Harper Collins, 2004.

Bradford, James C., ed. *Captains of the Old Steam Navy: Makers of the American Naval Tradition, 1840–1880.* Annapolis: U.S. Naval Institute Press, 1986.

———. *Quarterdeck and Bridge: Two Centuries of American Naval Leaders.* Annapolis: U.S. Naval Institute Press, 1997.

Bradsby, H. C. *History of Vigo County, Indiana, with Biographical Selections.* Chicago: S. B. Nelson & Co., 1891.

Breithaupt, Richard. *Aztec Club of 1847: Military Society of the Mexican War, 1847–1997.* Universal City, Calif.: Walika Pub. 1998.

Bruce, Robert V. *Lincoln and the Tools of War.* Indianapolis: Bobbs-Merrill, 1956.

Burlingame, Michael, ed. *Lincoln's Journalist: John Hay's Anonymous Writings for the Press, 1860–1864.* Carbondale: Southern Illinois University Press, 1999.

Caldwell, Robert G. *The Lopez Expeditions to Cuba, 1848–1851.* Princeton, N.J.: Princeton University Press, 1915.

Callahan, James Morton. *Cuba and International Relations: A Historical Study in American Diplomacy.* Baltimore: Johns Hopkins Press, 1899.

Chambers, John W., ed. *The Oxford Companion to American History.* New York: Oxford University Press. 1999.

Clift, G. Glenn. *History of Maysville and Mason County.* Lexington, Ky.: Transylvania Printing, 1936.

———. *Kentucky Obituaries, 1787–1854.* Reprint, Baltimore: Genealogical Pub., 1977.

Collins, Richard H., and Collins, Lewis. *History of Kentucky.* 2 vols. Covington, Ky., 1874. Reprint, Berea: Kentucky Imprints, 1976.

Connelly, Thomas L. *Army of the Heartland: The Army of Tennessee, 1861–1862.* Baton Rouge: Louisiana State University Press, 1967.

Cook, Michael L., and Bettie A. Cummings Cook. *Fayette County Records.* Vol. 3. Evansville, Ind.: Cook Pub., 1985.

Cooling, Benjamin Franklin. *The Campaign for Fort Donelson.* National Parks Civil War Series. Fort Washington, Pa.: Eastern National, 1999.

Cooper, Edward S. *William Babcock Hazen: The Best Hated Man.* Madison, N.J.: Fairleigh Dickinson University Press, 2005.

Cortissoz, Royal. *The Life of Whitelaw Reid.* 2 vols. London: Thorton Butterworth Ltd., 1921.

Coulter, E. Merton. *The Civil War and Readjustment in Kentucky.* Gloucester, Ma.: Peter Smith, 1966.

Cozzens, Peter. *General John Pope: A Life for the Nation.* Chicago: University of Illinois Press, 2000.

Cullum, George W. *Biographical Register of the Officers and Cadets of the United States Military Academy at West Point from Its Establishment in 1802, to 1890; with the Early History of the Untied States Military Academy.* 3rd ed. 3 vols. New York: Houghton, Mifflin & Co., 1891.

Cunningham, O. Edward,. Gary D. Joiner, and Timothy B. Smith, eds. *Shiloh and the Western Campaign of 1862.* New York: Salvas Beatie, 2007.

Current, Richard N. *Lincoln's Loyalists: Union Soldiers from the Confederacy.* Boston: Northeastern University Press, 1992.

Dana, Richard Henry, Jr. *Two Years Before the Mast.* New York: P. F. Collier & Son, 1909.

Daniel, Larry J. *Days of Glory: The Army of the Cumberland.* Baton Rouge: Louisiana State University Press, 2004.

———. *Shiloh: The Battle That Changed the Civil War.* New York: Touchstone, 1998.

Davenport, Charles Benedict. *Naval Officers, Their Heredity and Development.* 1919. Reprint,. Whitefish, Mont.: Kessinger Pub., 2008.

Davis, Burke. *The Civil War: Strange and Fascinating Facts.* New York: Fairfax Press, 1982.

Dawson, Henry B. *Battles of the United States, by Sea and Land.* New York: Johnson, Fry, & Co., 1858.

DeConde, Alexander, et al., eds. *Encyclopedia of American Foreign Policy.* 2nd ed. 3 vols. New York: Scribner, 2002.

Donald, David Herbert. *Lincoln.* New York: Simon & Schuster, 1995.

Draper, John William. *History of the American Civil War.* 3 vols. New York: Harper & Brothers, 1867–70.

Dudley, William S. *Going South: U.S. Navy Officer Resignations and Dismissals on the Eve of the Civil War.* Washington, D.C.: Naval Historical Foundation, 1981.

Dunn, Byron A. *General Nelson's Scout,* 7th ed. Chicago: A. C. McClurg "& Co., 1909. [Fiction]

Dyer, Frederick H. *A Compendium of the War of the Rebellion.* 3 vols. New York: Thomas Yoseloff, 1959.

Ellis, William Arba, ed. *Norwich University, 1819–1911: Her History, Her Graduates, Her Roll of Honor.* 3 vols. Montpelier, Vt.: Capital City Press, 1911.

Engle, Stephen D. *Don Carlos Buell: Most Promising of All.* Chapel Hill: University of North Carolina Press, 1999.

———. *Struggle for the Heartland: The Campaigns from Fort Henry to Corinth.* Lincoln: University of Nebraska Press, 2001.

Evans, Clement A., ed. *Confederate Military History.* 13 vols. Secaucus, N.J.: Blue & Gray Press, 1997.

Foner, Eric, and John A. Garraty, eds. *The Readers Companion to American History.* Boston: Houghton Mifflin, 1991.

Foote, Shelby. *The Civil War: A Narrative: Fort Donelson to Memphis.* 40th anniversary ed. Vol. 2. Alexandria, Va.: Time-Life Books, 1998.

Foulke, William Dudley. *Life of Oliver P. Morton, Including His Important Speeches.* Indianapolis: Bowen-Merrill Co., 1899.

Frazier, Donald, ed. *The United States and Mexico at War.* New York: Simon & Schuster, 1997.

Freeman, Douglas Southhall. *R. E. Lee: A Biography.* 4 vols. New York: Charles Scribner & Sons, 1934.

Frost, John. *The Mexican War and Its Warriors.* Philadelphia: H. Mansfield, 1850.

———. *Pictorial History of the Mexican War.* Philadelphia: Thomas, Cowperwait & Co., 1849.

Garraty, John A., and Mark C. Carnes, eds. *American National Biography.* 24 vols. New York: Oxford University Press, 1999.

Goodwin, Doris Kearns. *Team of Rivals: The Political Genius of Abraham Lincoln.* New York: Simon & Shuster, 2005.

Greve, Charles T. *Centennial History of Cincinnati.* Chicago: Biographical Co., 1904.

Griffis, William Elliot. *Matthew Calbraith Perry: A Typical American Naval Officer.* Boston: Cupples and Hurd, 1887.

Grimsley, Mark, and Steven E. Woodworth. *Shiloh: A Battlefield Guide.* Lincoln: University of Nebraska Press, 2006.

Hafendorfer, Kenneth A. *The Battle of Richmond Kentucky, August 30, 1862.* Louisville, Ky.: KH Press, 2006.

———. *The Battle of Wild Cat Mountain.* Louisville, Ky.: KH Press, 2003.

———. *They Died by Twos and Tens: The Confederate Cavalry in the Kentucky Campaign of 1862.* Louisville, Ky.: KH Press, 1995.

Hall, Clifton R. *Andrew Johnson: Military Governor of Tennessee.* Princeton, N.J.: Princeton University Press, 1916.

Hall, Susan G. *Appalachian Ohio and the Civil War, 1862–1863.* Jefferson, N.C.: McFarland & Co., 2000.

Hamilton, Frances Frazee. *Ancestral Lines of the Doniphan, Frazee and Hamilton Families.* Greenfield, Ind.: Wm. Mitchell Print Co., 1928.

Harris, Brayton. *Blue and Gray in Black and White: Newspapers in the Civil War.* Washington, D.C.: Brasseys [Potomac Books], 1999.

Harrison, Lowell H. *The Civil War in Kentucky.* Lexington: University Press of Kentucky, 1975.

Harrison, Lowell H., and James C. Klotter. *A New History of Kentucky.* Lexington: University Press of Kentucky, 1997.

Hatch, Alden. *Heroes of Annapolis.* New York: Julian Messner, 1943.

Hess, Earl J. *Banners to the Breeze: The Kentucky Campaign, Corinth, and Stones River.* Lincoln: University of Nebraska Press, 2001.

Hoppin, James Mason. *Life of Andrew Hull Foote.* New York: Harper & Brothers, 1874.

Hudson, Blaine J. *Fugitive Slaves and the Underground Railroad in the Kentucky Borderland.* Jefferson, N.C.: Borderland, 2002.

Hughes, Nathaniel Cheairs, Jr., and Gordon D. Whitney. *Jefferson Davis in Blue: The Life of Sherman's Relentless Warrior.* Baton Rouge: Louisiana State University Press, 2002.

Hughes, Susan Lyons. *Camp Dick Robinson: Holding Kentucky for the Union in 1861.* Frankfort: Kentucky Historical Society, 1990.

Jenkins, John S. *History of the War between the United States and Mexico, from the Commencement of Hostilities to the Ratification of the Treaty of Peace.* Auburn, N.Y.: Derby and Miller, 1850.

Johnson, Allen, and Dumas Malone, eds. *Dictionary of American Biography.* 11 vols. New York: Charles Scribner & Sons, 1958–64.

Johnson, Robert Erwin. *Thence Round Cape Horn: The Story of United States Naval Forces on Pacific Station, 1818–1923.* Annapolis: U.S. Naval Institute Press, 1963.

Kabdebo, Thomas. *Diplomat in Exile: Francis Pulszky's Political Activities in England, 1849–1860.* New York: Columbia University Press, 1979.

Katcher, Philip. *The American Civil War Source Book.* London: Arms & Armour Press, 1998.

Kettell, Thomas P. *History of the Great Rebellion: From its Commencement to Its Close; Giving an Account of Its Origin, the Secession of the Southern States, and the Formation of the Confederate Government, the Concentration of the Military and Financial Resources of the Federal Government; Embellished with over 125 Engravings, including 80 Portraits of Prominent Statesmen, Military and Naval Officers.* Cincinnati: F. A. Howe, 1865.

Kinard, Jeff. *Pistols: An Illustrated History of Their Impact.* Santa Barbara: ABC-Clio, 2003.

Kleber, John E., ed. *The Encyclopedia of Louisville*. Lexington: University Press of Kentucky, 2000.

——. editor-in-chief. *The Kentucky Encyclopedia*. Lexington: University Press of Kentucky, 1992.

Klotter, James C. *Kentucky Justice, Southern Honor and American Manhood*. Baton Rouge: Louisiana State University Press, 2003.

Komlós, John H. *Louis Kossuth in America, 1851–1852*. Buffalo, N.Y.: East European Institute, 1973.

Lambert, D. Warren. "The Decisive Battle of Richmond." In *The Civil War in Kentucky: Battle for the Bluegrass State*, edited by Kent Masterson Brown, 103–36. Mason City, Iowa: Salvas Pub. Co., 2000.

——. *When the Ripe Pears Fell: The Battle of Richmond*. Richmond, Ky.: Madison County Historical Society, 1995.

Langer, William L., ed. *An Encyclopedia of World History*. 5th ed. Boston: Houghton Mifflin, 1972.

Lee, Byron A. *Naval Warrior: The Life of Commodore Isaac Mayo*. Linthicum, Md.: Anne Arundel County Historical Society, 2002.

Lee, Lucy C. *A Historical Sketch of Mason County*, Kentucky. Louisville, Ky.: Press of the Masonic Home Journal, n.d. [1928].

Leech, Margaret. *Reveille in Washington, 1860–1865*. New York: Harper & Brothers, 1941.

Lewis, Lloyd. *Sherman: Fighting Prophet*. New York: Harcourt Brace, 1932.

Lowry, Thomas P. *Don't Shoot That Boy! Abraham Lincoln and Military Justice*. Mason City: Salvas Pub. Co., 1999.

Maclay, Edgar S., and Roy C. Smith. *A History of the United States Navy from 1775 to 1902*. New York: D. Appleton & Co., 1906.

Marolda, Edward J. *The Washington Navy Yard: An Illustrated History*. Washington, D.C.: U.S. Naval History Center, 1999.

Martin, David G. *The Shiloh Campaign: March–April 1862*. Conshohocken, Pa.: Combined Books, 1996.

Marryat, Frederick. *Peter Simple and the Three Cutters*. London: Little Brown & Co., 1834. [Fiction]

McBride, W. Stephen. *The Union Occupation of Munfordville, Kentucky, 1861–1865*. Munfordville, Ky.: Hart County Historical Society, 1999.

McDonough, James Lee. *War in Kentucky: From Shiloh to Perryville*. Knoxville: University of Tennessee Press, 1994.

McDowell, Robert E. *Louisville in the Civil War, 1861–1865*. Louisville, Ky.: Louisville Civil War Round Table, 1962.

Melville, Herman. *White Jacket; or, The World in a Man-of-War*. Boston: Harper & Brothers, 1850. [Fiction]

Meriwether, Colyer. *Raphael Semmes*. Philadelphia: George W. Jacobs & Co., 1913.

Merk, Frederick. *The Monroe Doctrine and American Expansionism, 1843–1849*. New York: Knopf, 1966.

Miles, Jim. *Piercing the Heartland*. Nashville, Tenn.: Rutledge Hill Press, 1991.

Miller, Caroline R., ed. *African-American Records: Bracken County, Kentucky, 1797–1999.* 2 vols. Brooksville, Ky.: Bracken County Historical Society, 1999.

Mitchell, Brig. Gen. William A. *Outlines of the World's Military History.* Harrisburg, Pa.: Military Service Pub. Co., 1931.

Morris, Richard B., ed. *Encyclopedia of American History.* New York: Harper and Row, 1998.

The National Cyclopedia of American Biography. 9th ed. New York: James T. White & Co., 1924.

Nevins, Allen. *The Emergence of Abraham Lincoln.* 2 vols. New York: Scribner's, 1950.

Niven, John. *Salmon P. Chase: A Biography.* New York: Oxford University Press, 1995.

Noe, Kenneth. *Perryville: This Grand Havoc of Battle.* Lexington: University Press of Kentucky, 2001.

Peck, Taylor. *Round Shot to Rockets: A History of the Washington Navy Yard.* Annapolis: U.S. Naval Institute Press, 1949.

Pell, Rosemarie Bonwell. *Bracken County, Kentucky, Marriages and Bonds, 1797–1859.* Brooksville, Ky.: Bracken County Historical Society, 1997.

———. *Bracken County, Kentucky, Tax Lists, 1797–1826.* 2 vols. Brooksville, Ky.: Bracken County Historical Society, 2002.

Penn, William A. *Rattling Spurs and Broad-Brimmed Hats: The Civil War in Cynthiana and Harrison County, Kentucky.* Cynthiana, Ky.: Battle Grove Press, 1995.

Perrin, William H., ed. *History of Bourbon, Scott, Harrison, and Nicholas Counties, Kentucky.* Chicago: O. L. Baskin & Co., 1882.

———. ed . *History of Fayette County, Kentucky.* Chicago: O. L. Baskin & Co., 1882.

Perrin, William H., J. H. Battle, and G. C. Kniffin, eds. *Kentucky: A History of the State.* Louisville, Ky.: F. A. Battey & Co., 1887. Reprint, Southern Historical Press, 1979.

Perry, Robert. *Jack May's War.* Johnson City, Tenn.: Overmountain Press, 1998.

Pickett, Thomas Edward. *The Quest for a Lost Race: Presenting the Theory of Paul B. DuChaillu, an Eminent Ethnologist and Explorer, that the English-speaking People of To-day are Descended from the Scandinavians rather than the Teutons, from the Normans rather than the Germans.* Louisville, Ky.: N.p., 1907.

Potter, David M. *The Impending Crisis, 1848–1861.* New York: Harper & Row, 1967.

Pratt, Fletcher. *A Short History of the Civil War: Ordeal by Fire.* 1935. Reprint, Mineola, N.Y.: Dover Publications, 1997.

Preston, John David. *The Civil War in the Big Sandy Valley of Kentucky.* Baltimore: Gateway Press, 1984.

Pulszky, Francis, and Theresa Pulszky. *White, Red, Black: Sketches of Society in the United States.* New York: Redfield, 1853.

Quisenberry, Anderson C. *Kentucky in the War of 1812.* Frankfort: Kentucky Historical Society, 1915.

———. *Lopez's Expeditions to Cuba, 1850 and 1851*. Louisville, Ky.: John P. Morton & Co., 1906.

Randall, J. G., and David Donald. *The Civil War and Reconstruction*. 2nd ed. Boston: D. C. Heath & Co., 1961.

Rives, George L. *The United States and Mexico, 1821–1848*. New York: Charles Scribner's Sons, 1913.

Rose, Annella Louise. *Fayette County Census, 1820–1850*. Utica, Ky.: McDowell Pub., 1982.

Sawyers, Sherry, et al., eds. *Mason County, Kentucky, Marriage Bonds and Permissive Notes*. 8 vols. Privately printed, n.d.

Schroeder, John H. *Matthew Calbraith Perry: Antebellum Sailor and Diplomat*. Annapolis: U.S. Naval Institute Press, 2001.

Shaler, Nathaniel Southgate. *Kentucky: A Pioneer Commonwealth*. Boston: Houghton Mifflin, 1897.

Sholk, Harry. *Drumbeats in the Valley: A Story of Life at Norwich University in the Early Nineteenth Century*. Haverford, Pa.: Infinity Pub., 2004. [Fiction]

Simon, John Y., ed. *The Papers of Ulysses S. Grant*. Vol. 31: *January 1, 1883–July 23, 1885*. Carbondale: Southern Illinois University Press, 2009.

Sisa, Stephen. *The Spirit of Hungary: A Panorama of Hungarian History and Culture*. Ontario: Vista Court Books, 1995.

Smith, Edward Conrad. *The Borderland in the Civil War*. New York: Macmillan, 1927.

Smith, Jean Edward. *Grant*. New York: Simon & Schuster, 2001.

Smith, Justin H. *The War with Mexico*. 2 vols. New York: Macmillan, 1919.

Speed, Thomas. *The Union Cause in Kentucky, 1860–1865*. New York: G. P. Putnam's Sons, 1907.

Spencer, Donald S. *Louis Kossuth and Young America: A Study of Sectionalism and Foreign Policy, 1848–1852*. Columbia: University of Missouri Press, 1977.

Stampp, Kenneth M. *Indiana Politics during the Civil War*. Indianapolis: Indiana Historical Bureau, 1949.

Stevens, Joseph E. *1863: The Rebirth of a Nation*. New York: Random House, 2001.

Street, James, Jr., and editors of Time-Life Books. *The Struggle for Tennessee: Tupelo to Stones River*. Alexandria, Va.: Time-Life, 1985.

Supplement to the Official Records of the Union and Confederate Armies. Edited by Janet B. Hewett et al. 100 volumes. Wilmington, N.C.: Broadfoot Pub. Co., 1994–2006.

Sweetman, Jack. *The U.S. Naval Academy: An Illustrated History*. 2nd ed. Annapolis: U.S. Naval Institute Press, 1979.

Taylor, Lenette S. *"The Supply for Tomorrow Must Not Fail": The Civil War of Captain Simon Perkins, Jr., a Union Quartermaster*. Kent, Ohio: Kent State University Press, 2004.

Time-Life Books. *The Battle Atlas of the Civil War*. Reprint, New York: Barnes and Noble, 1996.

Todorich, Charles. *The Spirited Years: A History of the Antebellum Naval Academy*. Annapolis: U.S. Naval Institute Press, 1984.

United States Naval Academy Alumni Association. *Register of Alumni, Graduates, and Former Naval Cadets and Midshipmen: Inclusive of the Naval Academy Class of 1956.* Annapolis: The Association, 1956.

Valle, James E. *Rocks and Shoals: Naval Discipline in the Age of Fighting Sail.* Annapolis: U.S. Naval Institute Press, 1980.

Warner, Ezra J. *Generals in Blue: Lives of Union Commanders.* Baton Rouge: Louisiana State University Press, 1964.

———. *Generals in Gray: Lives of Confederate Commanders.* Baton Rouge: Louisiana State University Press, 1960.

Webster's Biographical Dictionary. Springfield, Mass.: G & C. Merriam Co., 1943.

Wheelan, Joseph. *Invading Mexico: America's Continental Dream and the Mexican War, 1846–1848.* New York: Perseus Pub., 2007.

Wilke, Franc Bangs. *Pen and Powder.* Boston: Ticknor & Co., 1888.

Wimberg, Robert J. *Cincinnati and the Civil War: Off to Battle.* Cincinnati: Ohio Book Store, 1992.

———. *Cincinnati and the Civil War: Under Attack.* Cincinnati: Ohio Book Store, 1999.

Articles

Allen, Stacy D. "Crossroad of the Western Confederacy: Corinth." A Visitors Guide. *Blue & Gray Magazine* (2002): 1–76.

———. "Shiloh!" A Visitors Guide. *Blue & Gray Magazine* (1997): 1–76.

Bartman, Rev. Roger J. "Joseph Holt and Kentucky in the Civil War." *Filson Club History Quarterly* 40 (April 1966): 105–22.

Bearrs, Edwin C. "General Nelson Saves the Day at Shiloh." *Register of the Kentucky Historical Society* 63 (January 1965): 39–69.

Buckland, Ralph P. "Description of the Battle of Shiloh." In *Report of the Proceedings of the Society of the Army of the Cumberland at the Fourteenth Annual Meeting, Held at Cincinnati, Ohio April 6th and 7th, 1881.* Cincinnati: F. W. Freeman, 1885.

Campbell, Peter Scott. "The Civil War Reminiscences of John Marshall Harlan." *Journal of Supreme Court History* 32 (November 2007): 249–75.

Cist, Henry M., Jr. "Cincinnati with the War Fever, 1861." *Magazine of American History* 14 (July–December 1885): 138–47.

Clark, Paul C., Jr., and Edward H. Mosely. "D-Day Veracruz, 1847–A Grand Design." *Joint Force Quarterly* 10 (Winter 1995–96): 102–15.

Coburn, John. "General Recalls Civil War Experiences in Kentucky during 1861–1862: Action at Louisville, Frankfort, Wildcat Hill, and Cumberland Gap." *Kentucky Explorer* 12 (June1997): 46–50.

Cooper, Susan F. "Rear-Admiral William Branford Shubrick." *Harper's New Monthly Magazine* 53 (August 1876): 400–408.

Fahey, John H., M.D. "The 'Fighting Doctor': Bernard John Dowling Irwin in the Civil War." *North & South* 9 (March 2006): 36–50.

Feipel, Louis N. "The Navy and Filibustering in the Fifties." *United States Naval Institute Proceedings* 44 (April 1918): 769.

Fried, Joseph P. "How One Union General Murdered Another." *Civil War Times* 1 (June 1962): 14–16.

"General Nelson Was Noted for His Temper and Bad Talk." *Kentucky Explorer* 14 (September 1999): 8–10.

Griese, Arthur A. "A Louisville Tragedy: 1862." *Filson Club History Quarterly* 26 (April 1952): 133–54.

"Editor's Drawer." *Harper's New Monthly Magazine* 52 (January 1876): 3–12.

——. *Harper's New Monthly Magazine* 97 (September 1898): 499–664.

Hayes, John D. "Civil War Naval Officers, Southern Born." *Shipmate Magazine* 24 (March 1961): 15.

Haviland, John Von Sonntag. "The Gwin Fancy-Dress Ball (1858)." *Magazine of History with Notes and Queries*, Extra No. 23 (October 1913): 352–89.

Herring, Eliza A. "The Hoskins of Kentucky." *Register of the Kentucky Historical Society* 15 (May 1917): 9–14.

Jenkins, Kirk C. "A Shooting at the Galt House: The Death of General William Nelson." *Civil War History* 43 (June 1997): 101–18.

Kann, William J. "Mahlon D. Mason and the Civil War in Kentucky: The Politics of Martial Glory." *Register of the Kentucky Historical Society* 96 (Summer 1998): 221–47.

Kinkaid, Robert L. "Joshua Fry Speed, Lincoln's Confidential Agent in Kentucky." *Register of the Kentucky Historical Society* 52 (April 1954): 99–110.

——. "Joshua Speed, Lincoln's Most Intimate Friend." *Filson Club History Quarterly* 17 (April 1943): 63–129.

Klein, Maury. "When New York Became the U.S. Media Capital." *City Journal* 6 (Summer 1996): 1–11.

Koerting, Gayla. "For Law and Order: Joseph Holt, the Civil War, and the Judge Advocate General's Department." *Register of the Kentucky Historical Society* 97 (Winter 1999): 1–25.

Lafferty, W. T., ed. "The Civil War Reminiscences of John Acker Lafferty." *Register of the Kentucky Historical Society* 59 (January 1961): 1–28.

Messmer, Charles K. "Louisville and the Confederate Invasion of 1862." *Register of the Kentucky Historical Society* 55 (October 1957): 299–324.

——. "Louisville during the Civil War." *Filson Club History Quarterly* 52 (April 1978): 206–33.

Myers, Frank Elliott. "Died for Discipline." *Overland Monthly* 26 (March 1897): 303–6.

Oliver, John W. "Louis Kossuth's Appeal to the Middle West—1852." *Mississippi Valley Historical Review* 14 (March 1928): 481–95.

Paull, Joseph F. "A Most Unusual Alumnus." *Shipmate Magazine* 36 (September 1973): 15.

Peckham, Howard H. "I Have Been Basely Murdered." *American Heritage* 14 (August 1963): 88–92.

Quisenberry, A. C. "The Battle of Richmond, Kentucky, September 1862." *Register of the Kentucky Historical Society* 16 (September 1918): 9–17.

———. "Kentucky's 'Neutrality' in 1861." *Register of the Kentucky Historical Society* 15 (May 1917): 9–21.

"Resignations of Army and Navy Officers." *Skedaddle* 2 (February 12, 2005): 17, <http://www.pddoc.com/skedaddle/articles/index.html>.

Scalf, Henry P. "The Battle of Ivy Mountain." *Register of the Kentucky Historical Society* 56 (January 1958): 11–26.

Schneider, Frederick. "Civil War Murder Weapon." *North South Trader's Civil War* 26 (1999): 22–33.

Scroggs, William Oscar. "William Walker and the Steamship Corporation in Nicaragua." *American Historical Review* 10 (July 1905): 792–93.

Sheldon, N. L. "Norwich University." *New England Magazine* n.s. 20 (March 1899): 65–85.

Smith, William Farrar. "The Campaign of 1861–1862 in Kentucky Unfolded through the Correspondence of Its Leaders." *Magazine of American History* 14 (July–December 1885): 464–80.

Stampp, Kenneth M. "Kentucky's Influence upon Indiana in the Crisis of 1861." *Indiana Magazine of History* 39 (September 1943): 263–76.

Stauffer, Alvin P. "Supply of the First American Overseas Expeditionary Force: The Quartermaster's Department and the Mexican War." *Quartermaster Review*, May–June 1950, <http://www.qmfound.com/quartermaster_department_mexican_war.htm>.

Tapp, Hambleton. "The Assassination of General William Nelson, September 29, 1862, and Its Ramifications." *Filson Club History Quarterly* 19 (October 1945): 195–207.

———. "Incidents in the Life of Frank Wolford, Colonel in the First Kentucky Union Cavalry." *Filson Club History Quarterly* 10 (January 1936): 82–99.

"This Month in Our History: The Death of William Nelson." *Shipmate Magazine* 20 (September 1957): 18.

Truedley, Mary. "The United States and Santo Domingo, 1789–1866." *Journal of Race Development* 7 (October 1916): 220–74.

"Two Noted Civil War Recruiting Camps: A Look at Camp Dick Robinson and Camp Nelson." *Kentucky Explorer* 14 (March 2000): 60–65.

Zacharias, Donald W. "John J. Crittenden Crusades for the Union and Neutrality in Kentucky." *Filson Club History Quarterly* 38 (July 1964): 193–205.

Dissertations, Theses, Papers, and Miscellaneous Sources

Babcock, Elizabeth Rhea. "Unionist Activity in Louisville, Ky., Nov. 1860–Sept. 1861 inclusive." Typescript. April 1975. Filson Historical Society, Louisville, Ky.

Barnett, Bert. Review of *Annals of the Army of the Cumberland*, by John Fitch. H-CivWar, H-NetReviews (August 2004), <http://www.h-net.org/reviews/showrev.php?id=11084>.

Beszedits, Stephen. "The Nation's Guest: Lajos Kossuth in America, December 1851–July1852," 1–4, <http://www.hungarianamerica.com/harc/papers.asp>.

Burns, John E. "A History of Covington, Kentucky, through 1865." Typescript. 6 vols. Kenton County Public Library, Covington, Ky.

Camp Nelson Restoration and Preservation Foundation. "From the Camp Nelson Note Books." *Rally 'Round Camp Nelson* [Newsletter] No. 5 (Winter 2001); No. 6 (Winter 2002).

Ficklin Family in America, <http://www.ficklin.org/~ficklin/book/book.html>.

Hale, Jonathan D., and Civil War in Tennessee, <http://www.theborderlands.org/Stokely.htm>.

Hunneus, George. <http://www.famousamericans.net/georgehunneus>.

Hutchinson, Jack T. "Bluegrass and Mountain Laurel: The Story of Kentucky in the Civil War." Cincinnati Civil War Round Table (2000): 1–22.

Johnson, Wilson T., descendents of, <http://familytreemaker.genealogy.com/users/c/a/1 /Noreen-Callahan/GENE4–0002.html>.

Jones, James P. "Jefferson Davis in Blue: The Military Career, 1846–1866, of General Jefferson C. Davis, U.S.A." Masters thesis, University of Florida, 1954.

Kentucky Climate Center. "Weather during the Civil War: The Battle of Camp Wildcat," <http://kyclim.wku.edu/factsheets/civilwar/wildcat.html>.

Montt, Manuel. <http://www.famousamericans.net/manuelmontt>.

Murray, Edmundo. "Benjamín Vicuña Mackenna (1831–86)." *Dictionary of Irish Latin American Biography*, <http://www.irlandeses.org/dilab_vicuna.htm>.

The Rail Splitter: A Journal for the Lincoln Collector. Civil War Broadsides, Ephemera, Philately, Currency and Relics. No. 700. "To Arms!! Protect Your Home and Freedom," <http://www.railsplitter.com/sale11/cw-bdsides.html>.

Roth, Patrick H. "U.S. Navy Sailors Operating Ashore as Artillerymen: Four Vignettes," Burke, Va., 2005. Navy Department Library. Naval Historical Center, Washington, D.C., <http://www.history.navy.mil/library/online/sailor_art.htm#siege>.

Russell, Timothy McKnight. "Neutrality and Ideological Conflict in Kentucky during the First Year of the American Civil War." Ph.D. diss., University of New Mexico, 1989.

Schechter, Patricia Ann. "'The First Free Spot of Ground in Kentucky.' The Story of Camp Nelson." Honors Paper, Mount Holyoke College, 1986.

Williams, Glenn. "The Crowning Time: The International Slave Trade." Small Museum Association, <http://www.smallmuseum.org/articlecrime.htm>.

Electronic Resources

Abraham Lincoln Association, <http://www.hti.umich.edu./1/lincoln/>.

Abraham Lincoln Papers at the Library of Congress, Series 1, General Correspondence 1833–1916. Manuscript Division, Madison Bldg., Washington, D.C. Transcribed and annotated by the Lincoln Studies Center, Knox College, Galesburg, Ill. for the American Memory Project.

Accessible Archives, Inc. Primary Source Material from 18th- and 19th-Century Periodicals, <http://www.accessible.com>.

American Experience, "The Time of the Lincolns," Primary Sources, Responses to John Brown's Raid at Harper's Ferry, <http://www.pbs.org/wgbh/amex/lincolns/filmmore/ps_brown.html>.

Aztec Club of 1847, <http://www.aztecclub.com>.

Biographical Directory of the United States Congress, 1774–Present, <http://bioguide.congress.gov/scripts/biodisplay.pl?index=W000015>.

The Civil War Homepage, <www.civil-war.net>.

Corinth Information Database, Version 1.3, <http://www.corinth.net/NEW%20SITE/History/>.

Digital History. In collaboration with the University of Houston, the Gilder Lehrman Institute, the Museum of Fine Arts, Houston, American Voices, National Park Service, and Teaching American History.<www.digitalhistory.uh.edu>.

Documenting the American South, University of North Carolina, <http://docsouth.unc.edu/>.

Eighteenth- and Nineteenth-Century Journals Online, University of Texas, <http://www.lib.utexas.edu/refsites>.

Kentuckiana Electronic Texts Collection. <http://kdl.kyvl.org/cgi/t/text/text-idx?;page=simpleext&c=kynews>.

Naval Historical Center, Online Library of Selected Images: People––United States——Gustavus V. Fox (1821–1883), <http://www.history.navy.mil/branches/org11-2.htm>.

Naval Historical Center Washington Navy Yard. Officers of the Continental and U.S. Navy and Marine Corps, 1775–1900. <http://www.history.navy.mil/books/callahan/contmc.htm>.

Ohio Historical Society. Civil War Documents. Searchable Database. Correspondence to the Governor and Adjutant General, 1861–1866. Volumes 1A–35 and 37–43 of Series 147, <www.ohiohistory.org/resource/database/civilwar.html>.

Pennsylvania Civil War Newspapers, <www.libraries.psu.edu/digital/newspapers>.

Tennessee Civil War Source Book, <http://www.tennessee.civilwarsourcebook.com/>.

U.S. Army Military History Institute, <http://carlislewww.army.mil/usamhi/DL/chron/html>.

U.S. Naval Academy, <http://www.jcs-group.com/military/navy/usnaval.html>.

WorldCat. Online Computer Library Center, Inc., <http://www.oclc.org/worldcat/default.htm>.

Index

Page numbers in italics denote illustrations.

Davis, Garrett, 6, 38, 46–47, 49–51, 54–56, 59, 138, 141, 189n16; Nelson, view of, 61, 83
Davis, Jefferson Columbus, 24, 32, 33, 185n1; Army of the Cumberland, 159; under arrest, 151, 156; assassinates Nelson, 149–53, *150*, 163–64, 208n43, 210n24; failure to prosecute, 163–65; indictment and trial of, 156, 157, 162; Louisville and, 140, 141–42, 143, 144; Nelson, altercation with, 144–45, 148–49; promotion recommendation ignored, 160
Davis, Jefferson (Confederate President), 95
Davis, John B., 156
Deas, Zach C., *103*, 104
Decatur, Alabama, 87, 90
Democrats, 10–11, 23, 28–29, 35, 36 (Nelson); peace democrats, 157; 165, 174n78; states' rights, 37, 39, 42, 56; Union Democrats, 38
Desha, Joseph, 46
Diana (steamboat), 87
Dickey, Moses R., 116–17, 194n39, 200n60
Dilworth, Robert S., 119
discipline, 9, 12, 21, 34, 78, 79, 80, 82–83, 123; arrests of Confederate sympathizers, 67; arrests of officers, 85–86, 92, 131; Connell case, 80, 82, 85, 88–89, 98, 192n4, 194n34; court-martial, 126, 157–59, 194n34; executions, 88–89, 98, 127, 178n8; flogging, 9, 174n25; foraging abuses, 111, 125, 191n33; hazing, 173–74n14. *See also* court-martials
Donati's Comet, 33–34
Doniphan, Alexander, 2
Doniphan, Anderson, 1–2
Doniphan, Frances (Fannie), 3
Doniphan, George, 2
Doniphan, Joseph, 2, 73
Douglas, Stephen A., 23, 28, 32, 37
Draper, James N., 76
Dubois, William W., 105
Duck River Bridge, 90–91, 93–94
Duffield, William W., 90
Dumont, Ebenezer, 129, 132, 144, 145, 147
Duncan, Blanton, 45, 46, 51, 184n24
Du Pont, Samuel F., 37, 160

East Tennessee & Lynchburg Railroad, 79
East Tennessee expedition, 54–62, 66–68
Echo (brig Putnam), 32

Echagaray, Domingo, 18
Edgefield, Tennessee, 86
Edson, Alvin, 19–20
Ellis, Anderson Nelson, xii,148, 150, 201n8
Ethredge, Emerson, 52

Farragut, David G., 126
Faustin I, 28
Federal Army Departments: of the Cumberland, 58, 61, 190n25; Kentucky, 119; Mississippi, 89; Missouri, 84; Ohio, 47, 67, 129, 158, 160–61
Ficklin, John, 71
Fiji Islands, 8
Fillmore, Millard, 23
Finnell, John W., 50, 77, 122, 160
Fisher, Horace, 98, 99, 104, 107, 197n27
Fitch, Graham N., 84, 85
Fitch, John, 162
Foley, Bushrod W., 50
Foote, Henry S., 39
Forrest, Nathan Bedford, 107–8, 120, 123, 127
Fort Donelson, 63, 84, 85
Fort Henry, 63, 84
Fort Iturbide, 20
Fort Mitchell, 139, 141
Fort Sumter, 42–43, 43
Fort Zollicoffer, 87
Fox, Gustavus Vasa, 19, 42, 66
Fredonia (bark), 30, 36
Frémont, John C., 63, 64
French, E. B., 162
Fry, James B., xi, 24, 151,153, 164, 165
Fry, Speed S., 54, 56, 59, 161
Fugitive Slave law, 23–24
Fyffe, James Perry, 67, 73, 75, 159–60, 210n20

Gage, Charles P., *103*, 105
Gallatin, Tennessee, 126, 132
Garrard, Theophilus T., 54
Gaylord, Charles J., 111
Georgetown, Kentucky, 4
Gibson, Thomas W., 159
Gibson, Thomas Ware (Weir), 139, 149, 205n9, 208n43
Gibson, W. H., 194n39
Gilbert, Charles C., 132–33, 138, 140–41; on Nelson, 166; replaces Nelson, 153–54
Gill, Harrison, 70

Donald A. Clark is a native of Kentucky and a Centre College alumnus. He served as an army infantry officer in Vietnam, owned his own business for many years, and now devotes all of his energies to a lifelong interest in history. Clark is a member of various heraldry and historical organizations including the Kentucky Civil War Round Table. His recent work includes six entries for *Northern Kentucky Encyclopedia* and articles for the *Journal of the Illinois Historical Society* and *Tennessee Historical Quarterly*.